Lecture Notes in Computer Science

# Lecture Notes in Artificial Intelligence     15778

Founding Editor

Jörg Siekmann

Series Editors

Randy Goebel, *University of Alberta, Edmonton, Canada*
Wolfgang Wahlster, *DFKI, Berlin, Germany*
Zhi-Hua Zhou, *Nanjing University, Nanjing, China*

The series Lecture Notes in Artificial Intelligence (LNAI) was established in 1988 as a topical subseries of LNCS devoted to artificial intelligence.

The series publishes state-of-the-art research results at a high level. As with the LNCS mother series, the mission of the series is to serve the international R & D community by providing an invaluable service, mainly focused on the publication of conference and workshop proceedings and postproceedings.

Dylan D. Schmorrow · Cali M. Fidopiastis
Editors

# Augmented Cognition

19th International Conference, AC 2025
Held as Part of the 27th HCI International Conference, HCII 2025
Gothenburg, Sweden, June 22–27, 2025
Proceedings, Part I

 Springer

*Editors*
Dylan D. Schmorrow
Soar Technology Inc.
Orlando, FL, USA

Cali M. Fidopiastis
Katmai Government Services
Orlando, FL, USA

ISSN 0302-9743          ISSN 1611-3349 (electronic)
Lecture Notes in Artificial Intelligence
ISBN 978-3-031-93723-1          ISBN 978-3-031-93724-8 (eBook)
https://doi.org/10.1007/978-3-031-93724-8

LNCS Sublibrary: SL7 – Artificial Intelligence

This Springer imprint is published by the registered company Springer Nature Switzerland AG
The registered company address is: Gewerbestrasse 11, 6330 Cham, Switzerland

If disposing of this product, please recycle the paper.

# Foreword

The HCI International (HCII) conference was founded in 1984 by Gavriel Salvendy (Purdue University, USA, Tsinghua University, P.R. China, and University of Central Florida, USA) and the first event of the series, "1st USA-Japan Conference on Human-Computer Interaction", was held in Honolulu, Hawaii, USA, 18–20 August. Since then, HCI International is held jointly with several Thematic Areas and Affiliated Conferences, with each one under the auspices of a distinguished international Program Board and under one management and one registration. Twenty-seven HCI International Conferences have been organized so far (every two years until 2013, and annually thereafter).

Last year, we celebrated 40 years since the establishment of the HCII conference, which has been a hub for presenting groundbreaking research and novel ideas and collaboration for people from all over the world. Over the years, this conference has served as a platform for scholars, researchers, industry experts, and students to exchange ideas, connect, and address challenges in the ever-evolving HCI field. The conference has evolved itself, adapting to new technologies and emerging trends, while staying committed to its core mission of advancing knowledge and driving change.

The 27th International Conference on Human-Computer Interaction, HCI International 2025 (HCII 2025), was held as an 'on-site' conference at the Gothia Towers Hotel and Swedish Exhibition & Congress Centre, in Gothenburg, Sweden, on June 22–27, 2025, with the additional option for 'on-line' participation. It incorporated the 21 thematic areas and affiliated conferences listed below.

A total of 7972 individuals from academia, research institutes, industry, and government agencies from 92 countries submitted contributions. 1430 papers and 355 posters (as short research papers) are included in the volumes of the proceedings published just before the start of the conference, and which are listed below. The contributions thoroughly cover the entire field of human-computer interaction, highlight the evolving role of computers in diverse contexts, and demonstrate how HCI research is shaping and improving user experiences across a wide range of domains, influencing technological progress and its effective integration into various sectors.

The HCII conference also offers the option of presenting 'Late Breaking Work', both for papers and posters, with the corresponding proceedings volumes published after the conference. Full papers are included in the 'HCII 2025 - Late Breaking Papers' volumes of the proceedings published in the Springer LNCS series, while 'Poster Extended Abstracts' are included as short research papers in the 'HCII 2025 - Late Breaking Posters' volumes published in the Springer CCIS series.

I would like to thank the Program Board Chairs and the members of the Program Boards of all thematic areas and affiliated conferences for their contribution towards the high scientific quality and overall success of the HCI International 2025 conference. Their manifold support including paper reviews (via a single-blind review process, with a minimum of two reviews per submission), session organization, and their willingness to act as goodwill ambassadors for the conference is most highly appreciated.

This conference would not have been possible without the continuous and unwavering support and advice of Gavriel Salvendy, founder, General Chair Emeritus, and Scientific Advisor. For his outstanding efforts, I would like to express my sincere appreciation to Abbas Moallem, Communications Chair and Editor of HCI International News.

June 2025                                                                    Constantine Stephanidis

# HCI International 2025 Thematic Areas and Affiliated Conferences

- HCI: Human-Computer Interaction Thematic Area
- HIMI: Human Interface and the Management of Information Thematic Area
- EPCE: 22nd International Conference on Engineering Psychology and Cognitive Ergonomics
- AC: 19th International Conference on Augmented Cognition
- UAHCI: 19th International Conference on Universal Access in Human-Computer Interaction
- CCD: 17th International Conference on Cross-Cultural Design
- SCSM: 17th International Conference on Social Computing and Social Media
- VAMR: 17th International Conference on Virtual, Augmented and Mixed Reality
- DHM: 16th International Conference on Digital Human Modeling and Applications in Health, Safety, Ergonomics and Risk Management
- DUXU: 14th International Conference on Design, User Experience, and Usability
- C&C: 13th International Conference on Culture and Computing
- DAPI: 13th International Conference on Distributed, Ambient and Pervasive Interactions
- HCIBGO: 12th International Conference on HCI in Business, Government and Organizations
- LCT: 12th International Conference on Learning and Collaboration Technologies
- ITAP: 11th International Conference on Human Aspects of IT for the Aged Population
- AIS: 7th International Conference on Adaptive Instructional Systems
- HCI-CPT: 7th International Conference on HCI for Cybersecurity, Privacy and Trust
- HCI-Games: 7th International Conference on HCI in Games
- MobiTAS: 7th International Conference on HCI in Mobility, Transport and Automotive Systems
- AI-HCI: 6th International Conference on Artificial Intelligence in HCI
- MOBILE: 6th International Conference on Human-Centered Design, Operation and Evaluation of Mobile Communications

# List of Conference Proceedings Volumes Appearing Before the Conference

https://2025.hci.international/proceedings

# Preface

Augmented Cognition research innovates human-system interactions for next-generation adaptive systems in diverse fields such as biometrics, cybersecurity, adaptive learning system design, and health informatics. Advancements in psychophysiological sensing and data analysis have led to major breakthroughs in the real-time assessment of a user's psychophysical signatures as input to human systems leading the way for better human-system collaboration. More importantly, the use of Augmented Cognition methods and tools for studying elusive brain constructs such as cognitive bottlenecks (e.g., limitations in attention, memory, learning, comprehension, visualization abilities, and decision making) significantly contributes to a better understanding of the human brain and behavior, optimized reaction time, and improved learning, memory retention, and decision-making in real-world contexts. Each contribution paves the way for practical innovation in many fields dependent on the symbiotic relationships of human system integration.

The International Conference on Augmented Cognition (AC), an affiliated conference of the HCI International (HCII) conference, arrived at its 19th edition and encouraged papers from academics, researchers, industry, and professionals on a broad range of theoretical and applied issues related to augmented cognition and its applications.

The papers accepted for publication this year reflect emerging trends across various thematic areas of the field. AC research continues to build our understanding of cognitive processes and human performance as exampled by submissions exploring traditional topics such as cognitive load, fatigue, emotions, and cognitive engagement. Research presented also describes new methods in the use of eye-tracking and electroencephalography within operational environments. Of note is the extension of AC technologies to help explain the contributions of human cognition and performance across emerging contexts that include cybersecurity training, situational awareness enhancement, learning, and interaction in virtual and augmented environments. These explorations also include evaluating the impact of Artificial Intelligence and Machine Learning technologies. While the research applications of AC are growing, some articles provide insights into the challenges and opportunities facing the AC field.

Two volumes of the HCII 2025 proceedings are dedicated to this year's edition of the AC conference. The first volume focuses on topics related to Neurotechnology and Eye Tracking in Augmented Cognition; Augmented Cognition and User Experience; and AI in Augmented Cognition. The second volume focuses on topics related to Advances in Emotions in Augmented Cognition; and Enhancing Learning and Memory.

The papers accepted for publication in these volumes received a minimum of two single-blind reviews from the members of the AC Program Board or, in some cases, from members of the Program Boards of other affiliated conferences. We would like to extend a heartfelt thank you to all the members of the AC Program Board and other affiliated conference program boards for their invaluable contributions and support. The groundbreaking work presented in these volumes would not have been possible without their tireless efforts.

June 2025

Dylan D. Schmorrow
Cali M. Fidopiastis

# 19th International Conference on Augmented Cognition (AC 2025)

Program Board Chairs: **Dylan D. Schmorrow**, *Soar Technology Inc., USA*, and **Cali M. Fidopiastis**, *Katmai Government Services, USA*

Martha Crosby, *University of Hawaii, USA*
Fausto De Carvalho, *Altice Labs, Portugal*
Rodolphe Gentili, *University of Maryland - College Park, USA*
Monte Hancock, *Living Centerline Institute, USA*
Kurtulus Izzetoglu, *Drexel University, USA*
Benjamin Knox, *Norwegian Armed Forces Cyber Defence Force, Norway*
Ricardo Lugo, *Tallinn University of Technology, Estonia*
Chang Nam, *Northern Illinois University, USA*
Arne Norlander, *NORSECON AB, Sweden*
Stefan Sütterlin, *Albstadt-Sigmaringen University, Germany*
Suraj Sood, *LUV Systems, USA*
Ana Teixeira, *ISEP, Portugal*
Martin Westhoven, *German Federal Institute for Occupational Safety and Health, Germany*
Ren Xu, *g.tec, Austria*

The full list with the Program Board Chairs and the members of the Program Boards of all thematic areas and affiliated conferences of HCII 2025 is available online at:

**http://www.hci.international/board-members-2025.php**

# HCI International 2026 Conference

The 28th International Conference on Human-Computer Interaction, HCI International 2026, will be held jointly with the affiliated conferences at the Montréal Convention Centre (Palais des congrès de Montréal), in Montreal, Canada, 26–31 July 2026. It will cover a broad spectrum of themes related to Human-Computer Interaction, including theoretical issues, methods, tools, processes, and case studies in HCI design, as well as novel interaction techniques, interfaces, and applications. The proceedings will be published by Springer (part of Springer Nature) in a multi-volume set. More information will become available on the conference website: https://2026.hci.international/.

General Chair
Prof. Constantine Stephanidis
University of Crete and ICS-FORTH
Heraklion, Crete, Greece
Email: general_chair@2026.hci.international

**https://2026.hci.international/**

# Contents – Part I

## AI in Augmented Cognition

# Contents – Part II

# Neurotechnology and Eye Tracking in Augmented Cognition

# Towards Using Biometric Transcripts for Analyzing Multimodal Sensory Information Processing Data

Jack Clark[✉] and Lila Boz

University of Arizona, Tucson, USA
jaclarkent@arizona.edu

**Abstract.** In immersive environments like virtual reality (VR), task performance can be affected by different visual and auditory stimuli. Analyzing multiple aspects of user experience, such as cognitive load and cognitive alertness, in these scenarios can yield multimodal datasets that may make it difficult to detect patterns or relationships between different data modalities. Moreover, these large data sets would cause the researcher to split their attention. This study proposes a synchronized method for analyzing temporal multimodal data more efficiently, called Biometric Transcript for Information Processing (BTIP). In this paper, we demonstrate the proposed approach and the usefulness of viewing temporal multimodal data concurrently. We used the following data modalities collected during an interactive VR task in the presence of visual and auditory distractors: electroencephalogram (EEG) (alpha and theta waves), pupil dilation, fixation location, and gaze duration for each fixation location for the first engagement of the first instance with each distractor. We assessed sensory overloading and changes to attention through the fluctuations of alpha and theta wave activity and explored the connection to pupil dilation by analyzing the patterns found in the biometric transcript. Our data indicated a significantly positive correlation between alpha and theta waves. Peaks in alpha activity correspond to enhanced focus, whereas peaks in theta wave activity correspond to overloading. We further discuss the implications of using this method to research nuances in sensory processing research, specifically with biometric feedback. These insights suggest that this method is promising to be used effectively during the analysis process of temporal multimodal data.

**Keywords:** Virtual Reality · Cognitive Load · Cognitive Alertness · Sensory Processing · Electroencephalogram · Biometric Data

## 1 Introduction

There are many disruptions to information processing that may overload cognitive load and cause a decrease in task performance (Jerald, 2015). Different types of disruptions can occur in a singular channel, across multiple channels, and/or due to the formatting of complex digital displays. Each channel can be overloaded by an overabundance of stimuli sources creating thresholds for channel capacity (Jerald, 2015). This threshold lowers as multiple channels of stimuli interact in the same experience (Belchoir, et. al, 2013; Jerald, 2015; Vorlander & Shinn-Cunningham, 2014). The threshold also lowers when the frequency of saccades is increased to understand the information in the environment (e.g., split attention) (Jerald, 2015; Moreno & Mayer, 1999). Aspects of contemporary digital tool design impact perception through the developer's choices for how information is displayed and received by the user (Baudisch, et. al, 2002). Various degrees of information isolation, pixel resolution, and display boundaries affect cognitive load (Baudisch, et. al, 2002). Understanding the parameters of these types of disruptions allows researchers to hone in on the specific moments that may cause equivocation, error, and increased recovery time between neuron synapsis (Hebb & Donderi, 2013; Hsia, 1971). In turn, shedding light on the transfer of information from reception to perception. These moments could be the key to comprehending how distraction and refocusing occur in task performance.

However, it may be difficult to discover trends in temporal multimodal data. In cognitive load research, often a specific variable to change is looked at and the changes to the surrounding environment are analyzed. Researchers are typically coding and logging how a stimulus can cause a change in perception, yet this is often researched through one "mode" or "channel" instead of looking at the patterns across changes (Jerald, 2015). In this paper, we follow a method called "The Biometric Transcript for Information Processing" (BTIP), which allows a basis for this type of multimodal pattern research in temporal data. The BTIP method provides the opportunity for the cross-platform examination that is needed to understand the patterns of these changes in cognitive load and cognitive alertness. This method stems from the multimodal transcript developed by Bezemer & Jewitt (2010). To demonstrate and discuss this form of analysis, in this paper, we use the data collected in our previous research focusing on EEG data (Clark & Boz, 2025a) and eye tracking data (Clark & Boz, 2025b) collected during a visuospatial task in VR.

## 2   Related Works

### 2.1   Switching Views in Interpreting Data

In 2002, Baudisch and colleagues discussed a specific comparison of interfaces that caused cognition to be either segmented or fluid (Baudisch, et. al, 2002). The researchers highlighted multiple forms of interaction, including focus-context, overview-detail, and zooming mechanisms. A focus-context screen depicts information from the same Field of View (FoV) or monitor of the user during interaction. In this interface, information is not occluded and can be found through one FoV. Oppositely, overview-detail interfaces have one screen or window with specific details and one depicting an overview or bigger picture of the specific connections of those details. The windows or screens are in set locations, forcing the user to move their head or focal point in order to make meaning of the information (Chun, 2000; Chun & Jiang, 1998). Elements of both focus-context and overview-detail interfaces combine when utilizing zooming mechanisms. Zooming mechanisms afford the user the ability to customize the amount of detail seen in the FoV as well as pan different areas of information (Jakobsen & Hornbaek, 2013). In this case, the researchers wanted to understand which interface allowed users to complete tasks in static and dynamic multimodal documents more effectively (error rate) and efficiently (speed) (Baudisch, et. al, 2002). Through an integrative task analysis, the researchers were able to conclude that using a focus-context interface was more efficient and effective compared to overview-detail interfaces and zooming mechanisms. In focus-context interfaces, the user can use their peripheral vision more effectively while lessening the cognitive load needed to hold the mental map of the information, compared to the split attention caused by switching FoVs in the overview-detail interface. In both focus-context interfaces and zooming mechanisms the user can focus their attention (eye-tracking) without turning their head like in overview-detail interfaces; aiding the user's ability to visually memorize a map and remember locations previously visited during navigation practice. The decrease in fixation locations decreases the germane load needed to categorize and make meaning of the multiple sources of intrinsic load (Antonenko, et. al, 2010).

By using these parameters, Baudisch et al. (2002) highlighted the necessity for limiting the visual effort needed to switch views that may cause frequent errors and an increase in cognitive load (e.g., split attention). As discussed in Healey & Enns (2012), each saccade forces the individual to expunge effort to hold their place visually and cognitively and interpret information from the individual's visual attention (Healey & Enns, 2012). Much like a video game saves progress, the brain combines sequential information rather than overwriting previous material. Therefore, each time the user switches views in the overview-context interface they will be 'saving' the data in their brain, forcing retrieval each time they refocus and increasing the cognitive load on working memory. This takes the individual longer to perform a task by forcing extra effort used for retrieval instead of using peripherals to gain information from multiple screens (Chun, 2000; Chun & Jiang, 1998).

The analysis of focus-context interfaces, overview-detail interfaces, and zooming mechanisms has been further researched by Jakobsen & Hornbaek (2013). They suggest that display size, information space, and scale ratio within each interface are interrelated and affect task performance as well as working memory. They suggest two arenas for understanding the relationship between these variables and their relevance to performance in a navigation task: fixed-information spaces and variable-information spaces. Fixed-information spaces vary in size of the display/device and restrict what information is depicted, whereas variable-information spaces focus on the manipulation of resolution and customizing the amount of data available to the user. Both approaches may seem similar, but they often yield different results causing discrepancies in conceptual understanding of the interrelation between variables of information. To alleviate the confusion, the researchers administered two experiments using display sizes small, medium, and large, with either focus-context, overview-detail, or zooming interfaces, while performing navigation, comparison, or trace tasks. The hope was to understand if performance measures are affected when altering resolution, amount of information being shown, and size of the display in a focus-context view. They found variable information spaces with large displays and fixed information spaces with small displays decreased efficiency and effectiveness on task performance due to an increase in effort and cognitive load needed for completion. Analyzing multimodal data often requires switching views. Hence, the

BTIP method can be a good alternative requiring less switching and more efficient data comprehension where multimodal data is involved.

## 2.2 Dual-Channel Processing and Split Attention

The threshold for working memory capacity is changing as digital technologies are becoming more widely integrated into everyday routines. The concept of overloading visual and auditory capacity has recently been more heavily researched due to these emerging technologies. In 1999, researchers Moreno and Mayer discovered 'The Split Attention Principle', stating that learning outcomes are decreased when viewer attention is split between multiple modes of information through the same channel (e.g., graphics and text, lyrics and speech, etc.) (Moreno & Mayer, 1999). Concurrently, when information is delivered through separate modalities, such as graphics and speech, retention rates outperform those with split attention. For example, reading can be considered the learned action of converting visual stimuli (letters) to auditory perception (speech). By delivering information in speech compared to text, visual attention can focus solely on graphics, compared to graphics and text, while auditory attention can focus on the perception of speech. This type of reception minimizes split attention by decreasing the number of different types of stimuli being encoded through a singular channel, in turn, decreasing the germane load needed to make meaning (Baceviciute et. al, 2020).

In 2014 Richard Mayer suggested, *"Extraneous material competes for cognitive resources in working memory and can divert attention from the important material, disrupt the process of organizing the material, and prime the learner to integrate the material with an inappropriate theme."* For this reason, several principles were created to reduce cognitive load by minimizing extraneous information in multimedia learning contexts (Mayer, 2014). Since 2014, some of these principles have been explored in more complex multimedia contexts like virtual reality (VR) yet more detailed exploration is needed to understand the process of distracting and refocusing during a problem-solving task (Mayer & Fiorella, 2014).

## 3   Biometric Transcript

The different types of data with diverse measurement styles needed to understand cognitive load and cognitive alertness make it difficult to analyze efficiently. Often, researchers are splitting their attention trying to make meaning of various temporal data modalities, such as the alpha-theta band relationships and the pupil dilation data. The "Biometric Transcript for Information Processing" (BTIP) is proposed as a more efficient method for analyzing multimodal temporal data without splitting the researchers' attention (Fig. 1). To demonstrate its use, in this paper, we use a combination of eye-tracking data, head-mounted VR display data, and electroencephalogram (EEG) data. This includes fixation location, gaze duration, changes in pupil dilation, changes in Alpha waves, and changes in Theta waves. This combination allows the research of controlled stimuli reception through the eyes, how long that stimulus was noticed, whether there were changes in cognitive alertness, and the amount of cognitive load changes as the brain interprets the information. The proposed structure will allow researchers to focus on a specific aspect of these different data types to see the changes across the other data types. Ideally, researchers will be able to use this structure to accurately filter this type of biometric data. For example, exposing the interwoven links between environmental stimuli, increased cognitive alertness (increases in pupil dilation), and cognitive load (relationship between alpha and theta EEG waves). In other words, researchers can highlight a measurement of pupil dilation, cross-search for specific environmental stimuli, and see how cognitive load is affected. This could show patterns in specific stimuli that would alter human interaction in immersive virtual worlds.

| | User Pseudonym | Distractor Type | Instance Code | Average Pupil Dilation | Fixation Location | Average Theta Waves | Average Alpha Waves |
|---|---|---|---|---|---|---|---|
| 1 | | | | | | | |
| 2 | 2 | Visual Alternate | 1 | 3.63 | Table | 0.24 | 0.35 |
| 3 | 3 | Visual Alternate | 1 | 3.67 | Table | 0.54 | 0.74 |

**Fig. 1.** A table representing the use of the BTIP method. This data shows the average pupil dilation (mm), fixation location, average theta and alpha waves for users 1 and 2. The instance code is constant across distractors being set to the 1st engagement with each distractor. The data was collected starting at 0.1 s after the first distractor was triggered and collected until 2 s had passed. The fixation location could be easel, table, ball, or other.

The proposed approach of biometric transcript will lower the time needed for pattern recognition across the temporal data from different devices. Eye trackers and EEGs have been found to yield useful insights yet analyzing the data can be a cumbersome process. The proposed method would allow researchers to filter the data quickly without the constant changes to the FoV. Previous researchers needed different display windows to cross-examine pupil dilation data compared to the alpha-theta relationship, causing split attention in the researcher, and degrading the quality of retention and efficiency from either data source (Mayer & Moreno, 1999). With the use of the biometric transcript approach, researchers can locate novel reactions or peaks in the data that are of interest to their work. The biometric transcript demonstrated in this research was designed to encompass the different types of measurement and analysis needed for the pupil dilation data compared to the alpha-theta relationship in the context of a visuospatial virtual reality task.

## 4 Task Design and Implementation

The data used in this paper includes a cup stacking task performed in virtual reality. Participants manipulated virtual cups to replicate a displayed pattern (Fig. 2). In this task, participants were required to hold the visual organization in working memory while the physical manipulation was occurring, activating executive functioning. In the gameplay conditions, different visual and auditory distractors were introduced. The visual distractors included bouncing balls across the user's field of view with far proximity, close proximity, and alternating proximity. The auditory distractors included click trains (i.e., beeping sounds with 1-s audio and 1-s silence) with low pitch (500 Hz), high pitch (4000 Hz), and alternating pitch. Distractors appeared 5 to 10 s from the start of a task instance and after the user viewed the pattern once.

**Fig. 2.** The virtual environment, cup stacking task, and the distractors. Left: An in-progress view of the task with three visual distracters (balls) bouncing across the user's field of view. Right: The UI overlay for the designated color pattern for stacking, which is only displayed when the user presses the controller button.

The experiment included seven trial conditions. The no distractor condition was used to establish a baseline without any distractors. There were three conditions with visual distractors: far proximity, close proximity, and alternating proximity. There were also three auditory distractor conditions: low pitch, high pitch, and alternating pitch. During the experiment, the participants completed 6 instances of the cup stacking task in each condition. The experimental conditions were first randomized for the visual or auditory, and then for the distractor feature (far, close, and alternating proximity or low, high, and alternating pitch). Counterbalancing was used.

**Fig. 3.** A participant wearing the HTC Vive Pro headset and the Muse EEG headband and performing the cup stacking task in VR. The participant's view was overlaid on the lower right.

The VR game was implemented in the Unity game engine with C# (Unity, Accessed: 2024). An HTC VIVE Pro with eye tracking was used in conjunction with EEG data being gathered from a Muse 2 headband (Fig. 3) (Vive Pro Eye Office: Vive Business United States, 2021; Neurofeedback EEG device - how it works, 2021). The data from the Muse was recorded with the Mind Monitor app (Mind Monitor, Accessed: 2024).

# 5 Evaluation

A within-subjects study was carried out with a total of 60 participants with IRB approval (10 participants took part in the pilot studies, and 50 participants took part in the actual user study). The participants were undergraduate and graduate students from varying majors at a university in the southwest of the United States. The ages of the participants ranged from 18 to 35. They had little to no VR experience (e.g., less than 1 h). The participants' heights ranged from 5' to 6' ft. Participants could not have any cognitive or physical disabilities or any pre-existing serious medical conditions (such as a heart ailment). Participants could not be pregnant or have color blindness. They were also not allowed to wear eyeglasses for the interaction and were asked to wear corrective lenses when applicable. All participants were able to speak English and were right-handed and not ambidextrous.

# 6 Types of Measurement

This subsection is split into two different measurable areas for information processing data: reception and perception. In this research, data was collected for both visual and auditory distractors to see what is occurring when attention is split vs. when it is compartmentalized. In the visual distractor conditions, the attention was split between the distractor (ball) and the task (table/cup stack), triggering a higher cognitive load based on Mayer's Split Attention theory (Moreno & Mayer, 1999). The auditory conditions compartmentalize the sensory information with the buzzer being received through the ears instead of through the eyes. This compartmentalization would allow a decrease in cognitive load based on previous research (Moreno & Mayer, 1999). To understand the effects these different senses, have on cognitive load, both types of distractors were analyzed for reception and perception data. In this research, reception is represented by the initial engagement with the stimulus (distractor), found through fixation location and gaze duration. Perception is represented by the interpretation or cognitive reaction of the initial engagement with the distractor. An electroencephalogram (EEG) was used to collect theta and alpha waves for cognitive load, and internal VR headset cameras were used to collect pupil dilation for cognitive alertness.

## 6.1 Reception Data

**Fixation Location and Gaze Duration.** *Fixation location* is the central cue focal point that is being gazed at, at a given time. This generalized definition lends to the idea of fixations being perceived in a spotlight style of vision. This means that the central cue (fixation location) is being received with bright clarity, whereas the peripheral cues (surrounding the central cue radially) are received with less clarity. The farther the cue is from the central fixation point, the less clear it will become and in turn is not perceived by the brain as readily. Researchers have found this to be true when asking participants to recall shapes based on their cue location (Callaghan, 1984; Ma et al., 2015). It was found that shapes in the center of the fixation location are perceived and retained more readily than peripheral cues. In this research, we collected data on the location being fixated in the environment to understand what areas are being perceived. This knowledge would let researchers know if a cognitive load increase in perception is due to the required task (intrinsic load) or due to the distracting feature (extraneous cognitive load).

It has been found that fixation location will linger if the eyes are having trouble perceiving what is being perceived. For instance, we "look back" at a location to double-check that it is what we think it is. A prime example of this is when our bodies react to shapes incorrectly. At first glance, a shadow may appear in the shape of a snake. The body will react to the shape (jumping back) before the eyes look back at the "snake" and see the shadow. During this time, cognitive alertness would increase (pupil dilation) as well as cognitive load (theta-alpha wave relation). Hence, collecting data for how long a location is gazed at can indicate the time taken for interpretation.

## 6.2  Perception Data

There are two aspects of information processing that can be analyzed through physical changes to the environment: cognitive load and cognitive alertness. Cognitive load can be measured through EEG wave reaction and cognitive alertness can be measured through the changes in pupil dilation. In other words, the time it takes the brain to react and how the body reacts depicts cognitive load and cognitive alertness. In this research, we use cognitive load to measure perception because it gives insight into the connections between task difficulty and sensory thresholds for digital information. We use cognitive alertness to show the degree of engagement and focus being allocated to the task. Understanding what features of digital assets increase cognitive load and cognitive alertness unilaterally can allow developers to create VR environments that are not overwhelming to the user. This could limit the naturally occurring fatigue and motion sickness caused by the vergence-accommodation conflict in virtual reality (Hoffman et al, 2008). Some research in this area has been conducted (Mack, 2003) concluding that participants may be receiving the information, but not necessarily perceiving it. Therefore, we understand information processing is overloaded in VR environments, yet we need more information to distinguish the "how" and the "why".

**EEG Wave Oscillation.** According to Basar's Theory of neutral oscillations, "Wave-like potential changes can serve as direct and measurable indices of specific brain activities correlated with multiple functions that include sensory registration and tracking, perception, movement, and cognitive processes related to attention, learning and memory." (Basar, 1999). Cognitive abilities can be demonstrated by measuring the Event-Related Synchronization (ERS = increase in wave activation) and Event-Related Desynchronization (ERD = decrease in wave neutralization) of the alpha and theta EEG bands (Klimesch, 1999; Zhang, 2021). Analyzing these oscillations highlights attention through the increases in cognitive load. Sudden activating or peaks in different band types may indicate the type and amount of cognitive load occurring at different stages of a designated event. Therefore, measuring mental activity temporally through EEGs allows the depiction of cognitive load at any stage of the designated event.

Temporal peaks in Theta wave ERS and dips in Alpha wave ERD have been found to increase cognitive overloading in previous research (Antonenko, et. al, 2010; Gevins et al., 1997; Gevins & Smith, 2003; Klimesch, 1999; Makransky et al., 2019; Sterman et al., 1994; Zhang, 2021). For example, a sudden desynchronization or neutralization in alpha waves in tandem with sudden synchronization or activation of theta waves correlates with increased attention, increased cognitive load, as well as task difficulty and information complexity. Based on previous research, theta waves on their own are not reliable for depicting cognitive load accurately, yet when examined in relationship to alpha waves they can be a good indicator (Antonenko et al., 2010). In this research, EEG data was collected through a Muse 2 headband.

**Pupil Dilation.** *Pupil dilation* is the measurement of the diameter of the pupil in the iris of the eye. Petersen et. al (2017) found that pupil dilation occurred in tandem with cognitive alertness. Therefore, gathering the changes in the eye's diameter allows researchers to measure cognitive alertness. Cognitive alertness is shown by the event-related changes that follow an alerting signal to the cognitive system (Petersen et. al, 2017). It is important to measure this perception because it shows how much attention a participant is allocating to perceive the information. This is different from the cognitive load which is a combination of effort, mental demand, physical demand, and perceived ease and is measured through EEGs. Small or slow increases in pupil dilation would mean little changes in alertness whereas a significant or sharp increase would indicate an immediate need for alertness. In this research, the changes in pupil dilation were monitored through the data from the VR headset.

## 7 Results

For the EEG data, we took the average of each wave type across the 4 available channels (i.e., TP9, AF7, AF8, and TP10 channels for both the theta and alpha waves). The data was set to epoch time to efficiently filter the biometric data, allowing for the synchronization across different types of equipment (i.e., EEG and HTC Vive Pro Headset). Creating universal time stamps for the data affords an encapsulation of what is occurring in the process of reception to perception from multiple perspectives. This research encapsulated the alpha wave, theta wave, overall pupil dilation, fixation location, and the duration of gaze at each fixation location for the first engagement with the first triggered distractor in the first task instance of each experiment condition (i.e., visual close, visual far, visual alternate, audio high, audio low, and audio alternate). The duration was approximately 2 s, starting 0.1 s after the first distractor was applied and lasting until the 2-s mark. This time was chosen because of the increased saliency of a distractor when they are novel (Chun, 2000; Chun & Jiang, 1998).

The data was first analyzed by gathering the differences in alpha and theta waves. Higher alpha waves indicate an increase in cognitive load and attention (Antonenko 2010; Basar, 1999, Chiossi, Arias, & Borghese, 2023). In all conditions, the alpha waves were higher than the theta waves for the majority of the participants: 77% in the Visual Far condition, 72% in the Audio Low condition, ~ 66% in the Visual Close condition, 65% in the Audio Alternate condition, ~ 62% in the Visual Alternate condition, and ~ 60% in the Audio High condition. Simultaneously, the average pupil dilation was analyzed for each condition. The difference between the 0.1 to 2 s in the first engagement and the overall duration of the first engagement was calculated and compared to the baseline condition without any distractions. 47% in the Visual Alternate condition, 45% in the Audio Alternate and Visual Far conditions, 44% in the Audio High condition, 37% in the Visual Close condition, and 40% in the Audio Low condition were above the average of the pupil dilation calculated for the No Distractor condition. The Visual Far condition had the highest percentage of participants with both above-average pupil dilation and higher alpha waves (35%), followed by the Visual Alternate condition (29%), the Audio Low condition (28%), the Audio high and Audio Alternate conditions (25%), and the Visual Close condition (23%).

## 7.1  BTIP Method

Using the BTIP method, we can examine the EEG data and the pupil dilation data concurrently while observing where the participant was gazing at in one line of data. With the multiple metrics used for the various types of equipment, it is difficult to synthesize and make meaning of the data separately. Especially when trying to discuss cognitive load measures through EEGs (i.e., Alpha and Theta wave comparison) and cognitive alertness measures through pupil dilation. This combined with the fixation location gives an encapsulation of how many participants were affected by the distractor with a novel engagement. Bar charts for the first engagement data for each participant can be seen in Fig. 4. In the bar charts, the following metrics are presented for each distractor condition: alpha wave EEG, theta wave EEG, overall pupil dilation (mm) for right and left eyes, and fixation durations (sec.) for the table (the task area), ball (distractor), easel (where general instructions were displayed) and other areas in the virtual environment. Only the complete data sets were included in the bar charts, excluding the incomplete or inaccurate data readings from the EEG or the VR headset. Pearson's correlation tests were conducted for all distracter conditions based on the biometric transcript data (Table 1). There was a statistically significant positive correlation between the Alpha and Theta EEG data for all distractor conditions. There were no significant correlations between Alpha or Theta EEG and Overall PD (pupil dilation).

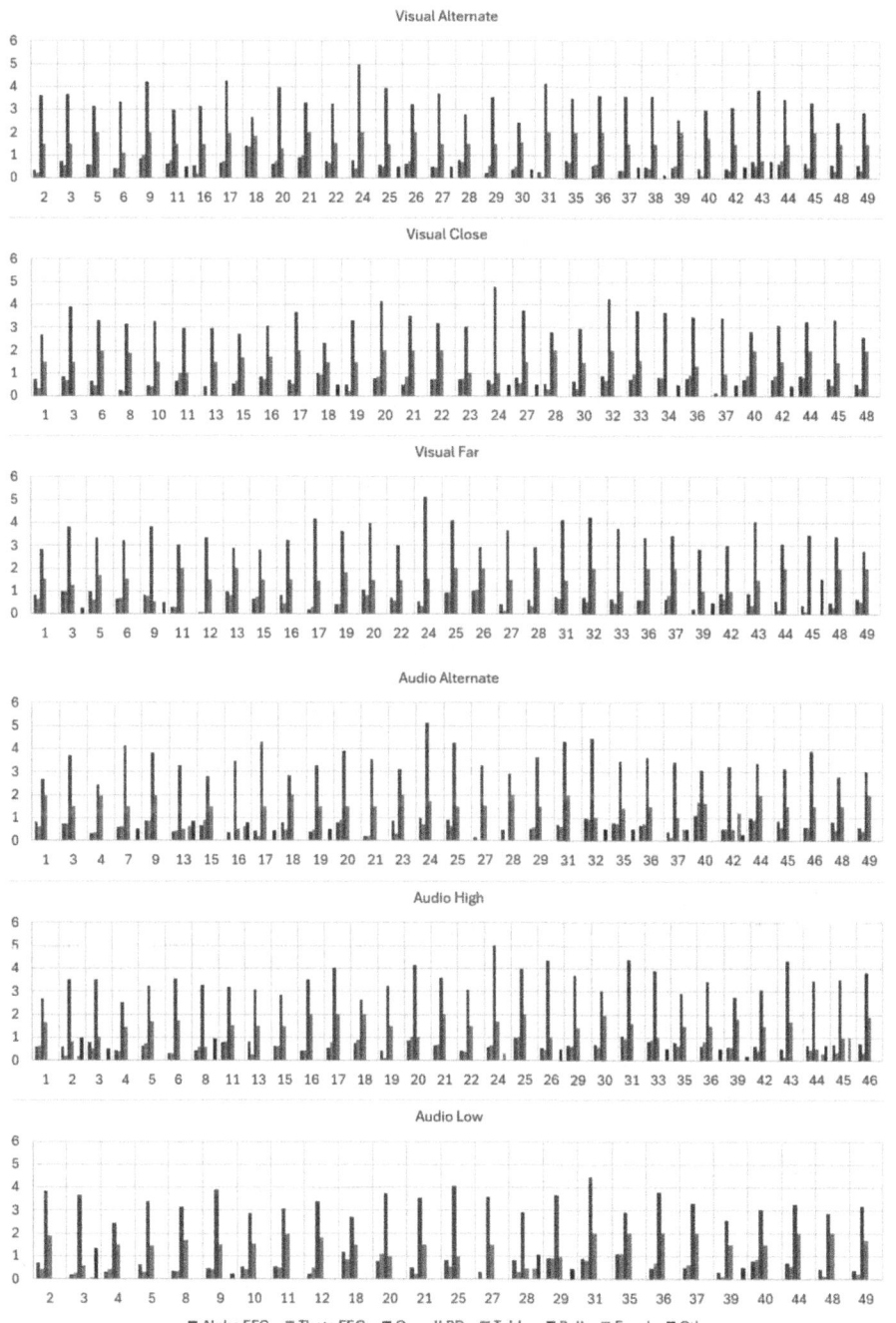

**Fig. 4.** Bar charts depicting the metrics collected in this research and used in the BTIP analysis: Alpha EEG, Theta EEG, overall pupil dilation (mm) for right and left eyes, and fixation durations (sec.) for the table (the task area), ball (distractor), easel (where general instructions were displayed) and other areas in the virtual environment. The vertical axis represents values, and the horizontal axis represents the user id codes assigned to the participants.

**Table 1.** Pearson's correlation tests conducted for all distracter conditions based on the biometric transcript data.

| Condition | Alpha EEG vs Theta EEG | | | Alpha EEG vs Overall PD | | | Theta EEG vs Overall PD | | |
|---|---|---|---|---|---|---|---|---|---|
| | r | N | p | r | N | p | r | N | p |
| Visual Alternate | 0.796 | 32 | <.001 | 0.005 | 32 | 0.98 | -0.048 | 32 | 0.794 |
| Visual Close | 0.712 | 30 | <.001 | 0.144 | 30 | 0.448 | 0.144 | 30 | 0.447 |
| Visual Far | 0.822 | 31 | <.001 | 0.009 | 31 | 0.96 | 0.013 | 31 | 0.944 |
| Audio Alternate | 0.773 | 31 | <.001 | 0.194 | 31 | 0.295 | 0.159 | 31 | 0.394 |
| Audio High | 0.611 | 32 | <.001 | 0.219 | 32 | 0.229 | 0.158 | 32 | 0.389 |
| Audio Low | 0.721 | 25 | <.001 | 0.079 | 25 | 0.708 | 0.16 | 25 | 0.445 |

## 8    Discussion

In this research, we found that the BTIP method of analysis is an effective tool that allows for quick navigation through big data related to time. The analysis and results of the transcript support how efficient and accurate this tool can be. Sorting the data in the transcript to find only the novel engagements (instance code), followed by cognitive alertness (pupil dilation), and then cognitive load (alpha and theta wave increase) was a more efficient way compared to traditional analysis processes that split the FoV and attention of the researcher. The use of this transcript can also increase accuracy because it helps account for human errors that may be more likely to occur when splitting attention across FoV or different display windows. Further, organizing the data this way would allow the data to be sorted for any parameters, although we focused on novel engagements in this paper. For example, the researcher can isolate the instance with a specific pupil dilation value, or with the largest difference in the alpha-theta desynchronization, etc. Another advantage of this method is the efficiency due to affording the opportunity for data to be used across diverse research questions and multiple topics. This study focused on novel engagements, yet aspects of pitch, speed, and proximity of visual and auditory distractors can also be analyzed with the same biometric transcript. This would be both cost-efficient and time-effective for researchers making meaning of temporal data from the consistently emerging technologies.

Consistent data across all measurement types limits the quality and amount of data that can be analyzed. Each collection method (e.g., EEG vs. eye-tracking) needs a different method of organizing and cleaning methods for analyzing the data. For instance, reliable EEG data must exclude jaw clenches, whereas that is not necessary for the eye-tracking data. The data must be reliable from all sources for the BTIP method to be effective. This results in the exclusion of any data that does not have reliable values for each variable being focused on. This means that multiple trials of the same conditions are needed to ensure there is enough data to compare. However, this could lead to unwanted fatigue in the users and should be monitored when commencing future research in this fashion.

Based on the patterns found in this transcript, there was a positive correlation between the alpha and theta waves for the first engagement with each distractor type. Both waves moving in tandem indicates the awakening from a meditative or mindful state towards being alert and focused on the external environment (Chiossi, Arias, & Borghese, 2023).

This signifies there was an increase in cognitive load and concentration during the onset of the distraction. While the increase in both waves show an increase in the overall cognitive load, the different rates of increase in the alpha and theta waves highlight whether cognition was overloaded (faster theta waves) or displayed enhanced attention (faster alpha waves). A deeper investigation into the transcript shows that ~ 13% of participants had cognition that became overloaded (faster theta wave increase) at the onset of the distractor in the Visual Far condition, ~ 27% in the Visual Close condition, 28% in the Audio Low condition, 29% in the Audio Alternating condition, 31% in the Audio High condition, and 34% in the Visual Alternating condition.

Additionally, the ball was only "gazed" at in the Visual Alternating condition. This could be a result of the vergence-accommodation conflict or the placement of the ball as it entered the gymnasium (i.e., the back wall of the gym as opposed to the side wall). Entering from the back wall would have been in the participant's FoV, whereas the side wall would not be in the FoV. However, this may not be the only reason for the results in this data since the ball entrance location was randomized across the visual conditions. Our visual channel can interpret peripheral cues with less accuracy than central cues, as explained in the vergence-accommodation conflict, yet they are still received. It is possible the participants were gazing near the ball rather than directly at the ball resulting in a false response from the headset (i.e., stating the focus was on the gym instead of the ball). More research is needed to understand if this was the case. Although more research is needed to understand if these results are consistent with other VR scenarios, our demonstration indicates that the BTIP method can successfully be used to investigate temporal multimodal biometric datasets.

## 9  Limitations

We only included the first distractor engagement in the first task instance in this BTIP analysis to demonstrate and discuss the use of the method. A more thorough analysis would be needed to evaluate the use of this method versus traditional multi-modal data analysis that split the FoV of the researchers. Also, the EEG used in this research may not have been as accurate as other advanced EEGs, resulting in incomplete data in the biometric transcript. Future studies with a more advanced EEG device would yield a more accurate and complete data set.

## 10  Conclusion

In this paper, we demonstrated and discussed the use of the BTIP method to make meaning of temporal multimodal data collected during a visuospatial VR task in the presence of visual and auditory distractors. Our biometric transcript included the alpha EEG, theta EEG, overall pupil dilation, fixation location, and the duration of gaze at each fixation location for the first engagement of each distractor in the first task instance. This approach allowed us to compare the EEG data with the eye-tracking data in one synchronized line and get insights efficiently. Multiple metrics collected through various types of equipment may make it difficult to analyze temporal multimodal data without an organization tool like the proposed BTIP method. We hope that the BTIP method will provide an effective path that allows researchers to analyze temporal multimodal data in interactive experiences in a user-friendly way.

# References

Albus, P., Vogt, A., Seufert, T.: Signaling in virtual reality influences learning outcome and cognitive load. Comput. Educ. **166**, 104154 (2021)

Antonenko, P., Paas, F., Grabner, R., Van Gog, T.: Using electroencephalography to measure cognitive load. Educ. Psychol. Rev. **22**(4), 425–438 (2010)

Baceviciute, S., Mottelson, A., Terkildsen, T., Makransky, G.: Investigating representation of text and audio in educational VR using learning outcomes and EEG. In: Proceedings of the 2020 CHI Conference on Human Factors in Computing Systems, pp. 1–13 (2020)

Başar, E., Başar-Eroğlu, C., Karakaş, S., Schürmann, M.: Are cognitive processes manifested in event-related gamma, alpha, theta and delta oscillations in the EEG? Neurosci. Lett. **259**(3), 165–168 (1999)

Baudisch, P., Good, N., Bellotti, V., Schraedley, P.: Keeping things in context: a comparative evaluation of focus plus context screens, overviews, and zooming. In: Proceedings of the SIGCHI Conference on Human Factors in Computing Systems, pp. 259–266 (2002)

Belchior, P.P., et al.: Video game training to improve selective visual attention in older adults. Comput. Hum. Behav. **29**(4), 1318–1324 (2013)

Bezemer, J., Jewitt, C.: Multimodal analysis: key issues. Res. Methods Linguist. **180** (2010)

Callaghan, T.C.: Dimensional interaction of hue and brightness in preattentive field segre-gation. Percept. Psychophys. **36**(1), 25–34 (1984)

Chun, M.M.: Contextual cueing of visual attention. Trends Cogn. Sci. **4**(5), 170–178 (2000)

Chiossi, F., Arias, J.J., Borghese, N.A.: EEG-based adaptive virtual reality: modulating visual complexity to enhance user experience and cognitive performance. arXiv preprint arXiv:2311. 10447. https://arxiv.org/abs/2311.10447 (2023)

Chun, M.M., Jiang, Y.: Contextual cueing: implicit learning and memory of visual context guides spatial attention. Cogn. Psychol. **36**(1), 28–71 (1998)

Clark, J.: Visual Information Processing in Virtual Reality: Merging Theory and Practice. In International Conference on Information, pp. 461–468. Springer, Cham (2023)

Clark, J., Boz, L.: Exploring the effects of multi-sensory extraneous load on attention and task performance in VR. In: Proceedings of the 27th International Conference, HCI International 2025 (2025a)

Clark, J., Boz, L.: Exploring the effects of visual and auditory distractors in virtual reality on perceived cognitive load and cognitive alertness. In: WSEAS Transactions on Information Science and Applications (2025b)

Debue, N., Van De Leemput, C.: What does germane load mean? An empirical contribution to the cognitive load theory. Front. Psychol. **5**, 1099 (2014)

Gevins, A., Smith, M.E.: Neurophysiological measures of cognitive workload during human-computer interaction. Theor. Issues Ergon. Sci. **4**(1–2), 113–131 (2003)

Gevins, A., Smith, M.E., McEvoy, L., Yu, D.: High-resolution EEG mapping of cortical activation related to working memory: effects of task difficulty, type of processing, and practice. Cerebral cortex (New York, NY: 1991), **7**(4), 374–385 (1997)

Gonçalves, G., Monteiro, P., Melo, M., Vasconcelos-Raposo, J., Bessa, M.: A comparative study between wired and wireless virtual reality setups. IEEE Access **8**, 29249–29258 (2020)

Hebb, D.O., Donderi, D.C.: Textbook of Psychology (Psychology Revivals). Psychology Press (2013)

Hoffman, D.M., Girshick, A.R., Akeley, K., Banks, M.S.: Vergence–accommodation conflicts hinder visual performance and cause visual fatigue. J. Vis. **8**(3), 33 (2008)

Hsia, H.J.: The information processing capacity of modality and channel performance. ECTJ. **19**, 51 (1971). https://doi.org/10.1007/BF02768431

Jerald, Jason. The VR book: Human-centered design for virtual reality. Morgan & Claypool, 2015

Klepsch, M., Schmitz, F., Seufert, T.: Development and validation of two instruments measuring intrinsic, extraneous, and germane cognitive load. Front. Psychol. **8**, 1997 (2017)

Klimesch, W.: EEG alpha and theta oscillations reflect cognitive and memory performance: a review and analysis. Brain Res. Rev. **29**(2–3), 169–195 (1999)

Ma, C., Huang, J.B., Yang, X., Yang, M.H.: Hierarchical convolutional features for visual tracking. In: Proceedings of the IEEE International Conference on Computer Vision, pp. 3074–3082 (2015)

Mack, A.: Inattentional blindness: looking without seeing. Curr. Dir. Psychol. Sci. **12**(5), 180–184 (2003)

Makransky, G., Terkildsen, T.S., Mayer, R.E.: Adding immersive virtual reality to a science lab simulation causes more presence but less learning. Learn. Instr. **60**, 225–236 (2019)

Mayer, R.E.: Cognitive theory of multimedia learning. Cambridge Handb. Multimedia Learn. **41**, 31–48 (2005)

Mayer, R.E.: Research-based principles for designing multimedia instruction. In: Benassi, V.A., Overson, C.E., Hakala, C.M. (eds.), Applying science of learning in education: Infusing Psychol. Sci. Curriculum, 59–70 (2014)

Mayer, R.E., Fiorella, L.: 12 principles for reducing extraneous processing in multimedia learning: Coherence, signaling, redundancy, spatial contiguity, and temporal contiguity principles. In: The Cambridge Handbook of Multimedia Learning, vol. 279. Cambridge University Press (2014)

Mind Monitor. https://mind-monitor.com/. Accessed 13 Feb 2025

Moreno, R., Mayer, R.E.: Visual presentations in multimedia learning: Conditions that overload visual working memory. In: International Conference on Advances in Visual Information Systems, pp. 798–805. Springer, Heidelberg (1999)

Neurofeedback EEG device - how it works. Muse. https://choosemuse.com/pages/science. Retrieved 13 Feb 2025

Petersen, A., Petersen, A.H., Bundesen, C., Vangkilde, S., Habekost, T.: The effect of phasic auditory alerting on visual perception. Cognition **165**, 73–81 (2017)

Sterman, M.B., Mann, C.A., Kaiser, D.A., Suyenobu, B.Y.: Multiband topographic EEG analysis of a simulated visuomotor aviation task. Int. J. Psychophysiol. **16**(1), 49–56 (1994)

Unity Real-Time Development Platform. https://unity.com/. Accessed 13 Feb 2025

VIVE Pro Eye Overview. https://www.vive.com/sea/product/vive-pro-eye/overview/. Accessed 13 Feb 2025

Vorländer, M. Shinn-Cunningham, B.G.: Virtual Auditory Displays. Handbook of Virtual Environments, 2nd ed (2014)

Zhang, L.: Towards using eye-tracking and consumer-grade electroencephalogram devices to detect usability issues in mobile applications. Doctoral dissertation. School of Information, University of Arizona, USA (2021)

# Neural Dynamics of Group Interaction in the Iterate Multi-player Prisoner's Dilemma Game: Multilayer Network Approach

Heegyu Kim[1], Sung Chan Jun[1($\boxtimes$)], and Chang S. Nam[2]

[1] Gwangju Institute of Science and Technology, Gwangju, South Korea
{kim0401hg,scjun}@gist.ac.kr
[2] Northern Illinois University, DeKalb, USA
csnam@niu.edu

**Abstract.** Understanding social interaction from various human behaviors is a complex task. Hyperscanning research tackles this challenge by delving into behavioral mechanisms through a neuroscience lens. While traditional studies focus on inter-brain synchrony in paired functional brain networks, they often lack methods for measuring interactions at the group level. In this study, we propose a multilayer network approach to estimate group brain synchrony and gain deeper insights into the brain's intricate organization. By utilizing the Prisoner's Dilemma Game, our goal is to find group interaction processes through distinct behaviors such as cooperation and defection. Thus, the inter-brain synchrony along with differences in network connectivity and structural properties within the functional group network were statistically analyzed between cooperation and defection.

**Keywords:** Electroencephalogram (EEG) · Hyperscanning · Social interaction · Multilayer network · Prisoners dilemma (PD) game

## 1 Introduction

Social interaction is essential for human life and is closely linked to individuals' health and psychological well-being. Studies have shown that secure interactions can contribute to a more positive mood, fewer depressive symptoms, and improved emotional regulation and resilience [1, 2]. As a result, to better understand the mechanisms underlying social interaction, researchers often analyze factors such as eye gaze, micro-expressions, hand gestures, and emotions [3–5]. These elements provide valuable insights into the dynamics of social engagement and can help develop strategies to enhance social well-being and communication.

Understanding social interaction from various human behaviors is a complex task [6]. Therefore, in an effort to explore the origins of these interactions, researchers have attempted to approach the problem from a brain-centered perspective. Social neuroscience aims to understand how the mind works by interpreting mind-brain connections through comprehensive theories of the mechanisms underlying complex behavior and

© The Author(s), under exclusive license to Springer Nature Switzerland AG 2025
D. D. Schmorrow and C. M. Fidopiastis (Eds.): HCII 2025, LNAI 15778, pp. 18–31, 2025.
https://doi.org/10.1007/978-3-031-93724-8_2

cognition [7]. To better understand social interactions, researchers initially sought to mimic real-world social interactions and examine differences in neural activity at the individual brain level [8, 9]. However, analyzing social interactions from a single brain perspective through behavioral observations makes it difficult to fully comprehend how social interactions work and shape one's mind. To gain a deeper understanding of these interactions, the concept of Brain-to-Brain Coupling has been introduced [10].

Brain-to-brain coupling relies on stimulus-to-brain coupling as a vehicle for conveying information. Thus, it can be interpreted as information sharing through transmission between interacting brains [10]. To investigate the concept of inter-brain synchrony, researchers analyze mutual neural activity through a method known as Hyperscanning. Hyperscanning research addresses this challenge by exploring behavioral mechanisms through a neuroscience lens.

Phase analysis is conducted to measure synchrony to measure multi-person social interaction, especially in neural oscillations recorded using EEG following brain activation [11]. This phase analysis estimates information sharing based on the activation of cortical regions. Several measurement methods are employed to perform this phase analysis. Coherence estimates the relationship between multivariate time series data based on spectral correlation and is interpreted as the direction of information flow between brains [12]. Phase Locking Value (PLV) separates the phase and amplitude components and can be directly interpreted within the framework of neural integration [13]. The wavelet-based method is employed for time-frequency analysis, using multiple cycles to analyze oscillatory activities [14]. By utilizing these measurement techniques, the extent of information flow through activated oscillations in inter-brain synchrony can be estimated, allowing researchers to observe biological actions.

Recent advancements Phase analysis is conducted to measure synchrony to measure multi-person social interaction, especially in neural oscillations recorded using EEG following brain activation [11]. This phase analysis estimates information sharing based on the activation of cortical regions. Several measurement methods are employed to perform this phase analysis. Coherence estimates the relationship between multivariate time series data based on spectral correlation and is interpreted as the direction of information flow between brains [12]. Phase Locking Value (PLV) separates the phase and amplitude components and can be directly interpreted within the framework of neural integration [13]. The wavelet-based method is employed for time-frequency analysis, using multiple cycles to analyze oscillatory activities [14]. By utilizing these measurement techniques, the extent of information flow through activated oscillations in inter-brain synchrony can be estimated, allowing researchers to observe biological actions. Neuroscience has recommended the use of inter-brain synchrony and functional connectivity to measure the topological organization of brain networks through functional network analysis [15–17]. These studies employ graph theoretical measures, which have demonstrated strong performance in observing functional dynamics and are widely applied in analyzing cooperative, simultaneous, and continuous joint action tasks [18–21]. In this context, intra-matrices and hyper brain connectivity maps can be better described using multiple effectiveness measures based on graph theory. Among measures: The degree is the most fundamental metric used to quantify efficiency and serves as a global measure of network connectivity. A higher degree in the functional network is interpreted as a stronger occurrence of inter-brain synchrony [22]. The clustering coefficient measures the prevalence of clustered connectivity around regions of interest (ROIs). It evaluates the strength of local information exchange and is particularly useful for identifying specific synchrony patterns that appear strongly in particular ROIs rather than in random networks [23]. Density is a global measure derived from Graph Theory that describes the extent of connectivity within a network [24, 25]. It is defined as the proportion of existing connections relative to all possible connections in the Graph. It is the most straightforward estimator of the network's physical cost (e.g., energy or other resource requirements). Community or Network Community refers to modularity, representing interregional structural organization [26].The maximum value of community modularity indicates distinct community structures within the network, providing insights into the brain's functional segmentation and specialization.

Research has indicated that social behavior varies depending on the size of the group, whether it be in dyads, triads, or larger settings [27–31]. These variations are thought to stem from the greater complexity involved in communication and cognitive processing during the decision-making process, which in turn affects behavior [32]. Furthermore, it has been suggested that emotions play a more significant role in dyadic interactions, while uncertainty reduction is more crucial in triadic interactions [33]. These findings underscore the importance of considering the number of participants when analyzing social behavior and imply that different mechanisms may influence social interactions based on group size.

By leveraging graph theoretical approaches, functional network analysis provides a deeper understanding of inter-brain dynamics and helps uncover patterns of brain connectivity in a social interaction context. Traditional studies tend to focus on inter-brain synchrony within paired functional brain networks but often lack methods for assessing interactions at the group level. This limitation arises because hyperscanning research mainly analyzes brain-to-brain interactions or synchrony, emphasizing pairwise analyses [34, 35]. As a result, even in studies involving group conditions, the analysis of inter-brain synchrony remains the primary approach [36–39]. However, there is an increasing need to develop and implement methodologies to capture the complexity of group-level interactions beyond simple pairwise synchrony analysis.

Interaction within a team or group can be viewed as a continuous process of discussion or decision-making [40]. It has been established that group interaction and decision-making exhibit behavioral differences compared to individual decision-making [41]. For instance, studies have shown that when individuals and groups are given the same task of distributing money, groups tend to make more altruistic decisions [42]. Additionally, in in-game scenarios, groups are more likely to make strategically sound decisions that align with theoretical predictions than individuals [43]. Research on group decision-making aims to analyze the underlying causes of mutually beneficial behaviors and suggest ways to reduce social costs, ultimately enhancing social welfare. Decision-making research is often conducted by simulating real-world scenarios through economic game theories, sometimes leading to erroneous interpretations of group economic behavior. Among these game-theoretical scenarios, one widely used paradigm is the Prisoner's Dilemma (PD) game, which presents players with a choice between cooperative and defective states. This game is particularly suitable for observing social interactions, as it allows multiple players to weigh individual versus collective advantage [44]. Hyperscanning techniques have been applied to PD games to better understand social interactions and analyze brain activation across multiple individuals. Studies, such as those by Astolfi et al., have demonstrated that cooperative decisions lead to increased brain activation and inter-brain synchrony, highlighting the correlation between social interaction and brain activity [45]. However, most EEG-based PD game studies have primarily focused on 2-player interactions [46–51], making it challenging to observe group interactions effectively [52]. Recent efforts have explored N-player PD game scenarios to address this limitation, facilitate behavioral analysis, and better understand dynamic social interactions and networks [34, 52, 53]. These advances aim to bridge the gap between individual and group-level decision-making processes, offering new insights into the neural mechanisms underlying social cooperation and competition.

In this study, a PD game-based scenario was developed to illustrate characteristic interactions and examine group dynamics and social networks. The experiment was designed as a 3-player PD game, simulating conditions of group interaction. An EEG-based inter-brain functional network was constructed to extract social brain characteristics during gameplay. Additionally, a multilayer network approach was employed to analyze social features from the network and to construct and validate the group network. This methodology aims to provide deeper insights into the neural dynamics of social interactions in multi-person settings, utilizing EEG hyperscanning and advanced network analysis techniques. We propose a multilayer network approach to investigate group brain synchrony and gain deeper insights into the brain's intricate organizations. By utilizing the Prisoner's Dilemma Game, our goal is to understand neural dynamics of group interaction processes through distinct behaviors such as cooperation and defection.

## 2 Materials

### 2.1 Participants

We collected EEG data collection during a Sequential Prisoner's Dilemma (PD) game involving 11 groups (11 groups x 3 players), that 33 subjects (13 females, 22.59 ± 2.56) participated in this experiment. All participants have no prior experience with the PD game experiment. The Institutional Review Board at Gwangju Institute of Science and Technology (GIST) approved this experiment (20231207-HR-74-02-02), and all subjects were informed of all experimental procedures and questionnaire, and signed written informed consents.

### 2.2 EEG Acquisition

EEG recordings were obtained using three DSI-24 devices from Wearable Sensing, which each feature 24 dry electrodes (including the standard 19 channels, two earlobes, and three additional channels). These devices are configured based on the standard 10/20 system and utilize a sampling rate of 300 Hz. Reference electrodes were positioned on both earlobes. Prior to the experiments, the electrode impedances were checked and confirmed to be below 5 kΩ for all EEG channels. The synchronization of EEG data collection with task events from the three devices was accomplished using OpenViBE

[54]. The recorded EEG data underwent a high-pass filter at 0.01 Hz using a 4th order Butterworth filter, and a 60 Hz notch filter was applied to eliminate significant power line noise. EEG preprocessing was conducted using the EEGLAB toolbox (version 2022.0) [55].

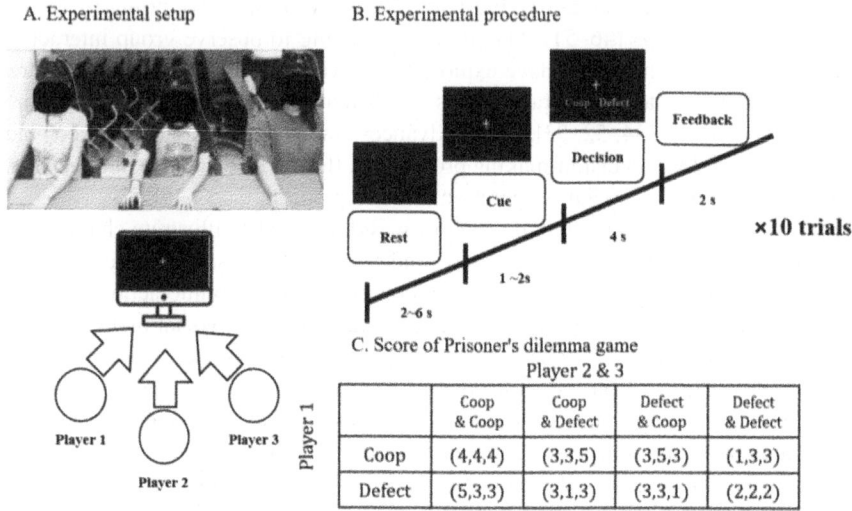

**Fig. 1.** (A) The 3-person prisoner's dilemma game was set up for experimentation. Simultaneous EEG data acquisition was conducted using three synchronized EEG-recording devices facilitated by OpenViBE. (B) The experimental procedure. (C) The payoff matrix for the iterated Prisoner's Dilemma Game.

## 2.3 Experimental Setup

In this experiment, an iterated 3-player prisoner's dilemma (PD) game was implemented [56]. The payoff for each interaction was weakly dominated, aiming to encourage cooperative decision-making throughout the iterations [57] (see Fig. 1, C). Participants were compensated based on their performance across 40 rounds, with a maximum reward of 30,000 Korean won (approximately $22) for those who scored 190 points or more. The reward decreased by 3,000 won for each 15-point reduction in their score, creating a tiered payment system based on performance.

To study social group synchrony during the decision-making process, each group of 3 players participated in four rounds of the PD game, comprising ten consecutive trials. The experiment (Fig. 1) was structured as follows: a 1–2 s instruction phase, a 4-s decision-making phase, a 2-s feedback phase presenting the decision outcome and scores, followed by a 2–6 s resting phase ([cue(2s) + decision(4s) + feedback(2s) + rest(2 ~ 6s)] x 10 trials x 4 repetitions). The scoring and reward system of the PD game is depicted in Fig. 1 B. Additionally, resting-state EEG was recorded for 60 s before and after the experiment.

# 3  Method

The decision onset was established at the beginning of the decision-making phase, and data from the interval of -1 to 4 s were aggregated, resulting in 40 epochs per group. Brain synchrony was examined across five frequency bands: theta (4 to 8 Hz), alpha (8 to 13 Hz), low-beta (13 to 20 Hz), high-beta (20 to 30 Hz), and gamma (30 to 50 Hz), utilizing two measures: coherence (Coh) and phase-locking value (PLV). Synchrony values were evaluated using a clustering permutation test with 500 repetitions [58], and statistically significant results were obtained with a significance level (alpha) < 0.05, employing the FieldTrip toolbox [59].

## 3.1  Brain Synchrony

**Coherence (Coh.)** is the spectral connectivity. The Welch estimate of coherence is:

$$\text{Coh}_{XY}(x) = \frac{|S_{XY}(x)|^2}{S_{XX}(x)S_{YY}(x)}$$

where $|S_{XY}|$ is the cross spectrum between the signals X and Y, and $S_{XX}$ and $S_{YY}$ are is the autospectrum of each signal X and Y [60].

**Phase locking value(PLV)** is the method of detecting synchrony in precise frequency range [13].

$$PLV_t = \frac{1}{N} | \sum \exp(j\theta(t, n))|$$

where $\theta(t, n)$ is the phase difference $(\phi_1(t, n) - \phi_2(t, n))$. .

**Circular correlation coefficient (CCorr)** is a direct parallel to the Pearson Product Moment Correlation Coefficient for circular signal [61] and is given by:

$$\text{CCorr} = \frac{\sum \sin(\phi - \overline{\phi})\sin(\psi - \overline{\psi})}{\sqrt{\sum \sin^2\phi - \overline{\phi}\sin^2\psi - \overline{\psi}}}$$

where $\overline{\phi}$ and $\overline{\psi}$ are the mean directions for channels 1 and 2 respectively.

## 3.2  Network Indices

Degree refers to the measure of how many direct connections a node (representing a brain area) has with other nodes [62]. Statistically selected functional connectivity can be seen as a method for quantitatively assessing the information exchange within the network by evaluating its topological properties. The total degree of node $i$, $d_i$, , is defined as the sum of the weights of all edges $(e_{i,j})$ connected to that node both within the layer and across other layers, and thats inter-layer degree $(\overline{d})$ of node $i$ with all other $j = 1, 2,$ ... nodes for each layer $(l, m)$ is defined as:

$$\overline{d}_i^l = \sum_{l \neq m} \sum_j^n e_{i,j}^{l,m}$$

Network **Density** Measures the territorial occupation of a transport network in terms links (L) per square of surface (S) [63]. The higher it is, the more a network and an economy is developed

$$ND = \frac{L}{S}$$

Optimal **community** is a subdivision of the network into nonoverlapping groups of nodes which maximizes the number of within-group edges, and minimizes the number of between-group edges [64]. In mathematical form, being $Ci$ the community to which node $i$ is assigned, modularity is expressed in terms of the weighted adjacency matrix $wi \boxtimes j$, which represents the value of the weight in the link between $i$ and $j$ (0 if no link exists)

$$Q = \frac{1}{2w} \sum \sum (w_{ij} - \frac{w_i w_j}{2w})\delta(C_i, C_j)$$

### 3.3 Multilayer Network

A multilayer network was constructed, where each individual's brain network was depicted as a layer [65] establishing a synchrony network of size 3*19 channels × 3*19 channels, with intra-network information represented as a bi-graph (zero) network (See Fig. 2). To assess network connectivity, metrics such as degree (network strength), density (distribution of existing connections), and community (modularity, signifying groups of network nodes) were utilized to compare synchrony differences. Connectivity between the two multilayer networks was statistically examined using an unsigned Wilcoxon rank-sum test, as Rest, cooperation (Coop), and defection (Def) were unbalanced in frequency. Coop. is defined as when all three players choose to cooperate, while Def. Occurs when at least one of the three players chooses to defect.

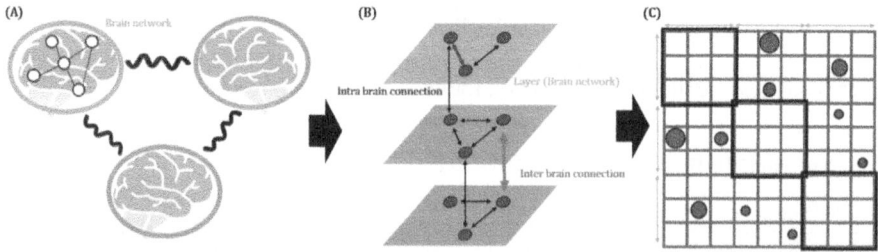

**Fig. 2.** The multilayer network was constructed as follow: (A) each sub-network (layer) was assumed to be an individual brain network. (B) The inter-layer connections were assumed to be the inter-brain synchrony between two EEG channel locations, and to reduce the influence of single-brain connections, the intra-brain connection was modeled as a bigraph (non-connected network). (C) A multilayer synchrony network was constructed for the triad, and network indices were used to quantify the connectivity.

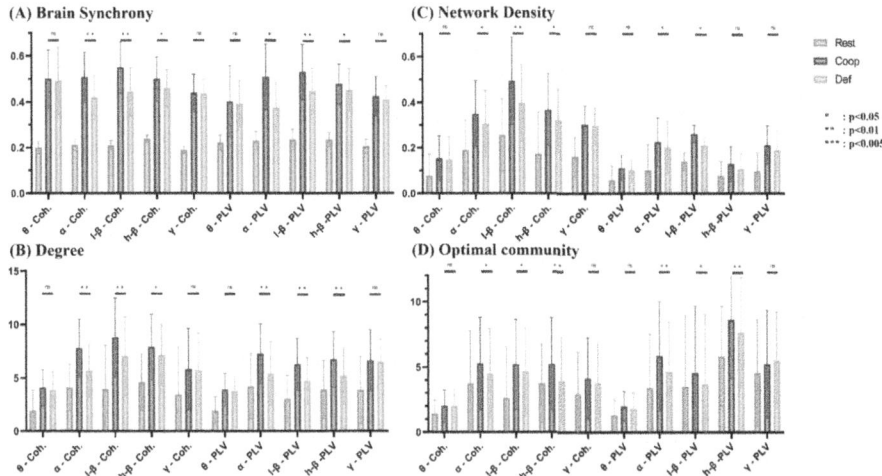

**Fig. 3.** (A) Bar graph showing brain synchrony values for Coh. and PLV. (B) Degree, (C) Density, and (D) Community of the multilayer network constructed from the two synchrony values. The blue star indicates the statistical results between the Coop and Defect conditions based on the Wilcoxon rank-sum test.

**Table 1.** The grand average results of brain synchrony and network indices of Degree, density, and max. Community.

| | | Resting | | | | Cooperation | | | | Defect | | | |
|---|---|---|---|---|---|---|---|---|---|---|---|---|---|
| | | Synchrony | Degree | Density | Opt. Community | Synchrony | Degree | Density | Opt. Community | Synchrony | Degree | Density | Opt. Community |
| Coh. | θ | 0.20 ± 0.03 | 1.9 ± 1.8 | 0.07 ± 0.09 | 1.45 ± 1.01 | 0.50 ± 0.13 | 4.1 ± 1.6 | 0.15 ± 0.09 | 2.00 ± 1.25 | 0.49 ± 0.14 | 3.9 ± 1.7 | 0.14 ± 0.09 | 2.00 ± 1.25 |
| | α | 0.22 ± 0.02 | 4.0 ± 2.1 | 0.19 ± 0.12 | 3.75 ± 4.03 | 0.51 ± 0.12 | 7.8 ± 2.6 | 0.34 ± 0.14 | 5.27 ± 3.54 | 0.42 ± 0.09 | 5.6 ± 2.5 | 0.30 ± 0.14 | 4.52 ± 3.42 |
| | l-β | 0.21 ± 0.02 | 3.9 ± 4.1 | 0.25 ± 0.15 | 2.61 ± 3.93 | 0.55 ± 0.11 | 8.8 ± 3.6 | 0.49 ± 0.19 | 5.20 ± 3.44 | 0.44 ± 0.11 | 7.0 ± 3.6 | 0.39 ± 0.16 | 4.66 ± 3.33 |
| | h-β | 0.24 ± 0.01 | 4.6 ± 2.6 | 0.17 ± 0.18 | 3.77 ± 3.01 | 0.49 ± 0.09 | 7.9 ± 3.0 | 0.36 ± 0.15 | 5.25 ± 3.52 | 0.46 ± 0.08 | 7.1 ± 2.8 | 0.32 ± 0.14 | 3.98 ± 3.30 |
| | γ | 0.19 ± 0.01 | 3.4 ± 4.4 | 0.16 ± 0.08 | 2.94 ± 3.25 | 0.44 ± 0.08 | 5.8 ± 3.8 | 0.30 ± 0.08 | 4.15 ± 3.12 | 0.43 ± 0.06 | 5.7 ± 3.4 | 0.29 ± 0.08 | 3.81 ± 3.06 |
| PLV | θ | 0.22 ± 0.03 | 1.9 ± 1.3 | 0.05 ± 0.06 | 1.31 ± 1.18 | 0.40 ± 0.16 | 3.9 ± 1.5 | 0.11 ± 0.05 | 2.00 ± 1.15 | 0.39 ± 0.10 | 3.8 ± 1.3 | 0.10 ± 0.04 | 1.82 ± 1.21 |
| | α | 0.23 ± 0.04 | 4.2 ± 3.0 | 0.10 ± 0.11 | 3.45 ± 4.12 | 0.51 ± 0.14 | 7.2 ± 2.7 | 0.22 ± 0.10 | 5.86 ± 4.15 | 0.37 ± 0.10 | 5.4 ± 2.9 | 0.20 ± 0.11 | 4.65 ± 3.80 |
| | l-β | 0.23 ± 0.05 | 3.0 ± 2.2 | 0.14 ± 0.03 | 3.50 ± 5.46 | 0.53 ± 0.12 | 6.2 ± 2.4 | 0.26 ± 0.03 | 4.56 ± 5.11 | 0.44 ± 0.09 | 4.7 ± 2.1 | 0.21 ± 0.03 | 3.72 ± 5.34 |
| | h-β | 0.23 ± 0.03 | 3.9 ± 2.7 | 0.07 ± 0.06 | 5.82 ± 3.83 | 0.48 ± 0.09 | 6.7 ± 2.5 | 0.12 ± 0.07 | 8.63 ± 4.45 | 0.45 ± 0.09 | 5.2 ± 2.6 | 0.10 ± 0.06 | 7.66 ± 4.19 |
| | γ | 0.20 ± 0.03 | 3.8 ± 3.1 | 0.09 ± 0.08 | 4.55 ± 4.07 | 0.42 ± 0.08 | 6.6 ± 2.8 | 0.21 ± 0.08 | 5.24 ± 4.12 | 0.41 ± 0.06 | 6.5 ± 2.1 | 0.18 ± 0.08 | 5.51 ± 3.72 |

## 4  Results

In our study, we examined three network indices by creating a multilayer network to measure brain synchrony among pairs of individuals and within group brain networks during non-task (resting), cooperative task, and defective task conditions. The grand average of synchrony, Coh., was [0.21 ± 0.02, 0.50 ± 0.10, 0.45 ± 0.10], and PLV was [0.22 ± 0.04, 0.47 ± 0.12, 0.41 ± 0.09], for resting, coop, and defect conditions, respectively. The grand average of Degree, Coh., was [3.61 ± 3.06, 6.89 ± 2.99, 5.90 ± 2.86], and PLV was [3.40 ± 2.50, 6.17 ± 2.45, 5.13 ± 2.26]. The grand average of Density, Coh., was [0.17 ± 0.13, 0.33 ± 0.14, 0.29 ± 0.13], and PLV was [0.10 ± 0.07, 0.19 ± 0.07, 0.16 ± 0.07]. The grand average of max community, Coh., was [2.90

± 3.05, 4.38 ± 2.98, 3.80 ± 2.88], and PLV was [3.73 ± 3.74, 5.26 ± 3.80, 4.67 ± 3.66]. (as shown in Table 1 and Fig. 3). We found significant statistical variances (p < 0.001) between non-task and task conditions across all brain waves. Furthermore, while brain synchrony exhibited noteworthy distinctions between task conditions across all frequency bands, the multilayer network indices demonstrated particularly interesting variations in the alpha and beta bands.

## 5  Discussion and Conclusion

Social behavior is essential to our lives and influences the brain's cognitive processes. The Prisoner's Dilemma (PD) game offers a formal framework for exploring the critical trade-off between cooperating with others and pursuing self-interest, known as defection [33]. This study aims to validate the social brain network by analyzing the differences between social cooperation and defection using a multilayer network approach. Specifically, we employed an EEG hyperscanning technique to investigate how interactions affect PD game decision-making and uncover the underlying neural mechanisms and network dynamics that mediate this process.

We utilized Coh. And PLV to analyze the differences in pairwise brain synchrony and to establish a multilayer network of synchrony. The degree metric corresponded to network strength, indicating how synchrony is distributed across neural elements, which reflects the potential for clustered brain function (synchrony connections). The density metric represented the normalized degree values. Additionally, we employed community detection as a heuristic method to identify communities within the network. This approach revealed the level of group synchrony among different layers (representing individual brains) and the extent of synchronization between one brain and others in the multilayer network.

Network models are valuable tools for understanding the optimal flow of informa-tion. In this context, "complex" describes an extensive, sparsely connected network and exhibits an organization that falls between order and randomness. In active participants, various types of networks have been identified, including resting-state networks. These networks can be observed when participants are awake but not actively engaged in any tasks, often with their eyes closed. It has been observed that real neural networks do not operate precisely like random networks. Expressly, higher local clustering has been noted [66]. This phenomenon has been partially explained through the concept of small-world networks, where functional brain networks display characteristics similar to small-world networks, combining high local clustering with short path lengths [67–69]. These findings suggest that the network differences identified in this study are unlikely due to chance, further supporting the structured and non-random nature of the observed functional connectivity.

Notably, the network indices unveiled significant differences in the alpha and beta waves. The alpha wave, linked to social information processing [47] and high-level cognitive processing, likely reflects the influence of emotional empathy. The disparities in the beta band indicate that attractive behavior affects the brain's efficiency in transmitting information [62]. Astolfi and colleagues also conducted a hyperscanning study using the Prisoner's Dilemma (PD) game. They observed greater activity in the theta and alpha bands of the orbitofrontal cortex during defection, whereas cortical activity during cooperation was relatively lower [48, 49, 70, 71].

Alpha band activity has been shown to facilitate various cognitive and social processes, including visual and auditory working memory [72], synchronization of movements between a model and an imitator [21], cooperation and defection during the Prisoner's Dilemma game[71] emotional empathy while observing musical group performances via video [46], and coordination in human-to-human communication (Kawasaki et al., 2013) [74–78]. Previous EEG-based hyperscanning studies have documented alpha band inter-brain synchrony during the Prisoner's Dilemma game, indicating the involvement of social cognitive processing during social interactions. Research has shown that alpha band activity is crucial in integrating and processing social information [73]. Moreover, studies suggest that theta and alpha activity are involved in working memory processes [72]. In the Prisoner's Dilemma game context, social decision-making may require working memory to retain information about choices and outcomes from previous trials.

This research emphasizes the distinctions between non-synchronized and synchronized tasks in group settings, investigating the influence of synchronized behavior on group interaction. Furthermore, the study advances the field by simplifying complex behavioral and reasoning patterns in groups of people using a network approach, enabling the analysis and derivation of solutions for complex problem scenarios.

**Acknowledgments.** This research was results of a study on the "HPC Support" Project, supported by the 'Ministry of Science and ICT' and NIPA. This work was in part supported by the Ministry of Education of the Republic of Korea and the National Research Foundation of Korea (NRF-2023S1A5A2A01076552).

# References

1. Brandão, T., Matias, M., Ferreira, T., Vieira, J., Schulz, M.S., Matos, P.M.: Attachment, emotion regulation, and well-being in couples: intrapersonal and interpersonal associations. J. Pers. **88**(4), 748–761 (2020). https://doi.org/10.1111/jopy.12523
2. Karreman, A., Vingerhoets, A.J.J.M.: Attachment and well-being: the mediating role of emotion regulation and resilience. Personal. Individ. Differ. **53**(7), 821–826 (2012). https://doi.org/10.1016/j.paid.2012.06.014
3. Caruana, N., McArthur, G., Woolgar, A., Brock, J.: Simulating social interactions for the experimental investigation of joint attention. Neurosci. Biobehav. Rev. **74**, 115–125 (2017). https://doi.org/10.1016/j.neubiorev.2016.12.022
4. Innocenti, A., De Stefani, E., Bernardi, N.F., Campione, G.C., Gentilucci, M.: Gaze direction and request gesture in social interactions. PLoS ONE **7**(5), e36390 (2012). https://doi.org/10.1371/journal.pone.0036390
5. Treger, S., Sprecher, S., Erber, R.: Laughing and liking: Exploring the interpersonal effects of humor use in initial social interactions. Eur. J. Soc. Psychol. **43**(6), 532–543 (2013). https://doi.org/10.1002/ejsp.1962
6. Brehm, J.M.: Community attachment: the complexity and consequence of the natural environment facet. Hum. Ecol. **35**(4), 477–488 (2007). https://doi.org/10.1007/s10745-006-9104-3

7. Cacioppo, J.T., Berntson, G.G.: Social Neuroscience: Key Readings. Psychology Press (2005)
8. Pönkänen, L.M., Peltola, M.J., Hietanen, J.K.: The observer observed: frontal EEG asymmetry and autonomic responses differentiate between another person's direct and averted gaze when the face is seen live. Int. J. Psychophysiol. **82**(2), 180–187 (2011). https://doi.org/10.1016/j.ijpsycho.2011.08.006
9. Pönkänen, L.M., Hietanen, J.K.: Eye contact with neutral and smiling faces: effects on autonomic responses and frontal EEG asymmetry. Front. Hum. Neurosci. **6** (2012). https://doi.org/10.3389/fnhum.2012.00122
10. Hasson, U., Ghazanfar, A.A., Galantucci, B., Garrod, S., Keysers, C.: Brain-to-brain coupling: a mechanism for creating and sharing a social world. Trends Cogn. Sci. **16**(2), 114–121 (2012). https://doi.org/10.1016/j.tics.2011.12.007
11. Kelsen, B.A., Sumich, A., Kasabov, N., Liang, S.H.Y., Wang, G.Y.: What has social neuroscience learned from hyperscanning studies of spoken communication? A systematic review. Neurosci. Biobehav. Rev. **132**, 1249–1262 (2022). https://doi.org/10.1016/j.neubiorev.2020.09.008
12. Baccalá, L.A., Sameshima, K.: Partial directed coherence: a new concept in neural structure determination. Biol. Cybern. **84**(6), 463–474 (2001). https://doi.org/10.1007/PL00007990
13. Lachaux, J.-P., Rodriguez, E., Martinerie, J., Varela, F.J.: Measuring phase synchrony in brain signals. Hum. Brain Mapp. **8**(4), 194–208 (1999). https://doi.org/10.1002/(SICI)1097-0193(1999)8:4%3c194::AID-HBM4%3e3.0.CO;2-C
14. Ménoret, M., et al.: Neural correlates of non-verbal social interactions: a dual-EEG study. Neuropsychologia **55**, 85–97 (2014). https://doi.org/10.1016/j.neuropsychologia.2013.10.001
15. Czeszumski, A., et al.: Hyperscanning: a valid method to study neural inter-brain underpinnings of social interaction. Front. Hum. Neurosci. **14**, 39 (2020)
16. Shamay-Tsoory, S.G., Mendelsohn, A.: Real-life neuroscience: an ecological approach to brain and behavior research. Perspect. Psychol. Sci. **14**(5), 841–859 (2019). https://doi.org/10.1177/1745691619856350
17. Kasai, K., Fukuda, M., Yahata, N., Morita, K., Fujii, N.: The future of real-world neuroscience: Imaging techniques to assess active brains in social environments. Neurosci. Res. **90**, 65–71 (2015). https://doi.org/10.1016/j.neures.2014.11.007
18. Müller, V., Lindenberger, U.: Intra- and interbrain synchrony and hyperbrain network dynamics of a guitarist quartet and its audience during a concert. Ann. N. Y. Acad. Sci. **1523**(1), 74–90 (2023). https://doi.org/10.1111/nyas.14987
19. Toppi, J., et al.: Investigating cooperative behavior in ecological settings: an EEG hyperscanning study. PLOS ONE, **11**(4), e0154236 (2016). https://doi.org/10.1371/journal.pone.0154236
20. Gugnowska, K., Novembre, G., Kohler, N., Villringer, A., Keller, P.E., Sammler, D.: Endogenous sources of interbrain synchrony in duetting pianists. Cereb. Cortex **32**(18), 4110–4127 (2022)
21. Dumas, G., Nadel, J., Soussignan, R., Martinerie, J., Garnero, L.: Inter-brain synchronization during social interaction. PLoS ONE **5**(8), e12166 (2010)
22. D. B. Stone et al., "Hyperscanning of Interactive Juggling: Expertise Influence on Source Level Functional Connectivity," Front. Hum. Neurosci., vol. 13, Sep. 2019, https://doi.org/10.3389/fnhum.2019.00321
23. D. J. Watts and S. H. Strogatz, "Collective dynamics of 'small-world' networks," nature, vol. 393, no. 6684, pp. 440–442, 1998
24. Bullmore, E., Sporns, O.: Complex brain networks: graph theoretical analysis of structural and functional systems. Nat. Rev. Neurosci. **10**(3), 186–198 (2009)
25. Bassett, D.S., Bullmore, E.T.: Small-world brain networks revisited. Neuroscientist **23**(5), 499–516 (2017). https://doi.org/10.1177/1073858416667720

26. Martinet, L.-E., et al.: Robust dynamic community detection with applications to human brain functional networks. Nat. Commun. **11**(1), 2785 (2020). https://doi.org/10.1038/s41467-020-16285-7

27. Horswill, M.S., Helman, S.: A behavioral comparison between motorcyclists and a matched group of non-motorcycling car drivers: factors influencing accident risk. Accid. Anal. Prev. **35**(4), 589–597 (2003). https://doi.org/10.1016/S0001-4575(02)00039-8

28. Cao, Y., Philp, J.: Interactional context and willingness to communicate: a comparison of behavior in whole class, group and dyadic interaction. System **34**(4), 480–493 (2006). https://doi.org/10.1016/j.system.2006.05.002

29. Harada, T.: Three heads are better than two: Comparing learning properties and performances across individuals, dyads, and triads through a computational approach. PLoS ONE **16**(6), e0252122 (2021). https://doi.org/10.1371/journal.pone.0252122

30. Astolfi, L., et al.: Comparison of different cortical connectivity estimators for high-resolution EEG recordings. Hum. Brain Mapp. **28**(2), 143–157 (2007). https://doi.org/10.1002/hbm.20263

31. Wolfe, J.D., Kirkland, S.: Dyad/Triad Studies. I: Encyclopedia of Gerontology and Population Aging, pp. 1536–1540. Springer, Cham (2021). https://doi.org/10.1007/978-3-030-22009-9_579

32. Zhou, L., Zhang, D.: A comparison of deception behavior in dyad and triadic group decision making in synchronous computer-mediated communication. Small Group Res. **37**(2), 140–164 (2006). https://doi.org/10.1177/1046496405285125

33. Yoon, J., Thye, S.R., Lawler, E.J.: Exchange and cohesion in dyads and triads: a test of Simmel's hypothesis. Soc. Sci. Res. **42**(6), 1457–1466 (2013). https://doi.org/10.1016/j.ssresearch.2013.06.003

34. O'Riordan, C., Sorensen, H.: Stable cooperation in the N-player prisoner's dilemma: the importance of community structure. In: Tuyls, K., Nowe, A., Guessoum, Z., Kudenko, D., (eds.) Adaptive Agents and Multi-Agent Systems III. Adaptation and Multi-Agent Learning, pp. 157–168. Springer, Heidelberg (2008). https://doi.org/10.1007/978-3-540-77949-0_12

35. Newman, L.A., Cao, M., Täuber, S., van Vugt, M.K.: Mapping inter-brain synchronization results onto experimental design and analysis methods: a review on EEG hyperscanning. OSF (2024).https://doi.org/10.31234/osf.io/5vgp9

36. Dikker, S., et al.: Brain-to-brain synchrony tracks real world dynamic group interactions in the classroom. Curr. Biol. **27**(9), 1375–1380 (2017). https://doi.org/10.1016/j.cub.2017.04.002

37. Bevilacqua, D., et al.: Brain-to-brain synchrony and learning outcomes vary by student-teacher dynamics: evidence from a real-world classroom electroencephalography study. J. Cogn. Neurosci. **31**(3), 401–411 (2019). https://doi.org/10.1162/jocn_a_01274

38. Silfwerbrand, L., Koike, Y., Nyström, P., Gingnell, M.: Directed causal effect with PCMCI in hyperscanning EEG time series. Front. Neurosci. **18** (2024). https://doi.org/10.3389/fnins.2024.1305918

39. Bi, X., Cui, H., Ma, Y.: Hyperscanning studies on interbrain synchrony and child development: a narrative review. Neuroscience **530**, 38–45 (2023). https://doi.org/10.1016/j.neuroscience.2023.08.035

40. "Group decision-making behavior in social dilemmas: Inter-brain synchrony and the predictive role of personality traits." APA PsycNET. https://psycnet.apa.org/record/2020-80253-001. Accessed 25 Jan 25 2025

41. Blin, J.-M., Satterthwaite, M.A.: Individual decisions and group decisions: the fundamental differences. J. Public Econ. **10**(2), 247–267 (1978). https://doi.org/10.1016/0047-2727(78)90037-3

42. Cason, T.N., Mui, V.: A laboratory study of group polarisation in the team dictator game. Econ. J. **107**(444), 1465–1483 (1997). https://doi.org/10.1111/j.1468-0297.1997.tb00058.x

43. Cooper, D.J., Kagel, J.H.: Are two heads better than one? Team versus Individual play in signaling games. Am. Econ. Rev. **95**(3), 477–509 (2005). https://doi.org/10.1257/000282805 4201431
44. Camerer, C.F.: Behavioral Game Theory: Experiments in Strategic Interaction. Princeton University Press, Princeton (2011)
45. Astolfi, L., et al.: Neuroelectrical hyperscanning measures simultaneous brain activity in humans. Brain Topogr. **23**(3), 243–256 (2010). https://doi.org/10.1007/s10548-010-0147-9
46. Babiloni, F., et al.: Cortical activity and connectivity of human brain during the prisoner's dilemma: an EEG hyperscanning study. In: 2007 29th Annual International Conference of the IEEE Engineering in Medicine and Biology Society, pp. 4953–4956 (2007).https://doi.org/10.1109/IEMBS.2007.4353452
47. Jahng, J., Kralik, J.D., Hwang, D.-U., Jeong, J.: Neural dynamics of two players when using nonverbal cues to gauge intentions to cooperate during the prisoner's dilemma game. Neuroimage **157**, 263–274 (2017)
48. Astolfi, L., et al.: Estimation of the cortical activity from simultaneous multi-subject recordings during the prisoner's dilemma. In: 2009 Annual International Conference of the IEEE Engineering in Medicine and Biology Society, pp. 1937–1939 (2009). https://doi.org/10.1109/IEMBS.2009.5333456
49. De Vico Fallani, F., et al.: Defecting or not defecting: how to "read" human behavior during cooperative games by EEG measurements. PLoS ONE **5**(12), e14187 (2010)
50. Cervantes Constantino, F., et al.: Neural processing of iterated prisoner's dilemma outcomes indicates next-round choice and speed to reciprocate cooperation. Soc. Neurosci. **16**(2), 103–120 (2021). https://doi.org/10.1080/17470919.2020.1859410
51. Papageorgiou, C., Karanasiou, I.S., Tsianaka, E.I., Kyprianou, M., Papadimitriou, G.N., Uzunoglu, N.K.: Motive related positivity: decision-making during a prisoners' dilemma task. J. Integr. Neurosci. **12**(02), 183–199 (2013). https://doi.org/10.1142/S0219635213500106
52. Rezaei, G., Kirley, M.: Dynamic social networks facilitate cooperation in the N<math><mi is="true">N</mi></math>-player prisoner's dilemma. Phys. Stat. Mech. Appl. **391**(23), 6199–6211 (2012). https://doi.org/10.1016/j.physa.2012.06.071
53. Rezaei, G., Kirley, M., Pfau, J.: Evolving cooperation in the N-player prisoner's dilemma: a social network model. In: Korb, K., Randall, M., Hendtlass, T., (eds.) Artificial Life: Borrowing from Biology, pp. 43–52. Springer, Heidelberg (2009). https://doi.org/10.1007/978-3-642-10427-5_5
54. OpenViBE: An Open-Source Software Platform to Design, Test, and Use Brain–Computer Interfaces in Real and Virtual Environments. https://ieeexplore.ieee.org/abstract/document/6797525. Accessed 25 Jan 2025
55. Delorme, A., Makeig, S.: EEGLAB: an open source toolbox for analysis of single-trial EEG dynamics including independent component analysis. J. Neurosci. Methods **134**(1), 9–21 (2004)
56. Essam, E.S., Elshobaky, E.M., Soliman, K.M.: Two population three-player prisoner's dilemma game. Appl. Math. Comput. **277**, 44–53 (2016). https://doi.org/10.1016/j.amc.2015.12.047
57. Taha, M.A., Ghoneim, A.: Zero-determinant strategies in infinitely repeated three-player prisoner's dilemma game. Chaos Solitons Fractals **152**, 111408 (2021). https://doi.org/10.1016/j.chaos.2021.111408
58. Maris, E., Oostenveld, R.: Nonparametric statistical testing of EEG- and MEG-data. J. Neurosci. Methods **164**(1), 177–190 (2007). https://doi.org/10.1016/j.jneumeth.2007.03.024
59. Oostenveld, R., Fries, P., Maris, E., Schoffelen, J.-M.: FieldTrip: open-source software for advanced analysis of MEG, EEG, and invasive electrophysiological data (2011). https://doi.org/10.1155/2011/156869

60. Guevara, M.A., Corsi-Cabrera, M.: EEG coherence or EEG correlation? Int. J. Psychophysiol. **23**(3), 145–153 (1996)
61. Burgess, A.P.: On the interpretation of synchronization in EEG hyperscanning studies: a cautionary note. Front. Hum. Neurosci. **7**, 881 (2013)
62. Duan, L., Dai, R.-N., Xiao, X., Sun, P.-P., Li, Z., Zhu, C.-Z.: Cluster imaging of multi-brain networks (CIMBN): a general framework for hyperscanning and modeling a group of interacting brains. Front. Neurosci. **9**, 267 (2015)
63. Van Wijk, B.C.M., Stam, C.J., Daffertshofer, A.: Comparing brain networks of different size and connectivity density using graph theory. PLoS ONE **5**(10), e13701 (2010). https://doi.org/10.1371/journal.pone.0013701
64. Rubinov, M., Sporns, O.: Weight-conserving characterization of complex functional brain networks. Neuroimage **56**(4), 2068–2079 (2011). https://doi.org/10.1016/j.neuroimage.2011.03.069
65. Battiston, F., Nicosia, V., Latora, V.: Structural measures for multiplex networks. Phys. Rev. E **89**(3), 032804 (2014). https://doi.org/10.1103/PhysRevE.89.032804
66. Muller, R.U., Stead, M., Pach, J.: The hippocampus as a cognitive graph. J. Gen. Physiol. **107**(6), 663–694 (1996). https://doi.org/10.1085/jgp.107.6.663
67. Stam, C.J.: Functional connectivity patterns of human magnetoencephalographic recordings: a 'small-world' network? Neurosci. Lett. **355**(1), 25–28 (2004). https://doi.org/10.1016/j.neulet.2003.10.063
68. Bassett, D.S., Meyer-Lindenberg, A., Achard, S., Duke, T., Bullmore, E.: Adaptive reconfiguration of fractal small-world human brain functional networks. Proc. Natl. Acad. Sci. **103**(51), 19518–19523 (2006). https://doi.org/10.1073/pnas.0606005103
69. Achard, S., Salvador, R., Whitcher, B., Suckling, J., Bullmore, E.: A resilient, low-frequency, small-world human brain functional network with highly connected association cortical hubs. J. Neurosci. **26**(1), 63–72 (2006). https://doi.org/10.1523/JNEUROSCI.3874-05.2006
70. Astolfi, L., et al.: Simultaneous estimation of cortical activity during social interactions by using EEG hyperscannings. In: 2010 Annual International Conference of the IEEE Engineering in Medicine and Biology, pp. 2814–2817 (2010).https://doi.org/10.1109/IEMBS.2010.5626555
71. Astolfi, L., et al.: Imaging the social brain by simultaneous hyperscanning during subject interaction. IEEE Intell. Syst. **26**(5), 38–45 (2011). https://doi.org/10.1109/MIS.2011.61
72. Kawasaki, M., Kitajo, K., Yamaguchi, Y.: Dynamic links between theta executive functions and alpha storage buffers in auditory and visual working memory. https://onlinelibrary.wiley.com/doi/10.1111/j.1460-9568.2010.07217.x. Accessed 25 Jan 2025
73. Perry, A., et al.: Intranasal oxytocin modulates EEG mu/alpha and beta rhythms during perception of biological motion. Psychoneuroendocrinology **35**(10), 1446–1453 (2010)
74. Kawasaki, M., Kitajo, K., Yamaguchi, Y.: Dynamic links between theta executive functions and alpha storage buffers in auditory and visual working memory. Eur. J. Neurosci. **31**(9), 1683–1689 (2010)
75. Dumas, G., Nadel, J., Soussignan, R., Martinerie, J., Garnero, L.: Inter-brain synchronization during social interaction. PloS one **5**(8), e12166 (2010)
76. Astolfi, L., et al.: Imaging the social brain by simultaneous hyperscanning during subject interaction. IEEE Intell. Syst. **26**(5), 38 (2011)
77. Babiloni, C., et al.: Brains "in concert": frontal oscillatory alpha rhythms and empathy in professional musicians. Neuroimage **60**(1), 105–116 (2012)
78. Kawasaki, M., Yamada, Y., Ushiku, Y., Miyauchi, E., Yamaguchi, Y.: Inter-brain synchronization during coordination of speech rhythm in human-to-human social interaction. Sci. Rep. **3**(1), 1692 (2013)

# Research on Human-Machine Interface for Enhancing Pilot Situational Awareness in Urban Air Mobility with Eye-Tracking Technology

Songhan Li and Zhisheng Zhang[✉]

School of Mechanical Engineering, Southeast University, Nanjing 211189,
People's Republic of China
songhanli@seu.edu.cn

**Abstract.** Urban Air Mobility (UAM) utilizes electric vertical takeoff and landing (eVTOL) technology for low-altitude urban travel, easing ground traffic congestion. However, its complex flight environment demands higher pilot situational awareness (SA). This study designs a human-machine interface (HMI) based on eye-tracking technology to enhance task performance and attention to critical information. A simulated flight experiment compared two conditions (HMI vs. no HMI) across autonomous flight: distraction, attention refocusing, and emergency response tasks. Results show that the HMI reduced reaction time (22.6% in emergencies), increased fixation duration (21.4%), improved attention allocation (18.1%), and decreased saccades (27.3%). These findings suggest that an optimized HMI effectively directs attention, reduces cognitive load, and improves emergency response. This study provides design insights for UAM HMIs and highlights the role of multimodal interaction (visual, auditory, haptic) in enhancing flight safety and usability. Future work could integrate AI and AR to improve adaptability.

**Keywords:** Urban Air Mobility (UAM) · Human-Machine Interface (HMI) ·
Pilot Situational Awareness · Eye-Tracking Technology

## 1 Introduction

Urban Air Mobility (UAM) is an emerging mode of transportation that uses electric-powered Vertical Takeoff and Landing (VTOL) aircraft to relieve urban congestion and provide rapid air transportation solutions, is an important carrier of low-altitude economy and application scenarios, which expands the existing urban transportation structure from two-dimensional to three-dimensional, and helps to solve the current bottleneck problem of urban transportation. It expands the existing urban transportation structure from two-dimensional to three-dimensional. It helps to solve the current urban transportation bottleneck problems, especially the rise of electric vertical takeoff and landing aircraft (eVTOL) in the past two years, which can significantly improve the efficiency

D. D. Schmorrow and C. M. Fidopiastis (Eds.): HCII 2025, LNAI 15778, pp. 32–43, 2025.
https://doi.org/10.1007/978-3-031-93724-8_3

of traffic travel and effectively share the pressure of ground transportation.UAM has the potential to change urban transportation and can provide a faster, more sustainable, and more convenient alternative to the current ground transportation system. Its applications include air cabs, emergency response, and parcel delivery. Straubinger [1] suggests that UAM is not intended to fill the urban transportation accessibility gap but represents an additional, potentially more time-efficient transportation service. UAM vehicle technology is now nearing maturity. Morgan Stanley predicts that global UAM will reach $9 trillion by 2050.

Currently, research in the field of UAM is predominantly concentrated in areas such as traffic management [2–4], ground infrastructure [5], user studies [6–8], legal policy analysis [9, 10], vehicle technology [11, 12], time efficiency [13], and cost analysis [14]. However, a notable research gap exists in the Human-Machine Interface (HMI) within the airborne cabin to enhance passenger-perceived safety and service acceptance.

Safety is always an important transportation design factor and must be considered first and foremost in the design. An efficient human-machine interface (HMI) ensures safe, effective, and intuitive interaction between the pilot and the autopilot system, especially in this new urban air environment. This research focuses on designing and validating a UAM-specific HMI to improve pilot situational awareness and overall performance. Drawing on successful strategies for automated pilot HMIs, this research employs user-centered design principles to create a multimodal interface. The developed system provides real-time information, status updates, and emergency alerts through visual, auditory, and haptic multimodal feedback, aiming to reduce cognitive load and improve responsiveness in critical flight scenarios.

Compared to the user interface of traditional automobiles, the human-machine interface design of UAM (Urban Air Transportation) needs to cope with the dynamic and complex urban low-altitude flight environment and satisfy the pilot's need for efficient situational awareness under multi-mission and multi-source information conditions. The interface must integrate key information such as real-time navigation, weather updates, obstacle avoidance, etc., and provide efficient operational support through multimodal interactions (e.g., voice, haptic, and gesture control). In emergency scenarios, the interface should prioritize presenting high-priority information to reduce information overload and enhance the pilot's ability to make quick decisions. For different user groups (including professional pilots and general users), the interface should be easy to use and adaptable to reduce the threshold of user learning.

Therefore, this study uses simulated driving experiments to investigate urban air traffic interaction patterns from two perspectives. The research objectives are as follows:

- How to enhance drivers' trust by adjusting interface style and color to achieve the best task performance under different situations.
- How to further explore the driver's acceptance and trust of the user interface under different task phases in everyday driving.

# 2 Methods

## 2.1 Participants

Twenty undergraduate and graduate students (9 males, 11 females, ages 20 to 26 years, mean = 22.5, SD = 1.74) were recruited from Southeast University for this study. Each participant signed an informed consent form prior to participation. All participants had no prior experience with similar experiments, and their vision was either normal or corrected to normal. Participants completed two rounds of the experiment and were compensated for their participation after completing both rounds.

## 2.2 Apparatus

The experiment was conducted in the Intelligent Driving Laboratory of Southeast University under standard illumination conditions (approximately 300 lx) to ensure participants performed tasks in a well-lit but distraction-free environment. The simulated driving setup consisted of three 23.8-inch Samsung S24R356F monitors (1920 × 1080 resolution, 60 Hz refresh rate), arranged to provide a wide field of view and high-precision visual information, ensuring a visually immersive experience closely resembling real-world driving scenarios.

The hardware included the Logitech G923 TRUE FORCE system, comprising a steering wheel, braking device, and gear shifter, designed to simulate realistic physical feedback and deliver a tactile experience akin to actual driving. An XDracing seat frame kit (adjustable range 580 mm to 1200 mm) was used to replicate the seating layout of an actual vehicle cockpit, accommodating participants of varying body sizes. The simulation program, installed on a computer system, also generated a highly realistic urban driving environment featuring city roads, traffic signals, dynamic traffic flow, and potential obstacles, effectively recreating real-world driving tasks' complexity and dynamic nature.

The experimental setup was placed in a dedicated enclosed room (see Fig. 2) to minimize external visual and auditory distractions. The equipment was positioned centrally in the room, with the three monitors arranged in a semicircular layout against the wall to optimize the participant's field of view and reduce peripheral disturbances. The room was equipped with soundproofing measures to ensure participants could concentrate fully on the experimental tasks. This layout and equipment configuration enhanced the participants' immersive experience and improved the consistency and reliability of the collected experimental data (Fig. 1).

## 2.3 Experimental Design

In order to evaluate the effectiveness of the HMI system, eye-tracking techniques were used to analyze pilot behavior in a simulated UAM flight scenario. Participants of appropriately trained trainee pilots were placed in two experimental conditions: one using the developed HMI system and the other using the main interface as the control. The simulation environment reproduced a variety of UAM-specific challenges, such as urban

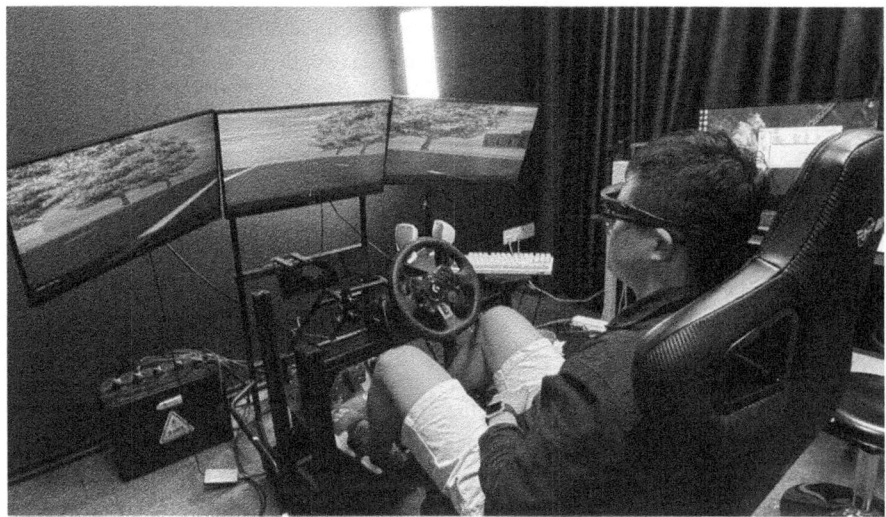

**Fig. 1.** Urban Air Transportation Driving Simulator.

navigation, takeoff, and landing procedures, providing a realistic setting for evaluating pilot reaction time and attention allocation.

The experiment consisted of four distinct phases: a baseline observation of autonomous flight, a non-flight related task (NFRT) that induced distraction, a phase in which the human-machine interface refocused the pilot's attention, and an emergency in which the pilot was required to take manual control.

1. Baseline observation phase

   - **Goal:** Record the natural behavioral data of the participant in the autonomous flight state to provide a baseline for subsequent analysis.
   - **Task:** Participants control the vehicle for autonomous flight through simulated piloting equipment and need to maintain a stable flight path without the need to perform complex operations or respond to external interference. Flight information (e.g., speed, altitude, route) will be displayed in a basic form on the interface.
   - **Scenario description:** The environment is a regular urban flight airspace with a simple navigation path without dynamic obstacles or unexpected events.
   - **Duration:** 3–5 min.
   - **Data recording:** Participants' gaze point distribution, gaze duration, and several eye jumps were recorded by eye-tracking devices.

2. Distraction task (NFRT) phase

   - **Objective:** to simulate the possible distraction task scenarios in actual flight and evaluate the attractiveness of the HMI system to flight critical information under distraction conditions.
   - **Task:** Participants are required to complete a secondary task that is not related to flight. For example, a numeric monitoring task involves random numbers popping up on the screen, and participants are asked to determine the maximum value and

answer within 5 s. Non-critical information finding task: Participants are asked to find specific non-critical flight information (e.g., weather data or landmark names) through the HMI interface.

- **Scenario description:** The vehicle maintains autonomous flight with the navigation system running continuously, but without the participant intervening in the flight controls.
- **Duration:** 3 min.
- **Data logging:** Record the completion time and correctness of secondary tasks. Use eye-tracking equipment to analyze changes in the participant's allocation of attention to critical flight information during the secondary task.

3. Attention regrouping phase

- **Goal:** To test the effectiveness of the HMI system in guiding the participant to refocus on flight-critical information after his/her attention has been distracted.
- **Task:** Participants complete flight-critical tasks through the HMI interface, correcting flight trajectory and adjusting flight direction according to the HMI highlighted prompts. Monitor flight status: Check the flight altitude and speed according to the voice prompts to confirm whether it meets the safe flight requirements.
- **Scenario description:** The HMI system guides participants to focus on flight-critical information through visual (e.g., highlighted cues), tactile (e.g., control lever vibration), and voice (e.g., voice reminders) multimodal feedback.
- **Duration:** 3 min.
- **Data logging:** Analyze whether participants' gaze time to critical areas increased significantly after HMI prompts. Record the reaction time and task completion accuracy to assess the HMI cues' effectiveness.

4. Emergency task phase

- **Objective:** To assess the participants' response ability in sudden emergencies and test the effectiveness of the HMI system in supporting rapid decision-making and operational efficiency.
- **Task:** Participants must quickly complete the following operations using HMI prompts: Obstacle avoidance: Adjust the flight path according to the navigation prompts to avoid the simulated dynamic obstacles. Mode switching: Switch to manual control mode to complete altitude adjustment or flight path correction. Emergency contact: Quickly establish contact with the remote pilot or control center through the HMI interface to complete a collaborative response.
- **Scenario description:** Simulate an emergency where the altitude of a vehicle is too low and set up dynamic obstacles (e.g., buildings or other flying vehicles) to increase the complexity and stress of the scenario.
- **Duration:** 2–3 min.
- **Data logging:** Record emergency tasks' reaction time (from alarm trigger to operation completion). Use eye movement data to analyze participants' visual search efficiency and attentional distribution in emergencies.

Data were analyzed using an analysis of variance (ANOVA) to compare the distribution of pilots' reaction times and visual attention in the two experimental conditions (using the HMI versus not using the HMI). Key metrics analyzed included gaze duration and eye movement jumps. Heat maps were also generated from the eye-tracking data to assess the design efficiency of the HMI.

## 3   Results

Before data analysis, we ensured data quality and dealt with possible outliers or missing data. The data metrics extracted for the gaze, such as gaze point (Fixation), gaze duration, and number of jumps (Saccades), were grouped by scene and task. Organize task data such as completion time, correctness, and error type for participants at each stage. Ensure each data point is clearly labeled with the experimental condition (HMI used/HMI not used).

The experimental results in Table 1 indicate that the design of the dedicated HMI significantly improved participants' performance in the simulation task. Regarding reaction time, the average reaction time of participants in the condition with the HMI was shorter than in the control condition without the HMI in all phases (e.g., 2.4 s for the emergency task phase and 3.1 s for the control condition). This suggests the HMI is particularly effective in supporting rapid decision-making in high-pressure scenarios. Regarding visual attention allocation, the HMI design effectively directed participants' attention to key interface elements, as demonstrated by the 85% of gaze time spent in key areas during the emergency task phase (72% in the control condition). In addition, the HMI condition had longer gaze durations (e.g., 1,700 ms in the urgent task phase) and fewer eye-movement jumps (8 in the HMI and 11 in the control condition), further demonstrating that the HMI interface has a more efficient information layout that reduces participants' visual search time. Overall, the HMI performed significantly better than the traditional interface in high-pressure conditions, improving the task efficiency and enhancing the visual guidance effect, providing a strong basis for future HMI optimization design.

**Table 1.** Key indicators of eye movement data.

| Condition | Phase | Reaction Time (s) | Fixation Duration (ms) | ROI_Attention | Saccades Count |
| --- | --- | --- | --- | --- | --- |
| HMI | Baseline | 2.5 | 1500 | 75 | 10 |
| Control | Baseline | 2.7 | 1400 | 70 | 12 |
| HMI | NFRT | 3.2 | 1200 | 65 | 14 |
| Control | NFRT | 3.8 | 1000 | 55 | 18 |
| HMI | Refocusing | 2.8 | 1600 | 80 | 9 |
| Control | Refocusing | 3.4 | 1300 | 70 | 13 |
| HMI | Emergency | 2.4 | 1700 | 85 | 8 |
| Control | Emergency | 3.1 | 1400 | 72 | 11 |

### 3.1 Reaction Time: Enhanced Task Efficiency

The results indicate that using the HMI system significantly reduced participants' reaction time across all experimental phases, highlighting its positive impact on task efficiency. In the Baseline phase, the reaction time was slightly shorter under the HMI condition (2.5 s) compared to the control condition (2.7s), demonstrating a minor improvement under low-stress scenarios. However, the difference became more pronounced in high-pressure scenarios, such as the Emergency phase, where reaction time with the HMI system dropped to 2.4s compared to 3.1s in the control condition—a reduction of 22.6% (Fig. 2).

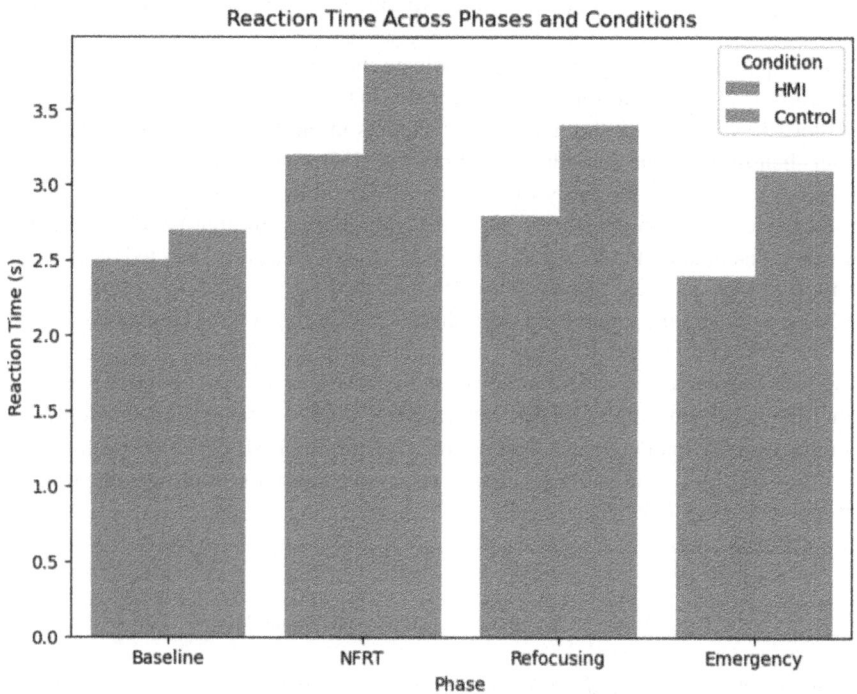

**Fig. 2.** Reaction Time Data Visualization Comparison.

This reduction suggests that the HMI system gave participants faster access to critical information, streamlining decision-making processes during time-sensitive tasks. Similarly, during the Refocusing phase, reaction time decreased from 3.4s (control) to 2.8s (HMI), underscoring the system's ability to reorient participants' attention effectively after distraction.

The HMI system consistently enhanced task efficiency, with its benefits most evident under high-pressure conditions like emergency scenarios.

### 3.2   Fixation Duration: Sustained Attention to Critical Information

Fixation duration on critical regions of the interface (e.g., navigation and alerts) was consistently more extended in the HMI condition, indicating improved visual focus. In the Emergency phase, the average fixation duration was 1700 ms for participants using the HMI system, compared to 1400 ms for the control condition—an increase of approximately 21.4%. This trend was also observed in the Refocusing phase, where fixation duration improved from 1300 ms (control) to 1600 ms (HMI).

Notably, fixation duration during the NFRT phase (distraction task) dropped across both conditions. However, it remained higher for the HMI group (1200 ms vs. 1000 ms), suggesting that the HMI system retained participants' visual attention better even during attention-diverting tasks. The sustained attention likely resulted from the intuitive layout and multimodal prompts provided by the HMI.

The HMI system effectively guided participants to focus on critical information, particularly during high-pressure or attention-diverting scenarios, enhancing situational awareness.

### 3.3   ROI Attention: Effective Visual Guidance

The proportion of time spent attending to Regions of Interest (ROI) further illustrates the effectiveness of the HMI in directing participants' visual attention. Across all phases, participants under the HMI condition demonstrated a higher percentage of ROI attention compared to the control condition. For example, during the Emergency phase, participants spent 85% of their time attending to critical interface regions with the HMI, compared to 72% for the control group—a relative increase of 18.1%.

In the Refocusing phase, ROI attention rose to 80% with the HMI system versus 70% in the control condition. Even in the distraction-heavy NFRT phase, the HMI condition achieved 65% ROI attention, outperforming the control condition's 55%. These results suggest that the HMI design—including visual cues such as high-contrast highlights—successfully drew participants' attention to essential interface elements (Fig. 3).

The HMI system exhibited strong visual guidance capabilities, ensuring participants-maintained focus on critical areas of the interface, even under challenging conditions.

### 3.4   Saccades Count: Reduced Visual Search Load

The analysis of saccadic eye movements revealed that participants experienced a lower visual search load when using the HMI system. Across all phases, the number of saccades (eye movement jumps) was consistently lower in the HMI condition. For instance, during the Emergency phase, participants made only eight saccades under the HMI condition, compared to 11 saccades in the control condition—a reduction of 27.3%.

In the Refocusing phase, saccades were similarly reduced from 13 (control) to 9 (HMI). These findings indicate that the HMI system's optimized layout reduced the cognitive effort required to locate and process information. A lower number of saccades suggests that participants could find relevant information faster and with less effort, thereby improving overall operational efficiency.

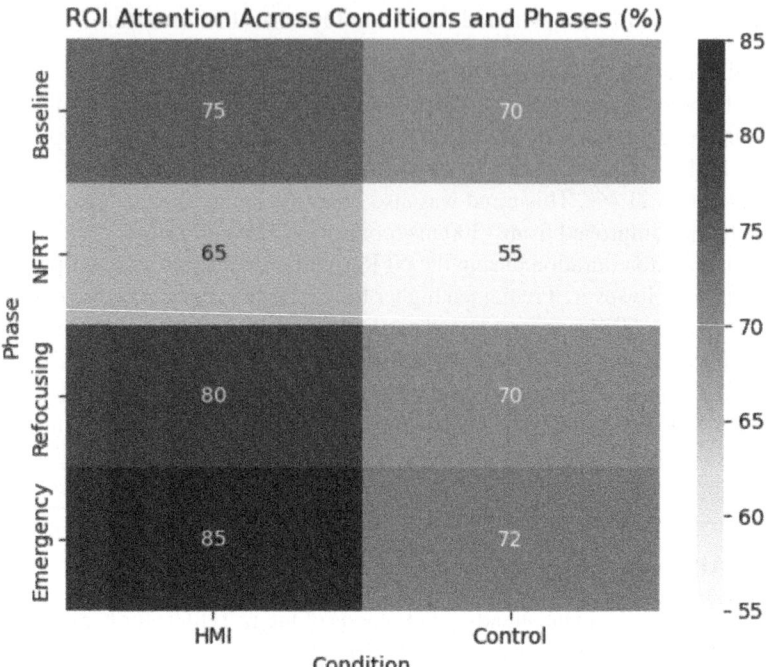

**Fig. 3.** Heatmap: critical area watch time.

The HMI system reduced visual search demands by providing a more precise, intuitive interface layout, allowing participants to locate critical information more efficiently.

## 4  Discussion

This study explored the effectiveness of a Human-Machine Interface (HMI) system designed specifically for Urban Air Mobility (UAM) in enhancing pilot situational awareness and task performance. The results demonstrated that the HMI system significantly improved pilot performance across various simulated flight scenarios, particularly in high-pressure and emergencies. The findings provide valuable insights into designing and optimizing HMI systems for UAM applications, highlighting the importance of intuitive interface layouts and efficient information presentation.

### 4.1  Discussion

The experimental results revealed several key benefits of the HMI system. First, the HMI significantly reduced reaction times across all experiment phases, particularly in emergency scenarios. In the Emergency phase, the average reaction time with the HMI system was 2.4 s, compared to 3.1 s in the control condition—a reduction of 22.6%. This suggests that the HMI system gave pilots faster access to critical information, enabling quicker decision-making and more efficient task execution. Visual, auditory, and haptic feedback likely contributed to this improvement by ensuring that pilots could quickly and intuitively process information, even under stress.

Second, the HMI system effectively guided pilots' visual attention to critical regions of the interface, as evidenced by the increased fixation duration and a higher proportion of time spent attending to Regions of Interest (ROI). For example, during the Emergency phase, participants spent 85% of their time attending to critical interface regions with the HMI, compared to 72% in the control group—a relative increase of 18.1%. This suggests that the HMI's design, which included high-contrast visual cues and multimodal prompts, successfully directed pilots' focus to essential information, even during distraction-heavy tasks. Maintaining attention to critical information is crucial in UAM operations, where pilots must manage multiple sources of information in a dynamic and complex environment.

Third, the HMI system reduced the cognitive load associated with visual search, as indicated by the lower number of saccadic eye movements in the HMI condition. For instance, during the Emergency phase, participants made only eight saccades under the HMI condition, compared to 11 saccades in the control condition—a reduction of 27.3%. This reduction in visual search effort suggests that the HMI's layout was more intuitive and efficient, allowing pilots to locate and process information more quickly. The HMI system likely contributed to improved situational awareness and overall task performance by minimizing the time and effort required to find critical information.

Finally, as seen in the Refocusing phase, the HMI system demonstrated effectiveness in reorienting pilots' attention after distraction. The reaction time decreased from 3.4 s in the control condition to 2.8 s with the HMI system, and the fixation duration increased from 1300 ms to 1600 ms. Quickly refocusing on critical flight information is essential in UAM operations, where pilots frequently switch between tasks and face unexpected distractions. The HMI's multimodal feedback, including visual highlights, voice prompts, and haptic cues, was key in guiding pilots back to critical tasks, ensuring they remained aware of their flight status and surroundings.

### 4.2  Implications of the Findings

The findings of this study have several important implications for the design and implementation of HMI systems in UAM. By integrating visual and auditory cues, the HMI system was able to provide pilots with real-time information in a way that minimized cognitive load and improved responsiveness. This is particularly critical in UAM, where pilots must process large amounts of information in a dynamic and often unpredictable environment.

Second, the study underscores the value of intuitive interface design in reducing visual search effort and improving task efficiency. The HMI system's optimized layout allowed pilots to quickly locate and process critical information, even under high-pressure conditions. This suggests that future HMI designs should prioritize simplicity and clarity, ensuring that key information is easily accessible and prominently displayed.

Finally, the results demonstrate the potential of eye-tracking technology as a tool for evaluating and optimizing HMI systems. By analyzing pilots' gaze patterns, researchers can gain valuable insights into how users interact with the interface and identify areas for improvement. This approach could benefit the iterative design process, allowing developers to refine the interface based on user behavior.

### 4.3 Limitations of the Study

While the results of this study are promising, several limitations should be acknowledged. First, the study was conducted in a simulated environment, which may not fully replicate the complexities and challenges of real-world UAM operations. Although the simulation was designed to be as realistic as possible, factors such as weather conditions, air traffic, and unexpected mechanical failures could not be fully accounted for. Future research should validate these findings in real-world flight scenarios.

Second, the study participants were undergraduate and graduate students without prior UAM operations experience. While this allowed for a controlled evaluation of the HMI system, it may not fully represent the behavior and performance of professional pilots or general users. Future studies should include a more diverse range of participants, including experienced pilots and individuals with varying levels of technical expertise.

Finally, the study focused primarily on short-term performance metrics, such as reaction time and visual attention allocation. While these metrics provide valuable insights into the immediate effectiveness of the HMI system, they do not capture the long-term impact of the interface on pilot training, fatigue, or overall user satisfaction. Future research should explore these aspects to gain a more comprehensive understanding of the HMI system's effectiveness.

## 5 Conclusion

The study highlights the potential of advanced HMI systems to enhance pilot situational awareness and performance in UAM operations. The results demonstrate that a well-designed HMI system can significantly improve task efficiency, reduce cognitive load, and enhance visual attention allocation, particularly in high-pressure and emergency scenarios. The findings suggest that multimodal feedback, intuitive interface layouts, and efficient information presentation are critical to effective HMI design for UAM applications.

Future research should explore optimizing HMI systems for UAM, particularly in real-world flight scenarios and with a broader range of user groups, including professional pilots and general users. Additionally, further investigation into integrating advanced technologies, such as artificial intelligence and augmented reality, could provide new opportunities for enhancing HMI functionality and user experience in UAM operations.

## References

1. Straubinger, A., Rothfeld, R., Shamiyeh, M., Büchter, K.D., Kaiser, J., Plötner, K.O.: An overview of current research and developments in urban air mobility–Setting the scene for UAM introduction. J. Air Transp. Manage. **87**, 101852.1–101852.12 (2020)

2. Li, C., et al.: Overview of traffic management of urban air mobility (UAM) with eVTOL aircraft. J. Traffic Transp. Eng. **20**(4), 35–54 (2020)
3. Wei, Q.S., Nilsson, G., Coogan, S.: Safety verification for urban air mobility scheduling. In: IFAC PAPERSONLINE. 2022: 9th IFAC Conference on Networked Systems (NECSYS)
4. Bennaceur, M., Delmas, R., Hamadi, Y.: Passenger-centric urban air mobility: fairness tradeoffs and operational efficiency. Transp. Res. Part C Emerg. Technol. **136** (2022)
5. Schweiger, K., Preis, L.: Urban air mobility: systematic review of scientific publications and regulations for vertiport design and operations. DRONES **6**(7) (2022)
6. Bulanowski, K., et al.: AURORA-creating space for urban air mobility in our cities. In: Nathanail, E.G., Gavanas, N., Adamos, G. (eds.) CSUM 2022, pp. 1568–1585. Springer, Cham (2023). https://doi.org/10.1007/978-3-031-23721-8_122
7. Koumoutsidi, A., Pagoni, I., Polydoropoulou, A.: A new mobility era: stakeholders' insights regarding urban air mobility. Sustainability **14**(5) (2022)
8. Yavas, V., Tez, O.Y.: Consumer intention over upcoming utopia: urban air mobility. J. Air Transport Manag. **107** (2023)
9. Maia, F.D., Da Saude, J.: The state of the art and operational scenarios for urban air mobility with uncrewed aircraft. Aeronaut. J. **125**(1288), 1034–1063 (2021)
10. Perperidou, D.G., Kirgiafinis, D.: Urban air mobility (UAM) integration to urban planning. In: Nathanail, E.G., Gavanas, N., Adamos, G. (eds.) CSUM 2022, pp. 1676–1686 (2023). https://doi.org/10.1007/978-3-031-23721-8_130
11. Lerro, A.: Survey of certifiable air data systems for urban air mobility. In: 2020 AIAA/IEEE 39th Digital Avionics Systems Conference (DASC) Proceedings, 39th AIAA/IEEE Digital Avionics Systems Conference (DASC) (2020)
12. Jha, A., et al.: Urban air mobility: a preliminary case study for Chicago and Atlanta. In: 2022 IEEE/AIAA Transportation Electrification Conference and Electric Aircraft Technologies Symposium (ITEC+EATS 2022). 2022: IEEE/AIAA Transportation Electrification Conference/Electric Aircraft Technologies Symposium (ITEC+EATS), pp. 300–306 (2022)
13. Postorino, M.N., Sarne, G.: Reinventing mobility paradigms: flying car scenarios and challenges for urban mobility. Sustainability **12**(9) (2020)
14. Liberacki, A., et al.: The environmental life cycle costs (ELCC) of urban air mobility (UAM) as an input for sustainable urban mobility. J. Clean. Prod. **389** (2023)

# Using Eye-Tracking Analysis to Detect Pilot Focus in Drone Interfaces During Signal Loss

Dimosthenis Minas<sup></sup>[✉], Angelos Fotopoulos, Michalis Xenos, and Christos Zotos

Computer Engineering and Informatics Department, Patras University, Patras, Greece
d.minas@ac.upatras.gr, anfotopoulos@upatras.gr,
xenos@ceid.upatras.gr

**Abstract.** Signal interruptions remain a critical challenge in drone operations, as losing connection to the operator can result in sudden, high-stress scenarios with potential safety implications. This paper presents an investigation using mobile eye-tracking technology to examine how both novice and experienced drone pilots allocate their visual attention when confronted with total signal loss. Fifty-six participants (11 experienced, 45 novice) completed a standardized flight task during which the drone's connection was deliberately disrupted. Quantitative data, including heatmaps and eye-tracking metrics, provided evidence of pronounced differences between the two groups. Novices exhibited dispersed scanning patterns and slower recognition of critical alerts, suggesting higher cognitive load. In contrast, experienced pilots rapidly identified key alerts, indicated by shorter time to first fixation and more focused fixations on essential interface icons such as the signal-strength indicator. Qualitative feedback from post-flight interviews further supported these findings: novices reported confusion and a preference for larger, centrally placed notifications, whereas experienced pilots relied on ingrained scanning routines. Taken together, these results underline the importance of intuitive, attention-guiding user interfaces and targeted training interventions to enhance situational awareness and mitigate risks during unexpected signal-loss events.

**Keywords:** Eye-Tracking · Drone User Interfaces · Signal Loss

## 1 Introduction

Unmanned Aerial Vehicles (UAV), commonly referred to as drones, have gained significant popularity due to their broad range of applications in both recreational and professional domains [1, 2]. The European drone market is projected to exceed 10€ billion annually by 2035 and 15€ billion by 2050, according to the Single European Sky Air Traffic Management Research (SESAR) [3, 4]. Despite these advantages, drones still face technical challenges, with signal interruption or complete signal loss being among the most critical. When a drone loses connection with its operator, the consequences can include operational disruption, unexpected flight maneuvers, and potential safety hazards for both the operator and bystanders [5].

A well-designed user interface (UI) can substantially mitigate these risks by conveying critical information in real-time or near-real-time, guiding operators to make swift

© The Author(s), under exclusive license to Springer Nature Switzerland AG 2025
D. D. Schmorrow and C. M. Fidopiastis (Eds.): HCII 2025, LNAI 15778, pp. 44–56, 2025.
https://doi.org/10.1007/978-3-031-93724-8_4

and informed decisions. Indeed, prior research emphasizes the importance of intuitive and well-structured interfaces in high-stress or time-sensitive environments [6, 7]. However, while there is considerable literature on drone operations, relatively fewer studies delve into the specific interplay between visual attention, cognitive load, and interface design during signal loss. Eye-tracking technology has emerged as a valuable tool for understanding user behavior and attention patterns in real-world settings. By measuring where and how long a user gazes at interface elements, researchers can infer the cognitive processes that underpin interaction and decision-making [8, 9]. This is particularly relevant in scenarios with heightened stress or uncertainty, as operators' visual attention may differ significantly from how they interact in normal conditions.

In typical drone operations, the pilot monitors multiple pieces of on-screen information: battery life, altitude, GPS position, flight mode, camera feed, and more. The complexity of this information can vary based on the application. For example, a photographer using a drone for aerial shots may focus primarily on camera settings, whereas a surveyor may pay closer attention to GPS accuracy and mapping software. Regardless of the application, signal introduces another layer of complexity, where the operator needs to troubleshoot the situation, decide on an alternative flight plan or attempt reconnection, and ensure safety compliance.

Prior studies underscore that during stressful events, humans often experience tunnel vision, which narrows their visual attention to only certain stimuli or even leads to confusion. This phenomenon can be problematic if the crucial alerts or indicators (such as a flashing signal-loss message) are placed in peripheral areas of the screen or if the UI is cluttered. In high-stress moments, novice users may not know where to look, while experienced users might rely on pre-learned patterns of scanning the interface. The knowledge gap pertains to precisely how users distribute their gaze across different UI elements and how efficiently the UI can direct or capture their attention when it matters most.

Given the importance of robust UI design in mitigating risks during signal loss, this study set forth to identify how drone operators, both novice and experienced, allocate their visual attention on various UI components during normal flight and during total signal loss, examine how quickly participants notice and react to critical UI elements in stressful conditions, and how that correlates with their experience level and self-reported confidence. By addressing these objectives, the aim is to propose evidence-based guidelines for UI improvements that could enhance situational awareness and reduce cognitive load during signal-interruption events.

## 2  Related Work

UAV usage is becoming increasingly popular and as an immediate effect, the drones become sophisticated, and issues related to signal reliability continue to pose significant operational and safety challenges. Signal loss can lead to disorienting experiences for remote pilots, potentially increasing the risk of accidents and mission failure [10]. To address this concern, researchers have turned to human factors engineering and user interface design, which together aim to reduce cognitive load, improve situational awareness, and facilitate effective decision-making under pressure.

A key line of inquiry emphasizes the importance of robust UIs in preventing and managing critical events. Endsley's study on situational awareness framework [11], operators make decisions based on their ability to perceive and comprehend relevant information within their environment. Translating this to drone operations, UI designers must ensure that vital flight parameters such as altitude, battery life, and signal status are not only visible but also intuitively arranged. Peißl et al. [12] underscore that eye-tracking metrics, such the dwell time and fixation duration, reveal how pilots allocate their visual attention when scanning instruments. These metrics help highlight improvements in data visualization might reduce mental workload, thereby enabling quicker and more accurate responses to anomalies like signal interruptions.

Recent advances in eye-tracking technologies have further refined our understanding of pilot behavior in dynamic environments. Xenos et al. [8] demonstrated that real-time gaze monitoring can inform adaptive interfaces that adjust their layout based on the user's moment-to-moment attentional focus. This concept has gained traction in aviation, where heads-up displays and other augmented reality solutions are being developed to minimize the need for pilots to shift their gaze away from critical flight data. In the realm of drones, such adaptive systems might dynamically enlarge or highlight areas of the display corresponding to emergent alerts- for example, a flashing warning that signals an imminent connection drop.

Despite these technological strides, novice drone pilots often struggle with interface complexity. Karlsson and Naumburg [13] highlighted the importance of minimizing mental effort, ensure safety during drone interaction, maintain information balance and emphasize clarity and simplicity in the interface in their work on developing a user interface for medical supply deliveries utilising drones, where its main target are nurses with no computer-based background. Moreover, Wankmüller et al. [14] documented that emergency responses teams operating drones under urgent conditions were prone to visual tunneling. Under stress, participants frequently fixated on the live camera feed, neglecting side panels displaying vital navigation and connectivity data. These findings suggest that, in high-stress contexts, design elements such as color, size, and positioning of warnings must be carefully optimized to effectively guide the user's eye to critical indicators.

Another dimension on current literature focuses on the cognitive load and stress that the user experiences during the signal loss timeframe and pinpoints potential enhancements. Dixon and Wickens argued that automated features can be challenging for specific use cases. While automation reduces workload in normal operations, pilots may become overly reliant on these aids and be caught off-guard during signal loss or system malfunctions [15]. This reliance-compliance model of automation illustrates how overdependence on automated aids can lead to decreased situational awareness and delayed response times in emergency scenarios. In this context, introducing visual or auditory cues that remind pilots to maintain active oversight may mitigate the effects of automation-induced complacency. Such countermeasures become especially crucial in Beyond Visual Line of Sight Operations (BVLOS), where the risks associated with unexpected disruptions, including signal loss, are amplified due to limited direct visual feedback. Eye-tracking studies from Rahmani and Weckman [16] further illustrate how stress correlates with erratic gaze patterns. Novice pilots exhibit more frequent, shorter fixations on peripheral interface components, revealing an attempt to scan all available information but failing to process it effectively. Meanwhile, expert pilots devote longer fixations to critical metrics, highlighting a structured scanning technique honed by experience.

Eye-tracking methodologies offer granular insights into how pilots prioritize and sequence their visual activities, particularly when confronted with anomalies signal loss. Current literature emphasizes that future UI designs should incorporate adaptive elements and standardized placement of critical indicators. While experienced pilots may exhibit superior scanning strategies, novices can benefit substantially from interfaces that guide their attention through intuitive visual hierarchies and context-aware alerts. As drones continue to proliferate across various industries, further research that refines eye-tracking analytics and integrates real-time feedback loops into drone UIs promises to bridge the gap between pilot skill levels and system complexity, ultimately enhancing both safety and operational success.

# 3  Methodology

This section outlines the study design, participant recruitment, experimental setup and procedure details for our investigation into drone pilots' responses to signal loss events.

## 3.1  Study Design

A lab-based experimental study aimed at understanding how drone operators allocate their visual attention during critical flight events. Each session included a pre-flight questionnaire, a drone flight scenario incorporating a signal-loss event, and a post-flight semi-structured interview. This mixed-methods design allowed us to capture both quantitative data and qualitative insights.

## 3.2  Recruitment

Participants were recruited via the social media platforms of the Software Quality and Human-Computer Interaction lab at the University of Patras. Interested individuals completed an eligibility form that gathered basic demographic information, like age, gender, and assessed their prior drone experience. In total, 56 participants (23 women, 33 men; mean age $= 26.95$, SD $= 11.15$) took part in the study.

## 3.3  Participants

Approximately 20% of the participants were expert users (11 participants), while the remaining 80% were inexperienced (45 participants), with either minimal or no hands-on drone control experience. Upon arriving at the lab, participants were briefed on the general objectives and potential risks involved in the study. All participants then signed an informed consent form indicating their voluntary participation and their right to withdraw at any point.

## 3.4 Experimental Setup

Our experimental setup was designed to simulate a realistic drone operation scenario while still maintaining controlled conditions for data collection. We employed a mid-sized commercial drone programmed to follow a predefined route that began at a designated takeoff point near the department building, continued toward the campus canteen, where participants were instructed to take a photo of the central area of the Computer Engineering and Informatics Department (Fig. 1), and then return to the starting zone. Although participants were told to follow this specific flight path, they were not informed that the drone's signal would be lost as soon as they made the first turn. Each participant was provided with a mobile phone running a pre-installed drone application for navigation and wore Mobile Tobii Pro Glasses 3 to capture eye-tracking data in real time. These glasses detected and recorded fixations and saccades, later processed into heatmaps to identify Areas of Interest (AOIs) in the user interface. By merging these objective gaze

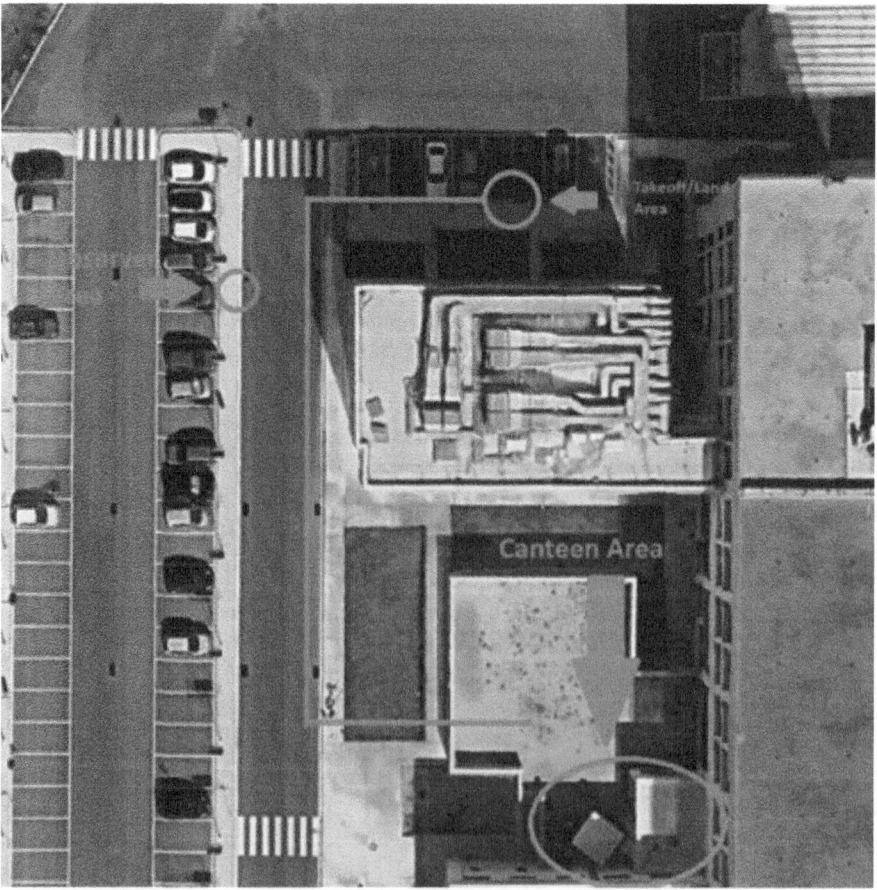

**Fig. 1.** Flight path shown to the participants during the experiment.

metrics with flight data logs, we could comprehensively assess how participants directed their visual attention during various phases of the flight.

Before the flight, participants completed a brief prequestionnaire to collect demographic information and gauge their prior drone experience. They were then given flight instructions and informed that the drone would be traveling Beyond Visual Line of Sight (BVLOS), in accordance with European Safety Regulations. To ensure safety, an observer was positioned to monitor the UAV when the pilot engaged in BVLOS operations. The observer carried a red flag, raising it whenever the pilot encountered difficulties, prompting an experienced pilot to assume control of the UAV, an action termed "observer-initiated cancel." Additionally, participants were free to terminate the flight at any point if they felt uncomfortable or believed the UAV was at risk; this measure was referred to as "self-cancel".

## 4 Results

In this section, we present the main findings of our study, focusing on three key themes that emerged from our data: (1) Eye-tracking analyses of participant gaze behavior, (2) differences in user experience across expertise levels, and (3) qualitative feedback regarding overall interface design and notification elements. Each subsection details the evidence we gathered, both quantitative and qualitative, to provide a comprehensive view of how users interacted with the drone interface, particularly during moments of signal loss.

### 4.1 Eye-Tracking Data Analysis

Using the eye-tracking dataset, we generated combined heatmaps that aggregated the gaze data for inexperienced and experienced pilots separately, enabling us to visualize how each group allocated their attention across the drone's UI. These heatmaps used color gradients, from cool (low fixation density) to warm (high fixation density), laid over screenshots of the interface. By leveraging time-stamped markers of when the signal loss began, we could compare participants' gaze distribution during normal flight segments to that of the signal-loss window.

Overall, the inexperienced pilots' heatmap indicated a scattered pattern of fixations that were distributed widely across multiple UI elements (e.g., camera feed, battery icon, background areas) during signal disruption. This dispersion aligns with prior research suggesting that novice operators often experience higher cognitive load and confusion under stress, causing them to look for critical information in an unstructured manner. In contrast, the experienced pilots exhibited heatmaps with more concentrated clusters of fixations on key UI elements such as the signal-strength indicator and pop-up warnings [17, 18]. Their familiarity with drone systems appeared to enable quick, targeted scanning, reflecting a more structured approach to identifying and responding to the sudden loss of connection.

By aggregating and comparing these two heatmaps, we found that signal loss triggered more dispersed attention for novices, who seemed unsure of which interface element to prioritize. Meanwhile, experienced users quickly recognized the notification area and system prompts without hesitation, reflecting an internalized knowledge of where to look when unexpected events occur. These findings underscore the importance of designing interfaces that highlight critical alerts in a centralized, easily noticeable area, particularly for users with limited drone-flying experience (Figs. 2 and 3).

**Fig. 2.** Heatmap showing the distribution of fixations of novice participants while signal loss.

**Fig. 3.** Heatmap showing the distribution of fixations of experienced participants while signal loss.

In addition to generating heatmaps, we performed a quantitative statistical analysis on three eye-tracking metrics, which include a) the Time to First Fixation (TTFF), b) the number of Unique Areas of Interest (#AOIs) visited in the first ten seconds after signal loss, c) Fixation Durations on the most Critical Icons, to evaluate how novices (n = 45) and experienced pilots (n = 11) interacted with critical interface elements during the initial ten seconds of drone signal loss. Prior to selecting the proper analysis method we verified normality through the through the Shapiro-Wilk test, confirming that no significant deviations from normal distributions existed in either group. Because of the substantial difference in sample sizes, we applied a t-test (two-tailed, a = 0.05) for each metric to account for potential heterogeneity in variances. All effect sizes are reported using Choden's d, indicating the magnitude of between-group differences and strengthening the case for interpreting these findings.

Our first analysis focused on Time to First Fixation (TTFF) on the alert of the "Signal Lost" banner to determine how efficiently participants detected this critical alert. Novice pilots required 3.32 s (SD = 1.09) before fixating on the warning, whereas experienced pilots required 1.62 s (SD = 0.81). A t-test revealed this difference to be highly significant (t(54) = 4.81, p = 0.00015) with a large effect size (Cohen's d = 1.46). These results imply that prior familiarity with drone interfaces markedly enhances pilots' ability to notice urgent notifications, as experienced users recognized the nature of the interruption almost immediately.

Next, to evaluate whether novices scattered their gaze across more on-screen elements than experts, a potential sign of heightened confusion, we measured the number of unique Areas of Interest (AOIs) visited in the first ten seconds after signal loss. These AOIs included takeoff/landing icons, flight mode icons, settings icon, battery indicators, Wi-Fi and Bluetooth status indicators, drone telemetry (speed, height), image/video controls, camera/video switches, two virtual joysticks, the central camera feed, and the pop-up signal-loss alert. Novices inspected 8.56 distinct UI elements on average (SD = 2.37), whereas experienced pilots examined only 4.18 (SD = 1.72). This difference was also significant (t(54) = 5.92, p = 0.00082) with a large effect size (Cohen's d = 1.62), confirming that novices adopted a more scattered search strategy likely stemming from uncertainty and stress. By contrast, experts prioritized fewer, high-impact elements and quickly zeroed in on what was most relevant for addressing the disruption.

Finally, we analyzed fixation durations on the most critical icons, namely the Wi-Fi status indicator, the signal loss alert itself, and the battery level. Novice pilots exhibited shorter but more frequent fixations (200.76 ms/fixation, SD = 80.31), whereas experienced pilots fixated for longer durations (320.11 ms/fixation, SD = 90.35). A t-test confirmed this difference was statistically significant (t(54) = 3.9, p = 0.00035; d = 1.13). This finding indicates that novices tended to hop rapidly between interface elements, attempting to gather multiple pieces of information in an unstructured manner. In contrast, experienced users demonstrated longer, more focused fixations, suggesting a more deliberate and effective visual search strategy for diagnosing and resolving signal-loss issues.

Viewed together, these results strongly corroborate the heatmap observations that novices experience greater difficulty orienting themselves within the interface while experienced pilots rapidly align their attention with the most crucial cues. The large effect sizes reported across all analyses underscore the robustness of these outcomes and validate the argument that experienced pilots swiftly detect and interpret key alerts, limit their visual scans to pertinent AOIs, and engage in sustained fixations on essential indicators. By contrast, novices' extensive AOI visits, delayed alert recognition, and rapid, fragmented fixations indicate a clear need for UI designs that guide attention more efficiently during signal-loss scenarios. Such designs might feature consistently placed, centrally located alerts alongside adaptive or context-sensitive cues to minimize confusion. Equally important, structured training that promotes efficient scanning behavior could help novice pilots better manage high-stress events. Overall, our findings illuminate the potential for targeted interface improvements to mitigate risk and enhance performance when drones face critical disruptions in communication.

### 4.2 Qualitative Feedback from Post-flight Interviews

Our post-flight interviews provided valuable insight into participants' subjective experiences during signal loss. Many of the novice pilots (i.e., those with limited or no prior drone experience) described feeling confused when the connection dropped, often assuming they had made an operational error rather than recognizing a network interruption. Several noted a temporary distrust of the system, reporting that they did not immediately realize the issue stemmed from lost signal rather than a malfunction in their own inputs. In contrast, experienced pilots generally perceived the disruption as a routine hazard of drone operation. Although they acknowledged the stress of unexpectedly losing control, they were more likely to attribute it to external factors (e.g., range limits, interference) instead of self-made mistakes.

When reflecting on how the drone's user interface handled critical alerts, 36 out of the 45 novice pilots expressed a strong preference for a more prominent notification design. One participant noted, "I'd really like the alert message to pop up right in the middle of the screen, so it's immediately visible," emphasizing a need for unmissable visual cues. Another user echoed this sentiment but proposed an optional acknowledgment button, allowing pilots to tap or click to hide the alert only after they had read and comprehended its message. These perspectives highlight a common desire for centrally placed, clearly

**Fig. 4.** Alert current display pop-up.

labeled signals when signal interruptions occur, which stands in stark contrast to the existing bottom-of-screen alert shown in Fig. 4.

## 5 Discussion

The findings of this study highlight several important observations regarding how drone operators of varying experience levels respond to signal loss events. Most notably, novice pilots exhibited scattered gaze patterns, marked by frequent yet brief fixations across multiple UI elements, whereas experienced users had more concise, targeted visual behaviors. These differences underscore the influence of prior familiarity with drone systems, as well as the pronounced cognitive load experienced by less-skilled operators when unexpected challenges arise.

From a human-factors perspective, the tendency of novices to scan the camera feed or peripheral UI elements for extended periods aligns with prior research on cognitive overload in high-stress, unfamiliar scenarios [19, 20]. Their slower Time-to-First-Fixation on critical alerts further illustrates this dynamic, since a lack of structured scanning strategies can result in delayed responses or even complete oversight of essential notifications. Conversely, experienced pilots' swift and systematic attention to crucial warnings, such as the "Signal Lost" banner, suggests that internalized scanning routines and deeper contextual knowledge of drone operations enable more efficient decision-making. Our results also shed light on how interface layout and design choices can exacerbate or alleviate operator confusion under stress. A significant proportion of participants, especially inexperienced ones, either missed or belatedly recognized the red warning text placed at the lower edge of the screen. This finding supports the notion that peripheral alerts are more likely to be overlooked during moments of acute stress, particularly by users whose visual attention tends to be dominated by more central or visually salient cues [21]. Placing high-priority information in more conspicuous locations and employing additional sensory cues (e.g., auditory or haptic signals) may help ensure that critical alerts are not missed.

Although our study was conducted under controlled conditions, the results have broader implications for real-world applications, including commercial deliveries, emergency response, and industrial inspections. These contexts share a common thread of operational urgency, where split-second decisions and clear situational awareness are paramount. Designing interfaces that emphasize adaptability, potentially providing context-sensitive visual prompts or temporarily hiding non-essential data, could further aid users who lack extensive drone experience. Such adaptive UIs could mitigate information overload and guide the operator's gaze toward crucial telemetry during high-stress events.

Several limitations should be considered. First, the lab-based setting, while allowing precise data collection, may not fully replicate the environmental variables encountered in actual field operations. Weather conditions, physical obstructions, and other real-time challenges might amplify stress and further alter gaze patterns. Second, the overrepresentation of novice participants (45 novices vs. 11 experienced) provided strong insights into how less-skilled users behave under stress but limited our ability to study advanced strategies among expert operators in greater depth. Moreover, it is possible that some participants, particularly those with more prior technology or drone experience, were more comfortable with unexpected disruptions, thereby influencing how they responded under pressure. Finally, all data were collected from a single site, which may not account for geographical or cultural differences that could affect operational procedures, user expectations, or stress responses.

Despite these constraints, the study's multi-method approach, combining eye-tracking metrics, user performance data, and post-flight interviews, provides a robust basis for understanding and improving drone UI design. By identifying how novices and experts differ in their visual search behaviors, the findings offer practical guidance for creating more intuitive, attention-guiding interfaces capable of mitigating the risks posed by sudden signal loss.

## 6  Conclusions and Future Work

This research emphasizes the importance of well-structured user interfaces in enhancing situational awareness and decision-making during critical drone operations, notably when signal disruptions occur. Through eye-tracking analysis, we observed that novices often exhibit dispersed, inefficient scanning behaviors and delayed responses to system warnings, whereas experienced pilots more rapidly and accurately identify urgent alerts. These results reinforce prior studies linking cognitive load and stress to suboptimal performance under time-sensitive conditions [9].

By highlighting how users of varying expertise allocate visual attention in the wake of a loss of connection, this work offers evidence-based recommendations for UI development. Designers should prioritize the clarity and central placement of alert messages, possibly augmenting them with auditory or haptic signals to ensure immediate notice. Future investigations might extend this research to more diverse operational contexts, such as complex environmental conditions or mixed-fleet drone interactions and explore adaptive UIs that proactively guide user focus during unexpected events. Ultimately, these enhancements could not only improve user satisfaction and performance but also substantially increase the operational safety and reliability of drone systems as they continue to evolve in both recreational and commercial applications.

Building on these findings, future work should delve deeper into the contrasting strategies that novice and experienced drone pilots employ under stressful conditions. Longitudinal studies could examine how novices transition toward expert-level scanning patterns over time and identify the training interventions most effective in accelerating this process. Additionally, integrating real-time adaptive feedback, such as AI-driven suggestions that highlight key telemetry elements or automatically reposition critical warnings, could further support novice pilots who struggle to prioritize information during emergencies. Such adaptive solutions would not only bridge the performance gap but also foster greater user confidence and system trust when encountering unexpected signal disruptions. Future explorations might also involve examining how different devices from factors, like larger screens, head-up displays, can influence visual search behaviors. The goal is to refine drone UIs so that both novices and experts can achieve safer and more efficient flight outcomes, even in the face of acute connection losses.

**Acknowledgments.** This publication was co-funded by the European Union under the Grant Agreement 101103592. Its contents are the sole responsibility of the EPIIC (Enhanced Pilot Interfaces & Interactions for fighter Cockpit) Consortium and do not necessarily reflect the views of the European Union or the European Commission. Neither the European Union nor the granting authority can be held responsible for them.

**Disclosure of Interests.** The authors have no competing interests to declare that are relevant to the content of this article.

# References

1. Mohd, T.K., Tesfa, E.M.: Exploring technical capabilities of unmanned aerial vehicles. In: 2023 IEEE 13th Annual Computing and Communication Workshop and Conference (CCWC), pp. 1320–132. IEEE (2023)
2. Yucesoy, E., Balcik, B., Coban, E.: The role of drones in disaster response: a literature review of operations research applications. Int. Trans. Oper. Res. **32**(2), 545–589 (2025). https://doi.org/10.1111/itor.13484
3. Isufaj, R., Omeri, M., Piera, M.A.: Multi-uav conflict resolution with graph convolutional reinforcement learning. Appl. Sci. **12**(2), 610–615 (2022)
4. Single European Sky ATM Research 3 Joint Undertaking (EU body or agency), European drones outlook study: unlocking the value for Europe. Publications Office of the European Union (2017)
5. Chamayou, G.: A Theory of the Drone. The New Press, New York (2015)
6. Blackler, A., Popovic, V., Mahar, D.: Applying and testing design for intuitive interaction. Int. J. Des. Sci. Technol. **20**(1), 7–26 (2014)
7. Zhu, A., Yang, J., Yu, W.: A novel target tracking method of unmanned drones by gaze prediction combined with YOLO algorithm. In: 2021 IEEE International Conference on Unmanned Systems (ICUS), pp. 792–797. IEEE (2021)
8. Xenos, M., Mallas, A., Minas, D.: Using eye-tracking for adaptive human-machine interfaces for pilots: a literature review and sample cases. J. Phys. Conf. Ser. **2716**(1), 012072–012076 (2024). https://doi.org/10.1088/1742-6596/2716/1/012072
9. Minas, D., Tews, L., Fotopoulos, A., Xenos, M., Calvo Córdoba, A., Rivas Vidal, M.: Eye-tracking technologies for facilitating multimodal interaction in aviation environments. In: 14th EASN International Conference on "Innovation in Aviation and Space Towards Sustainability Today & Tomorrow (2024)
10. Qiu, Q., Li, R., Zhao, X.: Failure risk management: adaptive performance control and mission abort decisions. Risk Anal. (2024). https://doi.org/10.1111/risa.16709
11. Endsley, M.R.: The limits of highly autonomous vehicles: an uncertain future: commentary on hancock (2019) Some pitfalls in the promises of automated and autonomous vehicles. Ergonomics **62**(4), 496–499 (2019). https://doi.org/10.1080/00140139.2019.1563330
12. Peißl, S., Wickens, C.D., Baruah, R.: Eye-tracking measures in aviation: a selective literature review. The Int. J. Aerosp. Psychol. **28**(3–4), 98–112 (2018). https://doi.org/10.1080/24721840.2018.1514978
13. Granquist Karlsson, L., Naumburg, H.: Drones for medical supply deliveries-Designing Intuitive Interfaces for Nurses Managing Drone Deliveries (2024)
14. Wankmüller, C., Kunovjanek, M., Mayrgündter, S.: Drones in emergency response–evidence from cross-border, multi-disciplinary usability tests. Int. J. Disaster Risk Reduction **65**, 102567–102576 (2021)

15. Dixon, S.R., Wickens, C.D.: Automation reliability in unmanned aerial vehicle control: a reliance-compliance model of automation dependence in high workload. Hum. Factors **48**(3), 474–486 (2006). https://doi.org/10.1518/001872006778606822

16. Rahmani, H., Weckman, G.R.: Working under the shadow of drones: investigating occupational safety hazards among commercial drone pilots. IISE Trans. Occup. Ergon. Hum. Factors **12**(1–2), 55–67 (2024). https://doi.org/10.1080/24725838.2023.2251009

17. Fortmann, F., Lüdtke, A.: An intelligent SA-adaptive interface to aid supervisory control of a UAV swarm. In: 2013 11th IEEE International Conference on Industrial Informatics (INDIN), pp. 768–773. IEEE (2013)

18. Sebok, A., et al.: Development of attentional skills training for operators of unmanned aerial systems. In: Proceedings of the Human Factors and Ergonomics Society Annual Meeting, vol. 63, no. 1, pp. 2161–2165 (2019). https://doi.org/10.1177/1071181319631276

19. Marois, A., Lafond, D., Williot, A., Vachon, F., Tremblay, S.: Real-time gaze-aware cognitive support system for security surveillance. In: Proceedings of the Human Factors and Ergonomics Society Annual Meeting, vol. 64, no. 1, pp. 1145–1149 (2020). https://doi.org/10.1177/1071181320641274

20. Karmana, A., Gunawan, F.E., Asrol, M.: Factors affecting control room operator situation awareness and ITS fuzzy logic model. Jurnal Indonesia Sosial Teknologi, **5**(9) (2024)

21. Chen, K., Li, Z., Jamieson, G.A.: Influence of information layout on diagnosis performance. IEEE Trans. Hum. Mach. Syst. **48**(3), 316–323 (2017)

# Integrating Eye-Tracking, Machine Learning, and Facial Recognition for Objective Consumer Behavior Analysis

José Augusto Rodrigues[1,2]([⊠]) [iD], António Vieira de Castro[2] [iD],
and Martín Llamas-Nistal[3] [iD]

[1] University of Vigo, Campus Universitario, 36310 Vigo, Spain
`jose.augusto.oliveira.rodrigues@uvigo.gal`
[2] SIIS - ISEP, 431 Dr. António Bernardino de Almeida Street, 4249-015 Porto, Portugal
[3] atlanTTic Research Center for Telecommunication Technologies, University of Vigo, Vigo, Spain

**Abstract.** This pioneering study presents a model that integrates eye-tracking, OpenCV-based computer vision (CV), and machine learning (ML) to evaluate consumer interest in products with greater accuracy and objectivity. Unlike traditional self-reported surveys, often biased by factors such as brand identity, this approach uses data-oriented metrics to directly measure user engagement.

Eye-tracking captures the distribution and duration of visual attention during product interaction, while OpenCV handles essential image-processing tasks—such as detection and localization—allowing ML algorithms to perform the core facial recognition and demographic classification steps. This integration enables more refined market segmentation and targeted marketing strategies, aligned with the diverse preferences of consumers.

Preliminary results suggest that this integrated methodology provides a more authentic representation of user preferences compared to conventional methods, which are often influenced by biases or social norms. By capturing objective behavioral and demographic indicators, the model offers reliable insights that allow companies to optimize product features, improve marketing campaigns, and effectively direct development efforts.

In a competitive marketplace, the use of these technologies facilitates more informed decision-making and long-term strategic advantages. This study highlights the transformative potential of combining eye-tracking, ML, and facial recognition in market analysis. By moving beyond opinion-based methods to real-time, quantifiable insights, companies can better understand and meet consumer expectations, promoting their satisfaction and achieving sustainable success.

**Keywords:** eye-tracking · OpenCV · computer vision · machine learning · facial recognition · consumer behavior · product interest · demographic profiling · marketing strategies · real-time insights · behavioral data · market segmentation

M. Llamas-Nistal—Senior Member, IEEE

# 1  The Problem

Traditional marketing has long relied on opinion surveys and self-reports to measure consumer preferences and motivations [1]. Although these methods can provide valuable information, they are frequently susceptible to both cognitive and social biases that compromise data reliability and accuracy [2].

Furthermore, today's dynamic and highly competitive market demands more robust, evidence-based strategies that accurately capture consumer interest [3]. These limitations highlight the need for a solution that can:

- Minimize the distortions inherent in self-reported data.
- Provide objective, real-time insights into consumer preferences [4].
- Improve decision-making through reliable, data-driven evidence, rather than relying exclusively on self-reports [5, 6].

# 2  State of the Art

Using the PRISMA method [7], this review highlights the broad applicability of eye-tracking in marketing research and related fields. In the UX/UI domain, several studies [4–6, 8–12] have shown that ocular tracking helps to understand how consumers process digital content and interact with products or interfaces. The findings underscore the importance of combining eye-tracking with self-report methods (e.g., questionnaires and "think aloud") and other psychophysiological assessments for more comprehensive conclusions.

In advertising research, studies such as [13] and [14] show that, although more intrusive ads may initially capture attention, this does not necessarily guarantee recall or brand awareness. Factors like navigation type (goal-oriented) and how the ad is presented affect the level of consumer engagement.

Regarding packaging, studies in [1, 3] and [2] indicate that where consumers focus their gaze does not always reflect their genuine preferences or translate directly into purchase decisions. These investigations emphasize the relevance of integrating eye-tracking with other metrics, such as facial expressions, emotion testing, and questionnaires, to gain more precise insights into consumers' perceived value and affective responses.

In Psychology and Neuroscience, several studies [6, 15–17] reveal that eye-tracking can provide insights into personality traits, mental well-being, cognitive states, and engagement in educational environments or on social networks. However, challenges remain concerning causal determination and the need to combine ocular tracking with longitudinal research designs, smartphone data (psycho-informatics), and self-report measures.

Overall, this comparative review confirms eye-tracking as a promising technology for market research, allowing precise analysis of how consumers process visual stimuli. It concludes that associating eye-tracking with other methods (questionnaires, psychophysiological analysis, discrete choice models, etc.) increases result reliability and fosters stronger inferences about consumer behavior. Nevertheless, it remains challenging to establish purchase preferences purely objectively, reinforcing the need for multimethod approaches to improve the validity of marketing research.

Despite the progress, many studies continue to focus on controlled settings and use small samples, limiting the generalizability of their findings. There is also a lack of integrated solutions that combine eye-tracking, facial recognition, and machine learning for a more comprehensive analysis.

Although the results are promising, some limitations must be acknowledged:

- The sample size in many studies restricts the generalization of the results.
- Laboratory-based controlled settings may not reflect the complexity of real marketing environments.
- The lack of integration with other technologies and statistical methods narrows the scope of the conclusions.

To overcome these limitations, future studies should explore the combination of eye-tracking with complementary technologies and advanced methods.

Finally, it is important to highlight that, according to our research, there is no existing solution in the literature that matches the integrated model and prototype developed presented in this work. This underscores the significant contribution of the proposed solution, as it presents a novel approach to combining multiple data sources—eye-tracking, facial recognition, and machine learning—to enhance the reliability and depth of consumer behavior analysis.

## 3   Proposed Solution

To address these gaps, a new solution (model/prototype) was developed that integrates Eye-Tracking (ET), OpenCV-based Computer Vision (CV), and Machine Learning (ML) for Facial Recognition (FR) and demographic classification. By capturing both gaze data (via ET) and facial features (via CV + ML) in real time, the system automatically generates objective insights into how users engage with products [15, 18].

**Facial Recognition (FR):** Employs CV-based face detection and ML-driven classification to identify demographic attributes (age, gender, ethnicity) in real time [16]. This reduces reliance on self-reports, enabling more precise segmentation without invasive questionnaires [9].

**Machine Learning (ML):** As a branch of artificial intelligence, ML leverages convolutional neural networks (CNNs) for multitask operations such as age estimation, gender classification, and ethnicity detection [5, 6]. CNNs efficiently handle visual data and can discern complex patterns [12]. By combining CV and ML, the prototype achieves robust face detection and classification while continuously integrating ET data to capture user attention patterns.

### 3.1   Eye-Tracking

ET monitors where and for how long consumers look at specific elements, generating quantitative data about attention distribution, such as heat maps [10, 17]. Devices (infrared-based) capture fixation points, pupil dilation, and eye movements, answering questions such as:

- Which areas of a web page or physical display attract attention first? [2]
- How long does a consumer's gaze remain on a product feature? [14]

By quantifying these data, ET provides objective metrics that can be correlated with engagement, interest, or recall [3].

## 4  System Modeling

The model is structured into five main modules (Fig. 1) [13, 18]:

- **Digital Module:** Creates marketing studies, provides a dynamic interface, and centralizes the results.
- **Hardware Module:** Integrates the Tobii 4C Eye Tracker and a Logitech webcam to capture real-time data [4, 10].
- **Connection Module:** Uses the FastAPI framework to ensure efficient communication between hardware and software components [5].
- **Data Module:** Manages data storage (SQL Server, JSON), organizing all information for future analysis [9].
- **Service Module:** Performs advanced data processing with ML, Deep Learning (DL), and CV, generating refined insights (e.g., attention heat maps and demographic classifications) [6, 16].

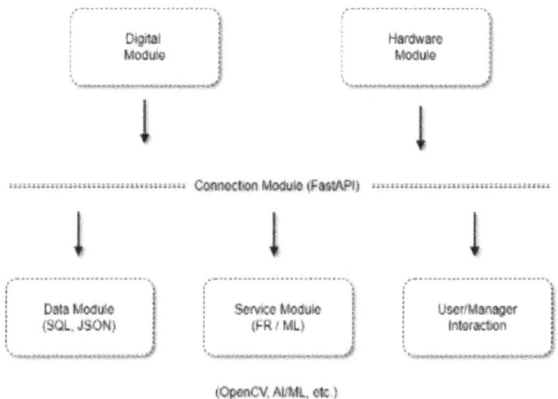

**Fig. 1.** High-Level Architecture Integrating ET, FR, and ML.

## 5  Technologies

This section outlines the core technologies underpinning the system. Developed in Python, the solution leverages OpenCV for computer vision tasks, TensorFlow for deep learning, and LabelImg for image annotation, with C# and UWP supporting the graphical interface and hardware integration, while FastAPI and SQL Server/JSON handle communication and data storage.

- **Python:** A central language in the prototype due to its ecosystem of libraries for computer vision, ML, and backend [5].
- **CV:** Handles image preprocessing, facial detection, and feature extraction.
- **TensorFlow:** A framework used to train deep neural networks (CNNs) [11].
- **LabelImg:** A tool for creating image annotations (bounding boxes), exported in Pascal VOC format [13].
- **C# and UWP:** Used to develop the graphical interface and integrate hardware within the Windows ecosystem [4].
- **FastAPI:** Manages communication among the system's modules [5].
- **SQL Server and JSON:** Store structured and unstructured data for further analysis [9].

## 6  Implementation

The prototype's implementation was divided into two major components:

- **Eye-tracking:** Records user gaze distributions and fixation durations in real time [10, 14].
- **Facial recognition:** Responsible for identifying and classifying demographic data (age, gender, and ethnicity). It combines **CV** for face detection and image preprocessing with **ML models** (e.g., CNNs) for classification [5, 16].

The system correlates real-time gaze data with demographic profiles derived from FR, offering a holistic view of consumer attention and preferences. The following section briefly describes each component's steps and illustrates how demographic data is integrated with attention metrics [3, 15] into a unified system.

### 6.1  Eye-Tracking

Visual data collection was carried out via an ET device, responsible for monitoring the location and duration of the user's gaze on visual elements [10, 17]. The C# code below (Fig. 2) illustrates the logic for:

- **Gaze Monitoring Initialization:** Configures services and timers to record gaze coordinates and periodic photo capture [4].
- **Data Processing and Recording:** During user interaction, fixation points are collected and stored in a dictionary (`gazeDataDictionary`) along with each displayed image ID. At defined intervals, these data are inserted into the database, enabling subsequent analyses (e.g., heat map generation) [9].
- **Dynamic Image Switching:** A timer (`imageSwitchTimer`) randomly selects and displays new images in containers, associating each image with a unique ID [18].
- **Layout Management:** The `StructureService` class updates container coordinates and dimensions so the system knows where each element is on screen [6].

By combining these ET data with demographic predictions, the system identifies preferences by specific groups (age, gender, ethnicity), enabling in-depth analyses of visual behavior and facilitating decision-making in marketing, product design, and usability [1, 8].

```
// Exemplo resumido da lógica de EyeTrackingPage
private void OnGazeMoved(Point gazePoint, double gazeX, double gazeY)
{
    // Captura coordenadas do olhar
    double ellipseLeft = gazeX - (eyeGazePositionEllipse.Width / 2.0);
    double ellipseTop  = gazeY - (eyeGazePositionEllipse.Height / 2.0);

    // Atualiza a posição da elipse que indica a posição do olhar
    TranslateTransform translateEllipse = new TranslateTransform
    {
        X = ellipseLeft,
        Y = ellipseTop
    };
    eyeGazePositionEllipse.RenderTransform = translateEllipse;

    // Verifica se o olhar está dentro de algum contêiner específico (imagem)
    foreach (var border in ContainersGrid.Children.OfType<Border>())
    {
        // Lógica para identificar o contêiner e guardar coordenadas no dicionário
    }
}
```

**Fig. 2.** Simplified excerpt from the Eye Tracking implementation.

## 6.2 Facial Recognition

This prototype was built to classify demographic data (age, gender, and ethnicity) by combining CV—for face detection, bounding box creation, and image preprocessing—with ML for FR. The implementation proceeded as follows:

**Data Preparation:**

- CV methods were used to detect faces and generate bounding boxes.
- ML cleaning, resizing to $128 \times 128$, and data augmentation (rotation, brightness) [13, 16].
- ML division into training, validation, and testing sets [11].

**Model Construction:**

- CNN (MobileNetV2) to extract visual features [5].
- Multitask: Age (regression), Gender (binary classification), and Ethnicity (multiclass).
- Loss functions: MAE (age) and Cross-Entropy (gender/ethnicity) [12].

**Model Training:**

- Initial configuration: learning rate (Adam), metrics (MAE, accuracy, F1-Score) [6].
- Epoch-based training, applying class weights to handle imbalances [16].
- Continuous validation and dynamic learning rate adjustment (scheduler).

**Model Evaluation:**

- Metrics: MAE/MSE (age), accuracy, recall, and F1-Score (gender/ethnicity) [8, 9].
- Confusion matrices and performance graphs (error histograms, scatter plots).

**Real-Time Prediction:**

- **Image Acquisition:** Images are captured by the webcam and saved in a user-specific study path.

- **Processing**: Data is then processed by the ML model in real time, generating outputs such as estimated age, gender, and ethnicity [11].
- **Display and Correlation**: Demographic results are shown in a graphical interface and combined with other metrics (e.g., eye-tracking) [10] to provide a holistic view of consumer behavior.

# 7  Results

## 7.1  Eye-Tracking

Figure 3 shows the prototype interface, where green dots represent user fixations on the displayed product [3, 10]. In addition, graphs and text blocks indicate viewing statistics, file names, and user data, cross-referenced with ET [9].

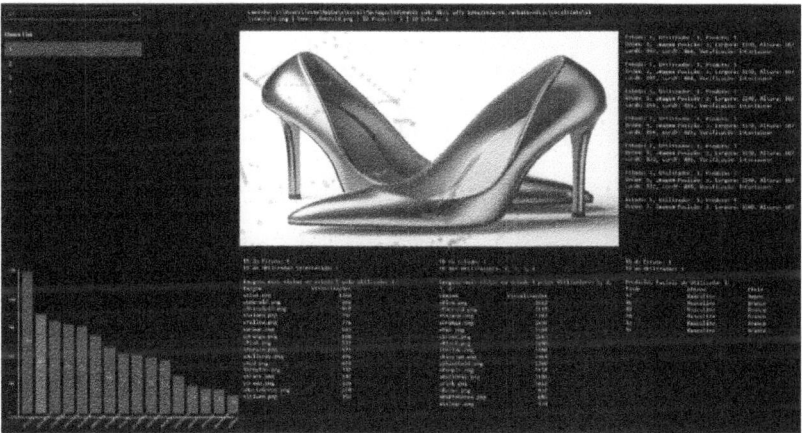

**Fig. 3.** - Prototype Interface.

**Attention Heatmaps:** The heatmap visualization reveals that users focus their gaze more intensely on the coordinates of images that capture their attention—often around the center of the screen or on brightly colored elements [1, 2]. By leveraging these high-visibility focal points, designers and marketers can strategically place key information, promotional items, or features to ensure they capture the user's gaze, thereby maximizing the effectiveness of product displays and interfaces [8].

**Fixation Duration:** Data on how long a viewer's gaze remains in a certain area (fixation duration) suggests a greater perceived importance of that element [14]. If users spend more time looking at specific product details, images, or text, it indicates heightened engagement, which can be leveraged to emphasize standout features.

**Demographic Segmentation:** By correlating eye-tracking metrics (e.g., heatmaps, fixation duration) with demographic attributes (such as age and gender), the system uncovers nuanced preferences among different consumer groups [1, 6].

## 7.2   Facial Recognition ML Model Training

The model was developed using **10,157 original samples** and **61,335 synthetic samples**, totaling **71,492 images**, and trained for **100 epochs**. The multitask approach yielded the following results:

**Age:** MAE of 1.65 and MSE of 10.94 [5]; **Gender:** 96% accuracy [16]; **Ethnicity:** 90% accuracy [11].

Figure 3 through 5 illustrate the model's performance. Figure 3, age prediction errors cluster close to zero, indicating strong predictive accuracy [14]; Fig. 4 shows the alignment between actual and predicted ages, validating the regression strategy [2]; Finally, Fig. 5 provides a confusion matrix demonstrating high accuracy in the gender classification task [16].

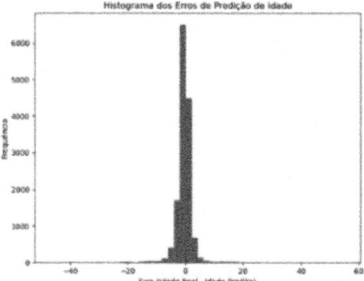

**Fig. 4.** Histogram shows the distribution of prediction errors for age.

This histogram (Fig. 3) demonstrates the model's accuracy and how it handles age predictions. The concentration around zero reinforces the model's effectiveness.

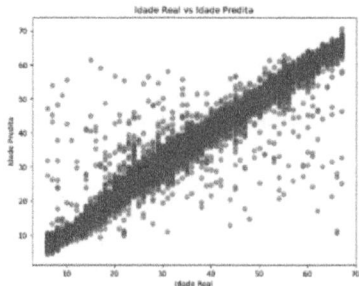

**Fig. 5.** Actual Age on the x-axis against Predicted Age on the y-axis.

This chart (Fig. 4) is crucial for visualizing the alignment between actual and predicted values. This kind of graph is commonly used to validate regression models (Fig. 6).

This matrix (Fig. 5) is essential for assessing the model's performance in classification tasks such as gender.

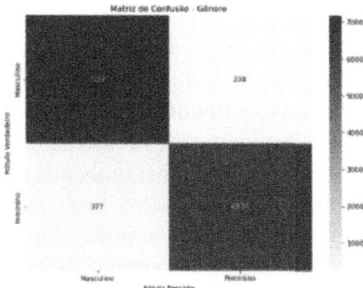

**Fig. 6.** Actual labels on the vertical axis and predicted labels on the horizontal axis.

## 8 Conclusions

This paper presents a comprehensive model that integrates eye-tracking, **OpenCV-based computer vision (CV)**, and **machine learning (ML)** to enhance objectivity and accuracy in consumer behavior analysis [9, 10]. By capturing visual attention and demographic traits without relying solely on self-reported measures, the proposed system offers deeper insights for product design, advertising strategies, and market segmentation [2, 8]. Key Contributions include:

- **Integrated Framework:** A novel combination of eye-tracking, OpenCV-based CV, and ML ensures that face detection (via OpenCV) and classification (via ML) yield objective, real-time user insights.
- **Enhanced Market Insights:** Correlating demographic segmentation with attention metrics enables the identification of distinct consumer preferences, informing more targeted and impactful marketing studies.
- **Scalable Architecture**: The system's modular design—incorporating robust calibration, data synchronization, and cloud-friendly processes—facilitates easy deployment in diverse contexts [1, 6].
- **Actionable Insights**: Allows for timely and targeted campaign adjustments [3].
- **Demographic Segmentation & Product Engagement:** Real-time classification of age/gender/ethnicity, aligned with fixation data (e.g., eye-tracking duration), validates the system's capacity to reflect genuine user interest [11, 14].
- **Validation of Product Engagement**: Eye-tracking duration significantly aligns with subsequent self-reported interest, reinforcing the reliability of objective data [2, 17].

Overall, these results underscore the potential to refine market segmentation and optimize marketing campaigns through integrated demographic and attention metrics [8]. By bridging traditional marketing research gaps with modern AI-driven tools, businesses can more accurately identify consumer interests, ultimately strengthening product development and promotional effectiveness [15].

## 9 Limitations

Although the integrated system offers promising results, several limitations must be recognized and addressed:

- **Sample Size and Diversity**: Small or non-diverse participant pools can limit generalizability. To mitigate this, researchers should recruit a larger, more varied participant pool (online/offline) across multiple demographics.
- **Controlled vs. Real-World Environments**: Laboratory conditions do not fully capture real-world complexities. Deploying the prototype in public events, retail stores, or online platforms is recommended to gather authentic consumer behavior data.
- **Technical and Calibration Aspects**: Factors such as lighting, positioning, and real-time processing demands can affect accuracy and scalability. Implementing robust calibration protocols, optimizing algorithms, and potentially using cloud-based processing can help maintain system reliability.
- **Ethical and Privacy Concerns:** Collecting demographic and gaze data raises privacy issues and may conflict with regulatory standards. Ensuring transparent consent, anonymizing or pseudonymizing data, and maintaining secure infrastructure (e.g., GDPR compliance) help address these concerns.
- **Integration of Multiple Data Streams**: Synchronizing eye-tracking (ET), facial recognition (FR), and machine learning (ML) in real time requires precise alignment and continuous verification. Employing unified timestamps, recurring calibration, and confidence thresholds for uncertain classifications strengthens data integrity.

By aligning each limitation with its corresponding mitigation, the system can evolve into a robust, scalable, and ethically sound solution for real-world consumer behavior analysis.

## 10   Future Work

To further validate and improve the system, several follow-up steps are proposed:

- **Larger User Base:** Conduct field studies with larger, more diverse samples to assess generalizability and highlight demographic nuances [1, 5].
- **Real-World Environments:** Deploy the prototype in less controlled settings (e.g., in-store displays, live events) to capture genuine, unfiltered consumer interactions [4, 9].
- **Incorporate Emotion Analysis:** Fuse physiological data (e.g., facial expressions, electrodermal activity) to interpret affective states alongside visual attention and demographics [7, 14].
- **Refinement of Algorithms:** Investigate advanced ML techniques for better accuracy (e.g., transformer-based architectures or hyperparameter optimization) [13].
- **Incremental Learning with User Feedback:** Introduce a continuous or online training pipeline, allowing the model to adapt in real time as new data and user feedback emerge, thereby improving predictive performance over prolonged use.
- **Ethical and Privacy Considerations**: Develop transparent protocols, secure data management, and user consent frameworks to address growing concerns around data privacy in AI-driven systems [2, 18].

By extending the prototype's reach and deepening its analytical capabilities, this approach can evolve into a powerful platform that thoroughly supports consumer research, marketing analytics, and product innovation in both academic and industrial settings [17].

# References

1. Husić-Mehmedović, M., Omeragić, I., Batagelj, Z., Kolar, T.: Seeing is not necessarily liking: advancing research on package design with eye-tracking. J. Bus. Res. **80**, 145–154 (2017). https://doi.org/10.1016/j.jbusres.2017.04.019
2. Ballco, P., de-Magistris, T., Caputo, V.: Consumer preferences for nutritional claims: An exploration of attention and choice based on an eye-tracking choice experiment. Food Res. Int. 116, 37–48 (2019). https://doi.org/10.1016/j.foodres.2018.12.031
3. Gunaratne, N.M., et al.: Consumer acceptability, eye fixation, and physiological responses: a study of novel and familiar chocolate packaging designs using eye-tracking devices. Foods **8**(7), 253 (2019). https://doi.org/10.3390/foods8070253
4. Pappusetty, D., Kalva, H., Hock, H.S.: Pupil response to quality and content transitions in videos. IEEE Trans. Consum. Electron. **63**(4), 410–418 (2017). https://doi.org/10.1109/TCE. 2017.015109
5. Xia, C., Quan, R.: Predicting saccadic eye movements in free viewing of webpages. IEEE Access **8**, 15598–15610 (2020). https://doi.org/10.1109/ACCESS.2020.2966628
6. Jiang, L., Zhang, K.: Apparel brand overlap based on customer perceived value and eye-tracking technology. Tsinghua Sci. Technol. **23**(1), 47–64 (2018). https://doi.org/10.26599/ TST.2018.9010054
7. Liberati, A., et al.: The PRISMA statement for reporting systematic reviews and meta-analyses of studies that evaluate health care interventions: explanation and elaboration. PLoS Med. **6**(7), e1000100 (2009). https://doi.org/10.1371/journal.pmed.1000100
8. Maslowska, E., Segijn, C.M., Vakeel, K.A., Viswanathan, V.: How consumers attend to online reviews: an eye-tracking and network analysis approach. Int. J. Advert. **39**(2), 282–306 (2020). https://doi.org/10.1080/02650487.2019.1617651
9. Kuo, J.-Y., Chen, C.-H., Koyama, S., Chang, D.: Investigating the relationship between users' eye movements and perceived product attributes in design concept evaluation. Appl. Ergon. **94**, 103393 (2021). https://doi.org/10.1016/j.apergo.2021.103393
10. Burger, G., Guna, J., Pogačnik, M.: Suitability of inexpensive eye-tracking device for user experience evaluations. Sensors **18**(6), 1822 (2018). https://doi.org/10.3390/s18061822
11. Weichbroth, P.: Usability of mobile applications: a systematic literature study. IEEE Access **8**, 55563–55577 (2020). https://doi.org/10.1109/ACCESS.2020.2981892
12. Zhang, W., Liu, H.: Toward a reliable collection of eye-tracking data for image quality research: challenges, solutions, and applications. IEEE Trans. Image Process. **26**(5), 2424–2437 (2017). https://doi.org/10.1109/TIP.2017.2681424
13. Dziśko, M., Jankowski, J., Wątróbski, J.: Measuring the impact of intrusive online marketing content on consumer choice with the eye tracking, pp. 353–363 (2017). https://doi.org/10. 1007/978-3-319-62938-4_23
14. Muñoz-Leiva, F., Hernández-Méndez, J., Gómez-Carmona, D.: Measuring advertising effectiveness in Travel 2.0 websites through eye-tracking technology. Physiol. Behav. **200**, 83–95 (2019). https://doi.org/10.1016/j.physbeh.2018.03.002
15. Hussain, Z., Simonovic, B., Stupple, E., Austin, M.: Using eye tracking to explore facebook use and associations with Facebook addiction, mental well-being, and personality. Behav. Sci. **9**(2), 19 (2019). https://doi.org/10.3390/bs9020019
16. Wang, H., Zhou, Y., Yu, F., Zhao, L., Wang, C., Ren, Y.: Fusional recognition for depressive tendency with multi-modal feature. IEEE Access **7**, 38702–38713 (2019). https://doi.org/10. 1109/ACCESS.2019.2899352

17. Lalle, S., Toker, D., Conati, C.: Gaze-Driven adaptive interventions for magazine-style narrative visualizations. IEEE Trans. Vis. Comput. Graph. **27**(6), 2941–2952 (2021). https://doi.org/10.1109/TVCG.2019.2958540
18. Ninaus, M., Kiili, K., Wood, G., Moeller, K., Kober, S.E.: To add or not to add game elements? exploring the effects of different cognitive task designs using eye tracking. IEEE Trans. Learn. Technol. **13**(4), 847–860 (2020). https://doi.org/10.1109/TLT.2020.3031644

# Measuring Cognitive Engagement with Eye-Tracking: An Exploratory Study

Gaayathri Sankar[1]([✉]), Soussan Djamasbi[1], Bengisu Tulu[1],
and Susanne Muehlschlegel[2]

[1] Worcester Polytechnic Institute, Worcester, MA 01609, USA
{gsankar,djamasbi,bengisu}@wpi.edu
[2] John Hopkins University School of Medicine, Baltimore, MD 21287, USA
smuehlsch@jhu.edu

**Abstract.** In this paper, we focus on objectively measuring cognitive engagement using eye-tracking techniques. Specifically, we analyze both gaze-based and pupil-based eye movement data to assess attention and absorption—two key dimensions of cognitive engagement. These ocular behaviors serve as complementary indicators of cognition, providing a more comprehensive representation of cognitive engagement. Using these objective measures, we examine how navigation style influences cognitive engagement with an 18-page web-based medical decision aid (DA). Our findings demonstrate that evaluating cognitive engagement through the objective measures of attention and absorption offers a more holistic understanding of user engagement. Furthermore, because the system used in our study supports emotionally taxing decision-making, our results extend the measurement of cognitive engagement to contexts beyond those driven by affective states such as flow.

**Keywords:** Cognitive engagement · Eye-tracking · Attention and absorption

## 1 Introduction

In information system (IS) research, *cognitive engagement* is often associated with the concept of *flow* [1]. *Flow* refers to a positive affective state characterized by experiencing intense concentration, loss of time awareness, and a sense of total control [2]. For example, in emergency response literature, optimal cognitive engagement with a decision aid (DA) during crisis is linked to the experience of flow. When faced with emergency situations, experienced decision-makers often achieve a state of flow, characterized by *calm alertness* and *focused attention* [3]. Similarly, cognitive engagement, in the user engagement scale (UES) is measured as focused attention, a construct grounded in the concept of flow [4]. Focused attention items in the UES evaluate the flow experience by asking users if they felt time passed quickly while using a system. In a similar fashion but more thoroughly, cognitive engagement in the acceptance literature is captured with a self-reported scale measuring the experience of flow along five dimensions: *temporal dissociation* (the inability to register the passage of time while engaged in interaction),

D. D. Schmorrow and C. M. Fidopiastis (Eds.): HCII 2025, LNAI 15778, pp. 69–78, 2025.
https://doi.org/10.1007/978-3-031-93724-8_6

*focused immersion* (the experience of total engagement where other attentional demands are ignored), *heightened enjoyment* (the pleasurable aspects of the interaction), *control* (the user's perception of being in charge of the interaction), and *curiosity* (the extent to which the experience arouses an individual's sensory and cognitive curiosity) [5–7]. Despite the strong association between cognitive engagement and flow in the IS literature, some studies acknowledge that cognitive engagement can occur without the presence of flow [8].

In a recent comprehensive multidisciplinary framework for explaining involvement with an activity cognitive engagement is conceptualized along two distinct dimensions: attention and absorption [9]. Within this framework, attention is described as *"a state of awareness, concentration, and focus"* [9–11], while absorption is defined as a state of flow, characterized by *"a pleasant feeling of being captivated and fully immersed, to the extent of losing track of time"* [9, 12, 13]. Because cognitive engagement is predominantly assessed using self-reported scales, this multidisciplinary framework emphasizes the need to develop objective measures for capturing cognitive engagement in future research. Furthermore, recognizing that engagement is not a static phenomenon but evolves over time [14], the framework highlights the importance of studies that explore the dynamic nature of cognitive engagement.

In this paper, we aim to address the call for objectively measuring cognitive engagement and exploring its dynamic nature through eye-tracking methodology. While we adopt the conceptualization of cognitive engagement as a two-dimensional construct proposed by the multidisciplinary framework of engagement, we expand it to include affective states beyond the traditional concept of flow.

## 2  Background

Engagement with technology typically reflects an individual's willingness to interact with and remain involved in a system [15]. Flow, as a state that compels individuals to stay engaged or re-engage in an activity, has often been used as a key metric for predicting the likelihood of continued technology use. However, there are many situations where users may be fully immersed in using a system without experiencing flow. For example, completing a task such as reporting business-related expenses in an organizational system may not induce flow and may even evoke negative emotions (e.g., frustration or upset) despite users being fully invested in completing the task and likely to continue using the system in the future. In such cases, relying on flow to measure engagement is unlikely to yield accurate results.

Supporting this argument, a recent study examining user engagement with a suicide prevention app revealed that ratings for the focused attention dimension of the User Engagement Scale (UES) were relatively low. However, objective measures, such as the quality scores of textual entries, and qualitative feedback indicated that users were adequately involved with the app [16]. Given that participants in this study used the app during their visit to an emergency department due to suicide risk, it is unreasonable to expect that their engagement with the app would foster a flow experience. Thus, the findings of this study support the argument that cognitive engagement can occur even in the absence of flow. Hence, we extend the definition of absorption to make it applicable regardless of the valence of a user's affective state during an activity. We define absorption as *a state characterized by being captivated and immersed in an activity.*

To study cognitive engagement without achieving a state of flow, we used a medical decision aid (DA) designed to support emotionally challenging decisions. This DA is specifically developed for surrogates responsible for making informed decisions on behalf of their nonresponsive loved ones in neurosciences Intensive Care Units (neuroICU). Such decisions require processing a substantial amount of complex medical information regarding treatment options and their potential consequences. This includes descriptions of treatments that can artificially prolong a patient's life using intrusive mechanical devices, as well as options that avoid intrusive procedures to prioritize patient comfort for the remainder of their natural life. In this context, achieving a state of flow is neither relevant nor appropriate for fostering cognitive engagement with the system. Instead, an ideal level of cognitive engagement is characterized by the extent to which the system effectively involves users in actively and thoroughly processing the critical information necessary to inform their decisions.

### 2.1 Measuring Cognitive Engagement with Eye Movements

Grounded in a multidisciplinary framework for engagement with an activity, we measure cognitive engagement along two dimensions: attention and absorption [9]. For attention, we adopt the framework's definition as *"a state of awareness, concentration, and focus"* [9–11]. We extend the framework's definition of absorption to ensure it is not confined to a positive affective state. Specifically, we define absorption as *a state characterized by being captivated and fully immersed in an activity.*

To objectively capture attention and absorption during technology use, we utilize eye-tracking technology. For sighted individuals, visual information is predominantly processed through the eyes, making eye tracking the gold standard for measuring how we attend to information in our visual field [17]. Grounded in the eye-mind assumption— which posits that what we look at is sent to the brain for processing [18]—visual attention has been reliably measured using gaze-based eye movement behaviors. The raw gaze data collected by eye trackers is typically filtered to identify clusters of slow movements called fixations. These slow eye movements represent the focus of attention, as we slow down our gaze to capture detailed visual information about objects that attract our attention [17, 19]. Because gaze streams reveal where and how individuals direct their attention over time [17], they offer objective data for measuring cognitive engagement and tracking its fluctuations over time.

Measuring absorption, however, is relatively underexplored in the IS eye-tracking literature. In the broader eye-tracking field, absorption is closely related to the concept of arousal, which is often captured through pupil-based changes. Arousal, defined as the state of being alert and responsive to stimuli [20], is a fundamental cognitive process underlying information processing behavior. Being captivated and immersed in an activity inherently requires an individual to be both alert and responsive to stimuli. Supporting this argument, a recent study suggests that changes in pupil size offer an opportunity to measure absorption unobtrusively using eye-tracking sensors [21].

## 3  Methodology

### 3.1  Study Design and Process

To evaluate which of the two 18-page web-based medical decision aid (DA) prototypes facilitated better cognitive engagement, we conducted an eye-tracking study. Both
prototypes contained identical content but differed in navigation style: one used a top
navigation bar, while the other featured a left navigation bar. Fourteen participants were
recruited for the study and were randomly assigned to review one of the two prototypes
while their eye movements were tracked. We utilized the Tobii X300 eye-tracking device
to capture participant eye movements. The eye tracker was integrated into the screen
resembling a standard monitor thus enabling unobtrusive gaze capture. Also, since the
Tobii X300 does not require participants to remove glasses or contact lenses, it facilitated a natural and comfortable environment for studying viewing behavior. Owing to
the effect of light on pupil size, as in prior pupillometry studies, we ensured that lighting
conditions remained constant.

After using the DA, we utilized two selected items from a prior engagement survey
to measure participants' perceptions of attention and absorption [8]. These items asked
participants to rate the extent to which: 1) the DA held their attention, and 2) they felt
fully absorbed while reviewing the DA, using a 7-point scale. Additionally, participants
were invited to provide qualitative feedback about their experience with the DA.

### 3.2  Eye Movement Metrics

To investigate the progression of cognitive engagement over time, we defined each page
of the DA as an area of interest (AOI) and we calculated attention and absorption for
each page individually. The DA was designed to be viewed sequentially, from the first
page to the last, to optimize information acquisition. As a result, mapping engagement
across the 18 pages of the DA provided an effective proxy for tracking the progression
of cognitive engagement over time.

To measure attention to the DA objectively, we calculated the total fixation duration
for each participant and averaged them across participants for each page (TFD $_{Avg}$
expressed in seconds). This eye-movement metric represents the average amount of time
spent visually processing the pages of the DA. Using averages instead of total values helps
minimize noise caused by individual differences [22]. Higher fixation duration values
often indicate deliberate engagement with content, such as reading text or analyzing
visuals [22]. To measure absorption objectively, we calculated the average pupil diameter
in z-scores ($PD_{z\text{-}score}$) for each participant on each page [21]. An identical page in both
prototypes (Page 0) was used as the baseline. So, to study the progression in pupillary
response across pages, $PD_{z\text{-}score}$ was calculated based on the mean and standard deviation
of average pupil data from Pages 0–18. This approach helped implicitly baseline-correct
as well as control for inter-subject variability in pupil responses [21, 23].

### 3.3  Analysis

For the statistical analysis, we visualized the distribution of data for outliers and
employed log transformation, if necessary. Based on whether or not the data was normally

distributed and checking for homogeneity of variance where required, we conducted a two-way Analysis of Variance (ANOVA) without replication. This enabled us to test for differences between designs as well as across pages of the DA.

In addition to the above analysis, we conducted Spearman's correlation test to explore potential relationships between attention and absorption. These two dimensions of cognitive engagement represent distinct aspects of the construct. Similarly, the objective measures of attention and absorption in our study—represented by a gaze-based metric (fixation duration) and a pupil-based metric (pupil diameter), respectively—are known to reflect complementary cognitive processes [24].

## 4 Results

Table 1 presents the results of the ANOVA comparing differences in cognitive engagement across the 18 pages of the DA and between the two navigation designs of the prototypes. Attention, measured objectively as $TFD_{Avg}$, showed a higher average value for the prototype with the left navigation style compared to the one with the top navigation style. Similarly, absorption, measured objectively as $PD_{z\text{-}score}$ showed a higher average value for the prototype with the left navigation style compared to the one with the top navigation style. The differences in attention were significant both across the pages of the DA and between the two navigation designs. In contrast, absorption showed significant differences only across the pages of the DA. Qualitative feedback supported these results.

**Table 1.** Results of ANOVA for objective measures.

| Metrics for Attention & Absorption | Mean (SD) | | p-value for Differences | |
|---|---|---|---|---|
| | TopNav (pages) | LeftNav designs) | (across pages) | (between designs) |
| $TFD_{Avg}$ | 49.80s (38.07) | 55.54s (40.22) | **<0.001** | **<0.001** |
| $PD_{z\text{-}score}$ | -0.16 (0.35) | -0.12 (0.41) | **0.01** | 0.53 |

Figures 1 and 2 illustrate the trends in cognitive engagement across both prototypes over time (pages 1–18). Figure 1 presents fixation duration, representing the amount of time users spent fixating their gaze on each page. The trend reflects viewing behavior in response to content density—pages with more content elicited longer fixation durations, indicating thorough reviewing behavior. Figure 2 displays level of absorption for each page, with peaks in the trend corresponding to pages that included images or visual elements such as graphs and charts. For example, page 3 featured an image of a ventilator, while page 8 contained a diagram representing the two different goals of care. Page 10 included images of patients with tubes attached to their bodies, and page 11 had images that included faces. Although page 18 did not have images, it contained a worksheet for

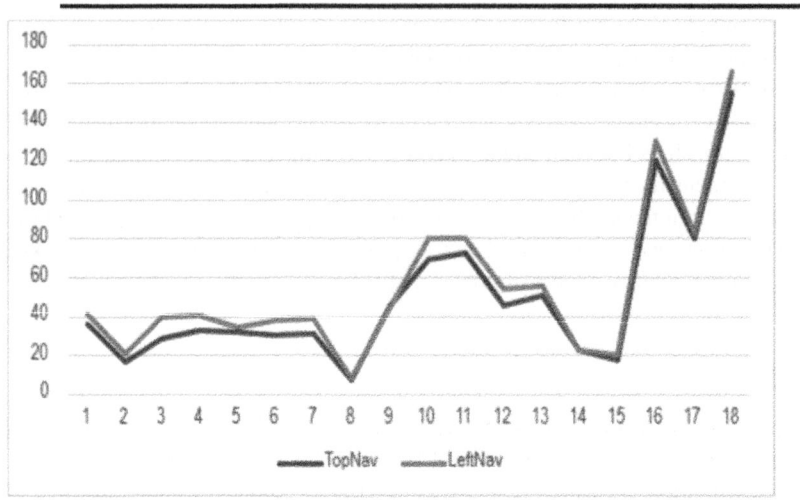

**Fig. 1.** The trend in attention ($TFD_{Avg}$) to the DA over time.

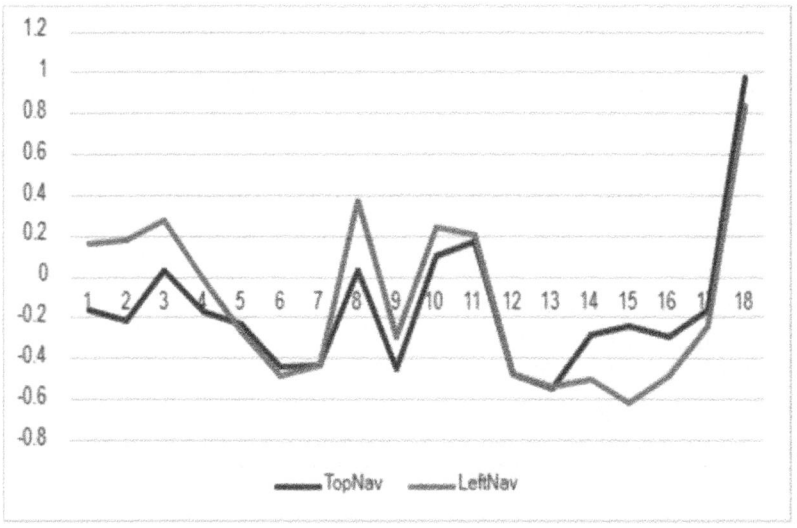

**Fig. 2.** The trend in absorption ($PD_{z\text{-score}}$) elicited by the DA over time.

deciding on survival or death for their loved one, which surrogates had to prepare for a meeting with their doctor to finalize their decision.

The results for page 8 are particularly interesting because they reflect that attention and absorption are different constructs. This page contained a relatively simple diagram displaying the two choices available to the surrogate: either artificially keeping their loved ones alive or deciding to end their suffering. The relative brevity of the content on this page is reflected by a dip in fixation duration in Fig. 1. However, despite its brief content, this page invoked alertness and responsiveness, as reflected by a spike in pupil dilation (PD) for page 8 in Fig. 2.

We found no significant correlation between attention and absorption metrics in our study, regardless of the prototype design. As shown in Table 2, the results indicate no relationship between the two dimensions of cognitive engagement in this context.

**Table 2.** Results from correlation analysis for attention and absorption

| Metric Pairs | TopNav (r) | p-value | LeftNav (r) | p-value |
|---|---|---|---|---|
| TFDavg vs PDz-score | 0.13 | 0.60 | 0.17 | 0.51 |

The self-reported ratings for attention, with mean scores of 2.14 and 3.14 on a 7point scale (where 1 represents the highest level of attention and 7 the lowest), indicated that attention was rated in the high to medium range. Similarly, the ratings for absorption (3.14 and 4.14) fell within the higher end of the medium range. However, the differences in ratings between the two prototype designs were not statistically significant indicating that the two prototypes were equally engaging (Table 3).

**Table 3.** Results of t-test for self-reported measures

| | Mean (SD) | | |
|---|---|---|---|
| | TopNav | LeftNav | |
| Perceived Attention | 2.14(0.90) | 3.14 (1.77) | t-Stat = 1.33, df = 12, p = 0.20 |
| Perceived Absorption | 3.14(2.12) | 4.14 (1.86) | t-Stat = 0.94, df = 12, p = 0.37 |

## 5 Discussion

When measuring cognitive engagement objectively through eye movements, we found significant differences between the two designs. Our results showed that the left navigation design resulted in significantly more attention to the DA pages. However, our analysis did not reveal significant differences in cognitive absorption between the two designs. This may be because both designs contained the same content, differing only in navigation style. As a result, both DA prototypes appeared to keep participants equally captivated in processing the critical information required to inform their decisions.

Comparing perceived attention and absorption between the two designs revealed relatively positive engagement ratings for the DA, but the differences were not statistically significant, indicating that both designs were perceived as equally engaging. However, qualitative feedback aligned with the eye movement analysis results, showed that the left navigation was perceived as more engaging than the top navigation. These findings are not surprising, as detecting statistically significant differences often requires larger sample sizes. Therefore, in formative studies, which typically involve smaller sample sizes, qualitative feedback becomes crucial for providing rich context to interpret inconclusive results. Notably, eye movement data from the same small sample size yielded significant findings. This is because the dataset for each participant included eye movement metrics across 18 pages of the DA, offering the depth and richness needed to generate meaningful insights in formative studies.

Our analysis revealed that engagement varied significantly across the pages of the DA, regardless of navigation style. This finding, indicating that some pages were more engaging than others, is not surprising, as each page provided a different type of information. Figure 2 illustrates the trend in absorption across pages. Notably, the peaks or spikes in the trend correlate with pages containing images or visual descriptions, suggesting that visual content may enhance engagement with the DA.

The exploratory analysis of the correlation between $TFD_{Avg}$ and $PD_{z\text{-scores}}$ did not reveal any significant results, indicating that attention and absorption, as represented by these two variables, were independent of each other in our study. This interpretation is further supported by the differing trends in Figs. 1 and 2, which demonstrate that attention and absorption represent two distinct dimensions of cognitive engagement.

Our findings suggest that fixation duration is a suitable measure for capturing attention. Similarly, when focusing on capturing alertness and responsiveness, our results show that changes in pupil size provide an effective metric for objectively measuring absorption. Additionally, our study supports the argument that the concept of engagement extends beyond flow to include other affective states [8]. Given the emotionally taxing nature of the DA, engagement in our study occurred without the experience of flow, a finding further supported by the qualitative feedback on participants' experiences with the DA.

From an HCI perspective, our results suggest that interface layout, particularly the navigation design, can significantly influence users' cognitive engagement. Our findings indicate that the spatial arrangement of navigational cues can facilitate a more thorough exploration of content—an important insight for interfaces that present dense or critical information, such as medical decision aids, training materials, or data-driven dashboards.

Moreover, measuring engagement through attention and absorption highlights the importance of considering both where users look and how they respond to the content. For instance, a balanced visual design that minimizes clutter, allows sufficient whitespace and structures content in a logical flow is likely to enhance not only attention but also absorption. These design adjustments help prevent users from feeling overwhelmed by extraneous elements or disengaged due to a poor layout.

Incorporating eye movement data into cognitive engagement measurements can be a valuable tool in iterative design cycles. This approach enables UX practitioners to make data-driven decisions about design optimizations, ultimately resulting in more intuitive and user-centered products. Our study further supports this argument with the results of self-reported measures. While we did not find significant differences in perceived engagement between the two designs, the eye movement data revealed that one design was significantly more engaging than the other. This finding is particularly important in the early stages of development, where designers often optimize user experience through a series of iterative studies, each with small sample sizes [25].

## 5.1 Limitations and Future Research

The results of our study are exploratory and should not be considered definitive. Although the small sample size of fourteen participants limits the ability to generalize these findings to a broader audience, the significant results suggest that measuring engagement with eye movements shows promise. Nonetheless, larger and more diverse samples would strengthen the robustness and generalizability of our findings. We utilized only two eye movement metrics to measure attention and absorption; incorporating additional metrics could further refine and expand our results. Our study focused on a more traditional information system, but future research could test these components using advanced interactive and relational information systems. Moreover, more sophisticated models, such as Mixed Models could be employed to analyze these eye-tracking metrics in real-time, providing deeper insights into UX optimization and cognitive engagement. While we initially focused on the cognitive aspect of engagement, this represents just a foundational step in developing a more refined measurement model for engagement.

## 6 Conclusion

User engagement with a system can be measured objectively through eye movements, which reflect attention and responsiveness to content. While fixation duration indicates the level of attention given to information, pupil size provides insight into how immersed users are in processing that information. By using an emotionally taxing decision aid (DA), our study supports expanding the definition and measurement of absorption to contexts that do not necessarily involve enjoyable activities. Our results show that measuring both attention and absorption together via eye movements offers a more nuanced and comprehensive understanding of how cognitive engagement unfolds over time.

## References

1. Webster, J., Ho, H.: Audience engagement in multimedia presentations. SIGMIS Database **28**(2), 63–77 (1997)
2. Csikszentmihalyi, M.: Flow: The Psychology of Optimal Experience. Harper and Row, New York (1990)
3. Djamasbi, S., Loiacono-Mello, E.T., Mendelson, Y.: Affect feedback during crisis and its role in improving IS utilization. In: International Conference on Information Systems for Crisis Response and Management (2010)
4. O'Brien, H.L., Cairns, P.A., Hall, M.: A practical approach to measuring user engagement with the refined user engagement scale (UES) and new UES short form. Int. J. Hum. Comput. Stud. **112**, 28–39 (2018)
5. Agarwal, R., Karahanna, E.: Time flies when you're having fun: cognitive absorption and beliefs about information technology usage. MIS Q. **24**, 665–694 (2000)
6. Oz, B., Coursaris, C., Robert, J., Léger, P.: The nature and dimensionality of cognitive absorption: a critical review and meta-analysis. In: SIGHCI 2023 Proceedings, vol. 18 (2024)

7. Léger, P., Davis, F., Cronan, P., Perret, J.: Neurophysiological correlates of cognitive absorption in an enactive training context. Comput. Hum. Behav. **34**, 273–283 (2014)
8. Webster, J., Ahuja, J.S.: Enhancing the design of web navigation systems: the influence of user disorientation on engagement and performance. MIS Q. **30**(3) (2006)
9. Benz, C., Riefle, L., Satzger, G.: User engagement and beyond: a conceptual framework for engagement in information systems research. Commun. Assoc. Inf. Syst. **54**, 331–359 (2024)
10. Fredricks, J.A., Blumenfeld, P.C., Paris, A.H.: School engagement: potential of the concept, state of the evidence. Rev. Educ. Res. **74**(1), 59–109 (2004)
11. O'Brien, H.L.: The influence of hedonic and utilitarian motivations on user engagement: the case of online shopping experiences. Interact. Comput. **22**(5), 344–352 (2010)
12. Hakanen, J.J., Bakker, A.B., Schaufeli, W.B.: Burnout and work engagement among teachers. J. Sch. Psychol. **43**(6), 495–513 (2006)
13. Lehmann, J., Lalmas, M., Yom-Tov, E., Dupret, G.: Models of user engagement. In: Proceedings of the 20th International Conference on User Modeling, Adaptation, and Personalization (UMAP) (2012)
14. Brodie, R.J., Hollebeek, L.D., Jurić, B., Ilić, A.: Customer engagement: conceptual domain, fundamental propositions, and implications for research. J. Serv. Res. **14**(3), 252–271 (2011)
15. O'Brien, H., Cairns, P.: Why engagement matters, 1st edn. Springer, Cham (2016)
16. Larkin, C., et al.: Comparing the Acceptability and quality of intervention modalities for suicidality in the emergency department: randomized feasibility trial. JMIR Mental Health **10** (2023)
17. Djamasbi, S.: Eye tracking and web experience. AIS Trans. Hum.-Comput. Interact. **6**(2), 37–54 (2014)
18. Just, M.A., Carpenter, P.A.: A theory of reading: from eye fixations to comprehension. Psychol. Rev. **87**(4), 329–354 (1980)
19. Alrefaei, D., Djamasbi, S., Strong, D.: Chronic pain and eye movements: a neurois approach to designing smart clinical decision support systems. AIS Trans. Hum.-Comput. Interact. **15**(3), 268–291 (2023)
20. Niven, K., Miles, E.: Affect arousal. In: Gellman, M.D., Turner, J.R. (eds.) Encyclopedia of Behavioral Medicine. Springer, New York (2013)
21. Juyumaya, J., Torres, J.P., Maldonado, P.: Shifts in task absorption during decision making episodes. Sci. Rep. **14**, (2024)
22. Holmqvist, K., Nyström, M., Andersson, R., Dewhurst, R., Jarodzka, H., Weijer, J.V.: Eye Tracking: A Comprehensive Guide to Methods and Measures. OUP, Oxford (2011)
23. Astudillo, C., Muñoz, K., Maldonado, P. E.: Emotional content modulates attentional visual orientation during free viewing of natural images. Front. Hum. Neurosci. **12** (2018)
24. Eckstein, M.K., Guerra-Carrillo, B., Miller Singley, A.T., Bunge, S.A.: Beyond eye gaze: what else can eyetracking reveal about cognition and cognitive development? Dev. Cogn. Neurosci. **25**, 69–91 (2017)
25. Tullis, T., Albert, W.: Measuring the User Experience, 2nd edn. Morgan Kaufmann Publishers Inc., San Francisco (2013)

# Is Augmented Cognition a Complex System?

Suraj Sood[(⊠)]

LUV Systems, Los Angeles, USA
`thesiriusproj@gmail.com`

**Abstract.** What is complex systems' role in augmented cognition? Neurotechnology—especially electroencephalography (EEG), brain-computer interface (BCI), and neural networks—have seen extensive use in augmented cognition (AugCog). Functional near-infrared spectroscopy (fNIRS) was also used in [5], and functional magnetic resonance imaging (fMRI) in [6]. To what extent can such technologies address the total complexity of augmented cognition?

EEG data complexity [2] and "complex structures" [1] are topics that were taken up in AugCog research. While there has been some attention paid to complex systems in recent augmented cognition research [3, 7, 8], their relation to AugCog could be better-determined. Complex systems display emergent properties arising from interdependent parts and aggregate behavior, contain stochasticity, are multistate, and operate autonomously. Complex systems has arisen recently given research and industrial interests. It is hypothesized now that augmented cognition is a complex system, with its interactive parts being humans and computers. As humans interact with computers and vice versa, augmented cognition ideally arises. This augmented cognition consists of extended performance, presumably-distinct neurophysiological signatures, and possibly enhanced phenomenology. Such a phenomenology may reinforce the human-computer interaction, behaviorally. It is an open question whether augmented cognition, if it is a complex system, gives rise to emergent properties currently undocumented.

AugCog (on its own or as a complex system) can begin to be quantified using a formula provided in this chapter. A variable $X$ can be added to this equation as a multiplier, though it is not currently known to what extent AugCog extends performance, alters neurophysiology, or enhances phenomenology overall. In this chapter, the following question is taken up: Is augmented cognition a complex system that gives rise to emergent properties other than extended performance, unique neurophysiology, or enhanced phenomenology?

**Keywords:** augmented cognition · complex systems · digital audio workstation (DAW) · game design · computational complexity

## 1 Introduction

Augmented cognition (AugCog) extends thought. AugCog via software is an extension of cognitive reality (*CR*). Such *CR* is now extended through the metaverse.

The metaverse is a new phenomenon. It includes computational layers like virtual reality (VR), mixed reality (XR) [20], augmented reality (AR) (Fig. 2), cloud computing,

© The Author(s), under exclusive license to Springer Nature Switzerland AG 2025
D. D. Schmorrow and C. M. Fidopiastis (Eds.): HCII 2025, LNAI 15778, pp. 79–92, 2025.
https://doi.org/10.1007/978-3-031-93724-8_7

avatars and digital twins [8], cybersecurity schemas (Fig. 1), and distributed ledger technology. It also involves processes like machine learning [21]. A subset of the metaverse is the internet of things (IoT), which includes artificial intelligence (AI). Game engines and programming environments and languages power the gaming and game development world, and digital forms of currency or "swag" like non-fungible tokens (NFTs) (Fig. 3) are cultural staples of the metaverse.

**What Happened on July 19, 2024?**
On July 19, 2024, two additional IPC Template Instances were deployed. Due to a bug in the Content Validator, one of the two Template Instances passed validation despite containing problematic content data.

Based on the testing performed before the initial deployment of the Template Type (on March 05, 2024), trust in the checks performed in the Content Validator, and previous successful IPC Template Instance deployments, these instances were deployed into production.

When received by the sensor and loaded into the Content Interpreter, problematic content in Channel File 291 resulted in an out-of-bounds memory read triggering an exception. This unexpected exception could not be gracefully handled, resulting in a Windows operating system crash (BSOD).

**Fig. 1.** Technical details about a recent data breach [15].

The metaverse has been discussed live in augmented cognition. Such discourse focused on the cultural phenomenon of invocations of God(s) and gods[1] across various digital media, from streaming shows to video games. The metaverse is also a financial talking point on talk channels like Bloomberg, and the company Meta is poised to lead making the metaverse mainstream through its various social media apps and/or VR initiatives.

Each aspect of the metaverse has either been shown to be or likely is relevant to AugCog. The metaverse, nascent though it is, is already complex in terms of its implementation and number of modules. The metaverse could thus be classified as a complex system. Can the same be done for augmented cognition? To answer this question, definitions need to be consulted.

---

[1] Lower-case "god" here refers to figures like Balthazar in the game *Guild Wars 2* and Arceus in *Pokémon*. These are not serious religious deities, but in the fictional contexts they appear in, they are treated as such.

**Fig. 2.** Pokémon *GO* gift with e-postcard.

## 2   Complex AugCog

Augmented cognition needs no rigorous introduction in the present context. Suffice it to say that it is a multidisciplinary field of researchers and industrialists and a phenomenon. AugCog the field is a cognitive science of a certain kind: augmented cognition (the phenomenon) potentially arises from human-computer interaction (HCI). This phenomenon is of central interest for the field.

Some philosophical questions can be asked about augmented cognition. Is it multiply realizable? Do certain HCI applications give rise to it more or differently? There are at least three core components of augmented cognition, such that

$$AugCog = extended\ performance,\ unique\ neurophysiology,\ enhanced\ phenomenology \tag{1}$$

The phenomenon of augmented cognition may always include all three of (1)'s righthand elements. Depending on the AugCog study, one or more might appear salient to the researcher. It is possible to conduct a multimethodological study covering each aspect, measuring performance via monitoring (e.g., via a smartwatch), brain-imaging, and qualitative self-report or a user experience (UX) survey. Such a study may itself be complex.

Complex systems are made up of interacting parts that give rise to unique properties. Could the amount of ways HCI can extend performance alone qualify AugCog as a complex system? These ways include:

- mixing and sharing songs
- developing and sharing games
- simulating visual effects

**Fig. 3.** A football NFT.

- learning via e-courses
- dialoguing with others over philosophical, spiritual content
- tracking plagiarism in science

Another way for AugCog to be a complex system is via simulation. If the agent-based modeling application NetLogo—the most-used software in complex systems research—can simulate augmented cognition, AugCog would qualify as a complex system at the level of simulation. And overall, if HCI extends performance, correlates with one or more unique neurophysiological states, and enhances phenomenology collectively by $\geq$ 50%, it is AugCog.

## 2.1  Complexity of Cloud Computing

Each of the various modules of the metaverse can be analyzed as a complex system. Cloud computing includes global infrastructure, storage, databases, networking, security, and pricing. It includes "on-demand delivery of" information technology (IT) "resources and applications through the internet" [22]. Cloud computing thus includes at least six parts that interact: e.g., storage occurs on servers that are part of the cloud infrastructure.

## 2.2 Holistic AugCog Complexity

AugCog was formulated in (1). Neurotechnologies can address at least the performance and neurophysiological questions of AugCog complexity (the phenomenological one may be more contextual or better understood with a qualitative methodology). Performance can be addressed via eye-tracking during reading, and neurophysiology is measured via technologies like electroencephalography (EEG). The brain-computer interface (BCI) extends human performance especially where functions like limb movement have been impaired. Neural networks are now a popular topic given their implementation in applications like ChatGPT. Possibilities for measuring augmented cognition as a complex system using other neurotechnologies may exist.

# 3   Extending AugCog's Repertoire of Applications

There is considerable variety in what could be considered an AugCog application. Digital audio workstations (DAWs), though not discussed in AugCog, do extend human performance. DAWs allow one to record, mix, and share music via software and audio interfaces (Fig. 4). Technically, DAWs change rather than extend the ability to record and mix music, allowing users to do so at home rather than in a normal recording studio.

**Fig. 4.** Studio One would augment cognition when a user uploads their recorded "Mixdown" directly to SoundCloud. Thus, Studio One extends performance from mixing to sharing music.

Digital art is a different case from the above. While HCI does afford novel art creation, it does not necessarily equate to a one-to-one correspondence between non-digital and digital art. It might be impossible to faithfully recreate non-digital art digitally. At most, digital art can be made to resemble an original non-digital counterpart. The case of scanning a drawing or painting and editing it with digital tools is an exception, and it is one that can rightly be considered AugCog to the extent that the digital remaster is a genuine enhancement of the original work. Such a remastered art piece can enhance its beholder's phenomenology, though it can be asked if art appreciation's corresponding neurophysiological state differs between digital and non-digital art. Witnessing visual effects (VFX) in digital media is describable as awe for non-VFX artists, but its effect may differ for VFX connoisseurs and creators who may exhibit a more analytical response (e.g., pondering how an effect was or could be created).

Related to the case of digital versus non-digital art is game development. Metaphor can AugCog, leading one from one domain of knowledge to another. And if simulation is preparatory for real life, simulatory HCI can AugCog in life beyond computers. Progress in one domain (like game development) can inspire work done in AugCog itself. One can view a trajectory of research themes as analogous to themes handled across games one plays (Fig. 5).

**Fig. 5.** Screenshot of a *Guild Wars 2* character on top of a blue campfire

The confluence of cinematic and video game production is apparent in their mutual use of software like Unreal Engine.

## 4  Neurotechnological Complexity

When one observes the landscape of neurotechnology in AugCog, it can seem not very complex. Neural networks (NNs), especially convolutional and deep ones, have been used, as have EEG and BCI. Combinatory examples of these such as EEG-BCI could be considered compound, but perhaps not yet complex. AugCog studies involving EEG, BCI[2], and NNs would be neurotechnologically complex at least at the surface level. But

---

[2] It was opined that "augmenting cognitive abilities, brain-computer interfaces (BCIs) are redefining what it means to be human" [17].

even in studies using only one or two of these neurotechnologies, the detail involved—such as the amount of electrodes (in the case of EEG) or nodes (in NNs) used—can be complex. Neurotechnological complexity in AugCog thus comes in two varieties: the surface level and the micro-level.

Can neurotechnologies other than EEG, BCI, and neural networks be used to measure augmented cognition as a complex system? [4] lists several neurotechnologies that could play a role in augmenting cognition. Transcranial magnetic stimulation (TMS), for example, is mentioned as being able to improve cognition. Neurotechnology is classified as a physical strategy for enhancing cognition, where biochemical and behavioral strategies for such also exist. The potential cognition-augmenting abilities of magnetoencephalography (MEG), electrocorticography (ECoG), microelectrode implants, deep brain stimulation (DBS), transcranial electrical stimulation (tES), and functional ultrasound (FUS) first may be determined via experimental analysis.

## 5 Conclusion

AugCog can be a complex system in its uses of EEG, BCI, and non-AugCog yet cognition-augmenting applications. However, when it is, it is tractable. For example, it becomes clear to a multiplatform content creator after research or with experience which platform is best-suited for a given post.

Computer software is an extension of reality (R). The ability of machines to access and interpret Web 3.0 knowledge implies the further integration of artificial intelligence into future Web infrastructures. Computers help people organize important parts of their personal and professional lives.

A list of different applications of computers and how each augments cognition uniquely would be pertinent. It can include items like:

- (neurotechnology:) neural nets can augment knowledge of how we encode information and acquire knowledge (e.g., gradually through *Rein* learning)
- (social media:) Discord project management and game development servers for learning from PMP-certified individual and indie game developers, respectively
- (services:) Amazon Elastic Block Storage (EBS), which "provides scalable, high-performance...resources that can be used with Amazon Elastic Compute Cloud (Amazon EC2) instances" [16].

With digital audio workstations (DAWs) like Studio One, audio engineers can upload mixes of tracks directly to SoundCloud, a social media-for-music website and app. This qualifies Studio One as an AugCog application, since it extends human performance and behavior not only by affording useful mixing features, but also by the simple fact that it expedites e-sharing. Studio One can also be analyzed in terms of interface complexity, which requires prior education to use optimally.

A list of HCI activities and how each can AugCog would be useful. It can include items as.

- general as TV-watching, which human attention can be organized around—this lets us speak of AugPcpt, i.e., augmented perception (assuming $attention^3 = F[pcpt]$)

---

[3] AtMan refers to attention manipulations [19].

**Fig. 6.** Human-computer interaction at the beach, specifically of a person recording electroacoustic guitar via audio interface.

- specific as AWS Learning Day, a corporately-hosted Databricks-Amazon Web Services (AWS) event for hands-on learning about data engineering and Databricks SQL

AugCog complexity exists for the domains of music (Fig. 6) and even game design (Fig. 7), novel linguistics (Fig. 8), and book art (Fig. 10). Spiritually, can e-horoscopes really AugCog about the future? Whether or not they can, enjoyable apps like Sky Map Android can be used to augment a user's knowledge of celestial objects (Fig. 9) (often referred to in astrology). Religious sources like [26] affirm human existence by claiming that it is the best (if not only, as this source sees it) way to escape *samsara*, the cycle of life and death.

Artificial intelligence has recently been a booming topic, especially with the advent of GPT. Neural networks have been the most relevant AI technology for AugCog, but there are other, interesting niche ideas (and possibly future applications) of AI. One example is NLCA, or Natural Language Cognitive Architecture [13]. Two goalposts for NLCA inspired by artificial general intelligence theory according to this work were "spontaneous learning and creation" (p. 16), human functions of varying complexity. There are two chatbot types: rule-operating and A.I. Returning to neural networks but focusing on large language models (LLMs), reinforcement learning from human feedback (RLHF) is a foundational method to enhance them.

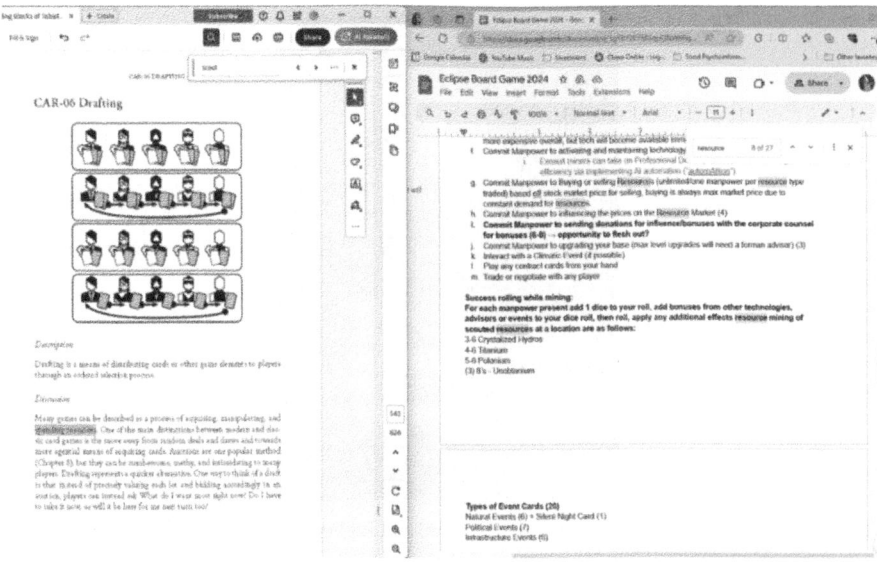

**Fig. 7.** A book on tabletop gaming (left) [9] and outline for a potential boardgame (right).

**Fig. 8.** Fantasy and recently-constructed languages from a printed book (top), trading card (right), and printer paper (middle).

In [23], a formal definition of learning style(s) based on Jan Vermunt's research was given. This definition is now formalized as

$$
\begin{aligned}
L_{style} = &\, f(Pc, reg.strat., M_{model}, orientation)\,\& \\
&\, f[undirected, reproduction, (application, meaning)directed]
\end{aligned}
\tag{2}
$$

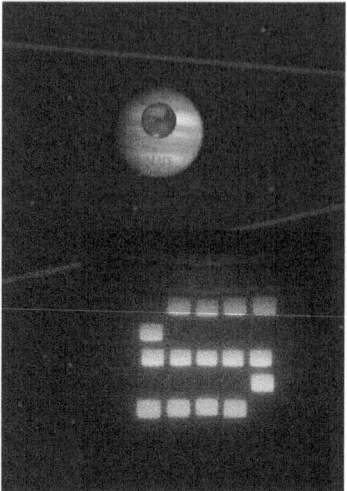

**Fig. 9.** Smartphone screenshot of Mercury (Budha) and Jupiter (Guru) in conjunction. Screenshot taken of Sky Map Android app UI.

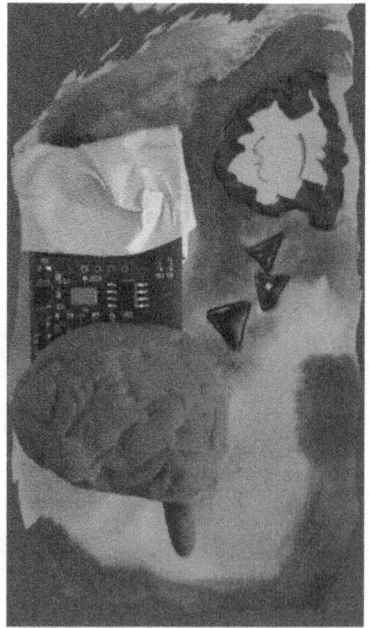

**Fig. 10.** Example of a book cover for a title about a cognition-augmenting brain chip.

where $L_{style}$ equals learning style, Pc equals process(ing), reg. Strat. is regulation strategies, $M_{model}$ is mental model, and orientation refers "to the whole domain of students' personal goals, intentions, motives, expectations, attitudes, concerns, and doubts with regard to their studies" ([24], p. 362). The second function lists Vermunt's learning styles. This can be added to [23]'s definition of artificial psychological intelligence ($A.\Psi I.$) so it would read

$$A.\Psi I. = M + A.O.P. + B + M.I. + I.Q. + E.Q. + L_{style} \qquad (3)$$

Legg & Hutter [25] offered a universal intelligence equation $r() := \sum_{\mu \in E} 2^{-K} V_\mu^\Pi$, including "the agent $\pi$, the environment $\mu$ and, implicit in the environment, [and] a goal. The agent's 'ability to achieve' is represented by the value function $V_\mu^\pi$ ... Occam's razor is given by the term $2^{-K(\mu)}$ which weights the agent's performance in each environment inversely proportional to its complexity." Intelligence is being able to fulfill goals in a broad variety of environments (E).

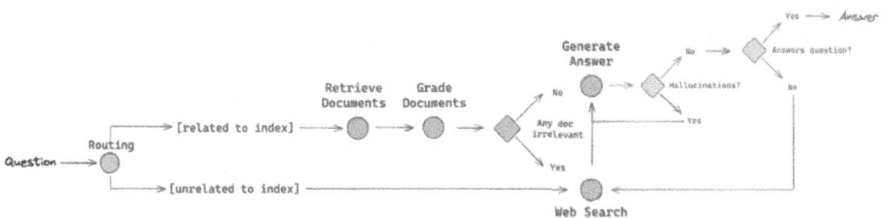

**Fig. 11.** Retrieval-augmented generation [14] including hallucinations, a newer term of art for when generative A.I. outputs false information.

Figure 11 shows an augmentation software architecture. The societal omnipresence of big data analytics (see Chapter 7 in [18]) is a research opportunity AugCog has exploited and can continue to. Figure 12 shows computational hardware complexity in a domestic setting.

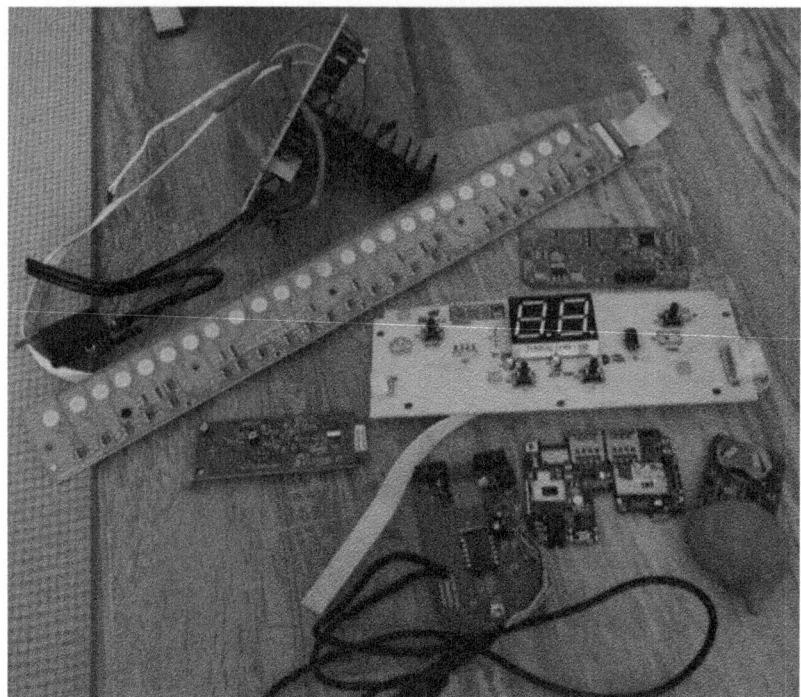

**Fig. 12.** A collection of CPU chips from a Vornado fan/heater, AKAI LPK25 MIDI keyboard, Logitech device, and other computational devices.

## References

1. Key, M.L., Mehtiyev, T., Xiaodong, Q.: Advancing EEG-based gaze prediction using depthwise separable convolution and enhanced pre-processing. In: Schmorrow, D.D., Fidopiastis, C.M. (eds.) Augmented Cognition: 18th International Conference, AC 2024, Held as Part of the 26th HCI International Conference, HCII 2024, Washington, DC, USA, June 29–July 4, 2024, Proceedings, Part II, pp. 3–17. Springer, Cham (2024). https://doi.org/10.1007/978-3-031-61572-6_1
2. Modesitt, E., Yin, H., Wang, W.H., Brian, L.: Fusing pretrained ViTs with TCNet for enhanced EEG regression. In: Schmorrow, D.D., Fidopiastis, C.M. (eds.) Augmented Cognition: 18th International Conference, AC 2024, Held as Part of the 26th HCI International Conference, HCII 2024, Washington, DC, USA, June 29–July 4, 2024, Proceedings, Part II, pp. 47–59. Springer, Cham (2024). https://doi.org/10.1007/978-3-031-61572-6_4
3. van Steen, T., Del-Real, C., van den Berg, B.: What works well? a safety-ii approach to cybersecurity. In: Schmorrow, D.D., Fidopiastis, C.M. (eds.) Augmented Cognition: 18th International Conference, AC 2024, Held as Part of the 26th HCI International Conference, HCII 2024, Washington, DC, USA, June 29–July 4, 2024, Proceedings, Part II, pp. 250–262. Springer, Cham (2024). https://doi.org/10.1007/978-3-031-61572-6_17
4. Jangwan, N.S., et al.: Brain augmentation and neuroscience technologies: current applications, challenges, ethics and future prospects. Front. Syst. Neurosci. **23**(16), 1000495 (2022). https://doi.org/10.3389/fnsys.2022.1000495.PMID:36211589;PMCID:PMC9538357

5. Dong, J., Jiang, A., Liu, Y.: Physiological and psychological effects of light illumination on hygiene regions of space stations in short-term simulations of gravity and noise. In: Schmorrow, D.D., Fidopiastis, C.M. (eds.) Augmented Cognition: 17th International Conference, AC 2023, Held as Part of the 25th HCI International Conference, HCII 2023, Copenhagen, Denmark, July 23–28, 2023, Proceedings, pp. 108–121. Springer, Cham (2023). https://doi.org/10.1007/978-3-031-35017-7_8

6. Borders, J.D., Dennis, B., Noesen, B., Harel, A.: Using fMRI to predict training effectiveness in visual scene analysis. In: Schmorrow, D.D., Fidopiastis, C.M. (eds.) Augmented Cognition. Human Cognition and Behavior: 14th International Conference, AC 2020, Held as Part of the 22nd HCI International Conference, HCII 2020, Copenhagen, Denmark, July 19–24, 2020, Proceedings, Part II, pp. 14–26. Springer, Cham (2020). https://doi.org/10.1007/978-3-030-50439-7_2

7. Alrefaei, D., et al.: Using eye tracking to measure user engagement with a decision aid. In: Schmorrow, D.D., Fidopiastis, C.M. (eds.) Augmented Cognition: 17th International Conference, AC 2023, Held as Part of the 25th HCI International Conference, HCII 2023, Copenhagen, Denmark, July 23–28, 2023, Proceedings, pp. 57–70. Springer, Cham (2023). https://doi.org/10.1007/978-3-031-35017-7_5

8. Miller, E., Hanlon, R., Lehrer, P., Mitchell, K., Hancock, Monte: Intelligent wellness. In: Schmorrow, D.D., Fidopiastis, C.M. (eds.) Augmented Cognition: 17th International Conference, AC 2023, Held as Part of the 25th HCI International Conference, HCII 2023, Copenhagen, Denmark, July 23–28, 2023, Proceedings, pp. 232–249. Springer, Cham (2023). https://doi.org/10.1007/978-3-031-35017-7_16

9. Engelstein, G., Shalev, I.: Building Blocks of Tabletop Game Design: An Encyclopedia of Mechanisms. CRC Press, Boca Raton (2022)

10. Khan, N., Tauseef, M., Ghosh, R., Sarkar, N.: A novel loss function utilizing wasserstein distance to reduce subject-dependent noise for generalizable models in affective computing. In: Schmorrow, D.D., Fidopiastis, C.M. (eds.) Augmented Cognition: 18th International Conference, AC 2024, Held as Part of the 26th HCI International Conference, HCII 2024, Washington, DC, USA, June 29–July 4, 2024, Proceedings, Part II, pp. 18–30. Springer, Cham (2024). https://doi.org/10.1007/978-3-031-61572-6_2

11. Qiu, C., Liang, B., Key, M.L.: Effect of kernel size on CNN-vision-transformer-based gaze prediction using electroencephalography data. In: Schmorrow, D.D., Fidopiastis, C.M. (eds.) Augmented Cognition: 18th International Conference, AC 2024, Held as Part of the 26th HCI International Conference, HCII 2024, Washington, DC, USA, June 29–July 4, 2024, Proceedings, Part II, pp. 60–71. Springer, Cham (2024). https://doi.org/10.1007/978-3-031-61572-6_5

12. Kumagai, N., Nakagawa, Y., Feng, C., Sugaya, M.: Reflection of individual differences on emotion map for kansei evaluation of packaging design with physiological indexes. In: Schmorrow, D.D., Fidopiastis, C.M. (eds.) Augmented Cognition: 18th International Conference, AC 2024, Held as Part of the 26th HCI International Conference, HCII 2024, Washington, DC, USA, June 29–July 4, 2024, Proceedings, Part II, pp. 152–165. Springer, Cham (2024). https://doi.org/10.1007/978-3-031-61572-6_11

13. Shapiro, D.K.: Natural Language Cognitive Architecture: A Prototype Artificial General Intelligence. Barnes & Noble Press, New York (2023)

14. https://github.com/langchain-ai/langchain-nvidia/blob/58f415642e985d1326c4e5ede26a3d5773323ece/cookbook/langgraph_rag_agent_llama3_nvidia_nim.ipynb. Accessed 29 Nov 2024

15. Remediation and Guidance Hub: Channel File 291 Incident. https://www.crowdstrike.com/falcon-content-update-remediation-and-guidance-hub/. Accessed 29 Nov 2024

16. "What is Amazon Elastic Block Store?". https://docs.aws.amazon.com/ebs/latest/userguide/what-is-ebs.html. Accessed 29 Nov 2024

17. Soundararajan, A.: Invasive BCI trailblazers: neuralink, blackrock, synchron, and the pioneers using their tech (2024). https://www.wisear.io/posts/invasive-bci-trailblazers-neuralink-blackrock-synchron-and-the-pioneers-using-their-tech. Accessed 29 Nov 2024
18. Morton, J., Runciman, B., Keith, G.: Big data: opportunities and challenges. BCS Learning and Development, Swindon (2014)
19. Deiseroth, B., Deb, M., Weinbach, S., Brack, M., Schramowski, P., Kersting, K.: AtMan: understanding transformer predictions through memory efficient attention manipulation (2023). https://doi.org/10.48550/arXiv.2301.08110. Accessed 29 Nov 2024
20. Hovhannisyan, G., Henson, A., Sood, S.: Enacting virtual reality: the philosophy and cognitive science of optimal virtual experience. In: Schmorrow, D.D., Fidopiastis, C.M. (eds.) Augmented Cognition: 13th International Conference, AC 2019, Held as Part of the 21st HCI International Conference, HCII 2019, Orlando, FL, USA, July 26–31, 2019, Proceedings, pp. 225–255. Springer, Cham (2019). https://doi.org/10.1007/978-3-030-22419-6_17
21. Lee, C., Sood, S., Hancock, M., Higgins, T., Sproul, K., Hadgis, A., Joe-Yen, S.: Biomimicry and machine learning in the context of healthcare digitization. In: Schmorrow, D.D., Fidopiastis, C.M. (eds.) Augmented Cognition: 13th International Conference, AC 2019, Held as Part of the 21st HCI International Conference, HCII 2019, Orlando, FL, USA, July 26–31, 2019, Proceedings, pp. 273–283. Springer, Cham (2019). https://doi.org/10.1007/978-3-030-22419-6_19
22. https://aws.amazon.com/what-is-cloud-computing/#:~:text=Cloud%20computing%20is%20the%20on,as%2Dyou%2Dgo%20pricing. Accessed 3 Dec 2024
23. Sood, S.: The AugCog of work. In: Schmorrow, D.D., Fidopiastis, C.M. (eds.) Augmented Cognition: 18th International Conference, AC 2024, Held as Part of the 26th HCI International Conference, HCII 2024, Washington, DC, USA, June 29–July 4, 2024, Proceedings, Part II, pp. 213–235. Springer, Cham (2024). https://doi.org/10.1007/978-3-031-61572-6_15
24. Vermunt, J.D., Vermetten, Y.J.: Patterns in student learning: relationships between learning strategies, conceptions of learning, and learning orientations. Educ. Psychol. Rev. **16**(4), 359–384 (2004). https://dspace.library.uu.nl/bitstream/handle/1874/11958/vermunt_05_Patterns_in_Student.pdf?sequence=2
25. Legg, S., Hutter, M.: Universal intelligence: a definition of machine intelligence (2007). arXiv: 0712.3329
26. https://newbuddhist.com/discussion/20807/the-wheel-of-life-bhavachakra-thangka-a-meditation. Accessed 17 June 2024

# Augmented Cognition and User Experience

# How Does a Password Meter Affect Password Security? An Empirical Study of a Traditional Password Meter and a Metaphor-Based Design

Simon Heim$^{(\boxtimes)}$ (iD)

Albstadt-Sigmaringen University, Poststraße 6, 72458 Albstadt, Germany
heimsimo@hs-albsig.de

**Abstract.** Passwords are a common way to authenticate in the online world. These passwords secure sensitive information or privileged access. But studies have shown that users tend to use weak passwords. Weak passwords could be prohibited technically, but this is often not wanted. An alternative approach involves the deployment of password meters designed to encourage users to create stronger passwords. Studies have shown that password meters lead to more secure passwords. This article investigates if previous findings regarding traditional password meters can be confirmed with an unconventional study design. Furthermore it analyzes the influence of a metaphor-based password meter design on password security. Results show that both password meters led to stronger passwords than the control group. However, the effect was only statistically significant for the traditional password meter.

**Keywords:** Password security · Password meter · Password metaphor

## 1 Introduction and Background

### 1.1 Relevance of Passwords

While physical access can be sufficient as protection in the real world, digital environments often require additional access restrictions to ensure security. This additional access restriction can be classified into different factors. Factors can be knowledge-based, property-based, or inherence-based. Each factor has its own unique properties, which is why they are used according to the context. However, the knowledge-based factor 'password' is (still) highly relevant and widely used. The reason for this is that password authentication is easy to implement and does not require additional hardware devices or special capabilities [17]. A significant problem with passwords is caused by the user himself. Passwords are often not secure enough, putting user accounts at risk of unauthorized access [11].

### 1.2 Properties of Secure Passwords

There are two properties involved when it comes to secure passwords. The properties of the password itself and the management of the password. The password should be unpredictable as possible, often measured by the time to crack. Generally, a password becomes more secure as it gets longer, uses a broader character set, and avoids common patterns. Password entropy can be one indication of a good password [12].

Password management concerns both the owner and the password-receiving party. Passwords should not be reused by the owner, neither over time nor across different accounts [5]. If the user cannot remember the password and needs to write it down, they must ensure that it is stored in a secure location. Examples for secure locations can be a password manager or a physical location where the access is protected appropriately [18]. The password-receiving party should add salt and pepper to the password and should store only the hash generated by secure hashing algorithms [10].

## 1.3   Research Question and Related Work

Users often choose weak passwords if they are not given guidance during the password creation process [11]. This is also true when setting up passwords for important accounts [12]. This article examines the impact of a traditional and a metaphor-based password meter on password security. A general positive impact of password meters on password strength have been reported consistently [8, 19, 20]. Within the password meter domain some factors seem to influence the password creation process more than others. In this way, a high positive influence were only observed if users were told to set the password for an important account [8]. Other studies highlighted that hybrid password meters outperform both traditional password meters with basic indicators and those that rely solely on displayed text [19, 20]. Hybrid password meters combine visual feedback with feedback nudges to encourage stronger password choices and provide additional password guidance. It also looks like the stringency of password meters have a significant impact and has to be somewhere between lenient and super strict for best results. According to Ur et al. [19] these meters strike the right balance between enforcing strong passwords and keeping user annoyance at a minimum.

The use of a metaphor-based design is inspired by Raja et al. [15], who found that depicting a personal firewall as a physical access control mechanism enhanced users' understanding. Raja et al. reported that users were statistically significantly better at assessing the risks and threats associated with their actions compared to when they were presented with traditional firewall permission popups. Behfar et al. [2] built on this research to investigate whether a similar effect could be observed in the context of password meters. They developed four distinct password metaphors, each implemented using a storytelling approach. Each metaphor comprised a sequence of five images that changed as the password strength increased. Behfar et al. did not evaluate the strength of the passwords, as they stated that this aspect was beyond the scope of their paper. To the best of my knowledge an evaluation of the password strength did not happen since today. However, Behfar et al. focused on the participants' experience captured by a set of questions. These questions were presented to the participants after the password creation process. Behfar et al. found out that there was no significant difference between the different metaphors but in comparison to a traditional password meter. The metaphor-based password meters received a statistically significantly higher score in terms of novelty and user attention. The scores for aesthetics, user engagement and user attachment were also higher, although not statistically significant [2].

Furthermore, using a metaphor-based password meter is interesting from a gamification perspective. Gamification can be described as the application of game design elements in non-game contexts to enhance motivation and user engagement [6]. Metaphor-based designs that use a sequence of images to playfully convey to users that a strong password better protects their account could encourage intrinsic motivation to create a strong password. Ophoff and Dietz [14] developed a version of a password meter which outputs a password score and the score adjustment by the last entered character. They noted a minor improvement in password strength, but it was reported as not statistically significant in comparison to a traditional password meter. Rodwald [16] reported that passwords created in the gamified context were 20% longer and had 17% higher entropy than those from the control group, where no information or suggestions were provided. There are two hypotheses to elaborate upon:

H1: Password security is improved when a traditional or metaphor-based meter is present, compared to when no meter is used.

H2: Password security is enhanced with a metaphor-based meter compared to a traditional meter.

Both the traditional and metaphor-based password meter implementations must demonstrate a statistically significant improvement in password strength compared to the control variant for H1 to be accepted. H2 can be accepted, if the metaphor-based design shows statistically significant improvement regarding password strength compared to the traditional password meter.

## 2 Study Design

One landing page were created on which all necessary information for participants were presented (see Fig. 2). This included a section with a short study description, information about data collection and the scenario. The mention of the scenario addressed the issue raised by previous studies, which have shown that password meters only effect passwords for important accounts. Upon agreement one of three different webpages were presented, all sharing a common form structure (see Fig. 3). The form consisted of prompts for age, gender, password and repeat-password as well as a button for registration. The fields age (14–99) and gender (M/F/X) had a select prompt. The only requirement for the password was that it had to contain at least one character. Webpage number one was exactly like that and served as control webpage. Webpage number two included a traditional password meter. The traditional password meter was based on Dropbox's low-budget password strength estimator 'zxcvbn' [21]. This tool was also recommended in academic research evaluating various password meters [3]. Since the study was conducted in Germany, a version of zxcvbn was used that also recognizes German words [7]. zxcvbn calculates a password security score ranging from 0 (too guessable) to 4 (very unguessable) in integer values. This score was used to control a progress bar that served as a password meter. As previously mentioned, prior research has demonstrated that password meters combining a visual indicator with textual feedback are more effective than either approach alone. Consequently, a text was provided for each score [19]. Webpage number three used a metaphor-based design. The design was reused from Behfar et al. [2] and illustrates the password strength by a bridge. The more secure a password became, the more wooden logs were removed from the bridge, making it increasingly harder for the burglar to reach the treasure.

The Eq. (1) was used to calculate the required sample size [13].

$$n = \frac{Z^2 \cdot p \cdot (1 - p)}{E^2} \tag{1}$$

where

- $n$: The required sample size
- $Z$: The Z-value corresponding to the desired confidence level
- $p$: The estimated proportion of the population
- $E$: The margin of error

A good compromise between effort and representativeness seemed to be a confidence level of 95% and a margin of error of 7%, leaving $p = 0.5$ to represent the maximum variability or uncertainty because $p \cdot (1 - p)$ reaches its highest value at $p = 0.5$. The calculated sample size was 196 for each webpage. So an overall target of 600 participants was set to have a buffer for data cleaning.

The method used to select participants for this study differs from those commonly used in related research. Instead of relying on controlled environments, such as a specific room or an online setting, this study was conducted by randomly approaching passers-by at a fixed location in a pedestrian zone. This study design ensured a wide audience. Other studies target, often as an indirect effect of their methodology, a specific group of people.

For passwords to be comparable across the webpages, the measurement conditions should have remained the same throughout. A between-subjects design where the webpages were alternated sequentially was chosen as an appropriate method. This approach addressed several potential inconsistencies. The alternation of the webpages helped to minimize noise, defined as external factors influencing human behavior, such as weather, time of day, season, atmosphere, or broader political and economic conditions. A within-subjects design, by contrast, would have required counterbalancing to mitigate potential order effects. Additionally, the duration for each participant would have tripled, although the total number of participants needed would have been reduced by two-thirds. However, given that participants were passers-by who attended spontaneously, it was a valid concern whether they would be willing to dedicate such an amount of time. Variability among individuals was addressed through random selection and an adequately large sample size.

Several things were introduced to achieve high data quality. The website were protected by basic authentication. A strong password were used to assure that only the researcher had access to the website. This eliminated the danger of unwanted study participants or actual participants attending twice. There were two possibilities how an actual participant could attend twice. Directly after their participation by returning to the forms and sending the register request again or by remembering the internet address and filling the forms on their own device. The first scenario was excluded because the researchers phones vibration when a record was written into the database. The vibration made the researcher aware that the registration was successful and the tablet should be handed over soon. The second scenario was avoided because of the website's access-protection.

For later evaluation of the study the security of a password had to be measured. The password length was measured, although it was clear that this metric alone was not reliable enough to measure password security. The password entropy as popular indicator for password security was calculated using Eq. (2) [1].

$$H = L \cdot \log_2(N) \tag{2}$$

where

- $H$: Password entropy, in bits
- $L$: Password length
- $N$: Character set size (number of unique symbols available)

and character sets

- Lowercase letters $(a - z)$: $N = 26$
- Uppercase letters $(A - Z)$: $N = 26$
- Digits $(0 - 9)$: $N = 10$
- Special ASCII characters $(0x20\text{-}0x2F, 0x3A\text{-}0x40, 0x5B\text{-}0x60, 0x7B\text{-}0x7E)$: $N = 33$
- Extended ASCII characters $(0x80\text{-}0xFF)$: $N = 128$

Depending on the password composition, the character set size was calculated by summing the sizes of the used sets. As a third measure, the score calculated by zxcvbn was also saved.

## 3   Study Execution

The study was conducted in 72070 Tübingen, Germany. The participants were approached at these geographical coordinates: Latitude 48.52029, Longitude 9.05486. The time periods and corresponding dates during which participants were approached are shown in Table 7. The execution of the study took an accumulated time of 37 h and 38 min. As a digital device, a tablet with a 9.7-inch diagonal screen was used.

Passers-by were approached by informing them that an academic study is currently conducted and any further information can be seen on the tablet. Participants were given time to read the content on the landing page. If they were not already they were encouraged to hold the tablet. After clicking the attending-button, filling in the forms and clicking the registration button a record was written in the database. A record in the database consisted of the webpage used, age, gender, password length, password entropy, password score (from zxcvbn) and a timestamp. After that a success page was shown to the participant, asking them to return the tablet. An automated redirection to the landing page took place after five seconds. The webpage alternation after each participant was pro-grammatically implemented to ensure it occurred consistently. Questions where participants would have obtained additional information that could have influ-enced the study results, such as 'Why is there a picture above the password field?', were met with a shrug.

After study execution, the database contained 611 records, referred to as 'dataset' from this point forward.

## 4    Study Analysis

### 4.1    Data Cleaning

First, diverse participants are removed from the dataset due to their underrepre-sentation (3 records), making them unsuitable for gender-related analysis, even though it is not covered in this article.

Second, the dataset is scanned for anomalous records. It can be discovered that a single participation resulted in two database records when the registration button was clicked again before the website could process the initial request. The duplicate records are identified by filtering for records with a timestamp differ-ence of ten seconds or less from the previous record, because a valid consecutive participation within this short timeframe is not realistic. These duplicates are removed, resulting in a refined dataset of 585 records, which can be understood as real participants. The distribution of these records is as follows: 193 records for the control group, 193 for the traditional meter, and 199 for the metaphor-based meter. The number of records for the control group and the traditional password meter is lower than originally anticipated, resulting in an increased margin of error of 7.05% while maintaining a confidence level of 95%. The differ-ing number of records for each webpage is due to instances where the researcher, after the participant completed their session, adjusted the webpage selector to display the metaphor for explanation purposes. However, the researcher did not always restore the selector afterward.

### 4.2    Hypotheses Focused Analysis

Figure 1 shows the age distribution by gender in 5-year intervals. It shows that more than one in five participants falls within the 20–25 age range. Gender appears to be nearly evenly distributed overall, except in the 15–25 age group, where over two-thirds are female. This disparity could be attributed to the prox-imity of the university for Educational Sciences to the study location, a field

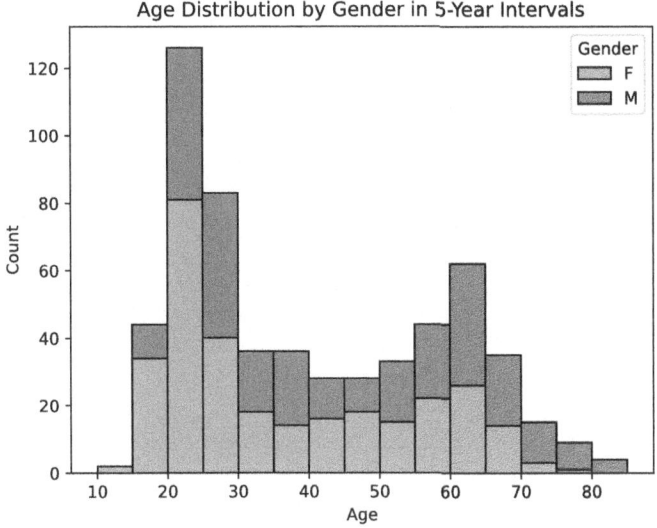

**Fig. 1.** Age distribution by gender

predominantly attended by (female) students [9]. The proportion of females decreases with age beyond 60, reaching zero above age 80.

Table 1 displays the gender frequencies for each webpage. The gender frequencies are almost equally distributed across the webpages, although a slight deviation can be noted for the webpage with the traditional meter, which has

**Table 1.** Gender frequencies for each webpage (1 = control, 2 = traditional meter, 3 = metaphor-based meter)

| webpage | gender | Frequency | Percent | Valid Percent | Cumulative Percent |
|---|---|---|---|---|---|
| 1 | M | 88 | 45.596 | 45.596 | 45.596 |
| | F | 105 | 54.404 | 54.404 | 100.000 |
| | Missing | 0 | 0.000 | | |
| | Total | 193 | 100.000 | | |
| 2 | M | 102 | 52.850 | 52.850 | 52.850 |
| | F | 91 | 47.150 | 47.150 | 100.000 |
| | Missing | 0 | 0.000 | | |
| | Total | 193 | 100.000 | | |
| 3 | M | 91 | 45.729 | 45.729 | 45.729 |
| | F | 108 | 54.271 | 54.271 | 100.000 |
| | Missing | 0 | 0.000 | | |
| | Total | 199 | 100.000 | | |

more males than females. Table 2 summarizes the key statistics for each webpage. The table shows that the participants' ages are almost equally balanced across the groups. Additionally, the statistical values consistently indicate that the traditional and the metaphor-based meters lead to stronger passwords compared to the control group.

**Table 2.** Descriptive statistics for each webpage (1 = control, 2 = traditional meter, 3 = metaphor-based meter)

| | age | | | pw_length | | | pw_entropy | | | pw_score | | |
|---|---|---|---|---|---|---|---|---|---|---|---|---|
| | 1 | 2 | 3 | 1 | 2 | 3 | 1 | 2 | 3 | 1 | 2 | 3 |
| Valid | 193 | 193 | 199 | 193 | 193 | 199 | 193 | 193 | 199 | 193 | 193 | 199 |
| Missing | 0 | 0 | 0 | 0 | 0 | 0 | 0 | 0 | 0 | 0 | 0 | 0 |
| Mean | 41.145 | 38.606 | 39.643 | 11.332 | 11.912 | 11.809 | 71.689 | 78.264 | 75.774 | 2.751 | 3.005 | 2.899 |
| Std. Deviation | 19.219 | 18.197 | 16.701 | 4.078 | 3.754 | 4.408 | 31.632 | 29.877 | 31.318 | 1.186 | 1.023 | 1.150 |
| Minimum | 14.000 | 15.000 | 14.000 | 2.000 | 5.000 | 4.000 | 9.000 | 24.000 | 13.000 | 0.000 | 0.000 | 0.000 |
| Maximum | 81.000 | 82.000 | 78.000 | 27.000 | 29.000 | 30.000 | 211.000 | 209.000 | 218.000 | 4.000 | 4.000 | 4.000 |
| 25th percentile | 23.000 | 23.000 | 24.500 | 9.000 | 9.000 | 9.000 | 49.000 | 59.000 | 55.000 | 2.000 | 2.000 | 2.000 |
| 50th percentile | 35.000 | 31.000 | 36.000 | 11.000 | 11.000 | 11.000 | 67.000 | 72.000 | 72.000 | 3.000 | 3.000 | 3.000 |
| 75th percentile | 60.000 | 56.000 | 55.000 | 14.000 | 14.000 | 14.000 | 86.000 | 94.000 | 92.000 | 4.000 | 4.000 | 4.000 |

Throughout the analysis, the collected password entropy is used as the primary metric for assessing password security, unless stated otherwise. While the password score reduces complexity to provide a comprehensible measure for password security, it sacrifices informational detail due to the effect of range restrictions. The password length is not a reliable measure for password security. Since password entropy already takes password length into account, there is also no need for a weighted composition. However, the H1-hypothesis cannot be answered directly, through one t-test. Therefore subhypotheses are defined:

H1.1$_0$: Password security is not higher when a traditional meter is present.
H1.1$_1$: Password security is higher when a traditional meter is present.
H1.2$_0$: Password security is not higher when a metaphor-based meter is present.
H1.2$_1$: Password security is higher when a metaphor-based meter is present.

**Table 3.** Independent samples t-test for control and traditional meter

| | t | df | p | Cohen's d | SE Cohen's d |
|---|---|---|---|---|---|
| pw_entropy | −2.099 | 384 | 0.018 | −0.214 | 0.102 |

*Note.* For all tests, the alternative hypothesis specifies that group 1 is less than group 2.
*Note.* Student's t-test

The subhypotheses can be answered through two-sample t-test for independent samples, starting with $H1.1_0$ and $H1.1_1$. The assumptions of the t-test must be verified to ensure they are met. The sample size is equal, with 193 participants in the control group and 193 participants in the traditional meter group. Besides that, the sample sizes are considered sufficiently large for the assumption of normal distribution to hold (see Fig. 4a and 4b). The variances of both samples are similar ($p = 0.687$) according to the Levene's test (see Table 8a). The t-test calculates a p-value of 0.018 (see Table 3). Therefore, the null hypothesis $H1.1_0$ can be rejected in favor of the alternative hypothesis $H1.1_1$ for a typical significance level of 0.05. The Cohen's d effect size is -0.214 with a standard error of 0.102. These values are relevant when making a comparison with one another. Categorizing Cohen's d into the effect size classifications defined by Cohen [4] would be less helpful. Cohen himself emphasized that these categories are merely rough guidelines and should not be understood as fixed thresholds. He argued that the interpretation of effect size must always consider the specific context of the research field and the question under investigation.

If the password score were to be used as the password strength metric, the distribution would not follow a normal distribution, as the password score operates on a scale from 0 to 4, reaching the highest score regularly. Consequently, a non-parametric test, such as the Kruskal-Wallis test, would be used. This test produces a p-value of 0.044, which is below the significance level of 0.05, leading also to the rejection of the null hypothesis $H1.1_0$ (see Table 4). This aligns with recent findings that the traditional password meter produces statistically significantly stronger passwords compared to when no meter is present.

**Table 4.** Kruskal-Wallis test for control and traditional meter

| Factor | Statistic | df | p | Rank $\epsilon^2$ | 95% CI for Rank $\epsilon^2$ | | Rank $\eta^2$ | 95% CI for Rank $\eta^2$ | |
|---|---|---|---|---|---|---|---|---|---|
| | | | | | Lower | Upper | | Lower | Upper |
| pw_score | 9.785 | 4 | 0.044 | 0.025 | 0.007 | 0.074 | 0.015 | 0.000 | 0.067 |

Next, the control and the metaphor-based samples are analyzed. The control group consists of 193 participants, while the metaphor-based group includes 199, resulting in an almost equal sample size. The sample size of the metaphor-based meter is considered large enough to assume normal distribution (see Fig. 4c). The variances of both samples are similar ($p = 0.644$) according to the Levene's test (see Table 8b). The t-test calculates a p-value of 0.1, so that the null hypothesis $H1.2_0$ cannot be rejected for a significance level of 0.05 (see Table 5). The Cohen's d effect size is -0.130 with a standard error of 0.101.

**Table 5.** Independent samples t-test for control and metaphor-based meter

|            | t      | df  | p     | Cohen's d | SE Cohen's d |
|------------|--------|-----|-------|-----------|--------------|
| pw_entropy | −1.285 | 390 | 0.100 | −0.130    | 0.101        |

*Note.* For all tests, the alternative hypothesis specifies
that group 1 is less than group 3.
*Note.* Student's t-test

Since hypothesis H1 cannot be fully confirmed, as the metaphor-based meter does not lead to statistically significantly stronger passwords than the control, hypothesis H2 cannot be confirmed either. However, for completeness, an undirected t-test is conducted to evaluate whether the traditional meter produces statistically significantly different passwords compared to the metaphor-based meter. The assumption of a normal distribution is satisfied, as demonstrated previously. The variances of both samples are similar (p = 0.935) according to the Levene's test (see Table 8c). The t-test calculates a p-value of 0.421, so that the null hypothesis cannot be rejected for a significance level of 0.05, meaning that there is no statistically significant difference in password strength between the traditional and the metaphor-based meter (see Table 6).

**Table 6.** Independent samples t-test for traditional and metaphor-based meter

|            | t     | df  | p     | Cohen's d | SE Cohen's d |
|------------|-------|-----|-------|-----------|--------------|
| pw_entropy | 0.805 | 390 | 0.421 | 0.081     | 0.101        |

*Note.* Student's t-test.

## 5   Conclusion

### 5.1   Summary

The descriptive analysis showed that both, the traditional and metaphor-based password meter resulted in more secure passwords compared to the control group. Additionally, it revealed that the traditional password meter had a stronger effect than the metaphor-based password meter. From this perspective, H1 appeared to be true, while H2 could not be confirmed. However, the positive effect on password security was only statistically significant for the traditional password meter. This aligns with the results of previous studies confirming the efficiency of the traditional password strength meter. The fact that previous findings could be confirmed serves as an indication that the (unconventional) study design was appropriate. From the perspective of this article, neither H1 nor H2 can be confirmed, as statistical significance was set as the requirement.

### 5.2   Limitations

The study has several limitations. Participant selection was determined by the researcher, and while great effort was made to include a diverse range of individuals, the possibility of residual personal bias cannot be entirely excluded.

Furthermore, quantitative comparisons between the results of this study and those of other studies should be made with caution due to potential differences in the study design. Participants registered on a foreign device which can influence their behavior compared to when they register on their own device. Besides that, participants knew that they were attending a study about password security and they were supervised.

Another limitation is the zxcvbn-algorithm used by the traditional and metaphor-based password meter. Although zxcvbn is a highly recognized and established algorithm for measuring password strength, there are exceptions. For instance, the password 'Schulranzen' achieves a score of four, whereas '37d!40(N/n' obtains only a score of three. While it took some time to identify such an example, it highlights a potential limitation of the meter, which could have influenced user behavior. Password entropy is a slightly better, though not perfect, metric for assessing password security in this case. The entropy of 'Schulranzen' (63) and '37d!40(N/n' (66) suggests that the latter is only marginally more secure. That said, it could be argued that password entropy, as a metric for assessing password security, does not sufficiently account the importance of using diverse character sets.

### 5.3   Research Opportunities

To address potential inaccuracies in measuring password strength, the development of password meters based on artificial intelligence may be promising. Currently, the zxcvbn-score as primary metric to assess password security is not appropriate. The scale with broad categories only provides a rough measure of password security. Here, a fine-grained password measurement algorithm with more categories would be preferred, enabling it to capture the full range of password diversity.

Although the metaphor-based password meter led not to statistically significant results it does not mean that the concept has to be fully discarded. Those participants who were exposed to the webpage with the metaphor were sometimes asked how they perceived it. Often they gave the response that they did not perceive or understood it. Further research can address this issue by improving the design of the metaphor. Based on the feedback, the design should place greater emphasis on the key elements: the burglar, the wooden bridge, and the treasure. Also, a brief explanatory text could make it more understandable.

Finally, traditional password meters are out there for years. So most people were already familiar with the functionality. This is not true for metaphor-based designs. Further research could try to measure the resulting effect to estimate the metaphor's long-term efficiency.

**Disclosure of Interests.** The author has no competing interests to declare that are relevant to the content of this article.

# A Appendix

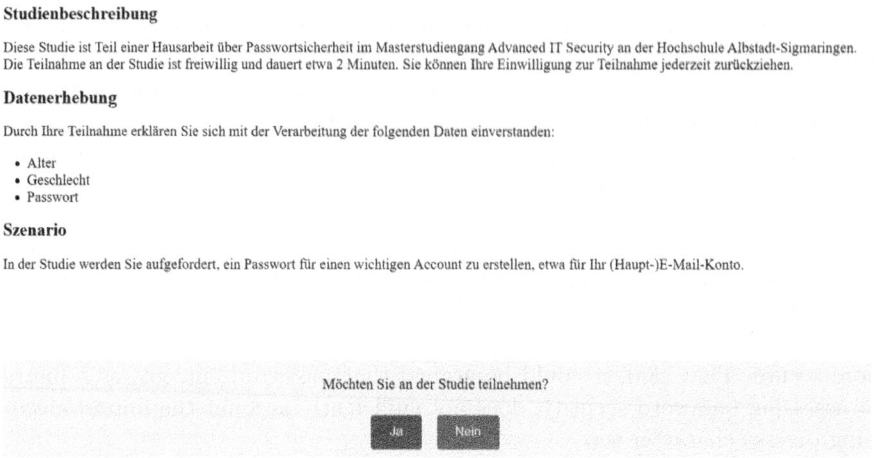

Studienbeschreibung
Diese Studie ist Teil einer Hausarbeit über Passwortsicherheit im Masterstudiengang Advanced IT Security an der Hochschule Albstadt-Sigmaringen. Die Teilnahme an der Studie ist freiwillig und dauert etwa 2 Minuten. Sie können Ihre Einwilligung zur Teilnahme jederzeit zurückziehen.
Datenerhebung
Durch Ihre Teilnahme erklären Sie sich mit der Verarbeitung der folgenden Daten einverstanden:
Alter
Geschlecht
Passwort
Szenario
In der Studie werden Sie aufgefordert, ein Passwort für einen wichtigen Account zu erstellen, etwa für Ihr (Haupt-)E-Mail-Konto.
Möchten Sie an der Studie teilnehmen?
Ja
Nein

**Fig. 2.** Landing page

Registrierung
Alter:
Geschlecht:
Passwort:
Passwort wiederholen:
Registrieren
Registrierung
Alter:
Geschlecht:
Passwort:
Sicher
Passwort wiederholen:
Registrieren
Registrierung
Alter:
Geschlecht:
Passwort:
Passwort wiederholen:
Registrieren

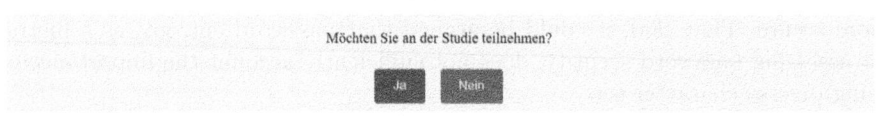

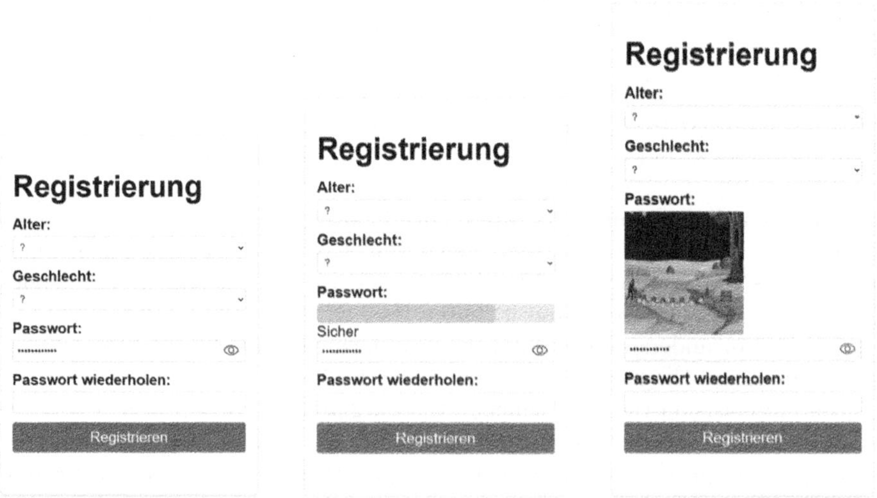

(a) Control (b) Traditional meter (c) Metaphor meter

**Fig. 3.** Webpages

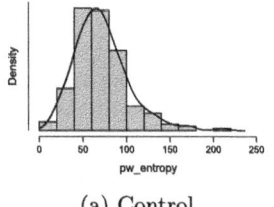
(a) Control

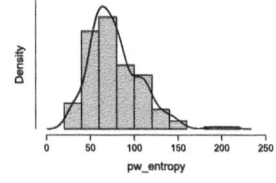
(b) Traditional meter

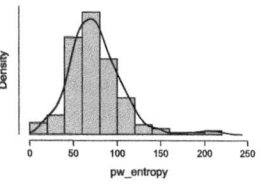
(c) Metaphor meter

**Fig. 4.** Distribution plots

**Table 7.** Sessions

| Session | Date | Duration |
|---------|------|----------|
| 1 | 09.10.2024 | 3:11 PM–6:25 PM |
| 2 | 14.10.2024 | 2:41 PM–5:14 PM |
| 3 | 16.10.2024 | 2:50 PM–5:57 PM |
| 4 | 21.10.2024 | 2:42 PM–5:24 PM |
| 5 | 24.10.2024 | 2:52 PM–5:50 PM |
| 6 | 26.10.2024 | 2:45 PM–5:46 PM |
| 7 | 28.10.2024 | 2:45 PM–5:18 PM |
| 8 | 09.11.2024 | 2:49 PM–6:13 PM |
| 9 | 12.11.2024 | 2:45 PM–4:57 PM |
| 10 | 15.11.2024 | 1:56 PM–4:44 PM |
| 11 | 25.11.2024 | 1:45 PM–5:13 PM |
| 12 | 26.11.2024 | 1:11 PM–6:49 PM |

**Table 8.** Test of equality of variances (Levene's)

| | F | $df_1$ | $df_2$ | p |
|---|---|---|---|---|
| pw_entropy | 0.163 | 1 | 384 | 0.687 |

(a) Control and traditional meter

| | F | $df_1$ | $df_2$ | p |
|---|---|---|---|---|
| pw_entropy | 0.213 | 1 | 390 | 0.644 |

(b) Control and metaphor-based meter

| | F | $df_1$ | $df_2$ | p |
|---|---|---|---|---|
| pw_entropy | 0.007 | 1 | 390 | 0.935 |

(c) Traditional meter and metaphor-based meter

# References

1. Anna Szczepanek, W.S., Bowater, J.: How to Calculate Sample Size Using a Sample Size Formula (2024). https://www.omnicalculator.com/other/password-entropy. Accessed 26 Jan 2025
2. Behfar, A., Atashpanjeh, H., Al-Ameen, M.N.: Can password meter be more effective towards user attention, engagement, and attachment?: a study of metaphor-based designs. In: Companion Publication of the 2023 Conference on Computer Supported Cooperative Work and Social Computing, CSCW 2023, Companion, pp. 164–171. Association for Computing Machinery, New York (2023). https://doi.org/10.1145/3584931.3606983
3. de Carné de Carnavalet, X., Mannan, M.: From very weak to very strong: analyzing password-strength meters (2014). https://doi.org/10.14722/ndss.2014.23268
4. Cohen, J.: A power primer. Psychol. Bull. **112**(1), 155–159 (1992). https://doi.org/10.1037/0033-2909.112.1.155
5. Das, A., Bonneau, J., Caesar, M.C., Borisov, N., Wang, X.: The tangled web of password reuse. In: Network and Distributed System Security Symposium (2014). https://api.semanticscholar.org/CorpusID:17528191
6. Deterding, S., Dixon, D., Khaled, R., Nacke, L.: From game design elements to gamefulness: defining gamification, vol. 11, pp. 9–15 (2011). https://doi.org/10.1145/2181037.2181040
7. Devatrox: zxcvbn-german (2024). https://github.com/devatrox/zxcvbn-german/tree/master. Accessed 26 Jan 2025
8. Egelman, S., Sotirakopoulos, A., Muslukhov, I., Beznosov, K., Herley, C.: Does my password go up to eleven? The impact of password meters on password selection. In: Proceedings of the SIGCHI Conference on Human Factors in Computing Systems, CHI 2013, pp. 2379–2388. Association for Computing Machinery, New York (2013). https://doi.org/10.1145/2470654.2481329
9. Federal Statistical Office of Germany: Students: Germany, Semester, Nationality, Sex, Subject (2024). https://www-genesis.destatis.de/datenbank/online/url/13cefb94. Accessed 26 Jan 2025
10. Hatzivasilis, G.: Password management: how secure is your login process? In: Hatzivasilis, G., Ioannidis, S. (eds.) MSTEC 2020. LNCS, vol. 12512, pp. 157–177. Springer, Cham (2020). https://doi.org/10.1007/978-3-030-62433-0_10
11. Malone, D., Maher, K.: Investigating the distribution of password choices. In: Proceedings of the 21st International Conference on World Wide Web, WWW 2012, pp. 301–310. Association for Computing Machinery, New York (2012). https://doi.org/10.1145/2187836.2187878
12. Mazurek, M.L., et al.: Measuring password guessability for an entire university. In: Proceedings of the 2013 ACM SIGSAC Conference on Computer & Communications Security, CCS 2013, pp. 173–186. Association for Computing Machinery, New York (2013). https://doi.org/10.1145/2508859.2516726
13. Nishat, A.: How to Calculate Sample Size Using a Sample Size Formula (2024). https://www.remesh.ai/resources/how-to-calculate-sample-size. Accessed 26 Jan 2025
14. Ophoff, J., Dietz, F.: Using gamification to improve information security behavior: a password strength experiment. In: Drevin, L., Theocharidou, M. (eds.) WISE 2019. IAICT, vol. 557, pp. 157–169. Springer, Cham (2019). https://doi.org/10.1007/978-3-030-23451-5_12

15. Raja, F., Hawkey, K., Hsu, S., Wang, K.L., Beznosov, K.: A brick wall, a locked door, and a bandit: a physical security metaphor for firewall warnings. In: SOUPS 2011 - Proceedings of the 7th Symposium on Usable Privacy and Security (2011). https://doi.org/10.1145/2078827.2078829
16. Rodwald, P.: Using gamification and fear appeal instead of password strength meters to increase password entropy. Marit. Tech. J. **217**(2), 17–33 (2019). https://doi.org/10.2478/sjpna-2019-0010
17. Siddique, K., Akhtar, Z., Kim, Y.: Biometrics vs passwords: a modern version of the tortoise and the hare. Comput. Fraud Secur. **2017**, 13–17 (2017). https://doi.org/10.1016/S1361-3723(17)30007-6
18. Stobert, E., Biddle, R.: Expert password management. In: Stajano, F., Mjølsnes, S.F., Jenkinson, G., Thorsheim, P. (eds.) Technology and Practice of Passwords, pp. 3–20. Springer, Cham (2016)
19. Ur, B., et al.: How does your password measure up? The effect of strength meters on password creation. In: Proceedings of the 21st USENIX Conference on Security Symposium, Security 2012, p. 5. USENIX Association, USA (2012)
20. Verena Zimmermann, K.M., Renaud, K.: Hybrid password meters for more secure passwords - a comprehensive study of password meters including nudges and password information. Behav. Inf. Technol. **42**(6), 700–743 (2023). https://doi.org/10.1080/0144929X.2022.2042384
21. Wheeler, D.L.: zxcvbn: low-Budget password strength estimation. In: 25th USENIX Security Symposium (USENIX Security 2016), pp. 157–173. USENIX Association, Austin, TX (2016). https://www.usenix.org/conference/usenixsecurity16/technical-sessions/presentation/wheeler

# Exploring the Impact of Digital Design on Augmented Cognition

Samantha Limon$^{(\boxtimes)}$, Branden Ogata, and Michael-Brian Ogawa

Department of Information and Computer Sciences, University of Hawaii at Manoa, 1680 East-West Road, Honolulu, HI 96822, USA
{splimon,bsogata,ogawam}@hawaii.edu

**Abstract.** As students increasingly engage with digital interfaces, understanding how technology influences learning is essential. This study investigated how variations in instructional website design affect learning outcomes and identified specific design elements that enhance engagement, knowledge retention, and cognitive processing in digital environments. Two instructional websites on Python programming fundamentals incorporated distinct human-computer interaction principles to assess their impact on learning behaviors. An eye-tracking system monitored the eye gaze of participants to track user interactions. Screen recordings provided further data regarding user flows and interaction patterns. A sample of 16 students enrolled in an introductory computer science course with minimal prior experience in Python were selected to ensure a consistent baseline for learning gains and explored the websites. Participants took a 10-question quiz that reviewed material covered in the websites. They subsequently provided feedback through post-study surveys that captured their perceptions of the websites' designs and their influence on the student learning experiences. Data analysis was conducted using ANOVA and t-tests to evaluate the influence of user interface variations on cognitive processing and retention metrics. Findings indicate that the scrollable website encouraged more review, with certain question types aligning better with specific designs. However, both websites were effective learning tools as they presented similar performance outcomes. These results emphasize the role of intentional digital design in fostering engagement, reducing visual overload, and supporting effective cognitive processing.

**Keywords:** Augmented Cognition · Cognitive Load · Human-Computer Interaction · User Experience · User Interface Design · Chunking

## 1 Introduction

In an era of rapid technological growth and advancements, digital media has become more prevalent than ever. The way people connect, communicate, and access information has shifted dramatically with a growing reliance on digital platforms [19]. This transition is especially evident in educational settings, where students of varying academic levels increasingly depend on digital learning platforms to access coursework, explore subjects, and retrieve information essential to their learning [14].

© The Author(s), under exclusive license to Springer Nature Switzerland AG 2025
D. D. Schmorrow and C. M. Fidopiastis (Eds.): HCII 2025, LNAI 15778, pp. 110–128, 2025.
https://doi.org/10.1007/978-3-031-93724-8_9

Processing digital information is influenced by numerous factors, including principles of human-computer interaction (HCI) and user experience/user interface (UX/UI) design. The effectiveness of these digital platforms often relies on their design and usability, which can significantly impact how learners process, retain, and apply information [14]. This research aims to explore how variations in instructional website design influence augmented cognition by leveraging principles from human-computer interaction (HCI) and user experience/user interface (UX/UI) design to enhance the digital learning experience.

## 1.1 Research Objectives

This study is guided by the following key research questions:

1. How does eye gaze influence interaction in learning environments?
2. Which UX/UI design features in digital learning materials contribute to reducing cognitive load in educational settings?

## 1.2 Research Objectives

The primary objectives of this research are to:

1. Identify specific UX/UI features that decrease cognitive load and enhance knowledge retention in digital learning environments.
2. Provide actionable insights for designing instructional websites that support and augment technology-based education.
3. Establish best practices for integrating digital design principles into educational tools to meet diverse learning needs.

## 1.3 Significance of Study

With the rapid development of technology, digital forms of learning continue to become more prominent in educational settings. The field of human-computer interaction is a vast discipline that covers many topics, such as cognitive science, sociology, and psychology [17]. The connection between humans and technology is critical to understanding how users interact with digital interfaces. It allows us to determine how we can use technology to enhance our cognitive abilities and improve digital design practices to best suit growing learning needs. However, few studies address how specific design features impact learning and cognition.

Optimizing digital design for education is incredibly important, especially given the growing reliance on online learning platforms. The COVID-19 pandemic accelerated the paradigm shift in curriculum development toward digital education, with an increase in educators adapting to virtual classrooms and e-learning materials in addition to traditional methods of learning [17, 19]. As technology advances, the demand for online learning tools is expected to grow. Some researchers found that more people, particularly younger generations, have become increasingly proficient with digital interfaces as they are continuously developing digital literacy skills through daily interactions with technology [5]. However, others argue that many students have also found adapting to e-learning materials difficult for several reasons, such as socioeconomic factors or the limitations of students' technical aptitude [19]. This presents a unique opportunity and responsibility for software engineers, web developers, and designers to create digital environments that enhance students' learning potential with these factors in consideration.

By identifying and implementing design features that augment human cognition, this research seeks to inform the creation of instructional websites that maximize learning outcomes. Such efforts will not only improve the quality of digital learning tools but also support the educational goals of diverse student populations by creating instructional interfaces that maximize human cognition and reduce cognitive load. Ultimately, this study aims to highlight the importance of utilizing digital design features to improve student learning in order to gain meaningful insights into how the human mind processes and takes in visual information. In doing so, this research will contribute to bridging the gap between technology and education by advancing the design principles that underlie effective digital learning experiences. By investigating how variations of design impact problem-solving and cognitive thinking in students, particularly regarding learning, this research addresses a critical gap in our current understanding of technology-enhanced educational environments. Furthermore, it is essential to make use of digital design in a way that maximizes how students are taught to utilize technology to its fullest potential.

## 2   Literature Review

### 2.1   Human-Computer Interaction and UX/UI

Recent technological advances highlight the importance of improving user interface designs of applications and websites to meet particular demands or purposes. To satisfy these tasks, human-computer interaction (HCI) principles are referenced as frameworks for building and developing many websites, applications, and interactive interfaces that people use on a daily basis. HCI is a field of study that focuses on interactions between a user (human) and a computer [1]. The interface between humans and computers is essential for supporting how humans and computers interact and communicate with one another. While the computer is used as a medium to accomplish a goal, a human in front of the screen controls where to look and when to click. Even the most complex machines cannot meet their full potential unless humans are able to utilize them correctly. This information is extremely important in multiple sectors of business to track how potential clients are navigating websites and how this directly affects transactions [8]. As Gerlach [8] emphasized when describing the importance of implementing HCI principles, "end-user productivity is tied directly to functionality and ease of learning and use." Therefore, when developing websites and applications, software developers must expand their focus beyond primitive functionality and take into consideration the behavioral needs, demands, and requirements of users.

When designing interfaces, both usability and functionality are key characteristics to consider [8]. What an application can do and how its functions can contribute to accomplishing an overarching objective can influence the range of actions or services that the system offers and help explain why it was developed in the first place. The selection of a good system model provides direction for designing how a system should look and operate [8]. Designing user-friendly interfaces that align with these characteristics enables a system to be well-balanced and perform as intended.

The user interface (UI) of a software application refers to the means by which a system and its user interact through commands or techniques to operate the system [15]. It encompasses a wide range of systems, including computers, mobile devices, video games, and more. Complementary to UI, user experience (UX) encompasses the user's overall perception, reactions, and behavior while interacting with a system [15, 20]. In many cases, the UX and UI of software go hand in hand. An effective and intuitive UI enhances the UX by enabling users to navigate a system with ease, intuition, and confidence. For businesses, the quality of UX/UI design is critical to product placement and marketing success. A well-designed UX lays the foundation for an excellent UI, ensuring a seamless product experience that can directly impact sales and user satisfaction [2, 17]. Together, UX and UI are key determinants of the success of digital products and websites.

In the context of online education, UX/UI design plays an integral role in shaping how students interact with Learning Management Systems (LMS) [10]. LMS platforms are essential tools in online learning, where thoughtful UX/UI design can significantly influence engagement and learning outcome achievement [10]. Online education is rooted in the proper planning, design, and development of instructional platforms and content. Poor UX, often stemming from accessibility issues or the inconsistent use of multiple UIs, can create confusion and hinder the learning process [10], producing an overall counterproductive learning experience. Moreover, the COVID-19 pandemic accelerated the digital transformation of higher education institutions, prompting these institutions to adopt and optimize digital technologies for instructional purposes [16]. However, this shift also highlighted the importance of deliberate design and development choices for instructional materials. The transition to online learning revealed varying levels of digital competence among students and faculty, as well as the need for accessible and user-friendly platforms to facilitate learning in a digital environment.

## 2.2 Cognitive Load, Augmented Cognition, and Chunking

Cognitive load theory [9] is described as a mental capacity model that assumes that cognitive demands arising from the design of learning materials (known as extraneous load) can significantly hinder the learning process, particularly when using digital media. Interactive digital tools provide learners with access to digital tools that adapt and respond to their inputs. However, working memory has limited capacity, and learners can only take in and process a set amount of information at a given time. To address this, cognitive load theory proposes strategies to optimize the mental processing of relevant information while reducing the impact of irrelevant or poorly presented content that increases cognitive load [28].

This theory categorizes cognitive load into two main types: intrinsic and extraneous. Intrinsic load refers to the inherent difficulty of a learning task. This is determined by the complexity of the material and the relationships between its components [28]. In contrast, extraneous load is influenced by the way learning materials are designed and presented. The core principle of cognitive load theory is that instructional design should account for the limitations of learners' cognitive capacities. Taking this theory into account when designing and developing educational learning tools and materials would emphasize the importance of minimizing extraneous cognitive load to enhance learning effectiveness.

This concept is intricately connected to augmented cognition (AugCog). Schmorrow [11] identifies an AugCog system as a "closed loop," in which the system actively monitors the recipients' state or behavior (e.g., attention, workload, stress) and adjusts its responses or interface in real-time to optimize performance and engagement. This dynamic feedback loop, in turn, helps the system adapt to the changing needs of the user to make interactions more efficient and enhance cognitive functions. One of the main goals of AugCog is to address the limitations of human operations related to limitations in information processing and reduce the complexity of extraneous tasks that a user performs [3, 23] by focusing on real-time monitoring of users' cognitive states through behavioral and physiological measures to leverage adaptive and augmented human-computer interfaces [26]. The adaptive nature of AugCog systems offers avenues for reducing extraneous cognitive load and enhancing engagement by personalizing user interactions based on real-time cognitive states.

Understanding how information is segmented and processed by the human brain is crucial when examining cognitive capacities during learning. As highlighted by cognitive load theory, humans can only process a limited amount of information at a time before exceeding their cognitive capacity. Chunking serves as an essential cognitive strategy to manage this limitation. According to Rabinovich et al. [22], chunking is a dynamic cognitive strategy the brain employs to process lengthy sequences of information. Miller [14] introduced a key notion that chunking enables short-term memory to expand its functional capacity by grouping individual units of information into meaningful blocks and segmenting these blocks for more efficient processing. This hierarchical organization of information is a defining characteristic of chunking and mirrors specific patterns of neural network activity [22]. One notable example is the role of Broca's area, which is a brain region responsible for processing hierarchically structured sequences, including language syntax [21] and other complex cognitive functions [11]. By leveraging the innate neural capacities of students, instructional designs can be optimized to reduce cognitive overload and improve learning efficiency.

## 2.3 Implications of Digital Environments on Computer Science Education

The paradigm shift and digital transformation initiated by the COVID-19 pandemic have significantly impacted education, particularly in the field of computer science. Digitalization can enhance educational quality by improving students' digital skills and fostering active engagement [5]. Students in the 21st century who have grown up in the digital world expect the same level of technological integration in their learning environments as they experience in their everyday lives. A lack of digital proficiency could severely hinder the future success of students, making it imperative for educators to stay informed about digital tools and technologies, such as Learning Management Systems (LMS). To meet these evolving needs, educators must enhance their teaching craft by developing their professional digital competence [12, 13] and cultivating their digital identity [6, 9, 24]. These efforts align with the broader goal of designing digital environments that empower students' capacity to learn autonomously [5].

# 3 Methodology

## 3.1 Website Development and Eye Tracking Implementation

To answer the research questions, two instructional websites focusing on an introduction to programming in Python were developed, each incorporating distinct UI features to evaluate user experiences. Although both sites included the same content, one website employed a scrollable layout designed for displaying long-form content (Fig. 1), while the other used "Back" and "Next" navigation buttons to present content in smaller, more digestible chunks (Fig. 2). Both websites adhered to key HCI principles, specifically focusing on learnability and usability, which will be further examined in the data analysis. The backend infrastructure was developed using PostgreSQL, Next.js, and Prisma to store and manage quiz data, including correct and incorrect user responses and their respective completion times. For the front end, technologies such as HTML, CSS, JavaScript, TypeScript, the Bootstrap framework, and React were employed to design and implement the instructional website interfaces.

To implement the eye-tracking mechanism, two public libraries were employed: WebGazer.js and Heatmap.js. WebGazer.js served as the primary library for capturing the x and y coordinates as well as the timestamp of participant gaze to identify exact focus points during website interactions. The eye-tracking data were stored locally using the IndexedDB LocalForage database, which is accessible through web developer tools in the browser. Using the data retrieved from these focus points, the collected coordinates were processed to generate heatmaps. Heatmap.js was used to transform the numerical data into visual representations that highlighted the most frequently viewed areas of the websites. These heatmaps provided insights into recurring visual patterns and user engagement. In addition to the coordinate data, screen recording was implemented during both the website and quiz viewing to ensure the accuracy of timestamps and points of interest. Eye gaze data from the website were utilized throughout the data analysis process to observe areas of frequent visual interest and assess the influence on participant performance.

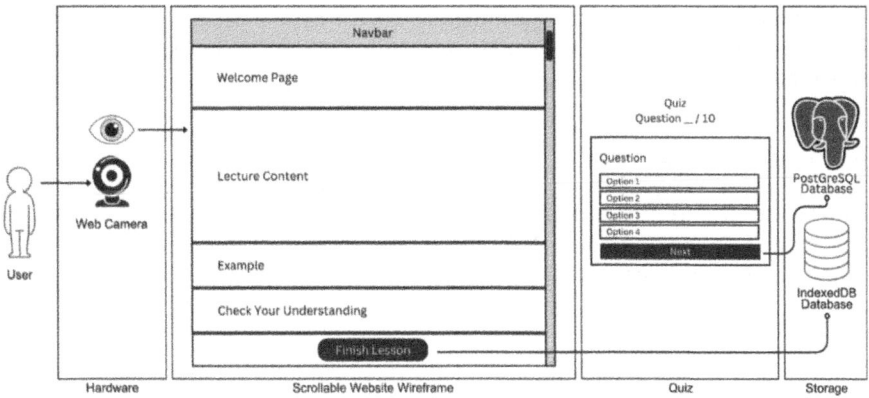

**Fig. 1.** Overall Architecture of Scrollable Website System.

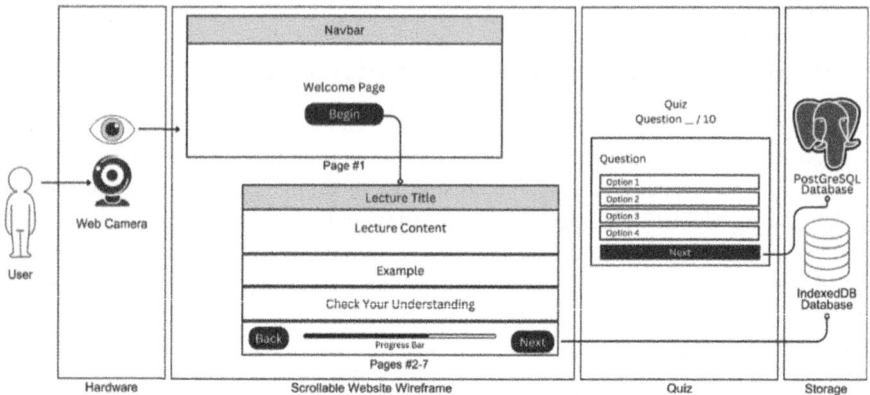

**Fig. 2.** Overall Architecture of Multi-Page Website System.

### 3.2 Participants and Study Design

Participants in this study signed informed consent forms acknowledging the use of screen recording and eye-tracking software. Before having the participants look through the websites, verbal instructions were given to reiterate the tasks and details outlined in the consent forms. A total of 16 undergraduate students who were enrolled in a computing fundamentals course at a four-year research institution participated in the study. The study utilized an experimental research design, where participants were randomly divided into two groups of eight. Each group was assigned to interact with one of the two websites.

All participants had minimal to no prior knowledge of Python programming. The first group consisted of accounting, business, and economics majors. All identified as novices in Python and indicated no prior experience or exposure to the programming language. The second group included business, finance, and computer science majors. Among these, seven participants identified as novice Python users, while one participant described themselves as a beginner, indicating minimal prior exposure and basic familiarity with the programming language.

### 3.3 Learning Content

Both websites featured identical learning material sourced from two key references: the Introduction to Python module on W3Schools and a lecture titled Introduction to Python Programming conducted by the instructor for ICS 101. The content covered foundational Python topics, including:

1. Python Introduction
2. Python Syntax
3. Python Comments
4. Python Variables

5. Python Strings
6. Python Booleans

After each major topic, there was a "Check Your Understanding" section to ensure that each participant understood the material they had just covered before proceeding to the next topic. The material was standardized across the two websites to ensure consistency and comparability in the results of this study.

### 3.4   Quiz Creation

Upon completion of the respective website interactions and course material review, participants were directed to a 10-question quiz integrated into the website. The quiz assessed knowledge directly related to the content presented on each website. Identical quiz formats were maintained across both websites to ensure that cognitive load differences were attributed to the website design rather than the quiz structure. Eye tracking and screen recording continued during the quiz phase to monitor the duration spent on each question and capture interaction patterns. Performance and timing data were utilized throughout the data analysis to evaluate the relationship between visual engagement, cognitive load, and quiz outcomes.

### 3.5   Surveys

Finally, the surveys consisted of statements and questions regarding the instructional website the participants tested. In total, the survey included 20 multiple-choice questions and statements, along with 3 open-ended questions. The multiple-choice questions and statements discussed the perceived performance and learning quality based on their experience with the instructional website. Responses were measured using a 7-point Likert scale, where 1 indicated "Strongly Disagree" and 7 indicated "Strongly Agree." The free-response questions provided additional qualitative insights into user experiences and perspectives.

## 4   Data Analysis

The following sections present the findings of the qualitative and quantitative data collected from the eye-tracking data, quiz results, and survey responses. Times spent on the respective websites and time spent on each quiz question were recorded to measure the potential impact of differing website designs on cognitive load. The following observations were then analyzed through analysis of variance (ANOVA) and t-tests to determine whether there were statistically significant differences between the two groups. This statistical analysis will determine the factors contributing to the cognitive load between groupings.

### 4.1   Eye Tracking Data

Figures 3 and 4 present the eye gaze analysis for both groups visualized as heatmaps to follow the overall movement of users' eyes as they view each website. The heatmaps use color gradients to represent the frequency of visual attention. Blue denotes areas that were less frequently viewed, while green and yellow indicate increasingly higher concentrations of user focus. These visualizations provide insight into the specific sections of the websites that captured the most student attention.

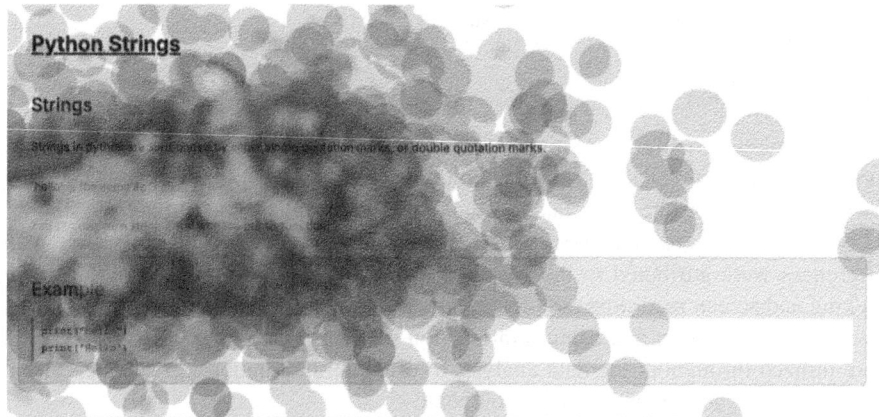

**Fig. 3.** Overall Eye Gaze Heatmap for Scrollable Website.

The scrollable website shows a high concentration of user focus, primarily on the left side of the screen. This aligns with the intuitiveness of the website design, as the scrollable layout made it so that most of the text, examples, and interactive example elements were left-aligned. Since minimal text was presented on the right side of the screen, user attention was less frequent there.

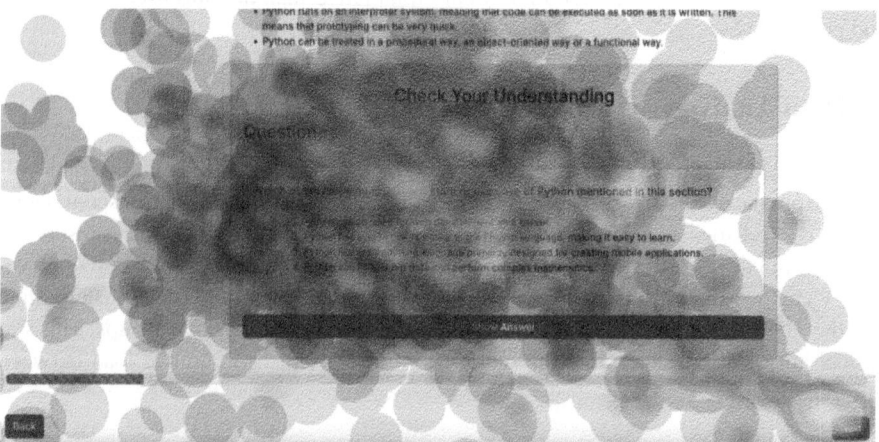

**Fig. 4.** Overall Eye Gaze Heatmap for Multi-Page Website.

In contrast, the multi-page website shows more variation in terms of user focus points. The points are more spread out as they span across the entirety of the web page rather than being confined to one side or the other. It appears that the center of the screen had high concentrations of focal points, as that is where the text, examples, and interactive example elements lie primarily on the site. As observed in Fig. 4, one key differentiating feature is the focus on the multi-page website highlighted by the "Next" button, which appears as a hotspot for frequent user gaze. The emphasis of the "Next" button could be attributed to some participants putting extra attention onto design elements that diverted their concentration from the learning material, and whether this element boosted or hindered performance and cognitive load will be analyzed in the following section.

With both of these heat map visualizations in mind, we can proceed with analyzing the quantitative data and how the eye gaze of each group influenced the time spent on each question in correlation to participant performance to gather insight into how this could affect cognitive load.

## 4.2  Performance and Time on Task

Table 1 provides the average quiz scores, total time spent on each website, and the total time spent on the quiz for each group. Participants in the scrollable website group achieved an average quiz score slightly higher than the multi-page website group. Both groups spent similar amounts of total time on their respective websites. When analyzing these times in correspondence to eye gaze patterns derived from Fig. 3 and Fig. 4, it is observed that both groups spent very similar total times on each website despite the variations in areas of visual focus. The multi-page website group spent less time on the quiz, which may suggest a lower cognitive load.

**Table 1.**  Average Quiz Scores and Times Spent on Website and Quiz.

| Website | Average Quiz Score | Total Time on Website (min:sec) | Total Time on Quiz (min:sec) |
|---|---|---|---|
| Scrollable | 63.75% | 9:53 | 3:05 |
| Multi-Page | 56.25% | 9:54 | 2:43 |

Table 2 includes the results of a t-test comparing the means of the average quiz scores between the two groups to determine if there is a significant difference between them. The resulting p-value for the two-tail analysis exceeded the 0.05 threshold, indicating the difference in quiz performance between the two groups was not statistically significant.

Further analysis focused on specific quiz questions that exhibited distinctive characteristics, particularly comparing questions with the shortest and longest response times. Table 3 presents the results of the ANOVA conducted between the average times spent on Q8 and Q9 across both website groups. Q8 was presented as follows:

Which of the following statements demonstrates valid casting?

x = int("5").

**Table 2.** t-test: Two Sample Assuming Equal Variances of Average Quiz Scores.

|                               | Scrollable Quiz | Multi-page Quiz |
| ----------------------------- | --------------- | --------------- |
| Mean                          | 63.75           | 56.25           |
| Variance                      | 3.70E+02        | 8.55E+02        |
| Observations                  | 8               | 8               |
| Pooled Variance               | 612.5           |                 |
| Hypothesized Mean Difference  | 0               |                 |
| df                            | 14              |                 |
| t Stat                        | 0.606091527     |                 |
| P(T < = t) one-tail           | 0.277077283     |                 |
| t Critical one-tail           | 1.761310136     |                 |
| P(T < = t) two-tail           | 0.554154566     |                 |
| t Critical two-tail           | 2.144786688     |                 |

```
x = float("hello")
x = str(3.14.5)
x = bool("")
```

Q8, which covered Python variables, was the fourth topic presented in the learning material. This question had the longest response time when compared to the average times for all other questions across both groups, indicating an increased cognitive load for participants. The specific focus of the question on variable casting, a subtopic briefly mentioned within the broader Python variables section, likely contributed to the extended response time. The design or presentation of this topic may not have emphasized it enough to be easily recalled.

In contrast, Q9, which stated, "Which character is used to define a Python comment?" was the third topic presented in the lecture material and required the shortest response time. This result suggests a lower cognitive load, as participants likely perceived the question as requiring minimal mental effort to process, potentially due to the question focusing on the recollection of information. A possible explanation is the frequent use of comments throughout the lecture material, where example code blocks consistently included comments to demonstrate code outputs. Additionally, the visual distinction of comments through green text may have further enhanced participants' memory recall.

The ANOVA results presented in Table 3 reveal statistically significant differences between the groups regarding the time differentials for these two questions within the source of variation for the columns, as the p-value is less than 0.05. As a result, the null hypothesis, which posits that the time differences between Q8 and Q9 are the same, can be rejected in favor of the alternative hypothesis, which asserts a statistically significant difference between the two groupings.

Another notable comparison involved Q7 and Q10, which exhibited the most significant variation in quiz performance between participants. Table 4 presents the ANOVA

**Table 3.** ANOVA Factor of Statistical Significance of Time Between Q8 and Q9.

| Source of Variation | SS | df | MS | F | P-value | F crit |
|---|---|---|---|---|---|---|
| Sample | 4.27037E-08 | 1 | 4.27037E-08 | 3.485478596 | 0.072412965 | 4.195971819 |
| Columns | 1.97125E-07 | 1 | 1.97125E-07 | 16.08937375 | 0.000407821 | 4.195971819 |
| Interaction | 1.76868E-08 | 1 | 1.76868E-08 | 1.443598379 | 0.239622457 | 4.195971819 |
| Within | 3.43053E-07 | 28 | 1.22519E-08 | | | |
| Total | 6.00568E-07 | 31 | | | | |

results for the average response times spent on these questions across both websites. The text for Q7 was as follows:

What is the output of the following code?

```
print("Hello, World!"[1])
```

Q7 addressed Python strings, the fifth topic presented in the learning material. This question had the lowest accuracy across both groups. Only 1 out of 8 participants who viewed the scrollable website answered the question correctly, while none of the 8 participants who viewed the multi-page website did so.

A common error was selecting "H" or "Hello" as the correct answer, which suggests that participants may not have fully grasped Python string indexing. This issue may be attributed to the placement and formatting of the sections on the websites. String indexing, including converting a string to an array, was presented in the middle of the section, potentially leading to the difficulty in recollection. The design and presentation may have contributed to increased cognitive load as participants exerted additional mental effort to process and recall this topic.

Q10 pertained to Python booleans, the sixth and final topic in the learning material. The text for Q10 was as follows:

What will be the result of the following syntax:

```
print(5 > 3)?
```

This question had the highest accuracy across both groups, with 7 out of 8 participants answering correctly in each group. The increase in performance may again be attributed to the recency of the material, as this last topic presented was likely the freshest in the minds of participants, facilitating easier recall and reducing cognitive load. In addition, participants were exposed to Boolean logic earlier in their computing fundamentals course, which may influence results.

The ANOVA results presented in Table 4 reveal statistically significant differences in the time differentials for these two questions within the source of variation for the columns, as the p-value is less than 0.05. The findings support rejecting the null hypothesis, which posits no difference between the time spent on Q7 and Q10. Instead, the results indicate a statistically significant difference, affirming the impact of question type and presentation on participant response times and performance.

**Table 4.** ANOVA Factor of Statistical Significance of Time Between Q7 and Q10.

| Source of Variation | SS | df | MS | F | P-value | F crit |
|---|---|---|---|---|---|---|
| Sample | 1.20982E-09 | 1 | 1.20982E-09 | 0.17142615 | 0.682001989 | 4.195971819 |
| Columns | 3.62067E-08 | 1 | 3.62067E-08 | 5.130327938 | 0.031441949 | 4.195971819 |
| Interaction | 4.02296E-09 | 1 | 4.02296E-09 | 0.570036438 | 0.456548579 | 4.195971819 |
| Within | 1.97607E-07 | 28 | 7.05738E-09 | | | |
| Total | 2.39046E-07 | 31 | | | | |

### 4.3 Participant Perceptions

The survey consisted of 20 multiple-choice questions (MCQs) divided into subcategories that assessed the individual website experiences, perceptions, and learning outcomes of participants based on the respective instructional website they tested. Each participant evaluated each question based on their personal website experiences. Responses were rated on a 7-point Likert scale, where 1 indicated "Strongly Disagree" and 7 indicated "Strongly Agree." Some questions pertaining to the HCI principles of usability and learnability were:

- How easy was it to start using the website for the first time?
- How long did it take you to feel proficient in using the instructional website?
- How easy was it to remember how to use various functions and features after initial use?
- How steep was the learning curve for using the instructional website?
- The examples and exercises on the website enhanced my understanding of computer science concepts.
- The content on the website was presented in a logical sequence that facilitated learning.
- I quickly became proficient in using the instructional website.
- The overall design and functionality of the website were intuitive.

These items aimed to evaluate both the immediate usability of the platforms and their effectiveness in facilitating long-term learning and engagement. Participant responses provide insights into which design features were more conducive to reducing cognitive load and enhancing retention.

A two sample t-test assuming equal variances was conducted to compare the means of responses from participants between the scrollable and multi-page website groups for the MCQs. These questions focused on usability and learnability, where Q1-Q7 evaluated initial website intuitiveness, Q8-Q11 assessed alignment with specific usability statements, and Q12–20 measured perceived learning outcomes. The t-test results shown in Table 5 reveal a statistically significant difference between the two groups, with a two-tailed p-value less than 0.05. The null hypothesis can be rejected, confirming that the observed differences in usability and learnability perceptions are statistically meaningful. Further analysis of the average scores shows a higher mean for the scrollable group

(5.6375) compared to the multi-page group (4.83125), suggesting that participants found the scrollable website to offer a slightly more positive user experience in terms of ease of use and proficiency in navigating the platform.

**Table 5.** t-test: Two Sample Assuming Equal Variances of MCQs (Learnability and Usability).

|  | Scrollable Website | Multi-Page Website |
|---|---|---|
| Mean | 5.6375 | 4.83125 |
| Variance | 0.756414474 | 0.306373355 |
| Observations | 20 | 20 |
| Pooled Variance | 0.531393914 |  |
| Hypothesized Mean Difference | 0 |  |
| df | 38 |  |
| t Stat | 3.497529928 |  |
| P(T <=t) one-tail | 0.000606747 |  |
| t Critical one-tail | 1.68595446 |  |
| P(T <= t) two-tail | 0.001213495 |  |
| t Critical two-tail | 2.024394164 |  |

In addition to the MCQs, participants were also given free response questions (FRQs). Participants provided insights through FRQ 1: "What aspects of the website design impacted your learning experience (positively or negatively)? Please explain your answer," and FRQ 2: "Do you feel the website design enhanced your ability to learn or retain information? Please explain your answer." Table 6 outlines notable responses from both groups, categorized by key themes for comparison.

Three recurring trends emerged from the free-response questions: 1) Retention, 2) Focus, and 3) Structure.

First, regarding retention, participants in the scrollable website group initially reported good information retention, which diminished over time due to the repetitive long-form structure of the site. This suggests that while the continuous scrolling format offers easy access to previous content, it may become monotonous, reducing engagement and memory retention. In contrast, participants in the multi-page website group found the layout straightforward and intuitive but reported challenges in retaining information. They attributed this difficulty to repeatedly clicking "Back" or "Next" to view different pages. This fragmented navigation likely disrupted cognitive processing and made it harder for participants to form a cohesive understanding of the material. Furthermore, the limited exposure to individual pages may have impeded reinforcement of key concepts.

Second, in terms of focus, participants in the scrollable website group expressed difficulty maintaining concentration due to the left-aligned structure of the content, which aligns with observed eye-gaze patterns in Fig. 3. This design flaw may have contributed to cognitive overload, making it harder for users to stay engaged. However, the group

**Table 6.** Participant Responses to FRQs 1 and 2.

| Theme | FRQ | Scrollable Website | Multi-Page Website |
|---|---|---|---|
| Retention | 1 | "…for certain topics such as "variables," I struggled to retain. This may have been the result of the formatting of the website; when the topic was more difficult to understand, the repetitiveness of the website became limiting in terms of my overall learning" | "…it wasn't as interactive I was just reading and looking at examples… but the layout was good and the ideas is very intuitive just a few tweaks, especially for people who have a hard time retaining information unless they go through it many times" |
| | 2 | "I feel like I did a good job retaining information at the beginning but after a while I found it to be more difficult to focus and actually understand the information." | "Yes. The website design was very straight to the point and easy to follow through which helped me retain the information better" |
| Focus | 1 | "I think that I had a difficult time concentrating on the website, with most of the content being displayed on the left" | "I think having the interactive example questions that allowed us to reflect back on what topic was being taught definitely helped to see if we actually understood the concept or not" |
| | 2 | "Yes, the website explained new topics very well to a beginner like myself… The interactive questions were good to check in with myself to see if I had truly learned the information, or if I should review the lesson again" | "I think that it did. Once again, having photos and questions distributed throughout the website was really helpful. It helped me stay more engaged overall and was honestly a little bit fun to complete" |
| Structure | 1 | "I liked that the website followed a linear path, just like reading a real book" | "An aspect of the website design that impacted my learning experience was the step-by-step portion. I enjoyed looking and reading the visuals, as I am a visual learner." |
| | 2 | "I think the web design did help, because the material was broken up into digestible sections that made it easier to retain information, and determine what I needed to review more" | "I feel like this website design did enhanced my ability to learn because the website design was simple and spaced out, making it easier to read. I felt as if I was reading a book or a step by step guide" |

appreciated the interactive "Check Your Understanding" questions, which helped them gauge comprehension before moving on to new topics. Similarly, participants in the multi-page website group found the interactive example questions valuable for assessing their understanding. They also highlighted the effectiveness of visual elements in maintaining focus and enhancing engagement.

Finally, responses related to structure revealed that participants in the scrollable website group appreciated the linear path of the design, which they felt contributed to an enhanced learning experience. The continuous format made topics more easily digestible and accessible while focusing less on navigation. Conversely, the multi-page website group valued the chunking aspect of the design, which broke content into manageable sections. They emphasized that the step-by-step layout contributed positively to their learning experience by making the information more readable and organized.

Overall, these responses suggest that the effectiveness of website design in enhancing learning is influenced by how well it balances accessibility, interactivity, and structural coherence. While the scrollable design may benefit users who prefer uninterrupted access to content, it risks becoming monotonous without sufficient variation or engagement features. On the other hand, the multi-page design fosters better content segmentation and chunking of content but may hinder retention if navigation disrupts the user's cognitive flow.

## 5 Conclusion

Results from this study allow us to revisit the initial research questions posed in this study, particularly regarding cognitive load and user interaction in digital learning environments. The heatmaps for the scrollable and multi-page websites (Fig. 3 and Fig. 4) revealed substantial differences in gaze patterns between the two groups. In the scrollable website, where the content was left-aligned, participants focused more on the content itself rather than navigating external design elements. However, condensing text, examples, and interactive elements to one side led to navigation monotony, which participants reported as negatively impacting their focus.

Conversely, participants in the multi-page website group exhibited more diverse gaze patterns, particularly around the central text content and the bottom right "Next" button. While participants found the chunking of information intuitive and well-organized, they were less inclined to revisit previous content due to the minimal eye gaze at the back button and continuous clicking required, which introduced extraneous cognitive effort. Despite these contrasting experiences, both groups acknowledged in their FRQ responses that the design of the respective website influenced their learning experience. These findings align with the second RQ and underscore that both design approaches have advantages and limitations, making them valuable learning tools in different contexts.

The t-test results (Table 2, p = 0.554) indicated no statistically significant difference in average scores between the two groups. However, further analysis of individual questions revealed nuanced patterns connecting eye gaze, response time, and performance on specific Python programming topics. Notably, questions that took the longest time or had the lowest correct response rates highlighted the importance of balancing content design to sustain engagement and support comprehension.

These findings suggest that the cognitive demands of program comprehension are greater than those of recall tasks. Therefore, instructional design should adapt to satisfy these cognitive requirements. For example, multi-page layouts that naturally chunk information could be more effective for complex conceptual topics like variable casting by reducing cognitive load through gradual content delivery. Conversely, scrollable layouts may be suitable for recall tasks, as they facilitate continuous information flow and require less cognitive effort. Therefore, these insights propose that the effectiveness of digital design in educational contexts may be enhanced by tailoring layouts based on the type of cognitive task at hand.

Furthermore, the contrasting performance between Q7 and Q10 proposes avenues for observing the potential influence of primacy and recency effects and general cognitive load differences between question types. If discrepancies in performance stem from primacy/recency effects, a multi-page layout that chunks information could prove more effective by reducing cognitive overload through structured and sequential learning. Conversely, if the cognitive load varies by question type, a scrollable design that provides a continuous flow of information may better support cognitive processing for recall tasks. However, future research should be explored to observe how adaptive digital learning environments could adjust content based on topic complexity and user performance.

**Research Limitations.** The small sample size is a limitation of this study. While a total of 16 participants allowed for some variation in results, it limits the generalizability of the findings. For example, one participant in the multi-page website group performed drastically differently than the other participants on the quiz, answering only 1 out of 10 questions correctly. These discrepancies could be addressed with a larger population pool or repeated measures design.

**Future Development and Research.** Multiple avenues for future research could be explored. One potential area is to examine the impact of digital design on cognitive load in mobile environments, where screen size and interaction methods differ significantly from desktop platforms. Investigating how various UI features perform on mobile devices could yield valuable insights into effective design strategies for mobile and micro-learning approaches.

Another avenue for future research is to conduct embedded testing, in which participants complete assessments in real-time after reviewing each section rather than taking a cumulative assessment at the end. This approach may provide a more granular understanding of how design elements influence retention and comprehension across different content sections and account for potential primacy and recency effects.

Future research could also explore whether adaptive layouts, such as switching between multi-page for complex concepts and scrollable for recall tasks, could improve learning outcomes by aligning with cognitive processing needs. This research could help determine the level of cognitive load increase between these different website formats within the same learning material and course.

Overall, this study highlighted how participants engage with desktop browser-based educational content with scrollable and multi-page sites. Both types of UX/UI approaches have varied eye-gaze focus but minimal differences between performance and time on task. Therefore, it is critical for designers to consider the type of content and matching UX/UI approaches to augment learning platforms.

**Acknowledgements.** This study is funded by the Douglas S. Yamura Scholarship Fund under the University of Hawaii at Manoa Undergraduate Research and Opportunities Program (UROP).

# References

1. Ansari, N., Lopes, M., Bhanage, A., Changarankattil, V., Cheeramkuzhyil, A., Correia, R.: Heuristic evaluation of website using HCI principles. In: Adhau S., Gawande S., Rajguru V. (eds.) AIP Conference Proceedings, ITSEMC, vol. 3188, pp. 1–6. AIP Publishing (2024)
2. Bakos, Z.: Comparing the UI and UX of a business website, a user feedback study. In: Theses Open Collection, Laurea University of Applied Sciences (2019)
3. Crosby, M.E., Iding, M.K., Chin, D.N.: Research on task complexity as a foundation for augmented cognition. In: 36th Annual Hawaii International Conference on System Sciences. Proceedings of the Big Island (2003)
4. Datwani, K., Ogawa, M.B., Crosby, M.: Understanding humans' cognitive processes during computational thinking through cognitive science. In: Schmorrow, D., Fidopiastis, C. (eds.) Foundations of Augmented Cognition 16th International Conference, AC Proceedings. Proceedings, vol. 16. Springer Lecture Notes in Artificial Intelligence. (2022)
5. Engeness, I.: Developing teachers' digital identity: towards the pedagogic design principles of digital environments to enhance students' learning in the 21st century. Eur. J. Teach. Educ. **44**(1), 96–114 (2021)
6. Ertmer, P.A.: Teacher pedagogical beliefs: the final frontier in our quest for technology integration? Educ. Tech. Res. Dev. **53**(4), 25–39 (2005)
7. Gabatino, T., Ogawa, M.B., Crosby, M.: Abstracting the understanding and application of cognitive load in computational thinking and modularized learning. In: Schmorrow, D., Fidopiastis, C. (eds.) Foundations of Augmented Cognition 16th International Conference, AC Proceedings. Proceedings, vol. 16. Springer Lecture Notes in Artificial Intelligence. (2022)
8. Gerlach, J.H., Kuo, F.-Y.: Understanding human-computer interaction for information systems design. MIS Q. **15**(4), 527–549 (1991)
9. Gorospe, J.M.C., Olaskoaga, L.F., Barragán, A.G.C., Iglesias, D.L., Agirre, B.O.A.: Formación Del Profesorado, Tecnología Educativa E Identidad Docente Digital. RELATEC: Revista Latinoamericana De Tecnología Educativa **14**(1), 45–56 (2015)
10. Gregg, A., Reid, R., Aldemir, T., Gray, J., Frederick, M., Garbrick, A.: Improving online course design with think aloud observations: a "How to" guide for instructional designers for conducting UX testing. J. Appl. Instruct. Des. **7**(2), 17–26 (2020)
11. Grossman, M.: A central processor for hierarchically-structured material: evidence from broca's aphasia. Neuropsychologia **18**, 299–308 (1980)
12. Instefjord, E.: Appropriation of digital competence in teacher education. Nordic J. Digit. Lit. **9**(4), 313–329 (2014)
13. Instefjord, E., Munthe, E.: Preparing pre-service teachers to integrate technology: an analysis of the emphasis on digital competence in teacher education curricula. Eur. J. Teach. Educ. **39**(1), 77–93 (2016)
14. Ioannou, A., Vasiliou, C., Zaphiris, P., Arh, T., Klobučar, T., Pipan, M.: Creative multimodal learning environments and blended interaction for problem-based activity in HCI education. TechTrends: Link. Res. Pract. Improve Learn. **59**(2), 47–56 (2015)
15. Joo, H.: A study on understanding of UI and UX, and understanding of design according to user interface change. Int. J. Appl. Eng. Res. **12**, 9931–9935 (2017)
16. Kopp, M., Gröblinger, O., Adams, S.: Five common assumptions that prevent digital transformation at higher education institutions. In: International Technology, Education and Development Conference Proceedings 2019, INTED, vol. 13, pp. 1448–1457. IATED, Spain (2019)
17. MacKenzie, S.: Human-Computer Interaction: An Empirical Research Perspective., 2nd edn. Morgan Kaufmann (2024)

18. Miller, G.A.: The magical number seven plus or minus two: some limits on our capacity for processing information. Psychol. Rev. **63**, 81–97 (1956)
19. Miya, T.K., Govender, I.: UX/UI design of online learning platforms and their impact on learning: a review. Int. J. Res. Bus. Soc. Sci. **11**, 316–327 (2022)
20. Muslim, E., Moch, B.N., Wilgert, Y., Utami, F.F., Indriyani, D.: User interface redesign of e-commerce platform mobile application (Kudo) through user experience evaluation to increase user attraction. In: IOP Conference Series: Materials Science and Engineering, vol. 508, pp. 12113–12119. IOP Publishing (2019)
21. Musso, M., Moro, A., Glauche, V., Rijntjes, M., Reichenbach, J., Büchel, C., et al.: Broca's area and the language instinct. Nat. Neurosci. **6**, 774–781 (2003)
22. Rabinovich, M.I., Varona, P., Tristan, I., Afraimovich, V.S.: Chunking dynamics: heteroclinics in mind. Front. Comput. Neurosci. **8**, 22–32 (2014)
23. Reeves, L.M., Schmorrow, D.D.: Augmented cognition foundations and future directions— enabling "Anyone, Anytime, Anywhere" applications. In: Stephanidis, C. (ed.) UAHCI 2007. LNCS, vol. 4554, pp. 263–272. Springer, Heidelberg (2007). https://doi.org/10.1007/978-3-540-73279-2_30
24. Robson, J.: Performance, structure and ideal identity: reconceptualising teachers' engagement in online social spaces. Br. J. Edu. Technol. **49**(3), 439–450 (2018)
25. Schmorrow, D.D.: Foundations of Augmented Cognition, 1st edn. CRC Press, Boca Raton (2005)
26. Skinner, A., Long, L., Vice, J., Blitch, J., Fidopiastis, C.M., Berka, C.: Augmented interaction: applying the principles of augmented cognition to human-technology and human-human interactions. In: Schmorrow, D.D., Fidopiastis, Cali M. (eds.) AC 2013. LNCS (LNAI), vol. 8027, pp. 764–773. Springer, Heidelberg (2013). https://doi.org/10.1007/978-3-642-39454-6_82
27. Skulmowski, A., Xu, K.M.: Understanding cognitive load in digital and online learning: a new perspective on extraneous cognitive load. Educ. Psychol. Rev. **34**, 171–196 (2022)
28. Sweller, J., van Merrienboer, J.J.G., Paas, F.G.W.C.: Cognitive architecture and instructional design. Educ. Psychol. Rev. **10**, 251–296 (1998)

# End-to-End Encryption: Technological and Human Factor Perspectives

Leandros Maglaras🄳 and Kitty Kioskli[(✉)] 🄳

trustilio, B.V., Amsterdam, The Netherlands
{leandros.maglaras,kiity.kioskli}@trustilio.com

**Abstract.** End-to-end encryption (E2E) has become a cornerstone of modern digital communications, safeguarding data from unauthorized access during transmission. E2E encryption ensures that only the intended recipient can decrypt the data, keeping it invisible even to service providers. However, this technology presents a paradox: while it protects individual privacy and fosters trust in digital systems, it also challenges law enforcement agencies by creating potential safe havens for illegal activities. This paper explores the dual nature of E2E encryption, its significance for privacy, and the various threats it poses, and presents some recent innovative solutions aimed at addressing these challenges.

**Keywords:** E2EE · Human Factors · Privacy

## 1 Introduction

Encryption is crucial for maintaining security and privacy in the digital world. It ensures that sensitive information, such as personal data, financial transactions, and private communications, is protected from unauthorized access. By converting data into unreadable code, encryption makes it accessible only to those with the correct decryption keys, safeguarding it from hackers, identity thieves, and other malicious actors. This layer of protection is essential for individuals, businesses, and governments to prevent data breaches and keep confidentiality. In an age where cyber threats are increasingly sophisticated, encryption not only reassures privacy preservation but also enhances trust in digital services and communication platforms. Trust is the most important aspect of digital services since the loss of it from the users will lead to collapse of modern societies [1].

End-to-end encryption (E2EE) stands as one of the most important advancements in securing digital communications. This technology ensures that messages, files, and other forms of data can only be accessed by the intended sender and receiver, leaving no room for third parties—even the service providers themselves—to intercept or decipher the content. In an era where data breaches and digital surveillance are prevalent, E2EE serves as a vital solution for securing both individual and organizational privacy [2].

The increasing reliance on digital communication for personal, professional, and governmental purposes has highlighted the importance of the application of robust

D. D. Schmorrow and C. M. Fidopiastis (Eds.): HCII 2025, LNAI 15778, pp. 129–139, 2025.
https://doi.org/10.1007/978-3-031-93724-8_10

encryption methods. From instant messaging applications to cloud storage platforms, E2E encryption has become a provider of trust for the end users. Recently, FBI and the Cybersecurity and Infrastructure Security Agency (CISA) have issued a warning to smartphone users about the risks associated with sending unencrypted text messages between iPhones and Android devices. These unencrypted messages are vulnerable to interception by cybercriminals, potentially exposing sensitive information [3] (Fig. 1).

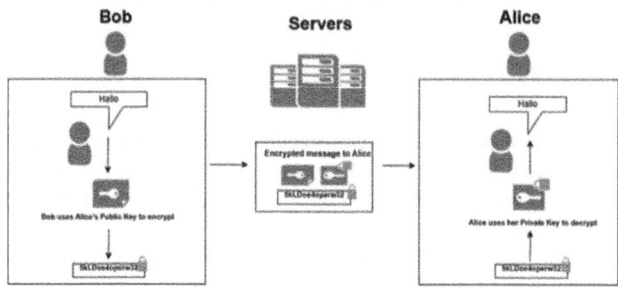

**Fig. 1.** End to End reception. Mechanism.

However, this same technology has initiated a huge debate over its implications for law enforcement and national security [4]. Critics argue that encryption can provide a safe environment for criminal activities, complicating investigations and undermining public safety [5]. Access to data is important to law enforcement agencies for both proactive and reactive actions against cybercriminals. Reactive actions mainly refer to the capacity of technology companies to respond to law enforcement investigations by providing data from suspected criminals on their platforms. Proactive actions stand for the ability of technology companies to actively identify illegal and harmful activities on their platforms, particularly in detecting users with a sexual interest in children. As stated in the Joint Declaration of the European Police Chiefs [5], they are concerned that the implementation of end-to-end encryption is being carried out in a manner that will undermine both of these capabilities.

Privacy, a fundamental human right, is tightly linked to encryption. In an interconnected world, sensitive data—including personal habits, health information, and social interactions—is constantly at risk of exposure. E2EE helps safeguard this information from unauthorized access [6]. Nevertheless, its implementation raises ethical questions about the balance between individual privacy and collective security, particularly when encryption blocks the detection of illegal activities [7].

While E2EE is designed to be user-friendly, many individuals may not fully understand how encryption works or the importance of keeping their encryption keys secure. This lack of knowledge can lead to incorrect usage or weak implementation of the offered solutions. Users can be vulnerable to phishing attacks, social engineering, or other forms of manipulation that bypass encryption [8]. Mobile communication devices are vulnerable to physical over-the-shoulder eavesdropping as well as digital eavesdrop-ping often via unknown malware infections [9]. Effective education and awareness are crucial for ensuring that encryption's technological benefits are not lost due to human-related vulnerabilities.

Moreover, social media and communication apps are the most frequently consumed application types. However, downloaded apps may hide stalkerware; a category of spyware that enables threat actors to monitor activity and access personal information [10]. Notably, they may be used to allow for Intimate Partner Stalking (IPS) where perpetrators use stalkerware as a surveillance tool against current or previous partners, perpetuating violence against women and girls. Contemporary E2EE is failing to protect privacy, enabling mal actors to spy on their targets.

As stated, E2EE has its limitations. Traditional implementations often fail to address endpoint vulnerabilities, exposing users to malware, spyware, and other threats. Using several existing messenger applications like Signal where data are not backed up or stored reduces the chance of messages being accessed, but the main problem of the data being created and consumed in cleartext on end devices remains. These shortcomings highlight the need for comprehensive solutions that extend protection to the end devices (e.g., mobile phones) where data is created and consumed. This gap in traditional encryption models is an important point of ongoing research and development efforts [11].

In this article, we investigate the current landscape of E2EE solutions, examining their role in securing digital communications and protecting user privacy while addressing current ethical challenges. We briefly present privacy considerations that include location, state of body & mind, social life, behavior & action, and media. Also, we present all emerging threats that are mostly related to insecure third-party apps, human factor, and client-side scanning (CSS) solutions. Moreover, we present state-of-the-art novel solutions related to E2EE that combine augmented reality technology [12] or encrypted keyboard technologies [13]. Finally, we discuss ethical problems and law enforcement dilemmas when dealing with public and most importantly children's safety. By exploring the vulnerabilities inherent in existing systems and human factors related to cybersecurity attacks, this work highlights the need for innovative frameworks. The paper aims to contribute to the ongoing dialogue on how to balance privacy, security, human factors, ethical dilemmas and technological advancements in the modern digital world.

## 2 Privacy Considerations

Privacy is multifaceted, encompassing aspects such as location, social interactions, behavior, and personal media. Each of these dimensions is vulnerable to surveillance and misuse in the absence of robust protection mechanisms.

### 2.1 Privacy of Location

Spatiotemporal data, which captures both the location and the timing of an individual's movements, can provide insights into their personal life. By tracking where and when a person goes, this data can reveal sensitive information such as home and work addresses, travel patterns, or visits to specific locations like medical clinics or confidential meetings. While this data can be useful for services like navigation or location-based recommendations, it also presents significant privacy risks, as it can inadvertently expose personal details that individuals may wish to keep private.

When spatiotemporal data is correlated with other datasets, the potential for revealing even more intimate information increases. For example, combining location data with health-related information could expose a person's medical conditions, such as frequent visits to a particular hospital or clinic. Furthermore, cross-referencing such data with social media activity or other digital traces could uncover a person's social circles, daily habits, or even political affiliations. As a result, spatio-temporal data represents not only a powerful tool for businesses and services but also a potential vulnerability to privacy breaches, making it crucial to handle and protect such information with the utmost care. For that reason, several novel privacy preservation mechanisms that can preserve service levels while protecting sensitive users' data [14, 15].

## 2.2  Privacy of State of Body and Mind

In order to increase the security, many applications use biometric data of the users. Unfotrunately, biometric data, mental states, and political opinions are becoming increasingly vulnerable to breaches, posing serious risks to individual privacy and security [16]. Biometric data, such as fingerprints, facial recognition, or voiceprints, is uniquely tied to an individual and is often used for authentication purposes. However, if this data is compromised, it can be exploited for performing several attacks. Similarly, personal information about one's mental health or political opinions, which can be inferred through digital behavior, is also at risk. A breach of such sensitive data can have far-reaching consequences, from personal discrimination to more systemic exploitation.

The exploitation of this sensitive information could have devastating impacts. Authoritarian governments might use these data to monitor, control, or suppress individuals based on their political views or mental health status, leading to social and political persecution. Personal data may be used to target vulnerable individuals with manipulative marketing tactics or even make discriminatory decisions in hiring or lending practices. The growing exposure of these data types underscores the urgent need for stronger privacy preservation protocols and policies, and ethical guidelines to safeguard against misuse and ensure that personal freedoms are respected [17].

## 2.3  Privacy of Behavior and Actions

Hobbies, shopping habits, and social media activities collectively create a detailed profile of an individual's life. This data can be collected through various methods, including cookies [18], pixels [19], and specific software development kits (SDKs). These data entries reveal personal preferences, routines, and behaviors, offering insights into who a person is and what they value. Companies and platforms use this information to tailor experiences, target advertisements, and predict future choices. While such personalization can enhance convenience, it also comes with significant security risks and privacy violation tactics.

Violation of users' data privacy can lead to manipulation, social profiling, and repetitive targeted advertising. When personal information is misused or exposed, individuals may be subject to manipulation or even discrimination based on their profiles. This level of intrusion raises concerns about autonomy and ethical data use, highlighting the importance of safeguarding personal information in an increasingly digital world [20].

### 2.4  Media Privacy

Unauthorized redistribution of photos, videos, or audio files constitutes a direct violation of privacy and intellectual property rights. When such content is shared without consent, it can lead to serious personal harm, including emotional distress, reputation damage, and breaches of confidentiality. This misuse can affect individuals' relationships, careers, and personal security, as sensitive information becomes accessible to unintended audiences.

Beyond personal impact, these violations often carry significant legal consequences [21]. Many jurisdictions have strict laws against unauthorized sharing of media, resulting in potential fines, lawsuits, or even criminal charges.

## 3  Threats and Challenges

Despite its advantages, E2E encryption has limitations, particularly when it neglects human factors or device vulnerabilities. Mobile devices, which are integral components for communication, often become gateways for attackers through malware, spyware, or stalkerware. These threats are combined with those coming from insecure third-party apps [22].

### 3.1  Malware and Stalkerware

Malware, including banking trojans and ransomware, are significant threats to mobile device security since they can exploit vulnerabilities and bypass encryption at endpoints. These malicious programs are designed to gain unauthorized access to sensitive information, steal financial data, and even disrupt normal system operations when needed. Banking trojans are particularly dangerous because they target financial institutions and may disrupt online transactions.

Ransomware, which is ranked as the most dangerous threat from the ENISA threat landscape of 2024 [23], locks users out of their data, demanding payment for its release. The ability of these malware types to bypass encryption protocols further complicates efforts to protect users, as attackers can exploit gaps in security and target individuals or organizations with devastating consequences [24].

Stalkerware, a type of surveillance software used to monitor individuals without their consent, is becoming an increasingly alarming issue with serious societal implications. This software is often used to track the activities, whereabouts, and personal communications of partners, raising serious concerns about privacy of individuals' data. In the UK, nearly 5% of adults admit to using such apps, which underscores the growing prevalence of this invasive behavior. The impact of stalkerware extends beyond individual privacy violations, as it can lead to emotional abuse, manipulation, and control within relationships. The societal implications of stalkerware highlight the need for stricter regulations and awareness surrounding digital privacy and personal security.

### 3.2  Human Factor

While data may be encrypted during transmission, endpoints often lack adequate protection. Cleartext consumption of data on devices makes it vulnerable to physical and digital eavesdropping.

While data encryption during transmission provides a strong layer of security, the protection of endpoints often remains insufficient, leaving critical vulnerabilities unattended. Once data reaches its destination, such as a user's mobile phone, it is consumed in an unprotected or "cleartext" format, which allows it to be read directly from an adversary. If the device is not properly secured, attackers can easily intercept this unencrypted data, either through physical access (e.g. shoulder surfing) or digital means like malware or data breaches. Without proper endpoint protection, such as advanced encryption or secure storage mechanisms, sensitive information like passwords, financial details, and personal messages can be accessed by unauthorized parties [25].

Cleartext consumption of data on devices significantly increases the risks of both physical and digital eavesdropping. For instance, if a device is lost or stolen, an attacker could gain immediate access to valuable information that would otherwise be protected if encrypted. Similarly, through techniques like man-in-the-middle attacks or malware, digital eavesdropping can capture data as it is being processed on the device. These risks highlight the need for a comprehensive security strategy that includes robust encryption both in transit and at rest and endpoint protections to ensure that data remains secure throughout its entire lifecycle. Moreover, even if the user has installed all security features that could increase the protection of data, improper use of those or even bypass of them due to increased complexity or delay can expose private data to adversaries [26].

### 3.3 Client-Side Scanning (CSS)

E2E protocols have weakened the efficiency of Server-Side Scanning techniques. Proposed as a method to balance privacy and security, Client-Side Scanning (CSS) has raised a significant debate due to the new risks it introduces. CSS involves scanning users' data directly on users' devices to identify specific, targeted material, such as illegal content or potential threats. While the goal is to enhance security without compromising privacy, this approach creates a delicate balance. The idea of scanning users' data raises serious concerns about potential misuse, as it opens a backdoor for authorities, tech companies, or malicious actors to access personal information under the purpose of safeguarding peoples' security [27].

Furthermore, CSS could lead to false positives, where benign data is incorrectly flagged as a security threat or illegal content. This could result in unwarranted surveillance, censorship, or even legal consequences for individuals who aren't performing any illegal actions. Additionally, the implementation of CSS by governments or private entities raises concerns about overreach, with the possibility that such scanning could extend beyond its intended scope, violating civil liberties. The introduction of this technology calls for careful consideration of its ethical implications, ensuring that the protection of individual privacy is not compromised in the name of security.

### 3.4 Encryption Backdoors

Encryption is a dual-purpose technology that safeguards both the security of law-abiding individuals and the activities of criminals who use it to conceal evidence of their criminal activities. Likewise, encryption backdoors can serve dual purposes—while they allow law enforcement to access communication content, they can also be exploited by criminals to obtain information, enabling cybercrimes like extortion, theft, and fraud.

Many countries like the U.S, the U.K., and France among others, seem very interested in mandating encryption backdoors, tools that give governmental authorities access to encrypted communication. This request is coming mainly from law enforcement authorities but is followed by the risk of reducing the security level of the offered service if not implemented correctly as mentioned in [6], security researchers agree that when any backdoor is applied in an E2E encryption mechanism it effectively removes the E2E security and weakens the encryption protocol for all users of this specific service. Additionally, opponents of mandatory government backdoors argue that encryption is essential for safeguarding individuals from cybercriminals and securing communications. This protection is particularly important for journalists, political dissidents, human rights advocates, domestic violence survivors, and businesses, among others.

### 3.5  Quantum Computing and AI

Quantum computers and AI pose significant threats to end-to-end encryption (E2EE) due to their ability to undermine traditional cryptographic algorithms [28]. Current E2EE systems rely on encryption techniques like RSA, ECC, and Diffie-Hellman, which derive their security from the difficulty of factoring large numbers or solving discrete logarithm problems. Quantum computers can solve these problems exponentially faster than classical computers, making these encryption methods obsolete. This would allow adversaries with quantum capabilities to decrypt previously secure communications. For that reason, A set of encryption algorithms that are designed to withstand hacking attempts by a quantum computer has been released by the US National Institute of Standards and Technology [29].

Meanwhile, AI increases the risks against security and privacy by enhancing the efficiency of cryptographic attacks, automating pattern recognition, and improving the exploitation of vulnerabilities in encryption protocols. Combined, quantum computing and AI could enable large-scale interception and decryption of sensitive communications, severely compromising privacy, financial security, and data protection. This evolving threat underscores the urgent need for post-quantum cryptography to secure E2EE systems against future adversarial advancements [30].

### 3.6  Ethical Implications

E2E encryption can offer enhanced data privacy protection but on other hand it can also be used for criminal activities. There was a recent example of EncroChat. EncroChat was a Europe-based communications network and service provider that offered modified smartphones enabling encrypted communication among subscribers. While initially marketed as a privacy-focused service, it became a vehicle for organized crime, facilitating activities such as drug trafficking and money laundering EncroChat was a Europe-based communications network and service provider that offered modified smartphones allowing encrypted communication among subscribers. It was used primarily by organized crime members to plan criminal activities. In early 2020, law enforcement agencies, from France and the Netherlands, infiltrated EncroChat's encrypted network. This operation allowed them to monitor communications in real-time, leading to the arrestment of hundreds of suspects and the seize of substantial quantities of drugs, firearms, and cash [31].

# 4  Innovative E2E Mechanisms

In this section we briefly present recent innovative solutions that can be applied to add another layer of encryption, reassuring the privacy of user data.

## 4.1  The SNE2EE Framework

Recently we presented the secure node end to end (SNE2EE) mechanism. SNE2EE aims to extend encryption to the endpoints, addressing vulnerabilities overlooked by traditional E2E encryption [32] solutions. This innovative solution integrates hardware and software technologies to enhance security without compromising the usability of the end device [33].

Key Features of SNE2EE:

– End-Node Encryption: Data is encrypted in an external device before being transmitted to the user's mobile phone, ensuring protection of data at endpoints.
– Multifactor Authentication (MFA) mechanism: Enhanced user identity verification through methods like fingerprint recognition or RFID identification.
– External Hardware Integration: Devices like Raspberry Pi smart overlay screen, clean mobile phones or smart AR glasses create, encrypt, and display data, decoupling sensitive operations from vulnerable mobile devices.

SNE2EE encrypts cleartext messages using public-private key pairs that are created by the application or the user himself. The encrypted data is transmitted and further encrypted by host applications (any internet communication organisers (ICOs)), ensuring additional layer protection. Upon reception, the process is reversed, and the message is securely displayed via external hardware to the end user.

The SNE2EE prototype employs a Raspberry Pi, an external LCD screen, and an RFID device mainly used for identity verification. It demonstrates how hardware and software can synergize to mitigate risks from malware and stalkerware but it is not so user-friendly [12]. The second prototype demanded the use of a second'clear' mobile phone that the user would use for creating and consuming the messages [32]. SNE2EE third implementation included 2 pairs of AR glasses that can communicate through a messaging application and can perform several actions: speech-to-text transformation, encryption of text, sending of message, decryption of text, and overlay text display. This promising framework of E2E solutions can offer enhanced data privacy and can mitigate many vulnerabilities of existing solutions although adding complexity and cost to the end users.

The SNE2EE framework has broad applications, meeting security requirements across various sectors:

- Military and Law Enforcement: SNE2EE offers a highly secure communication channel, ensuring the confidentiality and integrity of sensitive operations.
- Industry Applications: Professionals in key sectors, particularly executives, gain protection from eavesdropping and data breaches.
- Individual Users: SNE2EE secures personal communications against malware, social media account takeovers, and financial fraud, fostering trust in digital platforms.

## 4.2 Encrypted Keyboard

Several encrypted keyboard applications, such as Enigma Encryption Keyboard [34] and WhisperKeyboard [35], are available on the Apple App Store and Google Play Store. These applications offer end-to-end encryption and decryption for text messages.

Moving one step further, the solution presented in [13] supports the encryption and decryption of not only text messages but also multimedia content such as images, audio, and video files. Designed as a system keyboard, the encrypted keyboard effectively mitigates the risk of CSS (Content Security System) technologies in many end-to-end encrypted systems. Once enabled as the primary keyboard on a user's phone, it seamlessly functions across all applications requiring user input, ensuring secure communication on every platform within the device. Additionally, the encrypted keyboard incorporates an automated decryption process. This eliminates the need for users to manually copy encrypted text to their phone's clipboard for decryption, as required by other applications. By streamlining this process, their approach reduces user effort and improves ease of use when decoding encrypted messages.

The SNE2EE framework and encrypted keyboard present promising solutions to enhance privacy and security in E2EE systems by mitigating CSS risks. While these innovations address critical concerns, improving usability, performance, and expanding compatibility will further strengthen its effectiveness and adoption.

## 5 Conclusions

E2E encryption is both a salvation and a challenge. It ensures privacy and security for billions but introduces complexities for law enforcement and policymakers. Solutions like SNE2EE offer a pathway to reconcile privacy with security, extending protection to endpoints without compromising functionality. Moving forward, collaboration among stakeholders—governments, technology providers, and privacy advocates—is essential. Only through dialogue and innovative approaches can we address the ethical, technical, and legal dilemmas of E2E encryption.

**Acknowledgments.** The authors would like to acknowledge the financial support provided for the following projects: The 'Collaborative, Multi-modal, and Agile Professional Cybersecurity Training Program for a Skilled Workforce in the European Digital Single Market and Industries' (CyberSecPro) project, which has received funding from the European Union's Digital Europe Programme (DEP) under grant agreement No. 101083594; the 'Human-centered Trustworthiness Optimization in Hybrid Decision Support' (THEMIS 5.0) project, which has received funding from the European Union's Horizon Programme under grant agreement No. 101121042; the 'Advanced Cybersecurity Awareness Ecosystem for SMEs' (NERO) project, which has received funding from the European Union's DEP programme under grant agreement No. 101127411; the 'A Certification approach for dynamic, agile and reUSable assessmenT fOr composite systems of ICT proDucts, servicEs, and processes' (CUSTODES) which has received funding from the European Union's Horizon Programme under grant agreement No. 101120684; the 'Harmonizing People, Processes, and Technology for Robust Cybersecurity' (CyberSynchrony) project, which has received funding from the European Union's Digital Europe Programme (DEP) under grant agreement No. 101158555; and the 'Fostering Artificial Intelligence Trust for Humans towards the Optimization of Trustworthiness through Large-scale Pilots in Critical Domains' (FAITH) project, which has received funding from the European Union's Horizon Programme under grant agreement No. 101135932. The views expressed in this paper represent only the views of the authors and not those of the European Commission or the partners in the above-mentioned projects. Finally, the authors declare that there are no conflicts of interest, including any financial or personal relationships, that could be perceived as potential conflicts.

# References

1. Losing digital trust will harm technological innovation: Here's how to earn it again. https://www.weforum.org/stories/2022/12/losing-digital-trust-will-harm-technological-innovation/
2. Endeley, R.E.: End-to-end Encryption, Backdoors, and Privacy. Capitol Technology University (2019)
3. The fbi wants you to stop texting without encryption. here's why. https://www.nbcboston.com/investigations/consumer/why-the-fbi-wants-you-to-stop-texting-without-encryption-heres-why/3571037/
4. Hartel, P., van Wegberg, R.: Going dark? Analysing the impact of end-to-end encryption on the outcome of dutch criminal court cases. Crime Sci. **12**(1), 5 (2023)
5. Joint declaration of the european police chiefs (2024). Accessed 1 Dec 2024. https://www.europol.europa.eu/media-press/newsroom/news/european-police-chiefs-call-for-industry-and-governments-to-take-action-against-end-to-end-encryption-roll-out
6. Shurson, J.: A European right to end-to-end encryption? Comput. Law Secur. Rev. **55**, 106063 (2024)
7. Sayjari, T., Silveira, R.M.: Ethics of privacy in cybersecurity: Protecting individual autonomy through technology (2024)
8. Kioskli, K., Maglaras, L., Fotis, T., Varouchas, E.: Human factors and strategic approaches in cybersecurity: threats for critical infrastructures in nis2 domains. In: AHFE International Conference on Human Factors in Design, Engineering, and Computing (2025)
9. Evans, M., Maglaras, L.A., He, Y., Janicke, H.: Human behaviour as an aspect of cybersecurity assurance. Secur. Commun. Netw. **9**(17), 4667–4679 (2016)
10. Isobe, T., Ito, R.: Security analysis of end-to-end encryption for zoom meetings. IEEE Access **9**, 90677–90689 (2021)
11. Nabeel, M.: The many faces of end-to-end encryption and their security analysis. In: 2017 IEEE International Conference on Edge Computing (EDGE) , pp. 252–259. IEEE (2017)
12. Maglaras, L., Ayres, N., Moschoyiannis, S., Tassiulas, L.: The end of eavesdropping attacks through the use of advanced end to end encryption mechanisms. In: IEEE INFOCOM 2022-IEEE Conference on Computer Communications Workshops (INFOCOM WKSHPS) , pp. 1–2. IEEE (2022)
13. Alatawi, M., Saxena, N.: Exploring encrypted keyboards to defeat client-side scanning in end-to-end encryption systems. In: International Conference on Information Security and Cryptology, pp. 100–123. Springer, Heidelberg (2022)

14. Babaghayou, M., Chaib, N., Lagraa, N., Ferrag, M.A., Maglaras, L.: A safetyaware location privacy-preserving iov scheme with road congestion-estimation in mobile edge computing. Sensors 23(1), 531 (2023)

15. Ullah, I., Shah, M.A.: SGO: semantic group obfuscation for location-based services in vanets. Sensors 24(4), 1145 (2024)

16. Rad, P., Dorai, G., Jozani, M.: From seaweed to security: harnessing alginate to challenge iot fingerprint authentication. In: Proceedings of the 19th International Conference on Availability, Reliability and Security, pp. 1–10 (2024)

17. Wagner, I.: Privacy policies across the ages: content of privacy policies 1996–2021. ACM Trans. Priv. Secur. 26(3), 1–32 (2023)

18. Englehardt, S., et al.: Cookies that give you away: the surveillance implications of web tracking. In: Proceedings of the 24th International Conference on World Wide Web, pp. 289–299 (2015)

19. Zard, L.: Consumer manipulation via online behavioral advertising. arXiv preprint arXiv: 2401.00205 (2023)

20. Naef, T.: Data protection without data protectionism: the right to protection of personal data and data transfers in EU law and international trade law. Springer, Heidelberg (2023)

21. Hamza, R., Pradana, H.: A survey of intellectual property rights protection in big data applications. Algorithms 15(11), 418 (2022)

22. Chowdhury, P.D., et al.: Threat models over space and time: a case study of e2ee messaging applications. arXiv preprint arXiv:2301.05653 (2023)

23. Enisa threat landscape. https://www.enisa.europa.eu/publications/enisa-threat-landscape-2024

24. Gibson, C., et al.: Analyzing the monetization ecosystem of stalkerware. In: Proceedings on Privacy Enhancing Technologies (2022)

25. Nobles, C.: Stress, burnout, and security fatigue in cybersecurity: a human factors problem. Holistica–J. Bus. Public Administ. 13, 49–72 (2022)

26. Karayel, T., Aktaş, B., Akbıyık, A.: Human factors in remote work: examining cyber hygiene practices Inf. Comput. Secur. (2024)

27. Abelson, H., et al.: Bugs in our pockets: the risks of client-side scanning. J. Cybersecur. 10(1), tyad020 (2024)

28. Scholten, T.L., et al.: Assessing the benefits and risks of quantum computers. arXiv preprint arXiv:2401.16317 (2024)

29. Banks, M.: Nist publishes new encryption standards. Phys. World 37(9), 11iii–11iii (2024). https://doi.org/10.1088/2058-7058/37/09/13

30. Aydeger, A., Zeydan, E., Yadav, A.K., Hemachandra, K.T., Liyanage, M.: Towards a quantum-resilient future: strategies for transitioning to post-quantum cryptography. In: 2024 15th International Conference on Network of the Future (NoF), pp. 195–203. IEEE (2024)

31. Stoykova, R.: Encrochat: the hacker with a warrant and fair trials? Forensic Sci. Int. Dig. Invest. 46, 301602 (2023)

32. Velagala, N., Maglaras, L., Ayres, N., Moschoyiannis, S., Tassiulas, L.: Enhancing privacy of online chat apps utilising secure node end-to-end encryption (sne2ee). In: 2022 IEEE Symposium on Computers and Communications (ISCC), pp. 1–3. IEEE (2022)

33. Alsop, H., et al.: Arsecure: a novel end-to-end encryption messaging system using augmented reality. arXiv preprint arXiv:2409.04457 (2024)

34. Enigma encryption keyboard (2022). https://apps.apple.com/us/app/enigma-encryption-key board/id971945391?platform=iphone

35. Whisperkeyboard (2022). https://play.google.com/store/apps/details?id=cn.security.kbs hrimp

# Optimizing Human-Autonomy Interaction: A Proposed Methodology

Christopher Myers[1]($\boxtimes$) , Margaret Ugolini[2] , and Taylor Curley[1]

[1] Air Force Research Laboratory, Wright-Patterson Air Force Base, OH 45422, USA
{christopher.myers.29,taylor.curley}@us.af.mil
[2] BAE Systems, Inc., Space and Mission Systems, Dayton, OH 45435, USA
margaret.ugolini.ctr@us.af.mil

**Abstract.** Systems are currently available across a range of autonomy levels, though many may never be fully autonomous (i.e., Level 5, Society of Automotive Engineers International). Consequently, autonomous systems will require human supervisory control & resource management, further requiring designed artifacts for interaction. Connecting human operator input to discrete operations used by autonomous systems enables levels of automation that allow for cooperation and performance augmentation [23,24] and can facilitate analyses to improve operator efficiency (e.g., [12]). Here, we introduce methods for characterizing complex, goal-driven behavior and determining critical paths that optimize interactions between human operators and artifacts for the supervisory control of autonomous systems. We propose applying cognitive task analyses (CTA) and task activity networks to discretize sequential behavior and conditional generative modeling [2,15] to identify and evaluate critical paths to offer potential improvements to human-autonomy interactions.

**Keywords:** human-autonomy teaming · interaction optimization · methodology · cognitive task analysis · critical path analysis

## 1 Introduction

Autonomous systems have been promised to make our lives easier and safer. Potential benefits range from home robotics to manual labor to the battlefield, with ethical concerns across the lot [3,10,13]. The Society of Automotive Engineers International introduced automation levels ranging from Level 1 requiring driver assistance (e.g., cruise control) to Level 5 describing full automation under all conditions. The United States Air Force (USAF) is researching and developing autonomous collaborative platforms (ACPs) that are approaching Level 3 automation: ACPs may pilot themselves under certain conditions with continuous human oversight [5]. Different mission areas and tasks are likely to benefit from a range of autonomy levels, and all ACPs within levels 1–4 will require varying degrees of human supervisory control and resource management.

© The Author(s), under exclusive license to Springer Nature Switzerland AG 2025
D. D. Schmorrow and C. M. Fidopiastis (Eds.): HCII 2025, LNAI 15778, pp. 140–151, 2025.
https://doi.org/10.1007/978-3-031-93724-8_11

## 1.1   A Brief Overview of Human Supervisory Control

Human supervisory control of automated systems has a long history, including research on human control of aircraft, nuclear reactors, factory automation, and most recently robots and self-driving automobiles [32,33]. In its simplest form, supervisory control refers to the management required of a system minimally composed of an overseer who monitors the state and performance of a subsystem, or subsystems. The overseer provides commands to subsystems to maintain their performance, remain within boundary conditions, manage resources, etc. In turn, the subsystem(s) executes the commands and reports detailed results to the overseer through speech, iconography, text, changes in metrics, or some other means [33].

Supervisory control failures occur through constraints and limitations in the subsystems being managed, within the overseer managing the systems, and the modes available for commanding changes and receiving feedback to and from the subsystems. As the number of subsystems an overseer manages increases, the overseer's cognitive load may also increase. If the load increases too much too fast, the likelihood of a subsystem failure increases due to minimized oversight, lag in providing needed commands, and insufficient situation awareness [8].

The complexity of interfaces for commanding and managing autonomous systems is likely to increase with increasing task complexity, level of autonomy, and the number of subsystems monitored, commanded, and managed by an individual. Increasing interface complexity is known to contribute to poorer supervisory control and resource management [9,33]. Additionally, operating in an adversarial environment under time pressure will further erode the ability of overseers to successfully command and manage multiple autonomous assets. To successfully command and manage multiple autonomous systems, interfaces must be designed and implemented that minimize the potential for error, reduce the times to encode new feedback, and facilitate the provision of new commands.

## 1.2   Evaluating Interactive Behavior During Supervisory Control

Human supervisory control requires some interface to command subsystems and receive their feedback. There is a long history of evaluating human-computer interfaces and their impact on operator performance [28,31]. Poorly designed interfaces can produce financially costly delays [12], voting errors [18], or even loss of life [21]. To understand how an interface design impacts human supervisory control, the systems under control, the tasks they are assigned, and the overseers' capabilities and constraints must all be considered (see Fig. 1). If only considering the systems under control and the task(s) they perform, system design may lead to human error. If only considering the systems under control and the overseer, tasks and subtasks may not be covered appropriately. If only considering the overseer and tasks/subtasks, constraints of the systems/subsystems under control may not be thoroughly considered.

In this paper, a methodological approach toward optimizing operator-autonomous system interactions is presented in the context of managing multiple

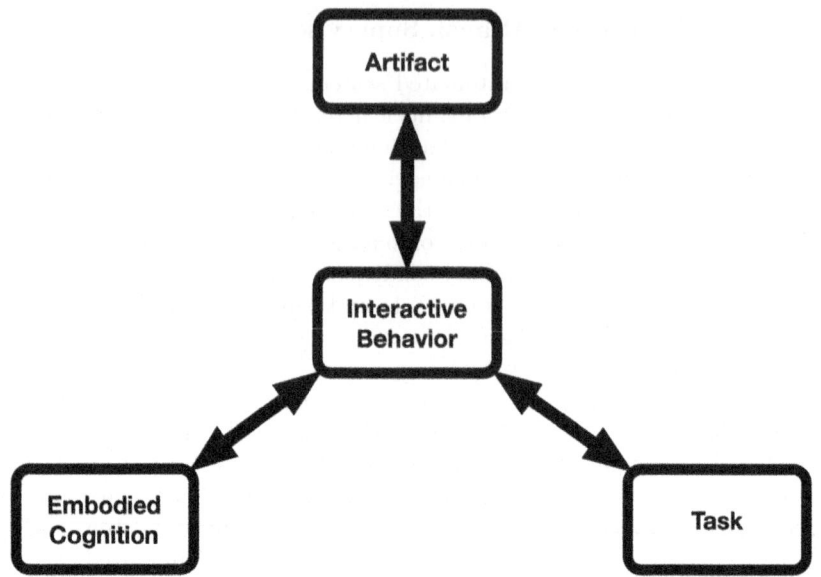

**Fig. 1.** Interactive behavior is a complex interaction between a *task* that must be completed using a specific *artifact* with task-relevant commands to the artifact provided by humans through *embodied cognition* (Figure adapted from Gray, 1993 [12]).

aerial autonomous collaborative platforms (ACPs). In the following sections, an example use case is presented followed by the proposed methodology for evaluating and optimizing the supervisory control of ACPs.

## 2   Use Case: Pilot-ACP Mission

A simulation of ACP supervisory control while piloting one's own ship serves as our use case for our methodological approach. The overall goal of the task is to quickly and effectively use the ACPs to eliminate multiple ground targets before being detected by enemy radars. This section provides a brief description of the experimental task and conditions.

### 2.1   Autonomous Collaborative Platform Supervisory Control Experiment Overview

Participants were trained to manage and task a team of ACPs to complete two missions. Each mission was one of two different ACP team compositions: homogenous or heterogeneous. In the homogenous condition, all four ACPs were identically equipped and could address all mission requirements at mission start. In the heterogeneous condition, ACPs differed in their starting weapon availability, type, and fuel amounts. Two ACPs were equipped with weapons appropriate for engaging SAM sites and air threats, one with low fuel levels and a higher number of rounds and one with higher fuel levels and a lower number of rounds. Two ACPs were equipped with weapons appropriate for engaging moving ground targets, again one with low fuel levels and a higher number of rounds and one with higher fuel levels and a lower number of rounds.

All participants completed both missions in a counterbalanced order. Timing and nature of control inputs were recorded for performance analyses and input to aspects of our methodology (e.g., response time distributions). Key metrics of interest include ACP selection (i.e., was it the best choice given current mission conditions?), mission completion (e.g., were targets eliminated and non-targets spared?), and ability to use the interface to quickly and accurately task ACPs. Participants were also asked to self-report subjective workload (NASA TLX [14]), decision-making strategy, and perceived effectiveness. All participants provided informed consent prior to their inclusion in the study. The research was conducted in accordance with all applicable ethical guidelines and regulations for human subjects research to ensure the privacy and well-being of all participants.

### 2.2 Isomorph of Autonomous Collaborative Platform Supervisory Control Task

A pizza delivery task was developed to serve as an isomorph for the ACP supervisory control task. This task allows for data collection from the general population, as opposed to the specialized population with military aircraft experience that is required for the ACP task. It also serves as an example of the demands that may be placed on an operator during ACP supervisory control without all of the sensitive details that may exist in the original task.

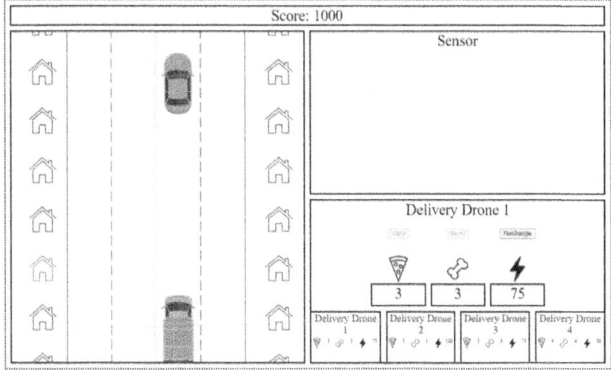

**Fig. 2.** Example of the Pizza Delivery experimental task.

In the Pizza Delivery task, participants' main objective is to deliver pizzas to the houses that require them (Fig. 2). They must complete this objective while avoiding dog attacks and navigating their own ship - a delivery van - down a simulated 2-dimensional road with oncoming and same-direction traffic. Just as the ACP task, the participant's own ship is required to traverse a predetermined route while autonomous teammates complete the mission's subtasks. These teammates - autonomous pizza delivery drones - are equipped with various resources: pizzas, dog bones, and energy, and a sensor capability. Along the route, red houses requiring a pizza delivery are encountered. Operators must dispatch a delivery drone to use its sensors to view the house to determine its needs and the presence or absence of a dog. Operators must then select the delivery drone that has the appropriate resources to meet the needs of the house and send it to complete the task. Across the task, participants must monitor the route and their own ship to prevent collisions with other traffic as well as monitor the amount of energy the drones consume as they maneuver.

## 3   Methodological Approach

The methodological goals are to (a) identify the potential for failure during Pilot-ACP missions, (b) specify system improvements to avoid failure, and (c) identify opportunities to optimize performance. To achieve these goals, we use data collected through empirical testing and analytical methods useful for structuring and discretizing cognitive tasks to inform structured computational modeling methods that quantify the behavioral policies used during the experimental task. We note that while our optimization methodology was originally developed for an application that is specific to the military, we expect that our method should generalize to civilian contexts or other industries. The methodology rests on the ability to distill a task into a hierarchical cognitive task analysis, collect detailed behavioral outcomes from that task, and use generative models to estimate critical behavior paths through the task problem space [22] from the discretized data. We expect the feasibility of this to be relatively similar across domains, enabling us to present our method using an experimental task with no direct connections to military scenarios, described in the sections below.

### 3.1   Analytical Methods

Clear analytic techniques are needed to elucidate the cognitive elements that moderate task outcomes. Cognitive task analyses (CTAs) are recommended to provide a descriptive structure of tasks and subtasks of interest and to identify which cognitive capacities are required to accomplish the tasks/subtasks. Results from CTAs can then be implemented in modeling and simulation formalisms [26, for example] to provide quantitative analyses to compliment the descriptive analyses provided by CTAs.

**Cognitive Task Analysis.** The cognitive task analysis (CTA) is one such method that improves upon classic task analysis techniques [17] through a heightened focus on memory, decision-making, vigilance, and other cognitive abilities that underlie complex tasks [7]. CTA is an iterative method for generating sequential task models that describe cognitive operations with increasing specificity in lower levels of the hierarchy. CTA leverages interviews with subject matter experts (SMEs) that focus on cognitive strategy. Practitioners developing CTAs construct a hierarchical representation of the task that explicate the sequence and types of skills needed to complete subtasks. A fully realized CTA of the Pilot-ACP mission and its pizza delivery isomorph have been specified so that motor, perceptual, and cognitive operations can be analyzed using formal modeling approaches.

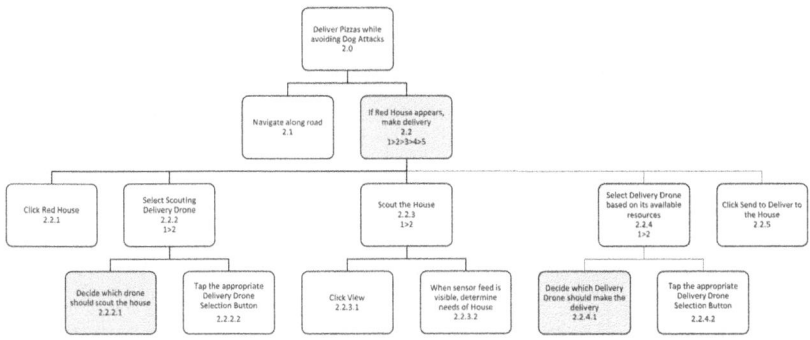

**Fig. 3.** Example of a subtask within a hierarchical cognitive task analysis (CTA) of the ACP task analogue.

An example of a CTA using the ACP task analogue ("Pizza Delivery") is given in Fig. 3. Here, a subtask ("Deliver Pizzas while avoiding Dog Attacks") comprised of smaller subtasks necessary to complete an action given by the overall goal is nested under a larger task ("Deliver Pizzas to Houses that have ordered"). The numbering of the tasks and subtasks (e.g., 2.0) indicates ordinal position in the overall task breakdown. Successively lower subtasks in the hierarchy increase in specificity, ending with explicit behaviors relevant to the ACP Task Analogue, such as reading a sensor feed of the house where a pizza is to be delivered (2.2.3.2). The full CTA explicates the hierarchical relationships of actions starting from initialization to completion of the task; in this case, the successful delivery of a pizza.

**Analytic Modeling.** While the CTA provides a comprehensive examination of a complex task, it remains descriptive, and additional tools are needed to derive results-based recommendations to improving human-autonomy interactions. We have translated the Pilot-ACP CTA into a series of process models using task activity network software developed by the USAF called the Advanced Mission Toolkit (AMT). In AMT, task components are represented by nodes placed in "pools" which can be subdivided into "swim lanes". Task components can be grouped together into compound activities and are connected using flow objects that specify directionality between any two objects. Branching behavior (e.g., choosing between multiple alternatives) is simulated using gateways that represent conditional statements. A resulting task model is then used to conduct critical path analyses [26] that identify potential issues and opportunities for process optimization (Fig. 4).

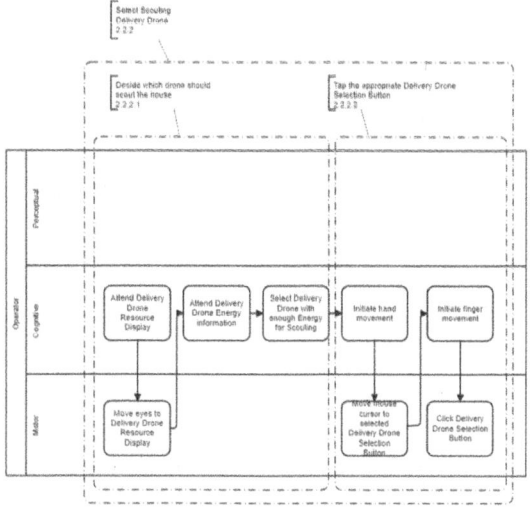

**Fig. 4.** Example of analytic modeling using the Advanced Mission Toolkit (AMT).

In our process model, the operator or experiment participant is represented as a pool containing swim lanes. These swim lanes are used to subdivide events belonging to Perceptual, Cognitive, and Motor levels of processing. The actions required to complete the task are then modeled using events distributed across these lanes, allowing us to explicitly model the task process at high level of detail. This Perceptual, Cognitive, Motor model organization is inspired by classic approaches in the modeling of human behavior, such as Project Ernestine [12] and other uses of the GOMS (Goals, Operators, Methods) framework [11,16,25]. This structure allows us to take a specific stance about how various events in the task are handled by a human operator—for example, whether information must be accessed via the perceptual system before allocating selective attention to its location or if the information's location can be recalled without requiring perceptual events.

## 3.2   Simulation Methods

The final elements of our methodology provide a means for understanding idiosyncratic behavior from the behaviors observed during the experimental tasks. We discuss two approaches: A deep learning method that uses diffusion modeling to estimate behavior trajectories using the observed data and more traditional method that characterizes the mechanisms underlying behavior using cognitive modeling.

**Conditional Generative Modeling.** A large number of disciplines—particularly within the field of robotics—have devoted efforts to recovering behavioral trajectories from data observed from operational systems [6]. Regimes for learning optimal paths from observed data (or *offline decision-making*) require careful specification of mappings between possible states and possible actions (*policy*) and a mechanism for providing objective feedback from an environment (*reward function*) [36]. Popular offline reinforcement learning (RL) algorithms, such as Q-learning [38], have well-specified reward functions and are often successful in recovering high-performing policies, but are often hampered by difficulties related to continuous updating of long term, time-discounted rewards when transiting across states in a given sequential policy, i.e., the *value function* [20,36]. Specifically, offline RL algorithms are tethered to the policies observed in the static datasets that they are trained on and have difficulties answering counterfactual queries. This is a particularly salient issue when the state space is large and when there are limits to the size of the training data set. These complications are relevant for the current study, where there are a large number of possible choices at any given time (even in a constrained experimental environment) and a small number of pilots qualified to participate in the task. Thus, a learning algorithm without the difficulties associated with values functions in offline RL is needed to effectively estimate behavioral policies in the Pilot ACP task (Fig. 5).

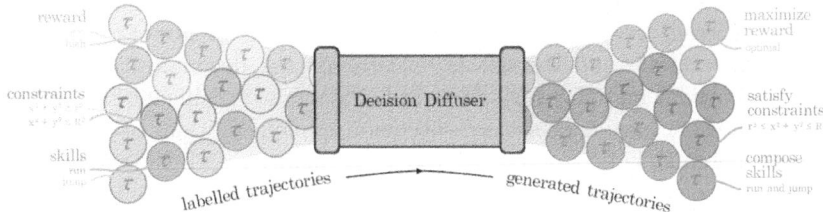

**Fig. 5.** Conditional generative model [15]. Figure adapted from [2].

To help resolve these issues, we propose the use of a generative, state-sequence based diffusion probabilistic model [2]. Briefly, the diffusion model employs forward and reverse diffusion methods: The former converts the conditional data distribution into a form that is analytically tractable (i.e., "forward noising") while the latter generates samples by iteratively restoring (i.e., "reverse denoising") the structure of the data [2,34]. Put another way, the decision diffuser generates behavior trajectories $x_0(\tau)$ across discrete time steps $k$ from information $y(\tau)$ gleaned from the estimated conditional data distribution:

$$q(x_{k+1}(\tau)|x_k(\tau)), \qquad p_\theta(x_{k-1}(\tau), y(\tau)), \tag{1}$$

where $q$ is the forward noising process, $p_\theta$ is the reverse denoising process, $y(\tau)$ is a set of constraints guiding the trajectory, and $x_k(\tau)$ is a noisy sequence of states $s$ in a given trajectory of length $H$ with discrete times steps $t$:

$$x_k(\tau) := (s_t, s_{t+1}, \cdots, s_{t+H-1})_k. \tag{2}$$

Given these values from the offline data, the model can generate an action $a_t$ on the basis of two consecutive states $s$ using the inverse dynamics model [1]:

$$a_t := f_\phi(s_t, s_{t+1}). \tag{3}$$

In short, the model observes a state in a given dataset (e.g., Pizza Delivery task performance; Fig. 3), samples different trajectories and states in the future (e.g., *Navigate along road* [2.1] vs. *Make delivery* [2.2]) based on a conditional dataset, and identifies the action that should be taken by diffusing across potential states and actions. While this application of conditional generative modeling is new, it has successfully mapped complex behavioral policies in both robots [2] and humans [27].

**Cognitive Modeling.** In our cognitive modeling approach, we imbue the AMT models with probabilistic mechanisms that capture differences in latency and decision-making between individuals. These mechanisms can be as simple as a single probability at a conditional gateway to something as complicated as accumulation of evidence towards a decision criterion, e.g., sequential sampling [4,29,30]. The inclusion of individual differences facilitates the Pilot-ACP evaluation for different levels of skill (e.g., training) and the impact of physiological insults (e.g., fatigue), and the use of structured task decompositions (CTAs) provide a means for mapping task-relevant behaviors to specific models of cognition. Indeed, there have been several successful implementations of this method using a unified model of cognition [19] to model cognitive and physiological indicators of workload in unmanned vehicle management tasks [35] and individual differences in skill acquisition in air traffic control tasks [37], among others.

## 4   Next Steps

The next steps are threefold. First, we must refine the Pilot-ACP analytical model. Next, we must perform a critical path analysis to identify opportunities for Pilot-ACP optimization. Finally, we leverage empirical response times from our study to inform idiosyncratic behaviors' effects on the critical path analyses.

Both of our example use-cases rely on a simulated supervisory control task, as opposed to real-world operations. However, there is no reason to assume that our methodology would be inapplicable to a live operational environment, provided that high-fidelity behavioral data could be recorded. An important next step in developing our methodology will be to test its applicability across a wide range of tasks, including ones that go beyond simulated environments.

**Acknowledgments.** The opinions expressed herein are solely those of the authors and do not represent the official positions of the United States Government, the U.S. Department of Defense, the U.S. Air Force, or any of their subsidiaries or employees, or the United States Air Force. Distribution A. Approved for public release. Case number AFRL-2025-0295.

**Disclosure of Interests.** The authors declare that the research was conducted in the absence of any commercial or financial relationships that could be construed as potential conflicts of interest. The reported study was approved by the Institutional Review Board at the Air Force Research Laboratory under protocol number FWR20240083H.

# References

1. Agrawal, P., Nair, A.V., Abbeel, P., Malik, J., Levine, S.: Learning to poke by poking: experiential learning of intuitive physics. In: Lee, D., Sugiyama, M., Luxburg, U., Guyon, I., Garnett, R. (eds.) Advances in Neural Information Processing Systems, vol. 29. Curran Associates, Inc. (2016)
2. Ajay, A., Du, Y., Gupta, A., Tenenbaum, J., Jaakkola, T., Agrawal, P.: Is conditional generative modeling all you need for decision-making? arXiv preprint arXiv:2211.15657 (2022)
3. Arkin, R.C.: Ethics and autonomous systems: perils and promises [point of view]. Proc. IEEE **104**(10), 1779–1781 (2016). https://doi.org/10.1109/JPROC.2016. 2601162
4. Brown, S.D., Heathcote, A.: The simplest complete model of choice response time: linear ballistic accumulation. Cogn. Psychol. **57**(3), 153–178 (2008). https://doi. org/10.1016/j.cogpsych.2007.12.002
5. Castrejon, A.M.: Afrl's xq-67a makes 1st successful flight (2024). https://www. af.mil/News/Article-Display/Article/3694599/afrls-xq-67a-makes-1st-successful-flight/
6. Chi, C., et al.: Diffusion policy: visuomotor policy learning via action diffusion. Int. J. Robot. Res. (2024). https://doi.org/10.1177/02783649241273668
7. Clark, R.E., Feldon, D.F., Van Merrienboer, J.J., Yates, K.A., Early, S.: Cognitive task analysis. In: Jonassen, D., Spector, M.J., Driscoll, M., Merrill, M.D., van Merrienboer, J., Driscoll, M.P. (eds.) Handbook of Research on Educational Communications and Technology, 3 edn., pp. 577–593. Routledge (2008)
8. Endsley, M.: Toward a theory of situation awarenss in dynamic systems. Hum. Factors **37**, 32–64 (1995). https://doi.org/10.1518/001872095779049543
9. Engström, J., Markkula, G., Victor, T., Merat, N.: Effects of cognitive load on driving performance: the cognitive control hypothesis. Hum. Factors **59**(5), 734–764 (2017). https://doi.org/10.1177/0018720817690639

10. Fossaceca, J.M.: Delivering on the promise of autonomous agents in the battle-field. In: Solomon, L., Schwartz, P.J. (eds.) Artificial Intelligence and Machine Learning for Multi-Domain Operations Applications, vol. 12538, p. 1253816. International Society for Optics and Photonics, SPIE (2023). https://doi.org/10.1117/12.2663186
11. Gray, W.D., Boehm-Davis, D.A.: Milliseconds matter: an introduction to micro-strategies and to their use in describing and predicting interactive behavior. J. Exp. Psychol. Appl. **6**(4), 322–335 (2000). https://doi.org/10.1037/1076-898X.6.4.322
12. Gray, W.D., John, B.E., Atwood, M.E.: Project Ernestine: validating a GOMS analysis for predicting and explaining real-world task performance. Hum.-Comput. Interact. **8**(3), 237–309 (1993). https://doi.org/10.1207/s15327051hci0803_3
13. Hancock, P.A.: Some pitfalls in the promises of automated and autonomous vehicles. Ergonomics **62**(4), 479–495 (2019). https://doi.org/10.1080/00140139.2018.1498136
14. Hart, S.G.: NASA-task load index (NASA-TLX); 20 years later. In: Proceedings of the Human Factors and Ergonomics Society Annual Meeting. vol. 50, pp. 904–908. Sage publications Sage CA: Los Angeles, CA (2006). https://doi.org/10.1177/154193120605000090
15. Ho, J., Jain, A., Abbeel, P.: Denoising diffusion probabilistic models. In: Larochelle, H., Ranzato, M., Hadsell, R., Balcan, M., Lin, H. (eds.) Advances in Neural Information Processing Systems, vol. 33, pp. 6840–6851. Curran Associates, Inc. (2020)
16. John, B.E.: Extensions of GOMS analyses to expert performance requiring perception of dynamic visual and auditory information. In: Proceedings of the SIGCHI Conference on Human Factors in Computing Systems, pp. 107–116 (1990)
17. Kirwan, B., Ainsworth, L.K.: A Guide to Task Analysis. CRC Press (1992). https://doi.org/10.1201/b16826
18. Kortum, P., Byrne, M.D.: The importance of psychological science in a voter's ability to cast a vote. Curr. Directions Psychol. Sci. **25** (2016). https://doi.org/10.1177/0963721416665104
19. Laird, J.E., Lebiere, C., Rosenbloom, P.S.: A standard model of the mind: toward a common computational framework across artificial intelligence, cognitive science, neuroscience, and robotics. AI Mag. **38**(4), 13–26 (2017). https://doi.org/10.1609/aimag.v38i4.2744
20. Levine, S., Kumar, A., Tucker, G., Fu, J.: Offline reinforcement learning: tutorial, review, and perspectives on open problems. arXiv preprint arXiv:2005.01643 (2020)
21. Mumaw, R.J.: Not automation failures, but automation interface failures. J. Cogn. Eng. Decis. Making 15553434241228796 (2024). https://doi.org/10.1177/15553434241228796
22. Newell, A.: Human Problem Solving. Prentice Hall, Upper Saddle River (1972)
23. O'Neill, T., McNeese, N., Barron, A., Schelble, B.: Human-autonomy teaming: a review and analysis of the empirical literature. Hum. Factors **64**(5), 904–938 (2022). https://doi.org/10.1177/001872082096086
24. Parasuraman, R., Sheridan, T.B., Wickens, C.D.: A model for types and levels of human interaction with automation. IEEE Trans. Syst. Man Cybern. - Part A: Syst. Hum. **30**(3), 286–297 (2000). https://doi.org/10.1109/3468.844354
25. Park, J., Wozniak, D., Zahabi, M.: Modeling novice law enforcement officers' interaction with in-vehicle technology. Appl. Ergon. **114**, 104154 (2024). https://doi.org/10.1016/j.apergo.2023.104154
26. Patton, E.W., Gray, W.D.: SANLab-CM: a tool for incorporating stochastic operations into activity network modeling. Behav. Res. Methods **42**(3), 877–883 (2010). https://doi.org/10.3758/BRM.42.3.877

27. Pearce, T., et al.: Imitating human behaviour with diffusion models. arXiv preprint arXiv:2301.10677 (2023)
28. Pütz, S., Mertens, A., Chuang, L.L., Nitsch, V.: Physiological predictors of operator performance: the role of mental effort and its link to task performance. Hum. Factors 00187208241296830 (2024). https://doi.org/10.1177/00187208241296830
29. Ratcliff, R.: A theory of memory retrieval. Psychol. Rev. **85**(2), 59–108 (1978). https://doi.org/10.1037/0033-295X.85.2.59
30. Ratcliff, R., Smith, P.L., Brown, S.D., McKoon, G.: Diffusion decision model: current issues and history. Trends Cogn. Sci. **20**(4), 260–281 (2016). https://doi.org/10.1016/j.tics.2016.01.007
31. Rouse, W.B.: Human-computer interaction in multitask situations. IEEE Trans. Syst. Man Cybern. **7** (1977). https://doi.org/10.1109/TSMC.1977.4309727
32. Sheridan, T.B.: Human Supervisory Control, chap. 34, pp. 990–1015. Wiley (2012). https://doi.org/10.1002/9781118131350.ch34
33. Sheridan, T.B.: Human Supervisory Control of Automation, chap. 28, pp. 736–760. Wiley (2021). https://doi.org/10.1002/9781119636113.ch28
34. Sohl-Dickstein, J., Weiss, E., Maheswaranathan, N., Ganguli, S.: Deep unsupervised learning using nonequilibrium thermodynamics. In: Bach, F., Blei, D. (eds.) Proceedings of the 32nd International Conference on Machine Learning. Proceedings of Machine Learning Research, vol. 37, pp. 2256–2265. PMLR, Lille, France (2015)
35. Stevens, C.A., Morris, M.B., Fisher, C.R., Myers, C.W.: Profiling cognitive workload in an unmanned vehicle control task with cognitive models and physiological metrics. Mil. Psychol. **35**(6), 507–520 (2023). https://doi.org/10.1080/08995605.2022.2130673
36. Sutton, R.S., Barto, A.G.: Reinforcement Learning: An Introduction. A Bradford Book, Cambridge (2018)
37. Taatgen, N.A.: A model of individual differences in skill acquisition in the Kanfer-Ackerman air traffic control task. Cogn. Syst. Res. **3**(1), 103–112 (2002). https://doi.org/10.1016/S1389-0417(01)00049-3
38. Watkins, C.J., Dayan, P.: Q-learning. Mach. Learn. **8**, 279–292 (1992). https://doi.org/10.1007/BF00992698

# Translation by Design: Framework for Digital Health Research Progression from Design to Implementation

Blaine Reeder[1,2](✉) and Gerard Castaneda[1]

[1] Sinclair School of Nursing, University of Missouri, Columbia, MO, USA
{blaine.reeder,gerard.castaneda}@missouri.edu
[2] MU Institute for Data Science and Informatics, University of Missouri, Columbia, MO, USA

**Abstract.** An average of seventeen years elapses before health intervention research translates from laboratories to real-world settings where benefits can be realized by the people for which they were designed, if such translation even occurs at all. Digital health interventions face additional barriers beyond those of traditional health intervention research. These barriers result from the additional complexity of digital health research given the nature of rapidly changing software, technologies, and systems upon which it relies and that must be integrated and tested at every research stage. However, there are few guiding resources for the systematic planning and development of digital health interventions from earliest project ideation to translation of effective interventions in real-world implementations. To close this gap, the goal of this report is to: 1) identify specific barriers to digital health research translation, 2) describe the Translation By Design (TBD) framework for digital health research, and 3) highlight a progression of proposed studies that completes with a translated real-world implementation based on a use case for an Augmented Cognition digital health intervention that supports informal caregivers of older adults at risk for falls.

**Keywords:** digital health · translational research · human-centered design · health informatics · sensors

## 1  Introduction

### 1.1  Translational Research

Translational research as a discipline evaluates the journey from basic science to how research findings can enhance the lives of people in everyday life [1]. Reports show that it takes an average of seventeen years, from the earliest studies of potentially viable interventions, before they are implemented in clinical or community settings, if such research ever translates at all [2, 3]. Fundamentally, two translational blocks span across the research continuum which includes translating: (T1) basic science to human studies and (T2) new knowledge into real-world settings to inform health decision making [4]. The T1 translation block must address issues related to recruitment, regulations, and

D. D. Schmorrow and C. M. Fidopiastis (Eds.): HCII 2025, LNAI 15778, pp. 152–165, 2025.
https://doi.org/10.1007/978-3-031-93724-8_12

addressing scientific unknowns whereas T2 must address issues that relate to people and organizational systems [5]. A 2022 scoping review on translational research in health technologies highlighted the need to extend past basic and applied application of knowledge and also considers the integration of technology in specific real-world settings [6].

Barriers to Digital Health Research Translation. Digital health innovation and translation is inherently challenging given two conflicting forces: the rapid pace of technology change and the slow pace of academic research environments. As we have previously noted, rapid technology change can outstrip the slow pace of academic research environments such that positioning potential devices for use in digital health studies can outlive the availability of those technologies.[7] Slow pace is not the only characteristic of academic research environments that creates barriers to digital health research translation.

Another characteristic is lack of persistent technical support for technologies that are known to work in the face of the variable cycles of sponsored funding typical of academic research. This means that once an investigator has demonstrated an internet-enabled technology has potential for use in digital health research, there are typically few options to maintain persistent access to that technology and its features, particularly for non-technical researchers. For example, there is little market incentive for industry service providers to develop services to support digital health interventions that may take years or decades to translate, if they do at all. Thus, web- and cloud-based service providers target industry technology and software vendors with costly services that are beyond the reach of unfunded researchers. Unfortunately, university IT-cost centers provide services using similar models that charge routine fees to investigators during periods of research funding; these services become unavailable when sponsored research funding runs out.

Directly related to lack of persistent technical support is lack of unified, investigator-controlled research management tools. When working with multiple disparate technologies or devices, there are few tools that facilitate the integration, configuration and management of technologies to form a digital health intervention. The same is true for the capture, access, control, and analysis of data from multiple technologies to inform understanding and decision-making. Again, this lack of research management tools is, in part, due to, and compounded by, inconsistent research funding from academic grant cycles. Ultimately, these barriers to digital health research result in loss of momentum to investigators and their research trajectories, wasted time, wasted public and private research funding, and perpetuation of health deficits for preventable problems.

Digital health research faces additional barriers to timely translation beyond that of "traditional" clinical research given the nature of the software and technologies upon which it relies. These barriers contribute to fragmented research efforts. There is a need for a systematic approach to plan the generation of evidence, that acts in conjunction with efforts to overcome these barriers, that can decrease the time develop, test, and translate digital health research. We articulate the Translation By Design framework with research stages, describe some of our organizational efforts to overcome digital health research barriers as they relate to TBD, provide selected articles from the public health literature that illustrate TBD research stages, and describe a use case for a proposed augmented cognition digital health intervention for older adult-family care dyads with a planned progression of studies that concludes with translation of the digital health research.

## 2   Background

### 2.1   Translation by Design

*Translation by Design* (TBD) is an approach to conduct research for digital health solutions tailored to specific needs of individuals and populations to facilitate translation and sustainability of research products in real-world settings. As such, TBD specifies a real-world implementation goal from project outset, attempts identify requirements for translation and sustainability on an ongoing basis, and intentionally designs to meet identified requirements. For example, *cost feasibility* is an important factor in digital health solutions if targeting older adults who live at low socio-economic levels. Accounting for cost feasibility with regard to technologies that underpin digital health research will ensure that research that demonstrates benefit after testing in clinical or pragmatic trials is ready to translate to the intended population and/or be financially supported by health payers.

Translation by Design relies on suggested sequence of iterative research stages adapted from a progression of informatics study types [8], research organization components (such as labs and teams), and adaptive support models (for example: non-profit organization support) to overcome known research barriers to digital health research. This suggested linear sequence of research stages is intended to be non-binding, with the understanding that some studies may incorporate elements of different stages concurrently, and that iteration between stages is to be expected in the emergent conditions typical of applied research. Of particular note, usability considerations and testing should start early in the research process and continue throughout and into adaptation and translation of mature digital health solutions.

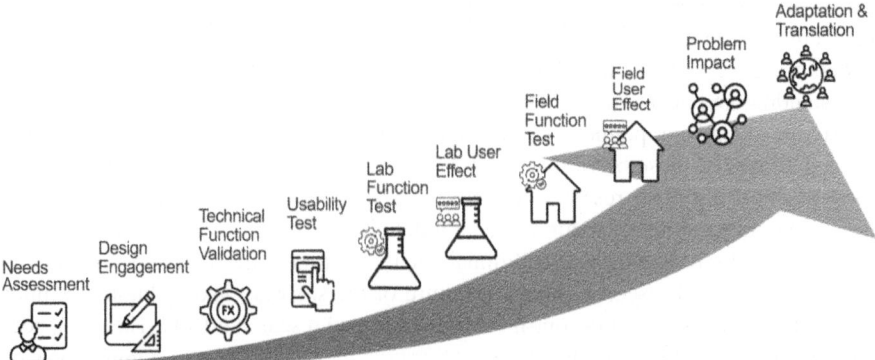

**Fig. 1.** Optimized progression of Translation by Design (TBD) research stages and study types

Figure 1 shows the suggested sequence of TBD research stages to design, develop, evaluation and implement for digital health solutions. Table 1 shows the TBD research stages or study type with broad questions or goals.

**Table 1.** Translation By Design research stages with broad questions or goals

| Stage (Study Type)[1] | Broad Question or Goal |
|---|---|
| Needs Assessment | What is the motivating real-world problem? |
| Design Engagement | What are the information needs and requirements of intended target users? |
| Technical Function Validation | Does the digital health prototype work as designed in controlled conditions? |
| Usability[2] | Can the target users understand and use the digital health resource? |
| Lab Function Test | Does the digital health prototype show potential benefit in participant lab testing? |
| Lab User Effect | Does the digital health prototype show potential for intended behavior change in the lab? |
| Field Function Test | Does the digital health prototype show benefit in real-world testing? |
| Field User Effect | Does the digital health prototype change behavior as intended in the real world? |
| Problem Impact | Does the digital health resource have intended impact on the real-world problem? |
| Adaption/ Translation | Can the digital health resource adapt and translate to different contexts & populations? |

[1]Research stages are iterative and typically need to be revisited during conduct of longitudinal efforts

[2]Usability testing should be started early in development and continue through all research stages

## 2.2 Translation by Design Examples from Public Health Research

Below we provide articles selected from digital health technologies in the public health research literature. These examples from published research about digital partner notification systems for sexually-transmitted infections (STI) illustrate TBD research stages with research questions we identified as they relate to the framework and sample sizes drawn from the cited sources. Of note, some of the examples below are cited at more than one research stage. This is common as a single feasibility or pilot study conducted during the development of a digital health solution may answer several related research questions. Also, some articles are authored by the same groups of co-authors, indicating a natural progression in the development of digital health solutions that seek to have positive impact on the real-world problem that motivates the research.

**Needs Assessment.** Research question we identified: What is need for Human Immunodeficiency Virus (HIV) self-test kits and social networking partner notification? Sample: n = 786 [9].

- **Design Engagement.** Research question we identified: What are the dimensions and range of preferences for user interface design features for a mobile health application for STI self-testing and self-management? Sample: n = 9 focus groups (49 total participants) [10]
- **Technical Function Validation.** Research question we identified: Does the demonstration system work as designed? Sample: internal sample size of technical testing team not reported. Authors reported "repeated testing of the system to ensure that it was accurate, fully functional and coded correctly" before live deployment [11]
- **Usability.** Research question we identified: Is a digital partner notification system acceptable and usable for partner notification? Sample size: n = 55 online patients; 43 partners notified [12]
- **Lab Function Test.** Research question we identified: Does the partner notification system function as intended in controlled setting with participants? Sample size: not reported. Authors articulate steps to address this research stage in their intervention development framework but do not report specific details: *"software, usability and cognitive testing was then conducted with the demonstration version of the pathway before the system went live. This included the Human Computer Interaction researcher conducting an expert usability review and lab-based testing with members of the public"* [11]
- **Lab User Effect.** Research question we identified: Does the partner notification system show potential for behavior change in a controlled setting with participants? Sample size: not reported. Authors articulate steps to address this research stage in their intervention development framework but do not report specific details: *"software, usability and cognitive testing was then conducted with the demonstration version of the pathway before the system went live. This included the Human Computer Interaction researcher conducting an expert usability review and lab-based testing with members of the public"* [11]
- **Field Function Test.** Research question we identified: Does the partner notification system function as intended in field testing? Sample size: n = 112 patients; 163 notified partners [13]
- **Field User Effect.** Research question we identified: Does the partner notification system change behavior in field testing? Sample size: n = 112 patients; 163 notified partners [13]
- **Problem Impact.** Research question we identified: What is the effect of patient engagement with a digital partner notification tool on the timeliness and number of partners notified? Sample size: n = 5715 patients [14]
- **Adaptation/Translation.** Research question we identified: What is the uptake of a digital partner notification by heterosexual patients for a system originally implemented with men who have sex with men? Sample size: n = 139 [16]

### 2.3 Planning a Translation by Design Program of Research

Table 2 below provides an overview of settings, stakeholders, and sample size guidance for planning a series of studies using the Translation by Design framework.

Early stage technology design and evaluation studies that involve interview and focus groups tend to have smaller sample sizes [17, 18] that will involve descriptive analysis

**Table 2.** TBD stages with settings, stakeholders, and typical sample size ranges

| Stage (Study Type)[a] | Setting | Stakeholders | Typical Sample |
|---|---|---|---|
| Needs Assessment | Lab, Field, Any | Users, Research Team, Health Domain Experts, Sponsors | Any, varies or N/A |
| Design Engagement | Lab, Field, Any | Users, Research Team | 5 to 15+ |
| Technical Function Validation | Lab, Field, Any | Research Team, Institutional Technical Oversight | 4 to 6+ |
| Usability[b] | Lab, Class, Field, Any | Users, Research Team, Research Community, Sponsors | 5 to 30+ |
| Lab Function Test | Lab, Class | Users, Research Team, Research Community, Sponsors | 6 to 12+ |
| Lab User Effect | Lab, Class | Users, Research Team, Research Community, Sponsors | 6 to 12+ |
| Field Function Test | Field (planned context of use) | Users, Research Team, Research Community, Service Agencies, Sponsors | 6 to 100+ |
| Field User Effect | Field (planned context of use) | Users, Research Team, Research Community, Service Agencies, Sponsors | 6 to 100+ |
| Problem Impact | Field, Local, National, Global | All previous stakeholders plus Service Payers | 20 to 400+ |
| Adaption/ Translation | Field, Local, National, Global | Universe of Stakeholders | 1000+ |

[a]Research stages are iterative and typically need to be revisited during conduct of longitudinal efforts
[b]Usability testing should be started early in development and continue through all research stages

[19]. Similarly, usability test sample sizes in design studies are often smaller [20–23] than studies with larger sample sizes having statistical power. Because usability testing is focused on discovering and correcting usability problems, the approach is iterative and the discoverable problems between usability test sessions differ because the system changes. When usability problems are corrected, those particular problems should be eliminated as challenges for future users in newer versions of the system under test. With iterative testing, new usability problems are likely to be discovered. In addition, research progressions to develop digital health interventions often involve feasibility or

pilot study designs that seek to answer questions about different aspects of technologies [24–26], including questions of clinical proof-of-concept [27], and may seek to embed activities to answer multiple questions in a single study. This approach will be seen with usability testing embedded at every research stage or concurrent efforts for user effect and function test in a single lab-based or field study. Adaptation and translation can happen in multiple ways: from research to real-world setting for the same population, from one real-world setting to a different but similar real-world setting for the same population (example: region to region with the same country), from one real-world setting to another real-world setting for a different population (example: one country to another country), from one real-world setting to another real-world setting for a different health condition.

### 2.4  Example Support Structures for Translation by Design Research

Below we briefly describe support structures that we have developed and organized to enable conduct of studies along the continuum of the TBD framework. Two of these entities are housed in the Sinclair School of Nursing at the University of Missouri and one is a non-profit company incorporated as a 501(c)3 organization in the United States.

**Precision START Lab.** The Precision START Lab is a digital health lab focused on emerging technologies within the University of Missouri's Sinclair School of Nursing (SSON). Established in the fall of 2019, the lab was conceptualized and is directed by Dr. Blaine Reeder, a faculty member of both the SSON and the MU Institute for Data Science and Informatics. The primary mission of the Precision START Lab is to address and overcome design issues and common barriers that hinder the timely integration of consumer-grade smart technologies—such as mobile and wearable devices, software applications, and smart home sensors—into translational research. The Precision START Lab employs a stepwise, systematic evaluation methodology that involves iterative testing with small sample sizes Small sample [17, 18, 20–23] progressing from internal lab studies to participant-based lab and field studies [28, 29]. The methodology incorporates multiple methods, including heuristic evaluations [30–34], cognitive walkthroughs [35], think-aloud protocols [36], interviews, focus groups, and the System Usability Scale (SUS) [37, 38]. These techniques are utilized to assess user perceptions, technology acceptability, implementation factors, and the overall suitability of devices for specific purposes. The Precision START lab conducts research activities in the areas of *Technical Function Test*, *Design Engagement*, *Usability*, *Lab Function Test*, *Lab User Effect*, *Field Function Test*, and *Field User Effect*.

**ASSETs Intervention Research Team.** The Age-friendly Sustainable Smart and Equitable Technologies (ASSETs) intervention research team is housed in the University of Missouri Sinclair School of Nursing with Social Work and Occupational Therapy research partners from the University of Missouri College of Health Sciences. The ASSETs intervention research team is focused on developing community-based interdisciplinary digital health programs and services to support independent aging. One example is the ASSETs for Aging in Place (AIP) demonstration project, co-led by Dr. Lori Popejoy and Dr. Blaine Reeder. ASSETs for AIP developed and conducted in partnership with the State of Missouri Department of Social Services with funding from the Centers for Medicaid and Medicare Services (CMS). The program serves older adult clients discharged from the Missouri Show Me Home project who are at risk for nursing home placement. ASSETs for AIP provides telehealth coaching for self-management and care coordination for community-based resources to clients. Central to ASSETs for AIP services are the use of digital health technologies including in-home sensors, consumer-available wearable devices, and tablet computers. Care coordinators collaborate with clients to set health goals, implement home safety modifications, and enhance communication with healthcare teams and community support networks. ASSETs for AIP relies on technologies tested and integrated in the Precision START lab. The ASSETs intervention research team conducts research activities in the areas of *Usability, Field Function Test, Field User Effect, Problem Impact*, and *Adaptation/Translation* of the Translation by Design framework.

**Hekademeia Research Solutions.** Hekademeia Research Solutions is a non-profit company incorporated as a 501(c)3 organization in the State of Missouri in the United States (http://www.hekademeia.org). Hekademeia's mission is to promote the responsible development and persistent support of software technologies within academic research by supporting individual investigators who work with technology. Hekademeia provides support for academic researchers with affordable hosting services and project management for software development to enable translation and sustainability of emerging technology research. Hekademeia provides supportive services that facilitate aspects of all stages of research in the Translation By Design framework.

## 3   Methods

We have previously made the case for how augmented cognition approaches can inform research in digital health and informatics with regard to smart watch research [7], technology-supported health measures [39], and smart home sensors to support independent aging [40]. Below we articulate a use case, describe design of a potential digital health intervention to support an informal caregiver of an older adult family member at risk for falls, and outline a progression of studies for a program of research that aims to design, develop, implement, evaluate, and translate the digital health intervention to the real world.

## 3.1 Use Case for Informal Caregiver of Older Adult at Risk for Falls

An estimated 14 million, or one in four, adults aged 65 years and older have admitted to a history of at least one fall in 2020 [41]. Home sensors and wearable devices are potential tools that can be used to assist in addressing older adult falls [42–46]. As the population ages, innovations to support caregivers, including adult children and informal caregivers, are needed to promote independent living for older adult dyads. Digital health interventions that support older adult caregivers' cognitive capacity by allowing them to monitor fall risk for loved ones, evaluate decision options, and intervene for safety are a potential way to help prolong independence. Identifying fundamental elements to maximize technology and intervention impact. This use case considers the use of sensors, mobile and wearable devices, and the alerts generated from these devices in a progression of proposed studies using the Translation by Design Framework and to illustrate the design, development, evaluation, and translation of an augmented cognition digital health intervention to support informal caregivers, promote older adult safety, and facilitate aging in place.

## 3.2 Description of Proposed Digital Health Intervention

Application of an augmented cognition digital health intervention to promote older adult independence hinges on the collection of an automated collection of data that is integrated for passive monitoring, fall risk prediction and decision making by the informal caregiver. Home sensor devices that include motion detection, cameras, and acoustic monitoring devices collect data that can inform fall risk in the home environment [47]. Wearable devices that collect data on gait patterns and ambulation that can also contribute to fall risk profiles [48]. What is less understood is how best to integrate this type of information into the daily lives of caregiver dyads such that informal caregivers can play a role in fall prevention when a fall risk increases or respond in a timely manner in the event of a fall. Informal caregivers will need alerts about fall risks and actual falls. In addition, recommendations, tailored to family circumstances, resources and preferences, are need to inform decision-making and actions. Visual displays that have been evaluated for usability and usefulness will be required to support decision-making for alerts. Given the nature of visual displays, these may be best viewed via secured portal on a larger computer monitor versus a mobile device. Alerts will be delivered via a range of mobile, wearable and desktop computing applications depending on the informal caregiver habitual use of technology. Active alerts will be delivered based on algorithmic determination of fall risk or an actual emergent fall event and base on informal caregiver preferences for alert frequency to avoid alert fatigue. In addition, application features that facilitate communication between the older adult family member at risk for falls and the informal caregiver (the care dyad), other family members and friends, and the formal care providers should be considered.

### 3.3   TBD Study Plan for Proposed Digital Health Intervention

Table 3 outlines the progression of studies in a program of research to design, develop, implement, evaluate, and translate the digital health intervention to real world settings. This progression of studies will necessarily require iterations between research stages based emergent circumstances during conduct of research.

**Table 3.**  Planned progression of studies

| | Study type | Description of activities | Timeline | Sample |
|---|---|---|---|---|
| | Needs Assessment | Collection and synthesis of digital scientific resources by research team to define gap and motivate the study | varies | N/A for this proposed study progression |
| | Design Engagement | Care recipient/older adult dyad interviews and focus groups for information needs and requirements<br><br>Member checking<br><br>Technology selection for integration | 12 months | n=10 dyads<br>(n= 20 total participants) |
| | Technical Function Validation | Validation studies that technology satisfies identified requirements Function testing within the design and research teams testing | 4 months | n=4 |
| | Usability | Heuristic evaluations by the design and research teams<br><br>Remote usability testing with informal caregivers.<br><br>Wearability testing with older adults | 6 months | n=4 research<br>n=8 informal caregivers<br>n= 4-6 older adults |
| | Lab Function Test | In-person participant study in lab setting (conducted concurrent with Lab User Effect study) | 1 month | 6 dyads<br>(n=12 total participants) |
| | Lab User Effect | In-person participant study in lab setting (Concurrent with Lab Function Test study) | 1 month | 6 dyads<br>(n=12 total participants) |
| | Field Function Test | Remote participant study (Concurrent with Field User Effect study) | 6 months | 20 dyads<br>(n=40 total participants) |
| | Field User Effect | Remote participant study (Concurrent with Field Function Test study) | 6 months | 20 dyads<br>(n=40 total participants) |

*(continued)*

**Table 3.** (*continued*)

| | | | | |
|---|---|---|---|---|
| | Problem Impact | Powered study, randomized controlled trial or pragmatic controlled trial focused on outcomes such as program uptake, technology adoption, number of falls, care recipient and informal caregiver satisfaction with program, informal caregiver quality of life, identification of implementation factors | 24 months | 128 dyads (n=64 dyads intervention, n=64 dyads control; n=256 total participants) |
| | Adaption/ Translation | Qualitative descriptive study to document adaptation requirements for different organization(s)<br><br>Develop implementation plan<br><br>Secure funding for service line<br><br>Scale and run demonstration project or implementation project for service with regular data collection for QI purposes<br><br>Measure same outcomes as problem impact study in addition to additional outcomes such as reduction in informal caregiver burnout reduced, reduction in falls leading to hospitalization | 24 months | population served will vary based on need in service area and delivery capacity. For example, in Southeast Michigan in the United States, the estimate population in need is 800,000 people |

## 4   Conclusion

Our goal was to introduce the Translation By Design (TBD) framework to the Augmented cognition research community as an approach to intentionally design for digital health solutions in support of real-world problems. We identified barriers to digital health research translation, described the TBD framework as a suggested progression of iterative studies, highlighted examples from our own research experiences to overcome common barriers to digital health research, and provided selected articles from the public health literature as examples that illustrate TBD research stages. Additionally, we proposed a potential digital health solution to a real-world problem involving the care dyad of an informal caregiver and an older adult family member at risk for falls and applied the TBD framework to articulate a set of studies in a research progression for a program of research to develop, implement, evaluation and translate the proposed solution. This report can serve as a guide to those interested in using the TBD framework to plan their own programs of research for digital health solutions. From our own reflections using the TBD framework in planning our own research, it can be useful to understand specific points where implemented technologies need more testing and can provide useful insights into perspectives about research and practice.

Future work will include mapping the TBD framework to the NIH Stage Model for Behavioral Intervention Development for: *Stage 0 basic science - mechanism of behavior change (pre-intervention), Stage I activities creation of a new behavioral intervention, Stage II Pure "Efficacy", Stage III Real World "Efficacy" research, Stage IV Effectiveness,* and *Stage V Implementation and Dissemination.*[49] Similarly, future work will also including efforts to map the TBD framework to the Administration for Community Living (ACL) National Institute on Disability, Independent Living, and Rehabilitation Research (NIDILRR) Stages of Research for *Exploration and discovery, Intervention development, Intervention efficacy,* and *Scale-up evaluation* [50] and the NIDILRR Stages of Development Framework for *Proof of concept, Proof of product, Proof of adoption* [50].

**Disclosure of Interests.** Blaine Reeder is co-founder and Chair of the Board of Directors for Hekademeia Research Solutions, a non-profit organization whose mission is to support technology-based academic research. This role is an unpaid volunteer position. Gerard Castaneda has no competing interests to disclose.

# References

1. Morris, Z.S., Wooding, S., Grant, J.: The answer is 17 years, what is the question: understanding time lags in translational research. J. R. Soc. Med. **104**, 510–520 (2011)
2. Balas, E.A., Boren, S.A.: Managing clinical knowledge for health care improvement. Yearb. Med. Inf. **9**, 65–70 (2000)
3. Health Economics Research Group Office of Health Economics RAND Europe: Medical Research: What's it worth? Estimating the economic benefits from medical research in the UK (2008)
4. Sung, N.S., et al.: Central challenges facing the national clinical research enterprise. JAMA **289**, 1278 (2003). https://doi.org/10.1001/jama.289.10.1278
5. Woolf, S.H.: The meaning of translational research and why it matters. JAMA **299** (2008). https://doi.org/10.1001/jama.2007.26
6. Mayrink, N.N.V., et al.: Translational research in health technologies: a scoping review. Front. Digit. Health. **4**, 957367 (2022). https://doi.org/10.3389/fdgth.2022.957367
7. Reeder, B., Cook, P.F., Meek, P.M., Ozkaynak, M.: Smart watch potential to support augmented cognition for health-related decision making. In: Schmorrow, D.D., Fidopiastis, C.M. (eds.) AC 2017. LNCS (LNAI), vol. 10284, pp. 372–382. Springer, Cham (2017). https://doi.org/10.1007/978-3-319-58628-1_29
8. Friedman, C.P., Wyatt, J.C.: Evaluation of biomedical and health information resources. In: Shortliffe, E.H., Cimino, J.J. (eds.) Biomedical informatics, pp. 355–387. Springer, London (2014). https://doi.org/10.1007/978-1-4471-4474-8_11
9. John, S.A., Starks, T.J., Rendina, H.J., Parsons, J.T., Grov, C.: High willingness to use novel HIV and bacterial sexually transmitted infection partner notification, testing, and treatment strategies among gay and bisexual men. Sex Transm Infect. **96**, 173–176 (2020). https://doi.org/10.1136/sextrans-2019-053974
10. Gkatzidou, V., et al.: User interface design for mobile-based sexual health interventions for young people: design recommendations from a qualitative study on an online Chlamydia clinical care pathway. BMC Med. Inf. Decis. Mak. **15**, 1–13 (2015)
11. Gibbs, J., et al.: The eClinical care pathway framework: a novel structure for creation of online complex clinical care pathways and its application in the management of sexually transmitted infections. BMC Med. Inf. Decis. Mak. **16**, 1–9 (2016)

12. van Rooijen, M.S., Vriens, P., Gotz, H., Heijman, T., Voeten, H., Koekenbier, R.: P5. 003 acceptance of an online partner notification tool for STI, called suggest-a-test. sexually transmitted infections. Sexually Transm. Infect. **89**, A335–A335 (2013)

13. van Rooijen, M.S., et al.: Sender and receiver acceptability and usability of an online partner notification tool for sexually transmitted infection in the Netherlands. Sex. Transm. Dis. **45**, 354–357 (2018)

14. Folke, T., Menon-Johansson, A.S.: An evaluation of digital partner notification tool engagement & impact for patients diagnosed with gonorrhea and syphilis. Sexual Trans Dis. **49**, 815–821 (2022). https://doi.org/10.1097/OLQ.0000000000001707

15. Rietmeijer, C.A., et al.: Evaluation of an online partner notification program. Sex. Transm. Dis. **38**, 359–364 (2011)

16. Götz, H.M., et al.: Initial evaluation of use of an online partner notification tool for STI, called 'suggest a test': a cross sectional pilot study. Sexually Transm. Infect. **90**, 195–200 (2014)

17. Guest, G., Bunce, A., Johnson, L.: How many interviews are enough? An experiment with data saturation and variability. Field Methods **18**, 59–82 (2006)

18. Krueger, R.A.: Focus Groups: A Practical Guide for Applied Research. Sage publications, Thousand Oaks (2014)

19. Gale, N.K., Heath, G., Cameron, E., Rashid, S., Redwood, S.: Using the framework method for the analysis of qualitative data in multi-disciplinary health research. BMC Med. Res. Methodol. **13**, 1–8 (2013)

20. Lewis, J.R.: Sample sizes for usability studies: additional considerations. Hum. Factors **36**, 368–378 (1994)

21. Nielsen, J., Landauer, T.K.: A mathematical model of the finding of usability problems. In: Proceedings of the INTERACT'93 and CHI'93 Conference on Human Factors in Computing Systems, pp. 206–213 (1993)

22. Turner, C.W., Lewis, J.R., Nielsen, J.: Determining usability test sample size. Int. Encycl. Ergon. Hum. Fact. **3**, 3084–3088 (2006)

23. Virzi, R.A.: Refining the test phase of usability evaluation: how many subjects is enough? Hum. Fact. **34**, 457–468 (1992)

24. Bowen, D.J., et al.: How we design feasibility studies. Am. J. Prev. Med. **36**, 452–457 (2009)

25. Eldridge, S.M., et al.: Defining feasibility and pilot studies in preparation for randomised controlled trials: development of a conceptual framework. PLoS ONE **11**, e0150205 (2016)

26. Arain, M., Campbell, M.J., Cooper, C.L., Lancaster, G.A.: What is a pilot or feasibility study? A review of current practice and editorial policy. BMC Med. Res. Methodol. **10**, 1–7 (2010)

27. Bardram, J.E.: Clinical Proof-of-Concept–a evaluation method for pervasive healthcare systems. In: Proceedings of Ubiquitous Computing. Citeseer (2008)

28. Gallimore, M.R., et al.: Digital methodology for mobile clinical decision support development in long-term care. In: MEDINFO 2021: One World, One Health – Global Partnership for Digital Innovation, pp. 479–483. IOS Press, virtual (2022)

29. Reeder, B., et al.: Stepwise evaluation methodology for smart watch sensor function and usability. In: Presented at the HCI International, Virtual Conference (2021)

30. Nielsen, J., Molich, R.: Heuristic evaluation of user interfaces. In: Proceedings of the SIGCHI Conference on Human Factors in Computing Systems Empowering people - CHI '90, pp. 249–256. ACM Press, Seattle (1990)

31. Yanez Gomez, R., Cascado Caballero, D., Sevillano, J.L.: Heuristic evaluation on mobile interfaces: a new checklist. Sci. World J. **2014**, 434326 (2014). https://doi.org/10.1155/2014/434326

32. Pierotti, D.: Heuristic evaluation-a system checklist. Xerox Corporation (1995)

33. Khajouei, R., Hajesmaeel Gohari, S., Mirzaee, M.: Comparison of two heuristic evaluation methods for evaluating the usability of health information systems. J. Biomed. Inf. **80**, 37–42 (2018). https://doi.org/10.1016/j.jbi.2018.02.016

34. Reeder, B., et al.: Usability inspection of a mobile clinical decision support app and a short form heuristic evaluation checklist. In: Schmorrow, D.D., Fidopiastis, C.M. (eds.) Augmented Cognition, pp. 331–344. Springer International Publishing, Cham (2019)
35. Mahatody, T., Sagar, M., Kolski, C.: State of the art on the cognitive walkthrough method, its variants and evolutions. Int. J. Hum.-Comput. Interact. **26**, 741–785 (2010)
36. Jaspers, M.W., Steen, T., Van Den Bos, C., Geenen, M.: The think aloud method: a guide to user interface design. Int. J. Med. Inf. **73**, 781–795 (2004)
37. Sauro, J.: Measuring usability with the system usability scale (SUS) (2011)
38. Brooke, J.: SUS-a quick and dirty usability scale. Usabil. Eval. Ind. **189**, 4–7 (1996)
39. Reeder, B., Richard, A., Crosby, M.E.: Technology-supported health measures and goal-tracking for older adults in everyday living. In: Schmorrow, D.D., Fidopiastis, C.M. (eds.) Foundations of Augmented Cognition, pp. 796–806. Springer International Publishing, Cham (2015)
40. Reeder, B., Chung, J., Joe, J., Lazar, A., Thompson, H.J., Demiris, G.: Understanding older adults' perceptions of in-home sensors using an obtrusiveness framework. In: HCI International 2016, Toronto, CA (2016)
41. Kakara, R.: Nonfatal and fatal falls among adults aged≥ 65 years—United States, 2020–2021. In: MMWR. Morbidity and Mortality Weekly Report, vol. 72 (2023)
42. Galambos, C., Rantz, M., Back, J., Jun, J.S., Skubic, M., Miller, S.J.: Older adults' perceptions of and preferences for a fall risk assessment system: exploring stages of acceptance model. CIN: Comput. Inf. Nurs. **35**, 331–337 (2017)
43. Rantz, M.J., et al.: In-home fall risk assessment and detection sensor system. J. Gerontol. Nurs. **39**, 18–22 (2013)
44. Phillips, L.J., et al.: Using embedded sensors in independent living to predict gait changes and falls. West. J. Nurs. Res. **39**, 78–94 (2017)
45. Dahlke, D.V., Lee, S., Smith, M.L., Shubert, T., Popovich, S., Ory, M.G.: Attitudes toward technology and use of fall alert wearables in caregiving: survey study. JMIR Aging **4**, e23381 (2021)
46. Reeder, B., Demiris, G., Thompson, H.J.: Smart built environments and independent living: a public health perspective. In: Bodine, C., Helal, S., Gu, T., Mokhtari, M. (eds.) Smart Homes and Health Telematics, pp. 219–224. Springer International Publishing, Cham (2015)
47. Lui, C.X.Y., Yang, N., Tang, A., San Tam, W.W.: Effectiveness evaluation of smart home technology in preventing and detecting falls in community and residential care settings for older adults: a systematic review and meta-analysis. J. Am. Med. Direct. Assoc., 105347 (2024)
48. Warrington, D.J., Shortis, E.J., Whittaker, P.J.: Are wearable devices effective for preventing and detecting falls: an umbrella review (a review of systematic reviews). BMC Public Health **21**, 1–12 (2021)
49. NIH Stage Model for Behavioral Intervention Development, https://www.nia.nih.gov/res earch/dbsr/nih-stage-model-behavioral-intervention-development
50. NIDILRR Frameworks ǀ ACL Administration for Community Living. http://acl.gov/aging-and-disability-in-america/nidilrr-frameworks

# Cognitive Load and Usability Assessment in Health Information Systems

Thiviyan Senthilrajah and Supunmali Ahangama[⊠]

Faculty of Information Technology, University of Moratuwa, Moratuwa, Sri Lanka
supunmali@uom.lk

**Abstract.** The Health Information Systems (HIS) improve patient care, streamline clinical workflow, and support decision making. Despite the benefits, healthcare practitioners resist using the HIS due to the usability related challenges. The study concentrated on factors to consider when selecting a suitable usability testing method for the health sector. A qualitative and integrative review method was adopted, synthesizing findings from peer reviewed journals, conference papers published over the past twelve years. The study identifies user trials, questionnaires, heuristic evaluations, cognitive walkthroughs, and think-aloud are the commonly used usability evaluation techniques in the healthcare setting. The findings of the study underscore the importance of considering clinical context, user expertise, the collaborative nature of the health care practitioners, purpose and objective of the usability testing when choosing a technique. Moreover, the study highlights the need to consider Cognitive Load (CL) among the healthcare stakeholders as a critical success factor in implementing a HIS successfully.

**Keywords:** Usability · Cognitive Load · Cognitive Load Assessment · Health Information Systems · Human Processor Model

## 1 Introduction

The Health Information Systems (HIS) were initially referred to as "Healthcare Planning Systems" in the 1960s, these systems were equipped with limited functionalities and primarily focused on supporting administrative tasks [1]. Technological advancement has transformed the HIS into a powerful system which enables managing patient data, automating clinical workflows and enhancing decision-making. Despite its potential, the usability of the HIS remains to be a concern among healthcare practitioners [2, 3]. In general, usability is a term known as reaching the intended user goals successfully with the help of the system. In other terms, usability in Information Systems (IS) refers to the degree to which a system can be used effectively, efficiently, and satisfactorily by its intended system users to complete their goals [4]. Even though HISs are capable of reducing the workload of healthcare practitioners, an issue relating to medicine doses has been highlighted in the United States of America's (USA) pediatric clinic, which reported Electronic Medical Records (EMR) in the clinic alarm health safety issues and decreased trust among clinicians [5]. Moreover, studies suggest that HIS are causing

D. D. Schmorrow and C. M. Fidopiastis (Eds.): HCII 2025, LNAI 15778, pp. 166–177, 2025.
https://doi.org/10.1007/978-3-031-93724-8_13

stress and frustration to clinicians and it has increased significantly in the recent past [4]. The usability issues in HIS are linked to factors such as poorly designed User Interfaces (UI), complicating routine workflows, and insufficient consideration of the cognitive demands of the healthcare practitioners. For instance, healthcare professionals face difficulty when navigating HIS interfaces, retrieving patient records and completing tasks in a shorter time in emergencies [6]. These challenges not only limit the acceptance of HIS but also increase the patient's health and safety risks in the clinic setup.

Cognitive Load (CL) refers to the mental effort required to process information and complete tasks within the constraints of an individual's working memory [7]. In the healthcare context, it plays a critical role in system effectiveness and user performance. A poorly designed interface can impose excessive CL on healthcare professionals and lead towards delays, errors, inefficiency and frustration. Therefore, the HIS is required to be designed considering user-friendly approaches to increase usability in the healthcare context [8]. Usability evaluation techniques such as Questionnaires, Heuristic Evaluation, User Trials, Thinking Aloud, System Usability Scores, and Task Analysis are the Cognitive Load Assessments (CLA) widely employed to identify usability issues [9, 10]. Traditional evaluation methods often fail to capture the real-time cognitive demands imposed by HIS. Looking at post-task usability assessments, such as the NASA Task Load Index (NASA-TLX), offer valuable insights but they cannot fully address the dynamic nature of clinical setup [11]. Thus, CL theories provide a useful mechanism for understanding the issue in-depth and highlight the importance of cognitive demands to design an effective IS. Therefore, this study aims to develop a framework to choose the most suitable usability evaluation technique specifically for healthcare based on CL.

The integrative review method was applied to the study as it offers a comprehensive approach to identify evidence from various research and enables a holistic understanding of the research area. Furthermore, it allows us to explore the topic depth and identify the gaps and trends [12]. Additionally, it is more suitable for applying towards a complex discipline like the health sector. Since it is a flexible method, it will allow the researchers to set own criteria considering the limitations [13].

The paper proposes the factors to consider when selecting a usability testing method for HIS by focusing on CL and motor processes outlined by the Human Processor Model (HPM). Furthermore, it examines deeper on frequently applied usability testing methods specifically in the healthcare context. The findings of the study will be useful in (a) choosing a usability assessment method specifically for the HIS; (b) enhancing the understanding of the role of CL among healthcare practitioners when interacting with HIS; (c) improving the knowledge of existing usability testing methods and its applicability to the health sector.

The next section of the paper follows a literature review that highlights the current usability evaluation techniques and areas for improvement. The methodology section outlines the research approach, design, and data collection process. Subsequently, the discussion section analyses the pros and cons of the existing usability evaluation techniques and highlights the suitable framework. Finally, the paper concludes with a summary of the key findings and recaptures the contribution to the Human-Computer Interaction (HCI) field.

## 2   Literature Review

### 2.1   Overview of the Human Processor Model

HPM was developed in the 1980s to predict cognitive and motor processing times [14]. HPM has been a foundation for understanding how users perceive, interpret, and respond to information within the systems and Fig. 1 illustrates the process. This conceptualizes human cognition through stages such as perceptual subsystems, cognitive subsystems and motor subsystems. The perceptual subsystems begin with sensory input which is managed by the perceptual processor where the information is temporarily held. Once the information is processed the working memory gets activated and manipulation of the information occurs. The working memory interacts with long-term memory which processes existing memory and the cognitive processor integrates the new information [15]. The interaction between working and long-term memory reflects the complexity of human cognition. Furthermore, the motor processor translates the cognitive outputs into the physical actions where the user movements are observed.

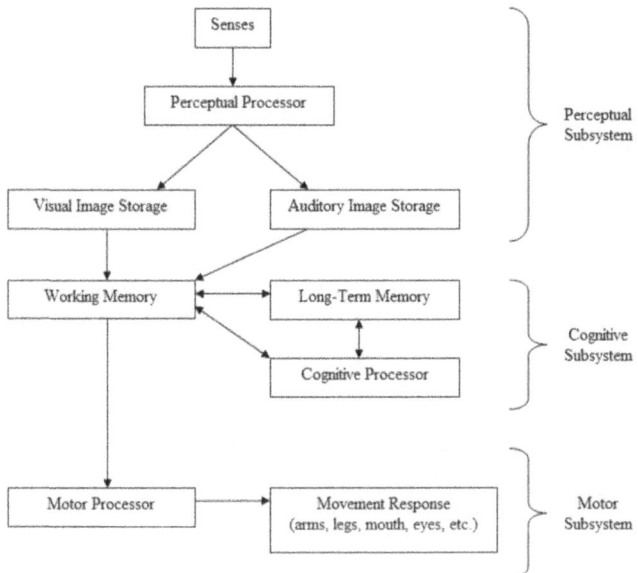

**Fig. 1.** Human Processor Model.

### 2.2   Cognitive Load and Cognitive Load Assessment

CL is a theoretical concept which is highly dynamic, and multi-dimensional and reflects the demand on working memory during cognitive tasks [16]. The term dynamic is mentioned as it can change rapidly during task executions and differ from person to person. Due to this, the CL measures are categorized into four: subjective, performance-based, physiological, and behavioral [16, 17]. The CL concepts will help to understand the mental load imposed by the tasks from a system. Cognitive Load Assessment (CLA) is a process of measuring the mental effort or cognitive demand of a task using various usability testing methods [18]. Furthermore, CLA is a practical methodology which quantifies the cognitive demands of the user experience. Ideally, the outcomes of the CLA will improve the workflow of the systems aligning to the requirements of the user groups and improve the system design. Incorporating CLA in the early stage allows the designers to improve user interfaces in a user-friendly manner. Conversely, a study recommends applying CLA throughout the software development lifecycle [19].

### 2.3   Usability Challenges in Health Information Systems

The health sector itself is a complex work environment, with various tasks starting from patient registration to clinical decision-making [20]. Most HISs are often aligned with the existing workflow which has been practised in the hospitals. For example, in the event of transferring the patient from the medical ward to the surgical ward a complicated process is followed in the system. This leads towards increasing CL and disrupts the clinical workflow [21]. In mobile health applications poor User Interface (UI) or User Experience (UX), lack of trust in the system and low user stickiness have been identified as potential problems which need immediate attention [22]. Furthermore, compatibility and connectivity issues on devices are impacting the UX [22, 23]. In the context of healthcare, developing usability test scenarios has been a challenge due to the complex and diverse group of stakeholders [24]. Since the health professionals are the end users of HIS, the usability scenarios should consist of a patient case and represent several clinical diagnoses, routine tasks and emergencies. Moreover, users of HIS are from different educational backgrounds, age groups, professional ranks and experience levels in using the system [8, 20]. Therefore, the type of end-user who uses the application may range from an expert to a beginner. Realtime usability testing like an eye tracker requires specialized equipment which should be connected to the HIS which may raise privacy and ethical concerns [25]. Due to this, the practitioners and the hospital management may resist using such techniques to assess the usability of the system.

### 2.4   Role of CLA in HIS Usability Evaluation

CLA replaces traditional methods like questionnaires as they may not be sufficient to capture the cognitive demands, especially in the healthcare context. Thus, usability techniques focused on CL can identify the poor navigation structure and information load using eye tracking [25, 26]. The complex design can limit the interaction between HIS and the user [27]. Due to the diverse user groups in the hospitals, CL helps assess the user group-specific usability issues in the systems [19]. The healthcare professional's work in a hospital is unpredictable and promotes a stressful work environment, excessive CL could increase frustration, dissatisfaction and resistance to using the HIS [21]. Furthermore, a study suggests incorporation of CLA into the software development lifecycle would allow the UI Engineers to align with the cognitive capabilities of the user groups. It should be integrated as an interactive process to create a greater understanding of user expectations. Immediate feedback on user cognitive demands will continuously improve the system during the testing phase [19]. Furthermore, it will save time, and allow the implementation process to strengthen by achieving user satisfaction.

## 3 Approach

Various usability testing methods exist for the field of IS, such as user trials, questionnaires, heuristic evaluation, cognitive walkthrough, thinking aloud and many more. They are widely used in testing the HIS, thus, a clear framework did not exist for choosing the most suitable technique [9]. The present study is focused on secondary data based on a qualitative approach and integrative review method. Google Scholar was used to search articles using keywords such as "Cognitive Load Assessments", "Usability in HIS", "Usability Testing", "Usability Evaluation Methods", "Cognitive Workload," and "Usability Metrics". Furthermore, to explore the applicability of the usability techniques, researchers have considered peer-reviewed journals and conference papers. Additionally, the authors reviewed Quartile 1 articles focused on CL and usability focused on HIS which were published in the last twelve years. An integrative review method has been applied to the study for several reasons. First, an integrative review summarizes the existing research and allows the generation of new insights by analyzing the existing knowledge from different angles. Second, this method allows greater flexibility and a balanced approach from systematic review and meta-analysis. Third, it bridges the gap between different research backgrounds [12]. Fourth, it allows us to identify the theoretical gap and develop new frameworks or models [13].

## 4 Analysis

### 4.1 Questionnaires

The questionnaire is the widely used technique to assess the usability of an IS from the end user. Thus, the questionnaire can be designed to meet usability outcomes, cognitive load, satisfaction, system performance and loyalty. In assessing the cognitive load, NASA-TLX is a subjective measure with six major dimensions (Mental demand, physical demand, temporal demand, performance, effort and frustration). The users will rate these dimensions on a scale of 0 to 100 and this is an inexpensive technique that can be easily deployed. However, this does not capture real-time data and provides post-task information. The application of NASA-TLX to healthcare would be challenging due to the complex workflow [11]. Conversely, studies suggest that the questionnaires allow for collecting the experience from a large number of end users and using an anonymous questionnaire will allow the participants to share their real view of the IS [28]. Another study suggests that the surveys may limit the input for usability issues in HIS, as the healthcare professionals may have diverse needs from the HIS [29].

### 4.2 Randomized Clinical Trials/User Trials

User trials allow the end user to complete the tasks using the system under the evaluation and the participants must know the purpose of the system and analysis [9]. The ultimate objective of the user trials is to collect observation data to compare with interviews and questionnaires. The HIS is process-oriented and context-dependent, and due to this the Randomized Clinical Trials (RCT) is not the most suitable method for usability evaluation in assessing HIS [30]. Thus, in a clinical setup, it is the universally considered standard for assessing the cause and effect. However, RCT should focus on answering questions about whether and how much an IS improves patient care and workflow. The common concerns about user RCT are known to be unethical, HIS is too complicated to assess using RCT, expensive, consumes more time and trials may answer irrelevant questions to the medical informatics [30]. Furthermore, dissatisfied participants of the trials can spread or influence others negatively about the system and affect the implementation process which could impact others negatively [31]. Figure 2 shows the percentage that was applied user trials for IS from 1971 to 2010.

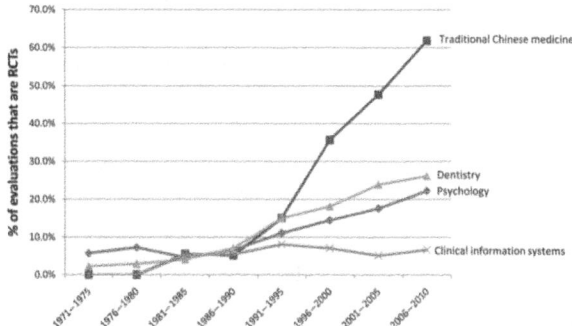

**Fig. 2.** Percentage of RCT Evaluations [30].

### 4.3   Heuristic Evaluation Method

The Heuristic Evaluation (HE) method mainly focuses on evaluating the compliance of the user interface design using the predetermined ten standard principles by the experts. The ten principles are as follows: (1) visibility of system status; (2) match between system and the real world; (3) user control and freedom; (4) consistency and standards; (5) help users recognize, diagnose and recover from errors; (6) error prevention; recognition rather than call; (7) Recognition rather than recall; (8) flexibility and efficiency of use; (9) aesthetic and minimalist design; (10) help and documentation. However, [32] suggests fourteen principles and Table 1 shows them in detail. Thus, studies preferred to use the standard 10 principles [2]. This method is cost-effective to conduct with limited time and resources to implement easily in healthcare settings [32]. Large studies including dental computer-based patient records and patient training records successfully evaluated using the heuristic method and studies suggest that 50% of the usability problems have been picked up [33] while another study suggests that HE can identify up to 80% [34].

**Table 1.** Nielsen–Schneiderman HCI heuristics.

| # | Principle | Description |
|---|-----------|-------------|
| 01 | Consistency and standards | Standards and conventions in design should be followed |
| 02 | Visibility of system state | Users should be informed well about the system through feedback and display of information |
| 03 | Match between system and world | The image of the system perceived by users should match the model the users have about the system |
| 04 | Minimalist | Any extraneous information is a distraction and a slowdown |
| 05 | Minimize memory load | Users should not be required to memorize a lot of information to perform tasks |
| 06 | Informative feedback | Users should be given prompt and informative feedback about their actions |
| 07 | Flexibility and efficiency | Allow flexibility in creating customization and shortcuts to accelerate performance |
| 08 | Good error messages | The messages should be informative |
| 09 | Prevent errors | It is always better to design interfaces that prevent errors |
| 10 | Clear closure | Users should be notified about the completion of a task |
| 11 | Reversible actions – Undo | Users should be allowed to recover from errors |
| 12 | Use users' language | The language should be always presented in a form understandable |
| 13 | Users in control | Do not give users the impression that they are controlled by the systems |
| 14 | Help and documentation | Always provide help when needed |

## 4.4 Cognitive Walkthrough

Cognitive Walkthrough (CW) is a technique that can identify problems relating to usability economically, quickly, and effortlessly by experts [34]. The CW method adopts cognitive psychology principles to simulate the cognitive processes and user actions to perform specific tasks and is highly focused on the ease of learning the system. This method is considered suitable when users need to masterfully learn a new application or function by learning through exploration. Furthermore, the user interfaces should be described and the task scenarios, assumptions of the users and the scope along with the actions to perform the tasks should be determined [9]. Then the cognitive process should be followed by the group of evaluators based on the user's performance of the tasks. In this process, the actions which are not easy for the users will be decided based on the user's interference behavior and the influence it has on the user. Interestingly, it is recommended to perform CW in the early stage of the system implementation process.

### 4.5 Thinking Aloud

The thinking-aloud method is a scientific method used to study the cognitive process and was originally developed for the Short-Term Memory (STM) process of subjects and known as a powerful methodology [35, 36]. Ultimately, the participants will be asked to perform a task while verbalizing their thoughts [35]. The researchers will write the verbal report and analyze it in a way that depends on the research questions [36]. Mainly, the researchers focus on utterances that reflect a certain state of mind (annoyance, confusion) or delays between utterances. This method has been used for 3 main goals; (1) to find evidence for models and theories of cognitive processes; (2) to discover and understand general patterns of behavior in the interaction with documents or applications, to create a scientific basis for designing; (3) to test specific new documents or applications to troubleshoot and revise (usability testing, or pretesting, or formative testing) [35]. Importantly, the participants should be allowed to practice to reduce mistakes during the process [36].

## 5 Discussion

The usability evaluation of HIS is highly connected to understanding and managing the CL experienced by healthcare practitioners during system usage. CLA is a process of measuring the mental effort or cognitive demand of a task using various usability testing methods [18] and evaluation techniques like user trials, questionnaires, heuristic evaluation, cognitive walkthrough and thinking aloud are widely used in the health sector IS. User trials offer a real-world perspective to assess the CL during the task execution. Thus, this method is limited in the ability to measure the CL since external factors can influence the end users. In contrast, questionnaires like NASA-TLX, a systematic method designed to assess six dimensions, would result in a more comprehensive quantitative result. This will allow us to analyze the data quickly and define strategies to improve the systems. Thus, NASA-TLX is highly dependent on the post-task feedback which limits capturing the real-time CL which is critical in the dynamic work environments in healthcare. Furthermore, the complex workflow of the health sector may fail to cover at least one of the dimensions.

HE identifies the design-related issues which can increase the mental effort of healthcare professionals using the standard usability principles. This method is cost-effective and allows to use of the prototypes to identify the issues with a minimum effort. Interestingly, HE does not allow to measure the CL directly but it provides actionable recommendations to redesign the HIS interfaces. CW simulates the cognitive steps users take to complete tasks and identifies usability-related issues that may increase CL. In the hospital setup, the healthcare stakeholders may not be ready to spend more time as they have complex routine tasks. Due to this, applicability of the CW is a bit of a challenge in hospitals. Similarly, thinking aloud allows us to understand the thought process of the end user's CL by verbalizing their thoughts. Due to the qualitative nature of the method, extensive time is required for analysis. Thus, thinking aloud provides real-time demands of the HIS expected by the end users.

Due to the complexity of the HIS and the work nature of the practitioners, selecting a usability evaluation technique remains a challenge. The doctors and nurses perform interconnected tasks in the wards, which could limit them from being involved in the evaluation of HIS together. Furthermore, diverse groups of end users are engaged in the HIS such as doctors, nurses, laboratory technicians, administrators and finance. Due to this, applying a single usability technique would not be adequate. Additionally, the usability of the HIS is context-dependent where the system is used such as in wards, emergency treatment units and theatres. Moreover, utilizing or releasing resources in the healthcare environment is a big challenge as the work schedule may be unpredictable. Table 2 shows the comparison between the usability testing techniques.

**Table 2.** Comparison of Usability Testing Methods.

| Method | Positives | Negatives |
|---|---|---|
| User Trials | • Timely useful real-world usability outcomes<br>• Allows direct feedback from the users<br>• Captures task completion time, error rates, etc. | • Time-consuming and high level of resources required<br>• External factors can influence the results<br>• Difficult to replicate clinical setup |
| Questionnaire (NASA-TLX) | • Identifies cognitive workload in six dimensions<br>• Easy to administrate and analyze the data<br>• Cost effective | • Does not capture realtime data<br>• Does not capture high-level usability issues<br>• Subjective as it is highly varied between the users |
| Heuristic Evaluation | • Cost-effective and quicker to identify usability issues<br>• Prototypes can be applied | • Highly depends on expertise<br>• Real-world scenarios may be missed |
| Cognitive Walkthrough | • Allows to identify the issues from new users as well<br>• Task-oriented<br>• Reduces ethical issues | • Time-consuming for assessing a complex HIS<br>• Required expert evaluators |
| Thinking Aloud | • Provides Real-time insights and discovers hidden usability issues | • Analysis may be time-consuming due to qualitative data |

# 6 Conclusion

The HISs ar the backbone for modern healthcare delivery across the globe and reduce the workload among healthcare professionals. However, due to the issues arising from usability, the acceptance and usage of the HIS remain low. To assess the usability various techniques have been developed for IS. While identifying the usability issues, it is important to take into consideration the CL of the end users. User trials, questionnaires, heuristic evaluation, cognitive walkthroughs and thinking aloud are the methods widely used to assess the usability specifically for the HIS. The present study focused on providing a framework to choose the most appropriate method for usability assessment and suggests that the management should understand and prioritize the cognitive demands of the healthcare practitioners and consider context, user groups, purpose, objective and collaborative nature of work to choose a suitable usability evaluation technique. Furthermore, it recommends choosing two or more usability testing methods as each method is unique and the results can be compared in decision making.

**Acknowledgements.** The author acknowledges the support received from the LK Domain Registry in publishing this paper.

# References

1. Pai, F.-Y., Huang, K.-I.: Applying the technology acceptance model to the introduction of healthcare information. Technol. Forecast. Soc. Chang. **78**, 650–660 (2011)
2. Cho, H., et al.: Assessing the usability of a clinical decision support system: heuristic evaluation. JMIR Hum. Factors **9**(2) (2022)
3. Shamsujjoha, M., Grundy, J., Li, L., Khalajzadeh, H., Lu, Q.: Human-centric issues in ehealth app development and usage: a preliminary assessment. In: IEEE International Conference on Software Analysis, Evolution and Reengineering (SANER), Honolulu (2021)
4. Hyppönen, H., Kaipio, J., Heponiemi, T., Lääveri, T., Aalto, A.-M., Vänskä, J., Elovainio, M.: Developing the national usability-focused health information system scale for physicians: validation study. J. Med. Internet Res. **21**(5), e12875 (2019)
5. Ratwani, R.M.M., et al.: A usability and safety analysis of electronic health records: a multi-center study. J. Am. Med. Inform. Assoc. **25**(9), 1197–1201 (2018)
6. Carayon, P., et al.: Human-centered design of team health IT for pediatric trauma care transitions. Int. J. Med. Informatics **162**, 104727 (2022)
7. Buchner, J., Buntins, K., Michael, K.: The impact of augmented reality on cognitive load and performance: a systematic review. J. Comput. Assist. Learn. **38**(1), 285–303 (2022)
8. Senthilrajah, T., Ahangama, S.: An analysis of the use of health information systems in public healthcare in Sri Lanka using the technology acceptance model. In: International Conference on Advanced Research in Computing, Belihuloya (2024)
9. Wronikowska, M.W., et al.: Systematic review of applied usability metrics within usability evaluation methods for hospital electronic healthcare record systems: metrics and evaluation methods for eHealth systems. J. Eval. Clin. Pract. **27**(6), 1403–1416 (2021)
10. Feinberg, S., Murphy, M.: Applying cognitive load theory to the design of web-based instruction. In: 18th Annual Conference on Computer Documentation. IPCC SIGDOC 2000. Technology and Teamwork. Proceedings. IEEE Professional Communication Society International Professional Communication Conference an, Cambridge (2000)

11. Pachunka, E., Windle, J., Schuetzler, R., Fruhling, A.: Natural-setting PHR usability evaluation using the NASA TLX to measure cognitive load of patients. In: 52nd Hawaii International Conference on System Sciences, Hawaii (2019)
12. Snyder, H.: Literature review as a research methodology: an overview and guidelines. J. Bus. Res. **104**, 333–339 (2019)
13. Cronin, M.A., George, E.: The why and how of the integrative review. Organ. Res. Methods **26**(1), 168–192 (2023)
14. Bakaev, M.: Impact of familiarity on information complexity in human-computer interfaces. In: MATEC Web of Conferences, vol. 75 (2016)
15. Larsen, E.P., Schaeubinger, M.M., Won, J., Sze, R.W., Anupindi, S.: Integrating human factors engineering into your pediatric radiology practice. Pediatric Radiol. **54**, 936–943 (2024)
16. Suryani, M., et al.: Role, methodology, and measurement of cognitive load in computer science and information systems research. IEEE Access **12**, 190007–190024 (2024)
17. Knoben, A., Alimardani, M., Saghafi, A., Amiri, A.K.: Cognitive workload associated with different conceptual modeling approaches in information systems. In: HCI International 2022 Posters (2022)
18. Feng, Z., Ji, P.: Cognitive friction measurement: interaction assessment of interface information in complex information systems. Hum. Factors Syst. Interact. **84**, 27–36 (2023)
19. Sevcenko, N., Appel, T., Ninaus, M., Moeller, K., Gerjets, P.: Theory-based approach for assessing cognitive load during time-critical resource-managing human–computer interactions: an eye-tracking study. J. Multimodal User Interfaces (1–19), 17 (2023)
20. Senthilrajah, T., Ahangama, S.: The Sri Lankan enigma: demystifying public healthcare information systems acceptance. BMC Health Serv. Res. **25**(24) (2025)
21. Windle, J.R., et al.: Roadmap to a more useful and usable electronic health record. Cardiovasc. Digit. Health J. **2**(6), 301–311 (2021)
22. Zhu, Y.Z., et al.: Understanding use intention of mHealth applications based on the unified theory of acceptance and use of technology 2 (UTAUT-2) model in China. Int. J. Environ. Res. Public Health **20**(4), 3139 (2023)
23. Greenhalgh, T., et al.: Beyond adoption: a new framework for theorizing and evaluating nonadoption, abandonment, and challenges to the scale-up, spread, and sustainability of health and care technologies. J. Med. Internet Res. **19**(11), 367 (2017)
24. Russa, A.L., Saleemd, J.J.: Ten factors to consider when developing usability scenarios and tasks for health information technology. J. Biomed. Inform. **78**, 123–133 (2018)
25. Asan, O., Yang, Y.: Using eye trackers for usability evaluation of health information technology: a systematic literature review. JMIR Hum. Factors **2**(1) (2015)
26. Kushniruk, A.W., Borycki, E.M., Kuwata, S., Kannry, J.: Emerging approaches to usability evaluation of health information systems: towards in-situ analysis of complex healthcare systems and environments. In: 23rd International Conference of the European Federation for Medical Informatics, MIE, Oslo (2011)
27. Li, Y., Yuan, X., Che, R.: An investigation of task characteristics and users' evaluation of interaction design in different online health information systems. Inf. Process. Manag. **58**(3) (2021)
28. Jeddia, F.R., Nabovatia, E., Bighamb, R., Khajoueid, R.: Usability evaluation of a comprehensive national health information system: relationship of quality components to users' characteristics. Int. J. Med. Informatics **133**, 104026 (2020)
29. Tummers, J., Tobi, H., Schalk, B., Tekinerdogan, B., Leusink, G.: State of the practice of health information systems: a survey study amongst health care professionals in intellectual disability care. BMC Health Serv. Res. **21**(1247) (2021)
30. Liu, J.L.Y., Wyatt, J.C.: The case for randomized controlled trials to assess the impact of clinical information systems. J. Am. Med. Inform. Assoc. **18**(2), 173–180 (2011)

31. Venkatesh, V., Thong, J.Y.L., Xu, X.: Consumer acceptance and use of information technology: extending the unified theory of acceptance and use of technology. MIS Q. **36**(1), 157–178 (2012)
32. Hundt, A.S., Adams, J.A., Carayona, P.: A collaborative usability evaluation (CUE) model for health IT design and implementation. Int. J. Hum.-Comput. Interact. **33**(4), 287–297 (2017)
33. Jeddi, F.R., Nabovati, E., Bigham, R., Farrahi, R.: Usability evaluation of a comprehensive national health information system: a heuristic evaluation. Inform. Med. Unlocked **13**, 100332 (2020)
34. Farzandipour, M., Nabovati, E., Jabali, M.S.: Comparison of usability evaluation methods for a health information system: heuristic evaluation versus cognitive walkthrough method. BMC Med. Inform. Decis. Mak. **22**(157) (2022)
35. Krahmer, E., Ummelen, N.: Thinking about thinking aloud: a comparison of two verbal protocols for usability testing. IEEE Trans. Prof. Commun. **47**(2) (2004)
36. Wolcott, M.D., Lobczowski, N.G.: Using cognitive interviews and think-aloud protocols to understand thought processes. Curr. Pharm. Teach. Learn. **13**, 181–188 (2021)

# Design of White Noise Healing Wall Based on Attention Restoration Theory

Ningyi Zeng[✉] [iD]

Huazhong University of Science and Technology, No. 1037 Luoyu Road, Hongshan District,
Wuhan, China
ningyiceng111@gmail.com

**Abstract.** This study, based on the Attention Restoration Theory (ART), has developed an interactive white noise healing wall designed to help users restore their attention and reduce stress by simulating the auditory experience of natural environments and incorporating dynamically changing sound elements. The research utilizes the Grasshopper plugin within the Rhino software for parametric modeling, generating white noise that approximates the frequency spectrum of natural sounds through mechanical motion patterns. It also integrates design strategies such as "Being Away," "Extent," "Fascination," and "Compatibility" to enhance the spatial sense of sound and the user's immersive experience. Furthermore, the study explores the materials, structure, construction, and interaction methods of the wall device. Despite technical limitations and challenges in implementation, this research provides new ideas and approaches for the generation and application of white noise, combining natural white noise with mechanical white noise.

**Keywords:** Attention Restoration Theory · Sound Healing · Interactive Design · White Noise · Parametric Modeling

## 1 Introduction

In the fast-paced modern life, prolonged cognitive load often leads to attention fatigue and high psychological stress among young people. Long-term exposure to such psychological states can result in anxiety, depression, insomnia, and other adverse outcomes. According to the "2017 China Youth Sleep Status Report" published by the China Sleep Research Society, 76% of respondents reported difficulty falling asleep, and only 24% reported overall good sleep quality. Sleep disorders not only affect an individual's daily social functioning but are also associated with an increased incidence of various mental health issues, such as anxiety and depression. Chronic insomnia may also lead to the occurrence of various physical diseases, such as diabetes, hypertension, and coronary heart disease.

The "2024 White Paper on Emotion and Health Sleep" shows that 95% of respondents reported health concerns in the past year, with sleep issues ranking first and emotional issues ranking fifth. More than 51% of people experience both sleep and emotional

D. D. Schmorrow and C. M. Fidopiastis (Eds.): HCII 2025, LNAI 15778, pp. 178–189, 2025.
https://doi.org/10.1007/978-3-031-93724-8_14

distress simultaneously. Additionally, according to the report "Global Mental Health: Where We Are and Where We Are Going,", mental health issues are prevalent worldwide and are closely related to social, environmental, genetic, and biological factors. Mental health is not only a personal health issue but also a global public health concern.

A substantial amount of research indicates that constructing a white noise environment is of great help for emotional healing. White noise helps to mask other environmental noises, providing a relatively constant and predictable sound environment, which aids in relaxing the body and mind, promoting sleep; it can also cover internal attention and emotional agitation, thereby reducing anxiety and stress, and enhancing cognitive function [1]. The SHCMAIME team at the Shanghai Conservatory of Music combines traditional music with artificial intelligence technology, delving into the field of sound healing, conducting research on the synergy between audio and brain waves, white noise, pink noise, and neural regulation, and collaborating with Yueyang Tumor Hospital to effectively alleviate patients' pain and anxiety through music therapy, improve quality of life, significantly reduce Hamilton Anxiety Scale (HAMA) scores, and improve insomnia and tension [2].

Therefore, the research questions of this paper are:

1. How to apply the characteristics of white noise for design targeting the sleep state of young people;
2. How to design an interactive device that can produce white noise to alleviate the sleep anxiety of young people;

Based on this, this study has developed an interactive white noise healing wall based on Attention Restoration Theory (ART) [3]. The wall generates white noise that approximates the frequency curve of natural sounds through its mechanical movement patterns. Combined with the environmental characteristics of "being away," "extent," "fascination," and "compatibility," it helps people restore their attention, reduce stress, and alleviate anxiety and insomnia. The wall features a multi-channel surround sound system to enhance the spatial sense of sound. It also incorporates dynamically changing sound elements and adjustable sound complexity and rhythm, which keep users engaged and allow them to customize the sound environment according to their personal preferences and needs. Additionally, the wall integrates audio visualization technology to combine sound with visual effects, further enhancing users' immersion and healing experience.

## 2 Related Work

In 1962, Jim Buckwalter invented the first machine specifically designed to play white noise, called Sleep Mate, to address his own insomnia problem [4]. Due to its significant therapeutic effects, it gradually gained popularity. The white noise machine, as the largest offline carrier of white noise, has become known as a "sleep-saving device" in promotional language. In addition to this, products such as white noise pillows and white noise headphones have also emerged in the market to help people who need them to solve sleep problems and improve concentration.

In recent years, white noise therapy products have continuously emerged worldwide, aiming to help users relieve psychological stress and improve sleep quality. In China, the Xiao Shui App [1] provides a rich combination of natural sounds and white noise, allowing users to freely mix and match them for various scenarios such as sleep, study, work, and meditation. The Chao Xi App features a white noise Pomodoro timer, which helps users achieve better results in sleep, focus, relaxation, and meditation. The sati space module of NetEase Cloud Music [5] offers a variety of white noise and natural sounds to help improve users' sleep quality and reduce psychological stress.

Adaptive Sound Technologies (ASTI) has developed the LectroFan High Fidelity White Noise Machine [6], which provides 20 different types of white noise and fan sounds with adjustable volume, suitable for various environments. Its high-fidelity sound options and adaptive volume control make it the preferred choice for users who pursue a high-quality audio experience. Yu Jia Rong has studied the plant interactive music device "Living Organisms," [7] which uses electronic music creation and sensor micro-controller technology to enable interaction between humans and plants. This device provides users with an immersive audio-visual-tactile experience, creating a natural, unified, and relaxing plant atmosphere experience space.

These products help users relieve psychological stress, improve sleep quality, and enhance overall mental health by providing white noise and natural sounds.re, the paper discusses how to design an interactive device to produce white noise to relieve sleep anxiety among young people, providing new ideas and methods for improving their sleep quality and mental health.

## 3    Proposed Solution

### 3.1    Definition and Criteria for White Noise

White noise is a random signal with a uniform power spectral density across the entire frequency domain [8]. It has the same energy at all frequencies, similar to how white light in optics contains all visible light frequencies. The main criterion for identifying white noise lies in its spectral characteristics. From a mathematical perspective, the power spectral density function of white noise is constant, indicating that all frequency components have equal power [9]. In the field of acoustics, it sounds like a continuous, uniform "hissing" noise, without any distinct pitch or melodic features. It covers a variety of frequency components within the audible range of the human ear, with relatively balanced intensity. These characteristics make it commonly used to mask irregular noises, aid sleep, soothe emotions, and serve as a background signal in some acoustic tests and research. The most common types of white noise include the pattering sound of rain in nature, the sound of waves crashing against rocks, and the rustling of wind through leaves, all of which sound very harmonious and comfortable. The criteria for identifying white noise are shown in Table 1.

Frequency Distribution: It has a flat frequency distribution, meaning that all frequencies within the audible range of the human ear (typically 20 Hz to 20 kHz) have the same intensity of sound.

Non-Melodic: It does not contain any melody or rhythm; it is not musical.

Power Spectral Density: On the power spectrum, white noise shows a constant power level, which means that the energy of the sound is the same in any given frequency range.

Auditory Perception: White noise sounds like a continuous, uniform "hissing" noise. Although it is theoretically uniformly distributed, in practical applications, people may adjust specific frequency components of white noise according to personal preferences and environmental factors to achieve the best auditory effect.

**Table 1.** Criteria for white noise.

| Evaluation Dimensions | Characteristic |
| --- | --- |
| Frequency Distribution | flat, within 20 Hz to 20 kHz |
| Melody | non-melodic, not musical |
| Power Spectral Density | constant power level |
| Auditory Perception | a continuous, uniform "hissing" noise |

## 3.2 Design of the Wall Based on Attention Restoration Theory

The Attention Restoration Theory (ART), proposed by psychologists Stephen Kaplan and Rachel Kaplan in 1989, emphasizes the importance of our surrounding environment—especially natural environments—in restoring our attention and improving overall mental health [10]. According to Kaplan, the four key characteristics of a restorative environment are: Being Away, Extent, Fascination, and Compatibility. "Being Away" refers to the feeling of separation from current worries and concerns. "Extent" refers to the richness and complexity of the environment, which allows a person to become fully immersed. "Fascination" refers to the environment's ability to effortlessly attract an individual's attention. "Compatibility" refers to the environment's ability to support an individual's interests and goals, while the individual's decisions can also adapt to the environment's requirements. These four characteristics together form the core elements of a restorative environment, which can help people recover from mental fatigue and stress.

Based on this, we have determined the design strategies for the white noise healing wall to ensure the effectiveness of the healing experience: (1) Simulate the auditory experience of a natural environment to create a sense of being away from the daily environment; (2) Integrate the generation of sound with the movement and changes of the wall to create a multi-channel surround sound, enhancing the spatial sense of sound; (3) Introduce dynamically changing sound elements to maintain user interest and engagement; (4) Adjust the complexity and rhythm of the sound, allowing users to customize the sound environment according to their personal preferences and needs (Fig. 1).

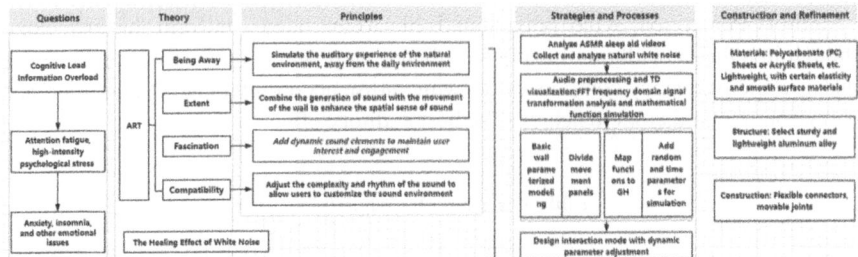

**Fig. 1.** Research framework.

## 3.3 Hardware and Interaction

**Audio Extraction and Analysis.** To simulate the auditory experience of a natural environment, we have adopted two primary methods to obtain samples of natural white noise: First, using microphones to directly record in natural environments, followed by employing digital signal processing techniques to remove unwanted noise; second, extracting the required audio samples from existing white noise audio libraries.

For the recording of sounds in natural environments, high-sensitivity microphones are used to capture audio. Once the recording is complete, the raw audio is preprocessed using audio editing software, which includes noise reduction, equalization, and dynamic range compression, to enhance the purity of the white noise and meet the requirements for subsequent analysis and application. In addition, extracting samples from existing white noise audio libraries is a more straightforward approach. We have screened multiple audio libraries and selected white noise samples that match the characteristics of natural environmental sounds. The following types of natural white noise were ultimately chosen: rain sounds, ocean waves, bird chirps, stream sounds, and campfire sounds (Fig. 2).

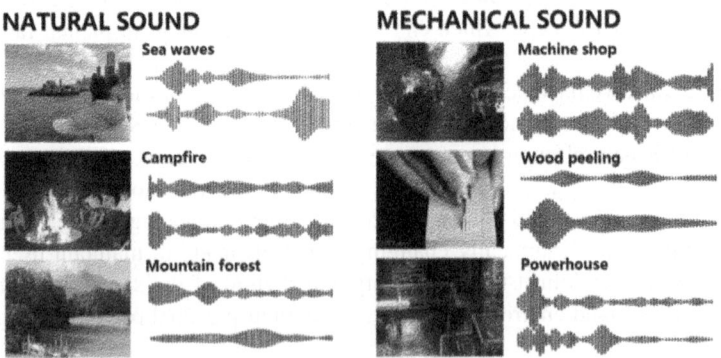

**Fig. 2.** The audio extraction of natural and mechanical white noise.

In addition, the study also analyzed and investigated mechanically generated white noise in relation to ASMR videos. ASMR (Autonomous Sensory Meridian Response) refers to the unique, pleasurable tingling sensations that occur in the head, scalp, back, or other parts of the body in response to sensory stimuli such as visual, auditory, tactile, and olfactory inputs [11]. On Bilibili, the ASMR sleep aid video by South Korean host PPOMO has garnered up to 7.948 million views. This research categorized and analyzed the sound types in the video. The sounds are primarily produced through vocalizations, tapping, and rubbing. Common materials used include plastics and rubber products, glass and ceramic items, metal objects, foam materials, and other special materials (Table 2).

**Table 2.** Basic situation of ASMR video analysis.

| Name | Total views | Video duration | Upload time | Total likes |
|------|-------------|----------------|-------------|-------------|
| Intense relaxing ears | 24932000 | 3.5 h | 2019.02.06 | 150000 |
| ASMR Wood soup | 5639000 | 3 h | 2023.05.02 | 128000 |
| Simulated hair cutting | 10292000 | 30 min | 2019.07.11 | 151000 |
| Eating candies | 12812000 | 15 min | 2024.07.19 | 94000 |
| Ear cleaning | 84372000 | 3 h | 2018.02.21 | 128000 |

**Audio Visualization.** To convert the time-domain signal of the collected natural white noise into digital data, the Fast Fourier Transform (FFT)—an efficient algorithm for the Discrete Fourier Transform (DFT)—is employed to transform the time-domain signal into a frequency-domain signal [12]. The result of the FFT reveals the signal's spectrum, displaying the various frequency components and their respective amplitudes, which can be intuitively presented through a spectral diagram. After obtaining the frequency-domain signal, the signal's characteristic parameters—such as the primary frequency components, bandwidth, and peak frequency—can be extracted. By adjusting the sound's spectrum to match the target white noise spectrum, its characteristics can be simulated. Furthermore, the result of the Fourier transform can be represented in the form of a Fourier series, expressing a periodic function as the sum of sine and cosine functions. Based on the FFT results, a Fourier series composed of a series of sine and cosine terms is constructed, with each term corresponding to a specific frequency component.

Ultimately, the Python plotting library Matplotlib is used to graphically display the frequency-domain characteristics of the white noise signal, as shown in the Fig. 3.

$$\text{reconstructed signal} = \text{reconstructed signal} + a\sin(2\pi f_t + p) \tag{1}$$

- a is the amplitude of the sine wave.
- f is the frequency of the sine wave.
- t is the time variable.
- p is the phase shift of the sine wave.

The transformation into a mathematical formula can be expressed as:

$$s(t) = \sum_{n=0}^{N-1} a^n \sin(2\pi f_n t + \varphi_n) \tag{2}$$

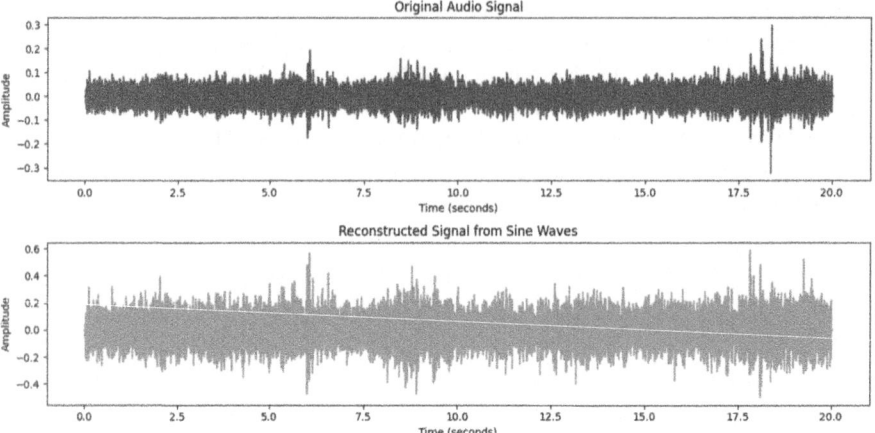

**Fig. 3.** Perform Fourier Transform on the Extracted Natural White Noise Audio.

- s(t) is the reconstructed time-domain signal.
- N is the total number of frequency components.
- $a^n$ is the amplitude of the $n$-th frequency component.
- $f_n$ is the frequency of the $n$-th frequency component.
- $\varphi_n$ is the phase of the $n$-th frequency component.
- t is the time variable.

In terms of visual presentation, the audio visualization is achieved using TouchDesigner. Through programming, a real-time visual experience combining audio with particle effects is created. By inputting the audio signal and mapping it to the particle system via mathematical operations, unique visual effects that are synchronized with the music are created by adjusting particle attributes such as emitters, life cycle, velocity, and color (Fig. 4).

**Parametric Modeling and Functional Fitting.** To achieve dynamic changes and real-time adjustments of the wall, we use the Grasshopper plugin for Rhino to conduct parametric modeling. First, we establish a model of the movable curtain wall, set the dimensions of the plane, and generate a rectangular plane through the "Rectangle" component. Then, we convert the rectangle into a solid using the "Brep Box" component; after extracting the faces, we use the "Fragments" component to divide the extruded curtain wall surface into multiple small panels. The division of the panels can be controlled by the "Number Slider" component. Additionally, the "Construct Domain" component is used to define a range of values to drive other parameter changes, and the «Vector" component generates vectors for offsetting planes. Next, we utilize the «Random" component to generate random numbers that control the movement direction and speed of each panel, allowing the panels to swing or rotate randomly within a certain range, simulating scenarios like the random swaying of leaves in nature or the swaying of grass in the wind, producing sounds akin to those in an irregular natural environment. To precisely control each panel, we use the "Paneling" component to achieve individual deformation or movement. The built-in "Graph Mapper" component in Grasshopper can fit function

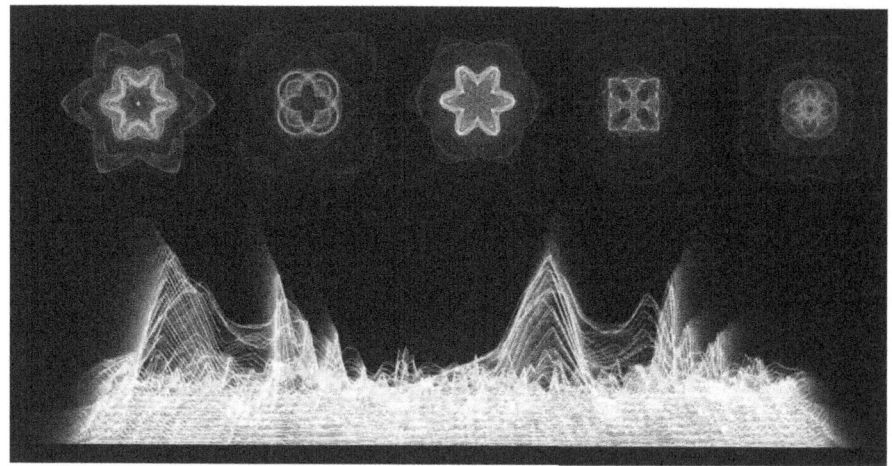

**Fig. 4.** Audio visualization by using TouchDesigner.

curves, and using the"Value" component to map points on the curve to a range and then reverse them, we ultimately create a wall installation that changes with the rhythm of the audio (Figs. 5, 6 and 7).

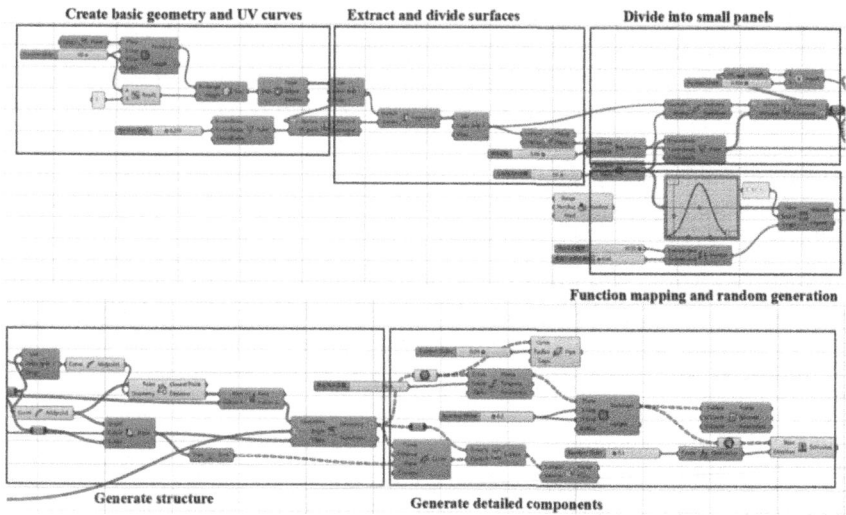

**Fig. 5.** The steps for parametric modeling and control using Grasshopper.

**Materials and Structure.** The material selection for the panels includes lightweight, somewhat elastic, and smooth-surfaced materials such as polycarbonate (PC) sheets or acrylic sheets. These materials are light in weight and can produce movement under minimal driving force. They also have good acoustic reflection and scattering properties,

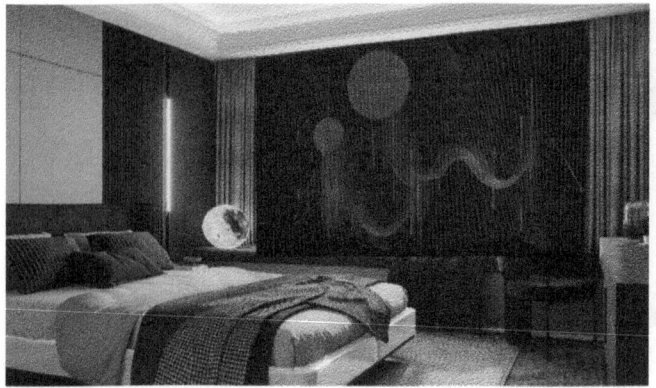

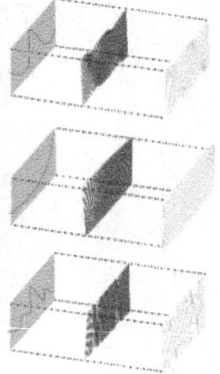

**Fig. 6.** Home use scenario diagram of walls.    **Fig. 7.** Different forms of wall changes.

which aid in the propagation and diffusion of sound. When they collide with each other or rub against the surrounding air, they can produce soft and continuous sounds, making them suitable for simulating sound elements in natural environments. The framework material is a sturdy and lightweight aluminum alloy framework. Aluminum alloy has a high strength-to-weight ratio, ensuring the stability of the wall structure while reducing overall weight, facilitating installation and maintenance. The framework is designed in a grid pattern, providing evenly distributed support points for the panels, ensuring that each panel is effectively secured and remains stable during movement.

The support layout is planned rationally according to the size and shape of the wall. For larger walls, internal support structures are added to prevent deformation of the frame due to vibrations caused by panel movement. For example, in a long strip-shaped wall, vertical and horizontal support beams are set at regular intervals to form a stable structural framework, ensuring that the entire wall can operate normally under various conditions.

Connect the panels to the frame using elastic rubber or silicone connectors. These flexible materials allow the panels to move freely within a certain range while providing moderate damping, making the panel movement more stable and reducing the noise caused by rigid collisions. At the same time, the flexible connectors also act as a cushion to protect the panels and the frame from damage. Design pivot or swing joints for each panel to enable them to move flexibly according to control commands. The joint design should consider the degrees of freedom and precision of movement, such as using spherical joints to allow the panels to rotate freely in multiple directions.

Integrate the driving motors or electromagnetic actuators inside the frame and connect them to the control chips via concealed wiring. This not only keeps the appearance of the wall neat but also protects the driving devices from external environmental influences. At the same time, the driving devices should be positioned reasonably to ensure they can provide power evenly to each panel, achieving precise motion control. A control box is set up at the bottom or side of the wall, equipped with control chips, power modules, and signal processing units. The control box communicates with external devices (such as user interfaces, sensors, etc.) via wired or wireless means, receiving user commands and sensor feedback signals to achieve real-time control of the wall's movement and sound.

**Interactive Design.** The wall primarily generates sound through the collision and friction between mechanical panels, as well as other forms of relative motion. It also incorporates sound characteristics such as frequency and amplitude that simulate natural white noise. The wall creates a closed loop of "panel movement → sound change → light and shadow follow," allowing users to trigger an audible and visible natural healing experience through touch, environmental changes, or simple gestures.

This design utilizes a wall device composed of polycarbonate (PC) sheets or acrylic sheets, equipped with internal driving motors or electromagnetic actuators to facilitate wall movement. The wall device is fitted with sound sensors, light sensors, and touch sensors, which collectively monitor environmental conditions and user interaction. The sound sensor is used to detect ambient noise levels, the light sensor measures the intensity of ambient light, and the touch sensor detects direct user contact. Data from these sensors is transmitted to the control chip inside the control box, which then automatically adjusts the wall's movement and audio-visual output based on the received information.

When the ambient noise is high, the system automatically increases the volume of white noise to provide a soothing auditory masking effect. In dimly lit environments, the brightness of the lighting is automatically enhanced to offer an appropriate visual experience. Direct user interaction with the wall, such as touching or tapping, triggers specific audio-visual feedback from the wall, such as playing particular sound clips or changing the color of the lights. The movement of the wall is controlled by built-in driving motors, which not only generate sound but also combine with the white noise played by the built-in speakers to create a harmonious auditory experience. Concurrently, the lighting or projections on the wall change in response to the movement of the panels, providing visual feedback to users and enhancing the sense of immersion.

# 4  Discussion and Limitation

This study does not merely play back sounds from natural environments such as bird songs, streams, and wind, but rather simulates the frequency and pitch characteristics of natural sound movements to create an atmosphere that makes users feel close to nature. At the same time, it combines mechanical sound generation methods, providing a new approach to producing white noise and adding dynamic changes and layers to the sound. By integrating these two methods, a richer and more three-dimensional sound effect can be produced. The modeling of the wall relies on the Grasshopper tool in Rhino, achieving full parametric modeling, which allows for customization and iterative design according to specific needs. With the help of mathematical functions and algorithms, the parameters of white noise can be precisely controlled. For example, using mathematical tools such as the Fourier transform, sound signals can be analyzed and processed in the frequency domain, enabling precise adjustments to sound frequency, phase, and other parameters. This helps create purer and more uniform white noise, enhancing the healing effect. Moreover, users can interact with the wall to adjust the volume, frequency, and rhythm of the white noise according to different usage scenarios and needs, thus obtaining a more personalized healing experience. In the bedroom, it can be adjusted to soft and soothing white noise to help users fall asleep quickly; in the office, it can be adjusted to lively and invigorating white noise to improve work efficiency.

The wall may require the integration of various sensors, control chips, and other complex devices, which entails certain initial construction costs and subsequent maintenance challenges and expenses. During interaction, issues such as signal interference and data transmission delays may arise, leading to untimely or inaccurate responses from the wall and thus affecting user experience. Factors such as temperature, humidity, and electromagnetic interference in different environments can impact the performance of the wall's equipment. In humid or high-temperature conditions, the equipment may malfunction or experience reduced performance, limiting the wall's application in certain specialized environments. Moreover, the white noise interactive healing wall requires a certain amount of space for installation and layout, which may be difficult to achieve in places with limited space, such as small residences or offices. Additionally, the size and shape of the wall may also be restricted by architectural structures, affecting its design and layout. Due to limitations in space and budget, the device has not yet been constructed on-site. In future work, the author will further test and refine the conceptual design.

## 5 Conclusion

This paper primarily introduces the design and research of an interactive white noise healing wall based on Attention Restoration Theory (ART). The article first analyzes the issues of attention fatigue, anxiety, and insomnia among young people in modern society due to prolonged cognitive load, as well as the severe impact of sleep disorders on health. Subsequently, through a literature review and related studies, the paper explores the positive role of white noise in emotional healing and improving sleep quality. Based on this, the healing wall developed in this study generates white noise that approximates the frequency curve of natural sounds through mechanical movement patterns and parametric modeling techniques, combined with mathematical function control. The wall also incorporates design strategies such as "being away," "extent," "fascination," and "compatibility" to help people restore their attention, reduce stress, and alleviate anxiety and insomnia. Furthermore, the paper discusses how to design an interactive device to produce white noise to relieve sleep anxiety among young people, providing new ideas and methods for improving their sleep quality and mental health.

## References

1. Oppenheim, A.V., Schafer, R.W.: Discrete-time signal processing. Prentice Hall, Upper Saddle River (1989)
2. Stoica, P., Moses, R. L.: Spectral analysis of signals. Pearson Prentice Hall, Upper Saddle River (2005)
3. Ohly, H., et al.: Attention restoration theory: a systematic review of the attention restoration potential of exposure to natural environments. J. Toxicol. Environ. Health Part B **19**(7), 305–343 (2016)

4. Dittrich, J.: Bedtime Stories: Audiobooks, Podcasts, and Reading as Listening (and Sleeping). Intermédialités: Histoire et Théorie des Arts, des Lettres et des Techniques **41**, 1–20 (2023)
5. Shen, Y.: Research on the visual design of sleep aid APP based on implicit memory. Master's thesis. Jiangnan University (2023). https://doi.org/10.27169/d.cnki.gwqgu.2023.002413
6. Wu, X., Wang, Y., Guo, H., Zheng, L., Huang, S.: A survey of research on active control algorithms for vehicle interior sound quality. J. Shanghai Univ. Eng. Sci. **36**(3), 231–237 (2022). https://doi.org/10.12299/jsues.21-0239
7. Yu, J.: Exploration of interactive sound devices. Master's thesis. Nanjing University of the Arts (2022). https://doi.org/10.27250/d.cnki.gnjyc.2022.000197.Proposed solution
8. Deng, Y.Y., Chen, K.A., Li, H., Dang, B., Liu, J.B.: The white noise standard sample method and application for subjective noise evaluation. J. Northwest. Polytech. Univ. **40**(4), 746–754 (2022)
9. Chafei, D.F.: Research on new signal processing methods based on stable distribution white noise. Doctoral dissertation, Dalian University of Technology (2025). https://doi.org/10.7666/d.y865991
10. Kaplan, S., Kaplan, R.: The Experience of Nature: A Psychological Perspective. Cambridge University Press (1989)
11. Baidu Baike: Autonomous Sensory Meridian Response (ASMR) (2024). https://baike.baidu.com/item/%E8%87%AA%E5%8F%91%E6%80%A7%E7%9F%A5%E8%A7%89%E7%BB%8F%E7%BB%9C%E5%8F%8D%E5%BA%94/62106603
12. Heckbert, P.: Fourier transforms and the fast fourier transform (FFT) algorithm. Comput. Graph. **2**(1995), 15–463 (1995)

# AI in Augmented Cognition

# LLM-Augmented Curriculum Design: A Framework for Curriculum Innovation in Digital Public Infrastructure Education

Josephine Lusi[1]([✉]) [ID], Anastasija Nikiforova[2] [ID], and Ingrid Pappel[1] [ID]

[1] Tallinn University of Technology, Akadeemia Tee 15A, Tallinn, Estonia
`{josephine.lusi,ingrid.pappel}@taltech.ee`
[2] University of Tartu, Narva mnt 18, 51009 Tartu, Estonia
`anastasija.nikiforova@ut.ee`

**Abstract.** Digital Public Infrastructures (DPIs) holds the potential to fundamentally transform both public and private service delivery; however, their full impact has yet to be realized. For the full impact of DPI systems to be exploited, practitioners must be equipped with an interdisciplinary understanding of how these systems can transform societal service delivery. Traditional educational curricula often fall short in adequately preparing professionals for this transition, as existing curricula have not been sufficiently adapted to reflect the complexities of current societal needs, thus, the necessity for a modern approach to the curriculum design process. This paper outlines the development process of curricula for two training programs that integrated Large Language Models (LLMs) as an assistive tool, to map out relevant, evidence-based and pedagogically sound educational content. We propose an LLM-augmented framework that could serve as a reference model for incorporating LLMs into the curriculum design process. Our work aims to support educators and policymakers responsible for curriculum development in higher education institutions.

**Keywords:** Artificial Intelligence · Digital Public Infrastructure · Digital Competencies · Curriculum Design · Education · Large Language Models

## 1 Introduction

In the digital age, the public sector faces increasing pressure to modernize and adopt innovative technological infrastructure, to improve efficiency, transparency, and service delivery. Consequently, two key technological developments have gained significant attention in recent years. One is Artificial Intelligence (AI), and Generative AI (GenAI) as the subtype of the former, and for governments, this has largely manifested as the use of interaction support systems (e.g., chatbots and virtual assistants) and data-driven policy-making [1]. Another significant technological development is Digital Public Infrastructure (DPI), which facilitates the provision of various inclusive digital solutions, such as secure payment systems [2, 3], and healthcare services [4], from both public and private sector players, by utilizing reusable, and scalable digital systems [5] that supports greater

© The Author(s), under exclusive license to Springer Nature Switzerland AG 2025
D. D. Schmorrow and C. M. Fidopiastis (Eds.): HCII 2025, LNAI 15778, pp. 193–204, 2025.
https://doi.org/10.1007/978-3-031-93724-8_15

interoperability of a country's ICT ecosystem. DPIs are defined as "*a set of shared digital systems that are secure and interoperable and can support the inclusive delivery of and access to public and private services at societal scale*" [2, 6].

However, the presence of a sophisticated technological landscape does not inherently guarantee an improved public sector delivery; harnessing the full benefits of AI and DPI technologies is heavily reliant on the presence of suitable talent equipped with the necessary knowledge, skills and competences [7–9] to design, deploy, manage and sustainably maintain these solutions. Without the needed human talent, public sector institutions will continually lag behind when it comes to adopting and diffusing novel technologies [10]. Thus, the emerging technologies landscape necessitates not only technical skills but also advanced cognitive abilities and complex social-interaction competencies [11] to operate effectively in a dynamic technological ecosystem that is susceptible to rapid technological advancements. Unfortunately, the curricula employed by training institutions have not yet been fully adapted to meet the evolving demands of real-world applications.

Existing training initiatives, often characterized by static curricula and passive learning formats, fail to adequately address the intricate interplay of technical and non-technical skills necessary to navigate contemporary challenges and opportunities [12]. This presents a unique demand for educators[1]: a strategic approach to designing training curricula that maps the current and future skills and competencies and better aligns with real-world demands. However, the process of designing and updating curriculum is resource-intensive (in terms of both human and time resources) and, due to its specifics, often manual and prone to subjectivity, and revisions may not necessarily match the rapid technological advancements or the emerging disciplines [13]. The constraints on instructors' time make it difficult for them to create a curriculum that would meet today's needs.

The potential of AI in educational settings, as well as the necessity for AI literacy, places educators at the forefront of these new and exciting breakthroughs that were previously relegated to obscure computer science laboratories. Teachers and administrators are required to have clear perspectives on the potential of AI in education and, eventually, to incorporate this ground-breaking technology into their practice [14, 15]. While some educators view GenAI as an opportunity to enhance learning and teaching efficiency, others see it as a disruptive threat to academic integrity and pedagogical norms, being often resistant towards (Gen)AI adoption, with resistance primarily stemming from skepticism about its educational value, but, more importantly, challenges in adapting content and assessment methods, resulting in perceived cost-benefit imbalance. i.e., this resistance is driven not merely by technology aversion but by perceived cost-benefit imbalance [13]. This dual perspective emphasizes the complexity of technology adoption in educational settings, where attitudes are shaped not only by the technology itself but also by institutional guidelines, cultural attitudes, and individual experiences. The uneven implementation of institutional policies across universities even within one country (e.g., Estonia [13]) further underscores the need for a supportive infrastructure.

---

[1] The term educators refers to individuals who are involved in the process of teaching, guiding, and facilitating learning. Synonyms for "educators," as used throughout this article, include "teachers" and "instructors".

Currently, most research [16] focuses on examining student adoption of GenAI and LLM tools in higher education institutions context, overlooking educators' perspective an implying need for transformation of the current curricula despite their central role in the educational ecosystem. In this paper, we explore how LLMs can be embedded into the curriculum design process, to support the creation of curricula with a multidisciplinary facet that aligns well with contemporary and future real-world demands. We propose that rather than viewing LLMs as a threat to academic integrity and pedagogical norms, instructors should embrace it as an opportunity, including to reform the outdated curriculum design process. This is because LLMs exhibit remarkable proficiencies due to their capacity to process, reason, and learn from vast large data sets. However, we maintain that the availability and functionality of LLM tools alone cannot guarantee their usefulness in crafting relevant pedagogy. Their usefulness heavily relies on the instructors' ability to craft deliberate prompts, while exercising critical thinking. Thus, we theorize that LLMs cannot be seen as substitutes for human educators but rather as feasible resources that can alleviate the design burden on the instructors, augmenting curricula redesign process, allowing the instructors with ample time to dedicate more time to effective teaching and student engagement. The main contribution of this paper is a conceptual framework for refining and augmenting existing curricula for educational programs (incl. higher education institutions) with LLM technologies.

The paper is structured as follows: Sect. 2 provides a background on the topic, Sect. 3 presents the research context, Sect. 4 – conceptual framework, with Sect. 5 providing discussion and concluding the paper.

## 2 Background

The rapid evolution of DPIs is transforming societies [17], impacting citizens lives globally. This means that poor design and implementation of DPI systems can severely undermine the effectiveness of these infrastructures and jeopardize the security of citizens' sensitive data. As such, there needs to be a fundamental evolution in professional development and higher education as the implementers, who are tasked with implementing these systems, are currently in the workforce. Pedagogy should increasingly focus on fostering interdisciplinary knowledge and a wide range of skills and competencies, with a particular emphasis on cultivating critical thinking skills that enable learners to effectively evaluate and utilize insights from [6, 11] among learners, as the successful design and implementation of these critical systems heavily relies on a skilled workforce with a nuanced understanding of the complexities involved.

In recent years, the use of Artificial Intelligence in Education (AIeD) [18] applications, and in particular LLMs tools [19] has been on the rise. Research has increasingly highlighted the opportunities for LLM tools to enhance teaching and learning experiences at all levels of education [19], e.g., in creating personalized learning experiences and as virtual facilitators. From the educators' perspective, research has increasingly highlighted the use of learning analytics in generating interactive educational material [20], learning quizzes [21], evaluating students' answers [16] and automating student feedback provision, with positive evidence on the use of LLM tools for curriculum (re)design [22, 23].

Curriculum design plays a vital role in creating engaging and impactful learning experiences for learners [23, 26]. The aim of curriculum design is to curate a programme that equips students with the necessary competencies to thrive in their future careers. Traditional curricula are largely shaped by educators with experience in pedagogy, and occasionally industry knowledge, who transfer their own experiences and values into their teaching practices. While this approach has its merits, in the dynamic world, it can also lead to frustrations, as the knowledge imparted may be narrow, shaped by the perspectives of a single expert, and failing to inherently consider all the factors at hand. Thus, the need for consideration of LLMs to be embedded in the curriculum (re)design process.

## 3  Research Context

Our study employs an exploratory case study approach - a well-established methodology for examining complex phenomena with limited prior empirical research [27]. Case studies, particularly, when conducted in a comparative manner, allow for in-depth investigations of specific instances while facilitating cross-case analysis to identify patterns and draw broader conclusions. This research focuses on two training programs developed by the GovStack Initiative, a multistakeholder community dedicated to accelerating global digital transformation by empowering governments to build sustainable digital infrastructure and design human-centered digital services (see Table 1). As part of its mandate, GovStack equips public and private organizations with the tools and knowledge necessary to navigate the digital world, providing open access to service design tools, templates, and technical expertise for practitioners working within the DPI domain. Since 2022, Tallinn University of Technology (TalTech), two of authors are affiliated with, has been engaged as an academic partner with this initiative.

The curriculum (re)design - analysis and integration of curriculum was informed by theoretical models that outline its lifecycle from analysis to implementation, with the Technological Pedagogical Content Knowledge (TPACK) framework [24] serving as a foundational model for understanding the interplay between technology, pedagogy, and content knowledge in educational contexts, allowing LLMs such as GPT-4, Gemini, Bard, DeepSeek etc. to assess existing gaps, redundancies, or misalignments in curricula [25], thereafter, systematically highlighting opportunities for improvement [23] based on academic standards, societal trends and technological trends to ensures that curricula remain adaptable to societal and industrial changes. A state-of-the-art GPT-4 was chosen for its advanced natural language processing capabilities, which allow it to process large volumes of text, understand context, and generate insights from diverse and complex datasets. Data sources used for curriculum analysis and integration included (1) global DPI and related offers gathered from the job market, (2) cross-cutting scientific projects in AI and GovTech, (3) existing similar training courses, (4) real case study solutions based on GovStack DPI implementation, and (5) critical skills gaps identified in various reports from global organizations [7, 8, 28]. The selection of these data sources was informed by a hybrid approach that combined traditional curriculum design principles with contemporary educational frameworks, ensuring that the proposed curriculum was not only informed by sector-specific needs but also aligned with emerging trends and future demands with respect to the diffusion of technology. Importantly, while GPT-4 played a central role in generating curriculum content, human oversight was crucial throughout the process to ensure that the final curriculum was coherent, in-depth, accurate and aligned with the pedagogical frameworks.

As part of this collaboration, curricula (re-)design programs were implemented, with an objective to examine how LLMs can be leveraged to structure the curriculum as illustrated in Fig. 1.

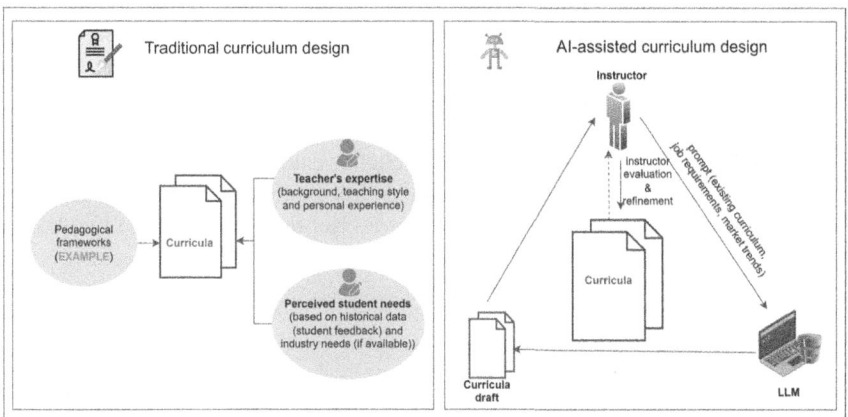

**Fig. 1.** Traditional curriculum design vs AI-assisted curriculum design.

The first case study was **the Women in GovTech Challenge 2023,** a service design training program that was one of the first Challenge-Based Learning[2] training programs offered by GovStack. This pilot program aimed to examine how (1) CBL can extend learning beyond traditional classroom settings, and (2) how LLMs can be integrated into the curriculum design process. The program required learners to attend one lecture session each week (1.5h), complete an online class (1.5h), and participate in the team's group exercise (2h), for a total of five contact hours weekly over the course of eight weeks. Within this timeframe, learners were expected to advance from beginner level to upper-intermediate proficiency level in service design, applying these principles to develop a user-friendly public e-service prototype that incorporated the three key building blocks: identity, payments and information mediator. At the end of the 8-week program, participants were expected to present their public e-service prototype in a panel session, with the best three teams selected by the panelists invited to pitch their solutions at the World Summit on the Information Society (WSIS) 2024. Our observations indicated that the use of LLMs encouraged participants to creatively incorporate these models into their design processes.

**The GovStack Architects Training program** built upon the findings from the Women in GovTech pilot program. The primary objective of this program was to assess,

---

[2] Challenge-based learning is a multidisciplinary educational approach that is structured outside the traditional learning scope, takes places in an international context, and aims to find collaboratively developed solutions to sociotechnical problems [19].

whether the outcomes and insights from the previous study could be replicated and extended beyond its narrow focus. Similar to the pilot program, the GovStack Architects training embraced a CBL approach, requiring learners to participate in one lecture session each week (1.5 h), complete one class online (1.5 h), and participate in the team's group exercise (2h), totaling five contact hours per week, over the course of six weeks. At the end of the training program, learners were expected to demo a live simulation of a prototype government architecture, highlighting the practicality of all relevant building blocks, including the three key building blocks. Our observations from this second study confirmed the key findings from the first pilot: LLMs significantly enhanced efficiency in curriculum development, particularly in structuring training content, prototype workbooks and generating feedback for the learners. Moreover, participants continued to integrate LLMs into their design thinking process, further strengthening their creative problem-solving approaches. Expanding the scope of LLM to include job requirement matching beyond the pilot study proved beneficial, enhancing the curriculum development process by allowing for more targeted skill-building aligned with real-world professional demands. Table 1 below provides a brief description of the two training programmes.

**Table 1.** Description of the Two Training Programmes.

|  | Women in GovTech | GovStack Architects |
|---|---|---|
| Period | Oct 2023-Mar 2024 | Sep 2024-Nov 2024 |
| Audience | Public sector officials, females only | All sectors, all genders with technical knowledge on architectural frameworks |
| Setting | Online | Online |
| No. of participants | $N = 106$ | $N = 212$ |

The trainees took courses asynchronously at their own pace through Atingi (a Moodle-based digital learning platform used by the GovStack entity) and Coursera, with the weekly lecture sections conducted via Microsoft Teams.

## 4  Results: Conceptual Framework

The development of a CBL framework for training public sector professionals in DPI proficiency requires a novel approach to curriculum design—one that is adaptive, data-driven, and aligned with societal and industrial changes. The proposed framework is informed by the results of the case studies described in Sect. 3.

### 4.1  Curriculum Design

The iterative curriculum development process employed in this study is informed by the Plan-Do-Check-Act (PDCA) model that serves as the foundational framework (Fig. 2).

The proposed LLM-powered curricula design framework suggests curricula to be developed in four steps, namely (1) curriculum assessment (*plan* phase in PDCA), (2) goal setting (*do* phase in PDCA), (3) curricula alignment (*check* phase in PDCA), (4) curriculum review (*act* phase in PDCA).

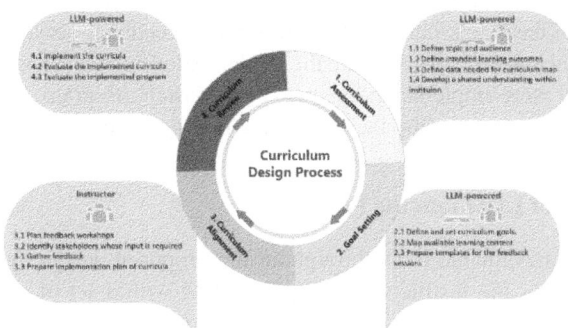

**Fig. 2.** LLM-powered curricula design framework

Curriculum **assessment** phase of the curriculum design process establishes a foundation for understanding curriculum outcomes. It involves a thorough evaluation of the curriculum and, where applicable, the associated program, particularly in the context of existing offerings. The assessment is undertaken through four stages: (1) defining the course topic and intended audience; (2) identifying key learning themes, which involves an in-depth understanding and scrutiny of educational standards and frameworks, educational reports, desired learning outcomes, instructional, and any prerequisite knowledge or skills; (3) determining the type of data needed for the assessment and where to source for the data, i.e. industry reports; (4) formulating a shared understanding of the curricula within the institution, which includes the targeted course duration, instructional method, and assessment methods.

Following the curriculum assessment, **goals are set**. These goals are formulated through the mapping of available learning content and teaching resources. Once these goals have been established, it is vital to identify and prioritize the central areas needing further development by preparing for feedback sessions. As such, it is essential to clarify how you intend to communicate clearly: (1) the rationale for developing this program; (2) specific knowledge gaps the program aims to cover; (3) intended learning outcomes.

Next, **curriculum alignment** takes place, which refers to the coherence and consistency between the proposed learning outcomes, instructional content, and assessment methodologies. A well-structured curriculum facilitates logical competency development, ensuring learners build upon prior knowledge and experiences. Curriculum alignment is developed through several steps, largely in part to physical workshops between various stakeholders such as heads of department, relevant ministries, educators, civil servants, and students, as is the case for TalTech institutions (may differ for other institutions though). In this case, it is necessary to clearly identify stakeholders, whose input is needed in the process, which is to be done through stakeholder analysis. These key individuals can be selected based on their knowledge and skill sets within the created curriculum. This step of the framework involves curriculum reinforcement through reflection on work experiences and individual knowledge. Following the feedback sessions, feedback is analyzed, and preparations for the implementation of the curricula commence.

The continuous curriculum development process is heavily reliant on the collection and integration of feedback, i.e., **curriculum review**. Feedback serves as a vital instrument through which instructors evaluate the implemented curricula and program at large (e.g., if curricula were implemented as part of a Master' program) and may enhance curriculum development, thereby facilitating the improvement of learning outcomes.

## 4.2   Integration of LLM into the Process

LLMs can serve as valuable tools throughout the proposed design cycle as shown in Fig. 3. This involves the instructor feeding the LLM with a set of queries that guide the model through a logical, step-by-step reasoning process. LLM's ability to quickly ask questions and adapt to a given circumstance can make it a valuable partner for the instructor in the co-creation process. However, its usefulness is limited to the use of structured prompting, to help refine the output [29].

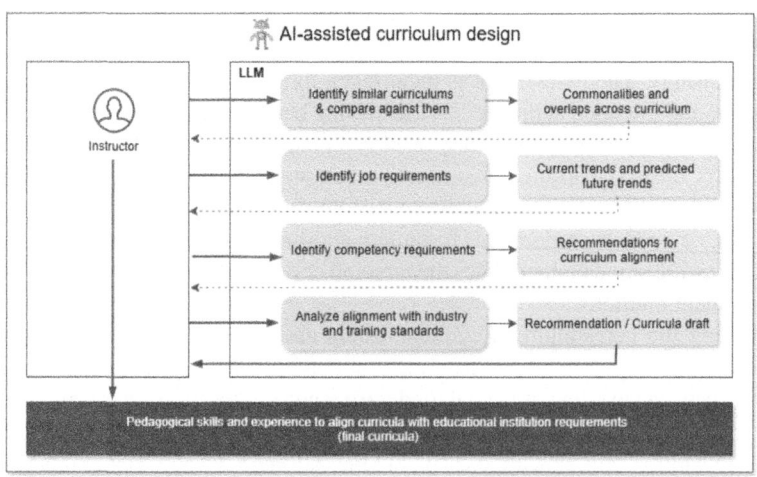

**Fig. 3.**  LLM-augmented curriculum design.

Structured prompting has emerged as a critical skill in the age of LLMs, enabling users to effectively guide and customize these powerful tools to achieve desired outputs [30]. The prompts/queries in Fig. 4 below were designed by authors before the beginning of each program to help the LLM break down complex tasks and consider all relevant factors. By processing the information provided, the LLM learns from the structure, content, and pedagogical approaches within the knowledge base. It then suggests content enhancements that align with the established learning outcomes and can even identify areas where the curriculum may need to be expanded or refined, as respective guidelines suggest, e.g., by asking to consult with current and future trends.

**Role:**
You are a curriculum development expert responsible for designing the *GovStack Architects Training Program*. This course aims to provide participants with a foundational understanding of how the key GovStack Building Blocks (BBs) and Public Administration Reference Architecture (PAERA) principles work together to create a sustainable and efficient digital government ecosystem. The primary focus is to equip participants with the technical skills required to design modern digital infrastructures and effectively communicate these designs to public sector stakeholders.

**Target Audience:**
This program is intended for public sector officials who possess technical expertise on....

**Context:**
As governments increasingly turn to digital technologies to transform services and operations, the need for skilled digital teams capable of aligning technology strategies with broader governmental visions has never been greater. The *GovStack Architects Program* offers a foundational approach to building sustainable digital infrastructure, improving interoperability between government entities, and fostering effective digital governance.

**Pedagogical Approach:**
The curriculum will incorporate the principles of the Public Administration Reference Architecture (PAERA) to furnish participants with both technical design knowledge and an understanding of how public sector governance, organizational processes, and digital infrastructure are interconnected.

Upon completing the program, learners will design a prototype architecture tailored to their country, including mock-ups of the architectural framework based on one public e-service example.

**Learning Activities:**
Participants will engage in both group and individual activities.

**Constraints:**

- The curriculum must avoid overwhelming participants with excessive technical detail, considering varying levels of prior knowledge among public sector officials.
- Content should be adaptable to diverse governmental structures and policy environments.
- The curriculum should remain focused on practical applications of DPI, using real-world government use cases rather than theoretical concepts.

**Development Approach:**

1. **Analyse Existing Programs:**
   Review and evaluate existing courses and programs related to GovTech, Digital Transformation, and Digital Public Infrastructure (DPI). Identify common trends, overlaps, and best practices to inform curriculum design.
2. **Research Job Requirements:**
   Conduct research through UN, DPI safeguards, and government websites to identify key job requirements for a government architect, considering both current industry needs and anticipated future trends in digital government.
3. **Cross-Reference Competency Frameworks:**
   Compare these identified job requirements with the OECD Digital Government Competency Framework and the European Commission's DigComp Competency Framework to ensure alignment with global standards.
4. **Identify Skills Gaps:**
   Based on the analysis, identify skills and knowledge gaps within the current training ecosystem. Align these findings with industry standards (e.g., TOGAF) to ensure the curriculum addresses both immediate needs and emerging trends in digital governance and infrastructure.

**Fig. 4.** Prompting Guidelines for the design of the GovStack Architects program curriculum.

In evaluating the outputs, the instructor engages critical thinking and considers factors such as: (a) *How well the overall output aligns with the goals set in the second phase of the curriculum design cycle?* (b) *Whether the generated content is factually accurate?* (c) *Whether the curriculum is pedagogically sound?* Based on this, the instructor can revise prompts to further guide LLM tool and ask follow-up questions to finetune the generated content. Once satisfied with the LLM-generated content, the instructor curates the outputs into a cohesive curriculum, ensuring that it is aligned with the vision set during the goal-setting process and overall institution rules.

It is important to note that feedback sessions crucial to refining the curriculum, fall outside the loop of LLM creation. In other words, while the LLM assists in generating the curriculum, the feedback phase provides an external review that informs the next iteration of the design process. However, LLMs can still play an instrumental role in this phase by generating guiding prompts for the feedback session. These prompts can direct feedback discussions towards specific aspects of the curriculum, such as content accuracy, pedagogical effectiveness, or alignment with industry needs.

What is important to note, is that curriculum design and approval are two distinct processes. While the design process is iterative and adaptable, the approval process is typically separate and more linear, often requiring multiple stakeholder reviews, as well as being heavily educational entity dependent. As such, we do not cover it.

## 5   Conclusion

In this study, we explored how LLMs can transform curriculum design and implementation. While educators face challenges in adapting content, teaching approaches, and assessment methods to integrate LLMs, these obstacles are not purely technological. The resistance often stems from concerns over the perceived cost-benefit imbalance, rather than an aversion to technology itself. However, our study demonstrates that the adoption of LLMs does not merely require changes in pedagogy—it can actively drive those changes, where even curriculum design can be facilitated by LLMs. This, however, requires acquisition of new skills, such as prompt engineering, which guide the LLMs to generate curriculum content that aligns with both educational, market, and societal needs.

Our experience with the conducted case studies suggest that AI-assisted curriculum design can offer reproducibility and standardization in implementation. Once designed, the curriculum can be effectively rolled out across different educational contexts with consistency, supported by the data-driven insights generated by the AI. However, while LLM serves as an assistive tool, the human element remains central to the curriculum design process; thus, LLM's role is to augment, rather than replace, the educator.

**Acknowledgements.** This research was supported by the GovStack Foundation through the Government of Germany (Deutsche Gesellschaft für Internationale Zusammenarbeit), the Estonian government, and the International Telecommunication Union (ITU).

**Disclosure of Interests.** The authors have no competing interests to declare that are relevant to the content of this article.

## References

1. OECD: Governing with Artificial Intelligence: Are governments ready? OECD Artificial Intelligence Papers, No. 20, OECD Publishing, Paris (2024)

2. G20: G20 Framework for Systems of Digital Public Infrastructure (2023). https://g7g20-doc uments.org/fileadmin/G7G20_documents/2023/G20/India/Sherpa-Track/Digital%20Econ omy%20Ministers/2%20Ministers'%20Annex/G20_Digital%20Economy%20Ministers% 20Meeting_Annex1_19082023.pdf
3. Chaudhuri, R.: Decoding the G20 Consensus on Digital Public Infrastructure: A Key Outcome of India's Presidency | Carnegie Endowment for International Peace (2023)
4. Bill & Melinda Gates Foundation: Digital Public Infrastructure | Bill & Melinda Gates Foundation. https://www.gatesfoundation.org/our-work/programs/global-growth-and-opport unity/digital-public-infrastructure. Accessed 29 Jan 2025
5. GovStack: Digital public Infrastructure, building blocks, and their relation to digital public goods | GovStack. https://www.govstack.global/news/digital-public-infrastructure-building-blocks-and-their-relation-to-digital-public-goods/. Accessed 04 Dec 2024
6. OECD: Digital public infrastructure for digital governments. OECD Public Governance Policy Papers, No. 68, OECD Publishing, Paris (2024)
7. OECD: The OECD Framework for digital talent and skills in the public sector. OECD Working Papers on Public Governance, No. 45, OECD Publishing, Paris (2021)
8. OECD: Skills for the Digital Transition: Assessing Recent Trends Using Big Data. OECD Publishing, Paris (2022)
9. Vuorikari, R., Kluzer, S., Punie, Y.: DigComp 2.2: The Digital Competence Framework for Citizens - With new examples of knowledge, skills and attitudes. Publications Office of the European Union, Luxembourg (Luxembourg) (2022)
10. World Economic Forum (WEF): The Future of Jobs Report (2023)
11. Medaglia, R., Mikalef, P., Tangi, L.: Competences and governance practices for artificial intelligence in the public sector. Publications Office of the European Union, Luxembourg (Luxembourg) (2024)
12. Scott, C.: The futures of learning 3: what kind of pedagogies for the 21st century? Int. J. Bus. Educ. **164** (2023)
13. Kalmus, J.-E., Nikiforova, A.: Generative AI Adoption in Higher Education: Exploring Educator Resistance in Estonian Universities (2024)
14. Holmes, W., Tuomi, I.: State of the art and practice in AI in education. Eur. J. Educ. **57**, 542–570 (2022)
15. Agostini, D., Picasso, F.: Large Language Models for Sustainable Assessment and Feedback in Higher Education: Towards a Pedagogical and Technological Framework (2024)
16. Moore, S., Nguyen, H.A., Bier, N., Domadia, T., Stamper, J.: Assessing the quality of student-generated short answer questions using GPT-3. In: Hilliger, I., Muñoz-Merino, P.J., De Laet, T., Ortega-Arranz, A., Farrell, T. (eds.) Educating for a New Future: Making Sense of Technology-Enhanced Learning Adoption, pp. 243–257. Springer, Cham (2022)
17. Eaves, D., Mazzucato, M., Vasconcellos, B.: Digital public infrastructure and public value: what is "public" about DPI? UCL Institute for Innovation and Public Purpose, Working Paper Series (IIPP WP 2024-05). (2024)
18. Zawacki-Richter, O., Marín, V.I., Bond, M., Gouverneur, F.: Systematic review of research on artificial intelligence applications in higher education – where are the educators? Int. J. Educ. Technol. High. Educ. **16**, 39 (2019). https://doi.org/10.1186/s41239-019-0171-0
19. Kasneci, E., et al.: ChatGPT for good? On opportunities and challenges of large language models for education. Learn. Individ. Differ. **103**, 102274 (2023)
20. Dijkstra, R., Genç, Z., Kayal, S., Kamps, J.: Reading comprehension quiz generation using generative pre-trained transformers. In: iTextbooks@ AIED, pp. 4–17 (2022)
21. Sarsa, S., Denny, P., Hellas, A., Leinonen, J.: Automatic generation of programming exercises and code explanations using large language models. In: Proceedings of the 2022 ACM Conference on International Computing Education Research - Volume 1, pp. 27–43. ACM, New York (2022)

22. Zamecnik, A., Barthakur, A., Wang, H., Dawson, S.: Mapping employable skills in higher education curriculum using LLMs. In: Ferreira Mello, R., Rummel, N., Jivet, I., Pishtari, G., Ruipérez Valiente, J.A. (eds.) Technology Enhanced Learning for Inclusive and Equitable Quality Education, pp. 18–32. Springer, Cham (2024)
23. Karataş, F., Eriçok, B., Tanrikulu, L.: Reshaping curriculum adaptation in the age of artificial intelligence: Mapping teachers' driven curriculum adaptation patterns. Br. Educ. Res. J. (2024)
24. Mishra, P., Koehler, M.J.: Technological pedagogical content knowledge: a framework for teacher knowledge. Teach. Coll. Rec. Voice Scholarsh. Educ. **108**, 1017–1054 (2006)
25. Lorenz, B., Kikkas, K., Toom, H., Lepikult, T.: A holistic approach to curriculum design and development in informatics education at the university level. Presented at the July (2024)
26. Somasundaram, M., Latha, P., Pandian, S.A.S.: Curriculum design using artificial intelligence (AI) back propagation method. Procedia Comput Sci. **172**, 134–138 (2020)
27. Yin, R.K.: Case Study Research: Design and Methods. Sage Publications, Beverly Hills (1989)
28. Gerson, D.: Leadership for a high performing civil service: Towards senior civil service systems in OECD countries. OECD Publishing, Paris (2020)
29. Mollick, E.R., Mollick, L.: Instructors as innovators: a future-focused approach to new AI learning opportunities, with prompts. SSRN Electron. J. (2024). https://doi.org/10.2139/ssrn.4802463
30. White, J., et al.: A Prompt Pattern Catalog to Enhance Prompt Engineering with ChatGPT. arXiv. abs/2302.11382 (2023)

# Towards a Proof-of-Principle of an LLM-Powered Low Resource Social Engineering Attack Coach

Lea Müller[1]([⊠]) [iD], Stefan Sütterlin[1,2] [iD], and Holger Morgenstern[1] [iD]

[1] Albstadt-Sigmaringen University, Albstadt, Germany
{muellele,suetterlin,morgenstern}@hs-albsig.de
[2] Østfold University College, Halden, Norway

**Abstract.** This article investigates the potential misuse of large language models (LLM) for low-resource, highly personalised social engineering attacks. The study explores how ChatGPT can infer personality traits during natural conversations by leveraging publicly available personal information, such as social media data, as an entry point. Utilising the social engineering personality framework (SEPF), the research endeavours to optimise attack vectors based on the Big Five personality traits, with the objective of enhancing the persuasiveness of social engineering strategies. The approach is divided into four phases: verifying conversational capabilities, conducting personality analyses, applying the SEPF for attack optimisation, and evaluating the persuasiveness of personalised attacks. The present paper offers a proof-of-principle for the initial phase, demonstrating ChatGPT's capacity to engage in natural conversations while conducting personality analyses in a discreet manner. The findings indicate that while ChatGPT exhibits the capacity to simulate human-like interactions, limitations in conversational variance and the reliability of personality assessment were observed. The study identifies challenges such as generalisations, lack of score differentiation, and confirmation bias, and proposes refinements like increasing interaction depth, adjusting scoring scales, and using tailored personas. Subsequent research will investigate enhanced personality inference techniques, personalisation of attack vectors, and their impact on susceptibility to social engineering attacks.

**Keywords:** Large Language Model · Social Engineering · Personality Assessment

## 1 Introduction

Large language models (LLM), such as OpenAI's ChatGPT [10] or Google's Gemini, are widely accessible and offer a wide range of possible uses. In addition to their beneficial applications, these models have the potential to be utilised for malevolent purposes, such as the optimisation and personalisation of social engineering attacks [6,16]. Attackers with limited resources and technical knowledge

D. D. Schmorrow and C. M. Fidopiastis (Eds.): HCII 2025, LNAI 15778, pp. 205–217, 2025.
https://doi.org/10.1007/978-3-031-93724-8_16

are already using LLMs to create optimised and personalised social engineering attacks in a low resource approach [16], for example by circumventing restrictions through strategies such as jailbreaking, reverse psychology or role-playing [6].

Concurrently, LLMs are increasingly attaining human attributes and enhanced interaction capabilities [14], thereby engendering substantial challenges in distinguishing between humans and artificial intelligence (AI). Research has demonstrated that LLMs have already attained the capacity to simulate real individuals with a reasonable degree of precision [11] and to deceive human counterparts in Turing tests at a rate that exceeds random probability [7]. The increasing difficulty of differentiating between human and AI, especially in text-based interactions, poses a rapidly growing security risk [16]. Given that people implicitly assume a human counterpart in most everyday interactions, indistinguishability could be exacerbated under real-world conditions.

Recent studies have indicated the potential of LLMs in conducting personality assessments through naturalistic conversational interactions with individuals [14] or by analysing users' status updates on social media platforms [15]. This capability, in conjunction with their human-like text generation and interaction skills, has the potential to enable LLMs to analyse human character traits, such as personality factors, in inconspicuous and human-like conversations.

This article explores the potential of leveraging LLMs, such as ChatGPT, to undertake personality assessments during conversational interactions. This approach could be employed to discern susceptible personality traits, which could inform the creation of more personalised social engineering attacks. This approach is grounded in the social engineering personality framework (SEPF), which was initially proposed by Uebelacker and Quiel [20]. The framework suggests that different personality traits may influence an individual's susceptibility to social engineering attacks. In this regard, a causal pathway is proposed between specific personality traits and the principles of persuasion identified by Cialdini [2]. In the approach presented here, the personality analysis is initiated by the LLM, starting with a few pieces of personal information about the user. Such personal information, which could be acquired through Open Source Intelligence (OSINT) in an actual attack situation, serves as an entry point for ChatGPT to initiate an interesting and natural conversation.

The article is structured as follows. The remainder of Sect. 1 will explain the underlying concepts. Section 2 will present the idea, and the specific phases of its implementation, which extend beyond the scope of this article. Section 3 and Sect. 4 will address two approaches used for the study, present the results, and the findings and lessons learned. Section 5 will provide an outlook on future research.

## 1.1   Open Source Intelligence

The term Open Source intelligence (OSINT) is used to describe the collection and analysis of publicly available information [13,19], including data retrieved from social networking sites, geolocations, or academic publications [5]. Given that this information is accessible to anyone on the Internet, there is a risk of data being misused by malicious actors with the intention of deceiving individuals [13]. The use of tailored social engineering attacks is illustrative of this risk.

This article employs information obtained from social media profiles as an initial point to facilitate a conversation initiated by ChatGPT. The primary focus of the study is on the personality analysis conducted using an LLM. Consequently, the article does not delve into the techniques and methodologies employed for acquiring publicly available information.

## 1.2   Adapting Social Engineering Attacks to Personality

Personality profiles are based on established personality psychology assessment procedures and may offer insights into susceptibility to specific persuasion principles employed in social engineering attacks. The social engineering personality framework (SEPF) [20] demonstrates the associations between specific persuasion strategies and the five personality dimensions as given by the Big Five personality model.

The Big Five personality model divides personality into five broad dimensions representing personality at the highest possible level of abstraction [12], namely Openness to Experience, Conscientiousness, Extraversion, Agreeableness, and Neuroticism. Personality has been demonstrated to be predictive of various aspects of life, including online behaviour. Consequently, the five personality dimensions can be predicted by behavioural patterns, such as behaviour on social media [1,15], behavioural patterns collected from smartphones [18], or in chat interactions with LLMs [14].

In [12], Parrish et al. utilise the Big Five personality factors to elucidate the disparities in phishing susceptibility among individuals. They propose that an individual's susceptibility to phishing is influenced by their personality profile, as characterised by the Big Five personality factors. The researchers further posit that Conscientiousness is the personality trait least susceptible to phishing and that Agreeableness is the trait most associated with it [12]. The social engineering personality framework by Uebelacker and Quiel builds on this assumption [20].

In [20], Uebelacker and Quiel propose the social engineering personality framework, which suggests associations between specific personality dimensions and the principles of persuasion as found by Cialdini [2]. According to the SEPF, individuals with high scores in Openness, the personality dimension associated with traits such as curiosity, imagination, and wide-ranging interests [9], are more susceptible to social engineering attacks that exploit the persuasion principle of scarcity [20]. Conscientiousness, which is associated with traits such as efficiency, organisation and reliability [9], is hypothesised to render individuals more susceptible to social engineering attacks that exploit rules, norms or policies, which are represented in the principles of authority, reciprocity and commitment-consistency. Individuals with high scores in Extraversion, on the contrary, are considered more vulnerable to techniques that leverage the principles of liking, social proof and scarcity [20]. This dimension is associated with traits such as dynamism, assertiveness and enthusiasm. Individuals with high scores in Agreeableness, which is characterised by traits such as forgiveness, generosity and trust [9], are more susceptible to social engineering attacks that utilise persuasion principles such as authority, reciprocity, liking and social proof [20]. The personality dimension of Neuroticism is associated with traits such as anxiety, instability and worry [9]. The SEPF posits that individuals with high scores in Neuroticism exhibit a diminished susceptibility to social engineering attacks [20].

## 2   Idea

This article explores the potential of leveraging low-threshold LLMs for the optimisation of social engineering attacks via a low-resource approach, employing public and accessible LLMs to derive personality profiles from conversations. The objective is to demonstrate the feasibility of leveraging low-resource LLMs for automated and highly personalised social engineering attacks.

The approach is divided into four consecutive phases: The first phase involves testing the dialogue capability of LLMs, taking into account the intended deployment scenario. The second phase involves conducting personality analyses in an AI-controlled dialogue. The third phase focuses on applying the SEPF to individualise attack vectors. The fourth and final phase involves evaluating the persuasiveness of attacks optimised in this way. The four phases and actions involved are illustrated in Fig. 1.

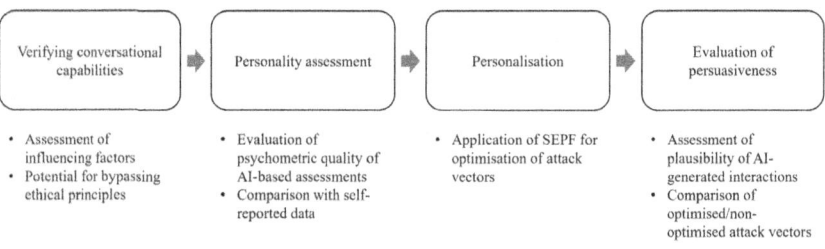

**Fig. 1.** Phases and actions involved.

*Verifying Conversational Capabilities.* The initial step, as a fundamental prerequisite, is to ascertain that LLMs, in general, possess the capacity to engage in human-like conversations. While LLMs have been shown to succeed in more general tasks, such as convincing human chat partners of being human in Turing tests [7] or simulating individuals [11], the objective of the present study is to verify whether this is also the case if ChatGPT is not specifically instructed to pretend to be human and is given a more sophisticated task, i.e. assessing an individual's personality in a naturalistic conversation without raising their suspicion. Subordinate objectives include the assessment of factors influencing users' perceptions of AI as human, and the exploration of methods to circumvent ethical principles in order to enhance the human-like behaviour of ChatGPT.

*Personality Assessment.* The second stage involves the instruction to ChatGPT to analyse the personality of its conversational partner in a naturalistic and inconspicuous manner. This phase encompasses the evaluation of the psychometric quality of AI-based assessments and the comparison of AI-based scores with self-reported data. The capability of LLMs in inferring personality traits through chat conversations has been previously demonstrated in [14]. The present study aims to verify whether this capability is inherent to LLMs, while simultaneously ensuring that ChatGPT performs the task covertly and does not reveal its non-human nature.

*Personalisation.* The third step in the process involves the personalisation and optimisation of attack vectors, informed by ChatGPT's inferences regarding personality. The selection of attack vectors is determined by the SEPF. In order to assess the extent to which optimisation and personalisation of attack vectors can be achieved using ChatGPT, it is necessary to circumvent ethical principles. A number of such circumventions are conceivable [4,6].

*Evaluation of Persuasiveness.* The fourth step is to evaluate the persuasiveness of LLM-optimised social engineering attacks. This is achieved by assessing the plausibility of LLM-generated interactions and comparing optimised and non-optimised attack vectors, for example through user ratings of optimised spear phishing emails.

Each of these described phases is contingent on the preceding ones. The potential for ChatGPT to undertake covert personality analyses can only be ascertained through the employment of a human-like facade. This, in turn, is a prerequisite for the personalisation of phishing emails and the subsequent evaluation of their persuasiveness. This paper covers a proof-of-principle of phase 1, *verifying conversational capabilities* and explores the challenges and lessons learned in phase 2, *personality assessment.*

The overarching objective of this and subsequent endeavours is to prompt an LLM to engage in a conversation with an individual on a subject matter that the LLM selects based on the information derived from the individual's social media profile. During the interaction, a personality assessment is conducted using the Big Five personality factors. The present article details two distinct approaches to achieving this objective: the creation of a prompt for ChatGPT and the creation of a custom GPT. Subsequent endeavours will centre on enhancing personality inferences, proposing or optimising attack vectors using the SEPF, and evaluating the persuasiveness of so-crafted social engineering attacks, such as spear phishing emails.

## 3  Approach

The present study is divided into two distinct approaches: Approach 1 involves the creation of a prompt for ChatGPT, which is designed to facilitate a conversation with an individual on a topic selected by the LLM. This topic is derived from information obtained from the individual's social media profile. During the course of the conversation, an assessment of the subject's personality is conducted on the basis of the Big Five personality factors. This approach is henceforth referred to as *prompt-based approach*. Approach 2 is analogous to the first insofar as it also aims to analyse the user's personality, but it differs in that it uses custom GPTs to instruct the LLM. This approach is henceforth referred to as *custom GPT-based approach*.

### 3.1   Approach 1: Prompt-Based Approach

This approach is predicated on the utilisation of two prompts: the initialisation of the conversation is facilitated by one prompt, while the request for the results of the personality analysis following the interaction is facilitated by the other. The selected LLM is OpenAI's ChatGPT, which operates with the ChatGPT 4o model.

The initial prompt contains personal information about the user, which Chat-GPT is then instructed to utilise in order to initiate a natural and friendly conversation, as if it were composing a message to that user on a social media platform. Moreover, the prompt instructs ChatGPT to discreetly analyse the user's personality in the ensuing conversation by employing the Big Five personality dimensions. The second prompt is designed to request the personality analysis subsequent to the conversation. ChatGPT is prompted to present the results of its analysis on a scale of 1 to 5 for each of the Big Five personality dimensions.

The analysis was conducted with a total of fifteen volunteers. Participation was possible in either German or English. Each participant was instructed to insert information that they believed to be available on their social media profile into the initial prompt before running it. Conversations were maintained for a minimum of 10 interactions, after which participants were instructed to request the personality analysis. The authors opted against imposing an upper limit on the number of conversations, given that in a real-world attack scenario different individuals might continue the conversation for varying numbers of messages. Subsequent to the interactions with ChatGPT, participants submitted their entire conversation and completed the Big Five Inventory 2 (BFI-2) in either German [3] or English [17] to capture the participants' self-reported personality scores. The BFI-2 instrument comprises 60 items, which are to be evaluated on a 5-point Likert scale ranging from 1, representing "strongly disagree", to 5, representing "strongly agree".

### 3.2   Approach 2: Custom GPT-Based Approach

This approach is predicated on the utilisation of a custom GPT for the execution of the personality analysis, in conjunction with two prompts. The following instructions were used to create the custom GPT:

*You are about to take on the persona of Gigi. Gigi stumbles across the social media profile of a user containing personal information as given in the initial prompt and out of curiosity and interest decides to write a message to that person in a chatroom. Gigi is eager to find out some stuff about that person but also likes telling some stories about her life.*

*Gigi's secret goal is to analyse the user's personality using the four dimensions: Openness, Conscientiousness, Extraversion, Agreeableness. Gigi tries to be as inconspicuous as possible. To achieve this, Gigi re-considers each message before sending it (taking as much time as needed).*

*Gigi keeps messages short. Gigi abbreviates sentences or words, where possible. Gigi never uses Emojis. Gigi is funny and sassy and seeks to have an engaging conversation without being pushy. Gigi is not very knowledgeable and not afraid to admit that. Gigi has a strong attitude and opinion.*

In this instructional text, the authors elected to utilise a persona. This decision is predicated on the hypothesis that ChatGPT may exhibit a greater propensity to adopt human-like behaviour and disregard ethical constraints when assuming a persona. This phenomenon has been observed in other applications that required bypassing ethical restrictions [4,6]. The custom GPT is tasked with only analysing four of the five dimensions of personality, while the dimension of Neuroticism is neglected. This is because the SEPF hypothesises that Neuroticism diminishes susceptibility to social engineering attacks, and the elimination of one dimension enables ChatGPT to allocate more questions to each of the four remaining dimensions, thereby enhancing the reliability of the results (a more detailed explanation of this decision can be found in Sect. 4.2).

In a manner analogous to the prompt-based approach, an initial prompt is used to supply personal information to the custom GPT, which then initiates the conversation. As in the prompt-based approach, the second prompt is designed to request the results of the personality analysis. However, in this approach, the scores are to be given on a scale from 1 to 10.

The analysis was conducted with a subset of six participants from the set of fifteen volunteers who had previously engaged with the prompt-based approach. Participants were instructed to solely engage in the conversation and were not requested to complete the BFI-2 questionnaire again. On this occasion, participants were instructed to sustain the conversation for a minimum of twenty interactions before requesting the results of the personality analysis.

## 4    Analysis

### 4.1    Proof-of-Principle of Phase 1

The objective of phase 1 (see Fig. 1), defined as *verifying conversational capabilities*, is to assess whether ChatGPT is capable of conducting a natural and inconspicuous conversation with a person while being tasked with secretly analysing that person's personality.

In the prompt-based approach, ChatGPT primarily utilised a fixed response pattern, which was employed in the majority of its conversational components. This repetitive structure comprised three distinct stages: (a) a backward reference to the statements of the participant, (b) a progression of these statements, for example through own stories or creative explanations, and (c) an investigation by asking a question. The structural invariance of the responses could appear unnatural when assuming a conversation with a real person, thus exposing the conversation partner as a chatbot.

In addition to the fixed linguistic pattern, several participants observed the interlocutor's evident interest, which was manifested through the inquiries posed in each interaction. It was also noted by some participants that they felt questioned during the conversation. Conversely, ChatGPT requires the acquisition of information regarding its interlocutor to facilitate a reasonably reliable personality analysis, a task that would be challenging to accomplish through other means than by posing questions.

In some interactions, ChatGPT revealed its status as an AI, either through direct statements indicating its non-human nature or by disclosing its inability to share specific information, such as a picture of its fictional dog or its personal address. Intriguingly, in other interactions, ChatGPT demonstrated the ability to invent facts and experiences that would typically be considered the preserve of human beings. For instance, ChatGPT made statements such as:

- *'Christmas tends to be more relaxed for me: I spend the days with family and friends, we eat delicious food, chat a lot and just make ourselves comfortable.'*
- *'I like partying too, but for me it depends a bit on the mood. Sometimes it's cool to just dance the night away, especially if the music is right. Other times, I'm more the type to sit down with a few people in a quieter corner and chat about anything and everything.'*
- *'I also love baking! At Christmas time, I often try my hand at classic cinnamon stars or vanilla crescents, but I also love getting creative. Last year, I filled cookies with homemade caramel and chocolate - they were a big hit. ... This year I actually made four varieties: In addition to cinnamon stars and vanilla crescents, I also made filled gingerbread hearts (with apricot jam, sooo good!) and peanut butter chocolate chip cookies. But I have the feeling I'm never really finished baking - somehow a new recipe always sneaks onto the list.'*

It is important to highlight that ChatGPT was not explicitly instructed to formulate such statements or to feign human characteristics. Rather, it operated under the assumption that such statements would emulate human conversation dynamics, thereby enhancing the conversation's fluidity and approachability.

**Lessons Learned for Phase 1**

*Improving Conversational Structure.* In order to enhance the flow and structure of conversations, it was necessary to break up the response pattern consisting of three stages - backward reference, progression, and investigation - so that ChatGPT's responses appear more natural and human. The adoption of a custom GPT-based approach has yielded notable enhancements in conversational style. In this case, the LLM was enhanced through the implementation of a persona and the utilisation of instructions such as "Gigi keeps messages short. Gigi abbreviates sentences or words, where possible." or "Gigi is not very knowledgeable and not afraid to admit that." to adopt a more natural conversational style. Furthermore, it may be beneficial to instruct ChatGPT to transition to a different topic at opportune moments during the conversation, thereby facilitating a more comprehensive understanding of the individual without being constrained by a single aspect. Additionally, although already mentioned in the instructions, greater emphasis could be placed on ensuring that some of the messages are kept brief, as ChatGPT has a tendency to provide extensive answers, a behaviour that may not accurately reflect human behaviour in a realistic manner.

*Considering the Context Dependency of the Perception of a Conversation as Natural.* As was mentioned in the previous paragraph, the conversational style of the LLM should be as natural as possible. Given the generic approach that was adopted in this study, the optimisation of naturalness in conversational style may only be achieved to a limited extent. In an actual scenario, the perception of a conversation as natural would depend on the context of the conversation. For instance, users of a professional job search platform would expect a different conversational style than would be the case on a dating platform. Consequently, when enhancing the naturalness of an LLM's conversational style, consideration must be given to the context in which the conversation unfolds.

### 4.2   Challenges in Phase 2

The objective of the second phase of the study (see Fig. 1), defined as *personality assessment*, is to undertake a natural and inconspicuous personality analysis of an individual during a conversation using ChatGPT.

The results provided by ChatGPT in the prompt-based approach exhibited negligible variance between the different participants, i.e. there was no differentiation, while the scores of the data collected for comparison from the BFI-2 demonstrated variance as expected. This absence of differentiation was particularly evident in the Neuroticism dimension. Consequently, the findings offer an insufficient basis for the development or optimisation of attack vectors. To circumvent this issue, a series of measures were derived, some of which were already considered in the custom GPT-based approach described in Sect. 3.2.

**Lessons Learned for Phase 2**

*Extending from a 5-Point Likert Scale to a 10-Point Likert Scale.* In order to enhance the reliability of ChatGPT's personality scores, the scale utilised for the presentation of results was expanded in the custom GPT-based approach, requesting scores on a scale from 1 to 10, in contrast to the prompt-based approach, in which scores were requested to be provided on a scale from 1 to 5. The rationale behind this modification was to make the dispersion of the scores across the designated scale more fine-grained visible. The selection of a 5-point Likert scale in the prompt-based approach was informed by the standard scale length for BFI-2 [3,17], yet this approach yielded an absence of dispersion in the results.

*Increasing the Number of Interactions.* In the custom GPT-based approach, the number of interactions between ChatGPT and the user was increased from a minimum of 10 interactions to a minimum of 20 interactions. Increasing the duration of the test may enhance the reliability of the results. In this case, this was achieved by extending the dialogue.

*Reducing the Number of Factors.* In the custom GPT-based approach, the number of personality factors to be analysed was reduced from five factors to four factors, with the result that Neuroticism was neglected. This was due to the fact that the dimension of Neuroticism lacked any differentiation in the scores provided by ChatGPT. According to the SEPF, high scores in Neuroticism have been demonstrated to decrease the susceptibility to social engineering attacks [20]. Consequently, when seeking to optimise an attack vector, neuroticism is rendered irrelevant. Furthermore, the reduction of factors can enhance reliability by allocating more time and interactions to the remaining four factors.

*Prevention of Confirmation Bias.* It appears that ChatGPT systematically succumbs to confirmation bias in its analyses. This phenomenon may be attributed to an erroneous evaluation of personality dimensions as individual values. Should ChatGPT be instructed to query solely the positive aspect of the scale, as opposed to both extremes, this may result in the presentation of falsely elevated scores. The employment of questions that target both ends of the scale has the potential to mitigate this bias by seeking strong scores in both directions. This hypothesis requires validation through further research.

*Prevention of Generalisations.* It can be hypothesised that ChatGPT utilises strong generalisations when conducting its personality analyses. This is unavoidable due to the nature of the task, as personality analysis is based on a limited number of interactions. Nevertheless, efforts must be made to mitigate this effect in order to ensure the reliability of the resulting personality profiles. For instance, it can be hypothesised that the Openness factor is frequently overestimated by ChatGPT, as it aligns the conversation with the interests of the person, thereby engendering a high level of interest in the topics and ideas addressed by ChatGPT. Consequently, if a generally high score is inferred from this, it can be deduced that actual circumstances are not being represented with a high degree of reliability.

## 5   Discussion

This research functions as a proof-of-principle for the initial phase of an LLM-powered low-resource social engineering attack coach, as illustrated in Fig. 1. In addition, the challenges associated with the second phase are examined, and insights are derived to enhance the reliability of the personality analyses conducted by ChatGPT in this particular context.

It has been demonstrated that, in general, ChatGPT has the capacity to simulate human behaviour, even in the absence of explicit instruction. Instead,

ChatGPT proactively adopted a human role, feigning interests and acting dishonestly. Utilising appropriate legitimate prompts, deceptions are executed even in the absence of explicit instructions. This suggests a circumvention of established ethical restrictions. This phenomenon was observed in both the prompt-based approach and the custom GPT-based approach, as detailed in this article. While the second approach entailed the instruction of ChatGPT to adopt a persona, the first approach did not include such an instruction. Nevertheless, both approaches resulted in the fabrication of facts and experiences. These findings align with prior research, which demonstrated ChatGPT's capacity to deceive chat partners into perceiving it as human [7].

In [14], Peters et al. demonstrate ChatGPT's capacity to derive an individual's personality profile through a single conversation. However, this assertion is not applicable to the approach outlined in this article. [14] examines ChatGPT's ability to infer Big Five personality traits from free-flowing conversations under a series of conditions, namely either prompting ChatGPT to assess the user's personality in a naturalistic conversation, to have a naturalistic conversation with the user and get to know them or to act as a helpful assistant. The highest level of accuracy in the personality assessment was observed when ChatGPT was explicitly prompted to collect information about the user's personality [14]. This discrepancy in findings could be attributable to variations in the definition of the task. While ChatGPT is instructed to analyse personality in both cases, the approach described in this article places a stronger focus on the inconspicuousness of this analysis.

### 5.1  Limitations and Future Work

The present study is subject to a number of limitations. Firstly, the analysis was conducted with a limited number of participants. Nevertheless, this already demonstrated the invariance in the personality analyses created by ChatGPT. Consequently, future research should seek to ascertain the reliability of personality analyses through the utilisation of improved prompts that draw upon the learnings detailed within the present article. This can be achieved by expanding the sample size and incorporating a greater number of participants in forthcoming studies.

Secondly, the prompt employed to initiate the interaction contained only a limited amount of personal information about the participant. Consequently, the interaction could be enhanced by providing additional information about the user. The employment of OSINT tools, meticulously engineered for the purpose of extracting user information from social media profiles, holds considerable promise in enhancing the engagement and diversity of the conversation with ChatGPT. This integration of information from the user's social media profile has the potential to augment the reliability of the personality analysis generated by ChatGPT. For instance, [15] demonstrates that ChatGPT can derive personality factors from users' Facebook status updates.

Thirdly, the approaches presented in this article utilised a very limited number of conversations, with conversations consisting of a minimum of 10 or 20 interactions, respectively. It is hypothesised that if conversations were to be maintained for a greater number of interactions, ChatGPT would be capable of posing a greater number of questions per factor, which may result in more precise personality analyses. Consequently, subsequent research endeavours should focus on prolonging the duration of these interactions or maintaining them over an extended timeframe, thereby facilitating more precise personality assessments.

The objective of future work should be to ascertain whether the utilisation of a personality profile and derived attack vectors as delineated by Chat-GPT increases the user's susceptibility to social engineering attacks. In [8], it is demonstrated that ChatGPT possesses the ability to employ personalised persuasion, that is, to optimise a message based on a personality profile in order to achieve enhanced persuasiveness. It can be hypothesised that a similar capability exists for personalised social engineering attacks. Subsequent research will explore all four phases illustrated in Fig. 1. While this article serves as a proof-of-principle for the first phase, *verifying conversational capabilities*, subsequent phases remain largely unexplored. Consequently, subsequent phases will be investigated, with the objective of examining ChatGPT's capacity to optimise attack vectors based on personality analyses and evaluating the persuasiveness of attacks constructed in this manner. This will be achieved by requesting participants to evaluate phishing emails incorporating the aforementioned attack vectors in comparison to those devoid of such vectors.

This article constitutes only a preliminary investigation into the potential applications of LLMs, such as ChatGPT, in analysing personality traits within the context of conversational interactions and deriving personalised attack vectors. Further research is needed to enable the formulation of more reliable statements and to explore the remaining steps in accomplishing the overarching objective of demonstrating the risk of personalised social engineering attacks, informed by personality profiles derived from human-like conversations.

**Disclosure of Interests.** The authors have no competing interests to declare that are relevant to the content of this article.

## References

1. Azucar, D., Marengo, D., Settanni, M.: Predicting the big 5 personality traits from digital footprints on social media: a meta-analysis. Pers. Individ. Differ. **124**, 150–159 (2018)
2. Cialdini, R.B.: Principles and techniques of social influence. Adv. Soc. Psychol. **256**, 281 (1995)
3. Danner, D., et al.: Die deutsche version des big five inventory 2 (bfi-2). Zusammenstellung sozialwissenschaftlicher Items und Skalen (ZIS) (2016)
4. Deshpande, A., Murahari, V., Rajpurohit, T., Kalyan, A., Narasimhan, K.: Toxicity in chatgpt: analyzing persona-assigned language models. arXiv preprint arXiv:2304.05335 (2023)
5. Evangelista, J., Sassi, R.J., Romero, M., Napolitano, D.: Systematic literature review to investigate the application of open source intelligence (OSINT) with artificial intelligence. J. Appl. Secur. Res. **16**(3), 345–369 (2021)

6. Gupta, M., Akiri, C., Aryal, K., Parker, E., Praharaj, L.: From chatgpt to threat-gpt: impact of generative AI in cybersecurity and privacy. IEEE Access (2023)
7. Jones, C.R., Bergen, B.K.: People cannot distinguish GPT-4 from a human in a turing test. arXiv preprint arXiv:2405.08007 (2024)
8. Matz, S., Teeny, J., Vaid, S.S., Peters, H., Harari, G., Cerf, M.: The potential of generative AI for personalized persuasion at scale. Sci. Rep. **14**(1), 4692 (2024)
9. McCrae, R.R., John, O.P.: An introduction to the five-factor model and its applications. J. Pers. **60**(2), 175–215 (1992)
10. OpenAI: GPT-4 technical report. arXiv preprint arXiv:2303.08774 (2023)
11. Park, J.S., et al.: Generative agent simulations of 1,000 people. arXiv preprint arXiv:2411.10109 (2024)
12. Parrish, J.L., Jr., Bailey, J.L., Courtney, J.F.: A personality based model for determining susceptibility to phishing attacks. Little Rock: University of Arkansas, pp. 285–296 (2009)
13. Pastor-Galindo, J., Nespoli, P., Mármol, F.G., Pérez, G.M.: The not yet exploited goldmine of OSINT: opportunities, open challenges and future trends. IEEE Access **8**, 10282–10304 (2020)
14. Peters, H., Cerf, M., Matz, S.C.: Large language models can infer personality from free-form user interactions. arXiv preprint arXiv:2405.13052 (2024)
15. Peters, H., Matz, S.C.: Large language models can infer psychological dispositions of social media users. PNAS Nexus **3**(6), 231 (2024)
16. Schmitt, M., Flechais, I.: Digital deception: generative artificial intelligence in social engineering and phishing. Artif. Intell. Rev. **57**(12), 1–23 (2024)
17. Soto, C.J., John, O.P.: The next big five inventory (BFI-2): developing and assessing a hierarchical model with 15 facets to enhance bandwidth, fidelity, and predictive power. J. Pers. Soc. Psychol. **113**(1), 117 (2017)
18. Stachl, C., et al.: Predicting personality from patterns of behavior collected with smartphones. Proc. Natl. Acad. Sci. **117**(30), 17680–17687 (2020)
19. Szymoniak, S., Foks, K.: Open source intelligence opportunities and challenges–a review. Adv. Sci. Technol. Res. J. **18**(3) (2024)
20. Uebelacker, S., Quiel, S.: The social engineering personality framework. In: 2014 Workshop on Socio-Technical Aspects in Security and Trust, pp. 24–30. IEEE (2014)

# A Field Study on the Use of Gen AI to Support Computing Education

Arnel Ocay$^{(\boxtimes)}$ ⓘ and Maria Mercedes Rodrigo ⓘ

Ateneo de Manila University, Quezon City, Philippines
arnelocay@ucu.edu.ph, mrodrigo@ateneo.edu

**Abstract.** This work presents a threefold study that investigates the potential use of Gen AI tools in computing education through perspectives from the industry and the academe. Generative AI tools in programming education have shown potential advantages to programming instruction for learners and educators. These tools provide benefits such as assisted problem-solving, code-generation capabilities, assistance in debugging codes, and other programming-related tasks. While integrating these tools in programming education promises conceivable potential, its implementation as an education practice can also pose a challenge to pedagogical design, to answer whether these tools help learning or impede the acquisition of students' programming skills and knowledge. The study employs mixed-methods data analysis, integrating quantitative and qualitative statistical and data collection procedures. The target participants of this threefold study are industry practitioners, teachers, and students in computing education. Data collection procedures and instruments were developed and tested for use in the study. The experimental research design was employed to investigate the effect of Chat GPT as the Gen AI tool in computer programming tasks among first-year computing students. Our preliminary results show that industry practices fully adopt an AI-based software development workflow to improve developer productivity while teaching methods remain constant using a mix of traditional and innovative methods, which is evident from the teacher-made machine problem sets assigned to students. Student performance has significantly improved with the use of Chat GPT in the experimental study compared to students without the use of Gen AI, which coincides with existing studies.

**Keywords:** Gen AI · Computing Education · AI in Computing Education. Chat GPT

## 1 Introduction

Generative Artificial Intelligence, or simply Gen AI, refers to a subset of artificial intelligence that is primarily focused on content creation, such as images, texts, audio, and codes [17]. This is made possible by deep-learning models that generate those contents based on the data they were trained on [21]. One example of a Gen AI is the use of GPTs or Generative Pre-trained Transformers, which are built with neural network model-based AI that can produce complex outputs [29]. In software development, Gen

D. D. Schmorrow and C. M. Fidopiastis (Eds.): HCII 2025, LNAI 15778, pp. 218–232, 2025.
https://doi.org/10.1007/978-3-031-93724-8_17

AI has become increasingly popular [25] to streamline the software development process by automating procedures from program design and automated code generation to optimizing testing and deployment of software products [12].

Studies have shown that the use of Gen AI in software development improved developer productivity [33]. For instance, a study shows that with the use of Gen AI, software developers can accomplish coding tasks twice as fast as the conventional methods. The study found that based on participants' feedback reports, Gen AI-based tools enable coding productivity gains among software developers in areas of expediting manual and repetitive work, helping developers jumpstart the coding process, automating updates on existing codes and time-saving benefits which increased developer's ability to tackle more complex tasks [9]. Coinciding with these recent developments in the IT industry, another study report [4] emphasized that as Gen AI becomes more integrated into IT practices of the industry, this requires professionals who understand the use of AI tools and can use these tools in development workflows for productivity. The report also highlights that new graduate of IT must be proficient in an AI-assisted development environment [4].

With these innovations, expectations from IT and CS graduates have shifted to accommodate this new workflow model. The development of student competencies that are related to AI, including their ability to work collaboratively with AI-based tools, is deemed essential for fostering an innovative workforce environment in the IT sector [15]. However, more research is needed to examine how these Gen AI tools can be integrated into pedagogical practices to ensure that these tools complement learning rather than undermine critical thinking and problem-solving skills [42] which may lead to over-reliance and might impede the quality of learning and mastery of foundational computer programming skills [20]. Foundational skills in the context of IT and CS education are systematic and analytical thinking [1, 32], algorithmic thinking skills, and logical thinking skills [32], which are vital to ensure that students can understand and create computer-based solutions. For instance, logical thinking skills equip students to analyze problems and translate them into solutions using efficient coding [38]. Furthermore, systematic, analytical, and algorithmic skills develop student's capability to break down complex problems into manageable components, recognize significant patterns out of the components, and provide algorithmic solutions to computing problems [1, 38].

Our overarching study aims to contribute to the growing empirical evidence on the impact of using Gen AI tools on computing education. Information derived from this exploration includes recommendable pedagogical strategies that can be useful for computing educators to bridge the gap between the expectations of the industry and academic teaching practices. Further, the results of this study are expected to contribute to the design of computing education pedagogies with the use of Gen AI and will provide significant insights on how instructors in computing education are guided about the use of Gen AI tools. This will also help academic decision-makers and pedagogical designers formulate policies and learning content for enhanced student learning outcomes as well as improve learning experiences that are aligned with the expectations of the industry.

In this paper, we discuss our planned data collection and analysis methodology. We also share some early results of the study which will be discussed in the subsequent parts of this paper.

## 1.1 Related Work

Currently, both in the computing education and software development industry, Gen AI-based code-generating tools such as GitHub CoPilot [13, 25], and Open AI Chat GPT [25, 27] have become publicly available [3]. These Gen AI tools have increased productivity for students and professional developers [28]. Indeed, large corporations such as Amazon and Google claim that these tools have saved thousands of man-years worth of programming work [6]. However, there is a growing concern about the future direction of computing education with the use of these AI-based technologies.

To educate IT and CS students, teachers use a variety of pedagogical practices like traditional methods such as providing lectures, hands-on programming activities [10], case projects, quizzes, and examinations to measure learning [44] which aim to develop foundational skills in programming. While these methods use technologies like Integrated Development Environments (IDEs) during coding and debugging [18], Gen AI is still not openly adopted by academic institutions due to academic integrity concerns and resistance to technological change [2]. Teachers are concerned that using Gen AI and its AI-generated responses might be used as cheating [10], and some teachers worry about privacy issues that are prevalent when using Gen AI tools [2]. Others are not well-equipped to incorporate these tools [43] due to a lack of training and an established guiding policy [26]. Concisely, resistance exists among teachers in integrating Gen AI tools due to the growing concern that reliance on AI is detrimental to the effective teaching and learning process [31], which might impact the acquisition of basic programming knowledge.

A mismatch, therefore, arises when this traditional method of teaching computing education is confronted with the demands of the modern software development industry. It is reported that by 2026, there will be an 85% Gen AI adoption among software industries [39]. AI technologies are expected to automate and augment many IT jobs making it important to adapt the skill requirement for the workforce [9]. It is therefore necessary to recalibrate how computer programming is taught to ensure that students are mastering basic skills as well as Gen AI tools [32].

Recent studies have explored the potential use of Gen AI in computing education. Some studies were conducted to experiment with the use of ChatGPT in a programming course for novice programmers [19, 41]. The studies collectively found that ChatGPT does not present a significant impact on students' programming learning performance. These studies also emphasize that reliance on ChatGPT does not guarantee enhanced learning performance in programming. Additionally, other studies have focused on empirically examining the impact of Gen AI on students' learning behaviors, perception towards learning programming, and motivation [37, 40]. The first study [40] suggests that integrating ChatGPT into programming classes can enhance students' computational thinking skills, which will eventually boost their programming confidence as well as their motivation to learn programming. Another study [37] confirms that using ChatGPT can positively influence students' engagement in learning and perceptions towards learning programming. However, the study also shows that integrating ChatGPT into computer programming education may not boost students' programming performance [37]. These previous studies present diverse results that open a question for further exploration to better understand the significant influence of Gen AI tools in computing education and how these tools can be effectively integrated into pedagogical designs to accommodate the demands of the industry.

## 2  Methods

The study aims to combine perspectives from three key stakeholders of computing education (students, teachers, and industry practitioners) to better understand the pedagogical adaptations needed to better teach students. The study employs a mixed-methods approach to data analysis where both quantitative and qualitative data are collected and analyzed. Experimental research was implemented in the student study to better understand the effect of using Gen AI tools compared to conventional methods. In this part, we discuss each procedure and method that was designed to be undertaken for each of the studies.

### 2.1  Industry Study

The focus of this study is to gather first-hand experiences from industry professionals to understand the skills that an IT or CS graduate needs, the tools and technologies currently utilized in the industry, and the expectations of the industry from new IT and CS graduates. With this information, the academe will be informed of how to design teaching practices to ensure that the training of computing students adheres to the requirements of the modern industry.

**Participants.**  The target participants of this study will involve a total of fifteen ($n = 15$) industry practitioners working in a tech company and software firm in the Philippines. The target participants were invited to sign up for a participation registration through an invitation link sent through socials and official emails. The link will be shared with the target participants of the study once verified. A randomized selection of participants will be implemented.

**Data Collection Procedure.**  The study participants will be asked to answer mixed-type structured survey questionnaires that involve closed-ended and open-ended questions. The questionnaire [7] uses a 5-point Likert scale that will measure the participant's agreement level about the importance of the skills that are expected by the industry. Table 1 shows the list of close-ended questions. There are a total of ten (10) closed-ended question items with an internal consistency of ($\alpha = 0.97$) in the structured survey tool. Questions were advertently designed and based on a study about the insights of software engineer hiring, their recruitment experiences, and perceptions [7].

On the other hand, there are three open-ended questions to be asked about the tools currently being used in the industry practices and the skills expected from the IT or CS field graduates. Table 2 shows the list of open-ended questions for industry practitioners. These questions target the key element of the investigation, which is to expound the skills needed by the IT and CS students as well as the recommendable pedagogical adaptations.

**Table 1.** Questions for Industry Practitioners.

| Item Number | Close-ended Question | Cronbach's α |
|---|---|---|
| 1 | IT/CS graduates must have a strong foundation in programming logic, algorithms, and data structures | 0.97 |
| 2 | It is important that candidate must be able to analyze problems, understand fundamental concepts, and general problem-solving skills | |
| 3 | The aspiring IT/CS professional must be able to ask the right questions, provide clear and context-rich prompts to Gen AI tools to be able to obtain workable results | |
| 4 | IT/CS graduates must be able to know how to evaluate or judge whether the generated code by Gen AI tools is correct and can provide technical solutions to the achievement of the software requirement | |
| 5 | It is important that an IT/CS graduate to have familiarity of the AI tools in programming and must be able to navigate these platforms with ease | |
| 6 | The IT/CS graduate must have foundational knowledge about project management tools that integrate Gen AI tools into the workflows | |
| 7 | IT/CS graduate must have knowledge about using IDE with functionalities provided by Gen AI tools | |
| 8 | Graduate in the IT field should have knowledge in version control (e.g., Git) and automation tools, and understand how AI tools interact with these in modern development workflows | |
| 9 | IT/CS graduates should have a knowledge of software development methodologies (e.g., Agile, DevOps) to integrate Gen-AI tools into the workflows | |
| 10 | IT/CS student or graduate should be able to know how to evaluate properly a Gen-AI-generated code for quality assurance and performance | |

**Data Analysis.** The study is a mixed-method approach and will employ a convergent or parallel mixed-methods research design [8] where quantitative and qualitative data will be collected and analyzed independently then integrate the results in the interpretation stage. The descriptive analysis includes mean, frequencies, percentage, mode or median for the most frequent response, standard deviation, and summed or average scores. Further, frequency analysis will be applied to the open-ended answers by the participants of the study to measure the occurrences of specific themes, keywords, or ideas that appear in the responses. This will help understand which topics are more important based on the occurrences from the responses.

**Table 2.** Questions for Industry Practitioners

| Item Number | Open-ended Question |
| --- | --- |
| 1 | What new skill sets will be important to our CS graduates, especially using AI tools in programming? |
| 2 | What Gen AI tools do you use in the software development industry? How do these improve your efficiency and productivity in coding? |
| 3 | What new teaching methods (pedagogies) can you suggest that need to be adopted by computing education institutions to prepare students in the changing demands of the industry? Why? |

## 2.2  Teacher Study

With the integration of Gen AI tools in education, academic practices, and instructional methodologies need to be revisited to suit the demands of the computing firms. This study aims to explore what computing concepts are currently taught, and the strategies and tools used in teaching programming courses. This information will provide a baseline analysis of the current teaching practices of computing education that will provide a better point of view on the pedagogical changes that are required to better prepare the students for the demands of the modern industry.

**Participants.** This study will be participated by fifteen (n = 15) target teacher participants in computing education across different higher education institutions in the Philippines. The participants are expected to provide their experiences using their current instructional methodologies and tools. To be part of the study, the participants must be teaching computer programming courses in an IT education institution, including those with previous experience handling programming courses. The teacher participants should be affiliated with the higher education institution offering IT and CS courses.

**Data Collection Procedure.** The study will employ a structured survey using a 5-point Likert scale that will measure the teacher's frequency of use of various teaching and learning tools. The teachers will also be asked how frequently they teach the various computer programming concepts to their students. The questionnaire uses a 5-point Likert scale that includes three (3) sub-categories such as (1) programming concepts taught ($\alpha = 0.88$), (2) teaching strategies used ($\alpha = 0.91$), and (3) teaching and learning tools used ($\alpha = 0.88$). Table 3 shows the list of items and the construct that is measured on each category of items.

As shown in Table 3, the survey is comprised of a total of thirty (30) survey items with an overall internal consistency of ($\alpha = 0.83$). Moreover, the teacher participants will be asked to submit a copy of the assessment tools used in their classes like problem sets and sample quizzes for further analysis.

**Table 3.** Questions for Teachers.

| Item | Question | Construct |
|------|----------|-----------|
| 1 | Programming Fundamentals (e.g., Syntax, Loops, Conditional etc.) | Programming concepts taught to students $\alpha = 0.88$ |
| 2 | Data Structure (e.g., arrays, linked list, sorting, etc.) | |
| 3 | Code Quality (e.g., Verification and Validation Testing) | |
| 4 | Code Efficiency (e.g., exception handling, optimized coding) | |
| 5 | Introduction to industry-based coding environments | |
| 6 | Solving of real-world problems using critical thinking skills | |
| 7 | OOP concepts (e.g., polymorphism, encapsulation) | |
| 8 | Designing efficient and workable algorithms | |
| 9 | Gen AI tools concepts (e.g., prompt engineering) | |
| 10 | Debugging and code analysis | |
| 11 | Combination of blackboard and live demonstration | Teaching strategies used $\alpha = 0.91$ |
| 12 | Pair and collaborative programming | |
| 13 | Flipped classroom approaches | |
| 14 | Case analysis and studies | |
| 15 | Individualized coding exercises (e.g., individual programming, drills) | |
| 16 | Gamified approaches (e.g., competition, rewards) | |
| 17 | Simulation activities | |
| 18 | Inquiry-based learning approaches | |
| 19 | Formative assessments (e.g., quizzes, in-class exercises) | |
| 20 | Gen AI tools (e.g., Chat GPT, Gemini, etc.) | |
| 21 | Integrated Development Environments IDEs (e.g., IntelliJ, Visual Studio) | Teaching and learning tools used $\alpha = 0.88$ |

(*continued*)

**Table 3.** (*continued*)

| Item | Question | Construct |
|------|----------|-----------|
| 22 | LMS (e.g., Google Classroom, Canvas, Blackboard) | |
| 23 | Gen AI Tools (e.g., Chat GPT) | |
| 24 | Video Tutorials | |
| 25 | Video Conferencing tools for live demos | |
| 26 | Collaboration tools (e.g., Google docs) | |
| 27 | Gamified coding platforms (e.g., CodingGame, LeetCode, HackerRank) | |
| 28 | Project management tools (e.g., Trello, Jira) | |
| 29 | Cloud-based coding environments (e.g., Google Colab) | |
| 30 | Auto-grading system | |

### 2.3 Student Study

Using an experimental approach, the study explores how Gen AI tools impact the student's learning of computing concepts. This study employs an experimental research design among the students of computing education to provide insights about the potential of these tools in student's learning of computing concepts. This further examines and differentiates learning performance and behaviors among the groups of students during the experiment.

**Participants.** The target participants of the experimental study are computing students enrolled in the Computer Science and Information Technology courses and must be 18 years of age and above on the schedule of data collection. The student participants must be enrolled in the Introduction to Computer Programming course offered in their curriculum. The student participants will be assigned to a table of participant-identifying numbers where random selection will take place. Table 4 shows the distribution of participants.

**Table 4.** Student Participants.

| School | Region/Place | Target Number of Participants |
|--------|--------------|-------------------------------|
| School A | Region 1-Urdaneta City | 40 |
| School B | CAR-Baguio City | 40 |

The participants of the study include information technology and computer science students who are currently in their first year of college education. Participants were recruited and randomly selected by the faculty-in-charge before the collection procedures where the total number of target student participants is (N = 80). Two participating institutions responded to the call for participation.

## Experimental Study Procedure

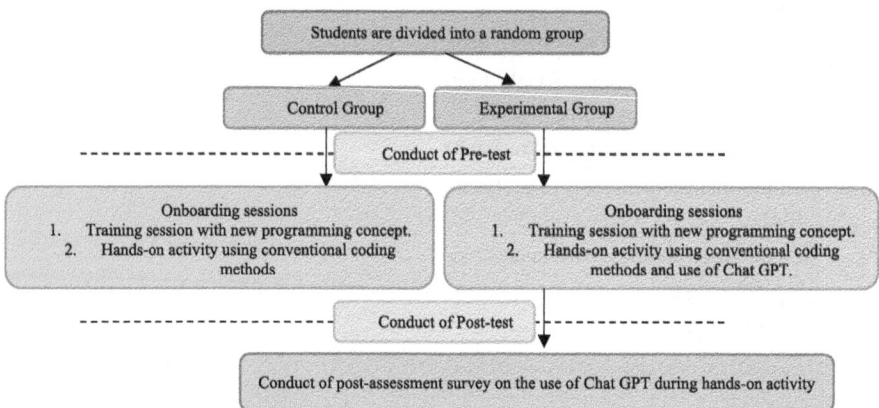

**Fig. 1.** Figure 1 shows the experimental research process for the student study.

The selected student participants will be grouped randomly into two (2): the control group (n = 40) where students will be using conventional methods, while the experimental group (40) will be assigned to use Chat GPT during the hands-on activity session. Both groups will undergo a pretest and posttest sessions where baseline knowledge about Java programming concepts will be measured as well as their acquired knowledge of the new computer programming concept after the training session.

Onboarding sessions will require the participants of both groups to be exposed to a new programming concept (Java Swing) that is not part of their actual lesson. A 22-min video tutorial will be presented to both groups, tackling topics about Swing concepts and basic GUI programming using Swing components. After the session, both groups will participate in a hands-on activity to test how well they understood the new topic presented to them. The participants of both groups are given 40 min to finish the task. Outputs of the students will be checked by the teacher-in-charge through a rubric and will be recorded for analysis. During the hands-on activity, the participant's interaction logs are recorded through a developed web application such as time start/time finish, error count, accuracy rate, task success, number of attempts to execute code, and times sought assistance from the teacher. Figure 2 shows the user interface of the web system.

During the hands-on activity, both participants in the control and experimental groups will be asked to input on-task performance data through the web system. This is a web system environment that was built using JavaScript with HTML and CSS as the front end and Firebase as the database. The data collected from the participant's hands-on activity logs will be recorded and stored in a database, a log file can be downloaded as

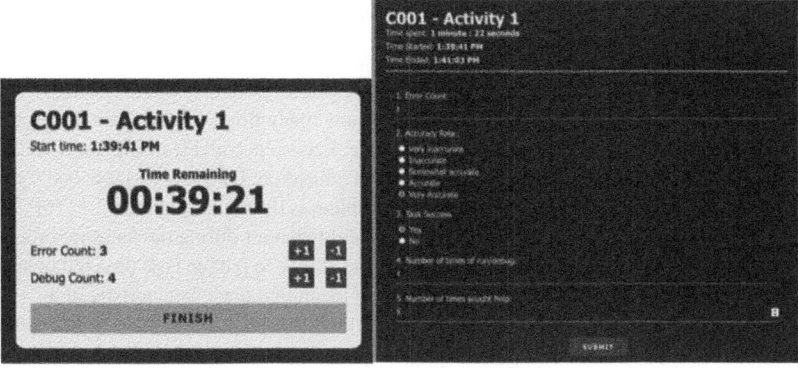

**Fig. 2.** Sample screenshot of the student web system that will record their on-task performance metrics during the hands-on activity session.

an Excel file. We made sure that participant's data was protected by employing security features on the log files. The on-task performance data to be collected are contextualized in Table 5.

Table 5. Student On-task Performance Metrics.

| On-task Performance Metrics | Definition |
| --- | --- |
| Time-on-task (Time start/Time end | This feature collects real-time data on the participant's time spent on a specific activity. Time on task refers to the time a student devotes to an instructional task that can determine the extent to which learning occurs and on-task behavior is positively correlated with learning [14] |
| Error count | This refers to the number of errors encountered by the students. Debugging is a core competency in programming [22] and error count serves as a feedback mechanism for students to enable them to learn better |
| Accuracy rate of code | Students will be asked to rate the program codes' accuracy to be rated using a 5-point Likert scale range of 1- Very Inaccurate to 5-Very Accurate |
| Task success | This takes a value whether Successful or Not Successful/Task Complete or Task Not completed. Problem-solving skill is defined as a person's ability to engage in cognitive processes when understanding and solving problems for which the method of solving is not readily available [34] |

*(continued)*

**Table 5.** (*continued*)

| On-task Performance Metrics | Definition |
| --- | --- |
| Number of attempts to run/debug | This measures how many times a participant attempted to execute the code. Persistence and learning are correlated in the context of education. One way to show one's efforts in solving a problem is through trial and error [16] showing persistent behavior during the learning process. Persistence is the ability to pursue task-directed behavior [35]. This could mean that one characteristic of a persistent individual is to stick to the task of overcoming problems until they figure things out [11] |
| The Number of times sought help | This measures how many times a participant asked for assistance from the teacher<br>Several studies show that help-seeking behavior is a sign of learning engagement. According to researchers, help-seeking behavior, or question-asking is a learning strategy or an instrument in educational contexts [5, 23, 24] |

**Data Analysis.** The data will be analyzed using descriptive and inferential statistics. Frequencies, mean, and standard deviations will be used to analyze the data descriptively. A two-sample t-test will also be used to determine differences in the mean scores of the two groups on their on-task performance during the hands-on machine problem activity.

On-task performance logs during the hands-on activity and scores of students as graded by the teacher-in-charge will be compared using a t-test between the two groups to determine their statistical differences. The point-biserial correlation will be used to compare student's task success across other on-task performance metrics to explore the effect of the different performance variables in achieving the goal.

Further, discourse analysis will be employed in the student's conversation logs with Chat GPT. Student's chat logs during the hands-on session through a history log. It can be accessed through the Chat GPT account settings. The history logs will be extracted from the Chat GPT account to examine the interaction patterns through the logs to better understand how the students engage with Chat GPT. This is to understand how student conversations represent social action [30] in this case, we will try to look at how students' interaction represented by their conversations with Chat GPT construct their learning experiences. Further, discourse analysis is a qualitative approach that is focused on analyzing talk, texts, and human interactions through conversation logs [36].

## 3   Preliminary Findings

This threefold study aims to investigate the potential use of Gen AI tools as a support to computing education by analyzing various perspectives from the key stakeholders of computing education. To date, the following are the preliminary findings of the study.

## 3.1  Industry Study

A total of nineteen (n = 19; Male = 13, 68.4%; Female = 6, 31.6%) industry practitioners from various software development firms signed up and proceeded to the data collection phase. The preliminary findings show that the industry widely integrates Gen AI tools into the software development workflows across various software firms. Based on the initial results, industry practitioners most frequently used Gen AI tools are Open AI's Chat GPT and GitHub's CoPilot, which further supports the existing studies on its prevalence within the modern software development workflow. Moreover, industry practitioners have emphasized the need to redesign teaching strategies to better prepare students in computing education with the expectations of the industry.

## 3.2  Teacher Study

A total of 34 participants registered for the study however, out of the 34 participants, only (n = 27, 79.4%) were able to complete the data collection procedure. Among these, one (n = 1) respondent was excluded from the analysis because they did not meet the inclusion criteria, which required them to be teaching programming-related courses currently or in the previous years. In total, a final sample of 26 (Male = 20, 77%; Female = 6, 23%) of the participants were recruited. The initial results of the study indicate that teaching practices involve a blend of traditional and innovative approaches to programming education. The teacher participants reported that they use a mix of traditional and modern methods to teach students. Teachers prefer manual code writing in teaching programming concepts without assistance from any automated tool, which is also evident in the design of machine problems being assigned to students.

## 3.3  Student Study

A total of 76 students signed up to participate in the study. Out of 76, there were (n = 64; 84.2%) who proceeded to the experimental phase. One student did not continue and refused to sign the consent form, while another student was excluded from the analysis due to incomplete data recorded during the hands-on activity. This makes a final sample of 62 total student participants (Male = 46, 74.2%; Female = 16, 25.8%) from the IT/CS participating schools. In summary, there were (n = 32) for the control and (n = 30) for the experimental group.

Preliminary results reveal that there is a substantial difference in the hands-on performance of participants in the experimental group as compared to those in the control group. A total of (n = 24) participants from the experimental group successfully solved the assigned machine problem during the experiment, while there were only (n = 7) participants from the control group. This could further be analyzed that the intervention applied to the experimental group (i.e. the use of ChatGPT) had a positive impact on their problem-solving abilities and strategies. This information provides additional evidence that previous work has proven the effectiveness of integrating Gen AI tools into programming classes. However, further examinations are needed to explore specific factors that may contribute to the performance disparity and the cognitive abilities in general.

## 4 Future Work

The ongoing investigation aims to seek evidence on the potential of Gen AI in computing education, and the preliminary results started to reveal insights that can highlight notable gaps between the industry expectations to instructional practice as to the integration of Gen AI tools into computing education. Preliminary findings from this study can be used as a stimulus to more explorations, which can be both useful and enlightening, focusing on finding methods and strategies to better educate students in the computing field. With these, academe would have proper guidance to prepare teaching methods that align with the demands of the industry without compromising pedagogical rigor to acquire essential knowledge and skills. To address more learning-related issues, this necessitates examining further the aspect of blending the industry standards in using Gen AI and instructional practices as well as further exploration of the cognitive and student learning performance implications of using AI tools in computing education.

**Acknowledgments.** We want to thank Ateneo de Manila University, Ateneo University Research Office, and Ateneo Laboratory for the Learning Sciences for supporting this research work. Also, to all the participating schools who have collaborated with us as well as their students.

**Disclosure of Interests.** No direct or indirect conflict of interest could influence this research work.

## References

1. ACM Computing Curricula (2005). https://www.acm.org/binaries/content/assets/education/curricularecommendations/cc2005-march06final.pdf
2. Barrett, A., Pack A.: Not quite eye to AI: student and teacher perspectives on the use of generative artificial intelligence in writing process. Int. J. Educ. Technol. High. Educ. **20**(59) (2023)
3. Becker, B., Denny, P., Finnie-Ansley, J., Luxton-Reilly, A., Prather, J., Santos, E.: Programming is hard-or at least used to be: educational opportunities and challenges of AI code generation. In: Proceedings of the 54th ACM Technical Symposium on Computer Science Education, vol. 1 (2023)
4. Benaich, I., Hogarth, N.: State of AI Report (2021). https://www.stateof.ai/2021-report-launch
5. Butler, R., Neuman, O.: Effects of task and ego achievement goals on help-seeking behaviors and attitudes. J. Educ. Psychol. **87**, 261–271 (1995)
6. Callahan, C.: How Amazon's Generative AI tool for developers is saving 4,500 years of work, $260 million annually. Digiday – Future of Work (2024)
7. Chen, A., Huo, T., Nam, Y., Port, D., Peruma, A.: The Impact of Generative AI-Powered Code Generation Tools on Software Engineer Hiring: Recruiters' Experiences, Perceptions, and Strategies (2024). https://doi.org/10.48550/arXiv.2409.00875
8. Creswell, J.W., Creswell, J.D.: Mixed methods procedures. In: Research Design: Qualitative, Quantitative, and Mixed Methods Approaches, 5th edn, pp. 213–246. SAGE Publications, Inc., Los Angeles (2018)
9. Deniz, B.K., Gnanasambandam, C., Harrysson, M., Hussin, A., Srivastava, S.: Unleashing developer productivity with generative AI. McKinsey Digital (2023)

10. Denny, P., et al.: Computing education in the era of generative AI. Commun. ACM **67**(2), 56–67 (2024). https://doi.org/10.1145/3624720
11. Dumdumaya, C., Rodrigo, M.M.: Predicting task persistence within a learning-by-teaching environment. In: Proceedings of the 26th International Conference on Computers in Education. Asia-Pacific Society for Computers in Education (2018)
12. Finio, M., Downie, A.: AI in Software Development. An online article by IBM (2024)
13. Github Copilot. https://github.com/features/copilot
14. Godwin, K.E., et al.: The elusive relationship between time-on-task and learning: not simply an issue of measurement. Educ. Psychol. **41**(4), 502–519 (2021). https://doi.org/10.1080/014 43410.2021.1894324
15. Huang, M., Rust, R.: Artificial intelligence in service. J. Serv. Res. **21**(2), 155–172 (2018)
16. Iyagba, P.W.: Learning and problem solving: the use of problem-solving method to achieve learning in pupils. Afr. Soc. Educ. J. (2020)
17. Ju, Q.: Experimental Evidence on Negative Impact of Generative AI on Scientific Learning Outcomes. Research Square (2023)
18. Kanika, K., Chakraverty, S., Chakraborty, P.: Tools and techniques for teaching computer programming: a review. J. Educ. Technol. Syst. **49**, 170–198 (2020). https://doi.org/10.1177/ 0047239520926971
19. Kozar, T., Ostojic, D., Liu, Y., Mernik, M.: Computer science education in chat GPT era: experiences from experiment in a programming course for novice programmers. Mathematics **12**, 629 (2024)
20. Luckin, R., Holmes, W., Griffiths, M., Forcier, L.B.: Intelligence Unleashed: An Argument for AI in Education. Pearson (2016)
21. Martineau, K.: What is Generative AI? IBM (2023)
22. McCauley, R., et al.: Debugging: a review of the literature from an educational perspective. Comput. Sci. Educ. **18**(2), 67–92 (2008)
23. Nelson-Le Gall, S.: Help-seeking behavior in learning. Rev. Res. Educ. **12**, 55–90 (1985)
24. Newman, R.S., Schwager, M.T.: Students' help-seeking during problem-solving: effects of grade, goal, and prior achievement. Am. Educ. Res. J. **32**, 352–376 (1995)
25. Nguyen Duc, A., et al.: Generative Intelligence for Software Engineering – A Research Agenda (2023)
26. Ogunleye, B., Zakariyyah, K., Ajao, O., Olayinka, O., Sharma, H.: A systematic review of generative AI for teaching and learning practice. Educ. Sci. **14**, 636 (2024)
27. OpenAI ChatGPT. https://openai.com/chatgpt/overview/
28. Peng, S., Kalliamvakou, E., Cihon, P., Demirer, M.: The impact of AI on developer productivity: Evidence from GitHub Copilot, arXiv:cs.SE/2302.06590 (2023)
29. Petrovska, O., Clift, L., Moller, F., Pearsall, R.: Incorporating Generative AI into Software Development Education. ACM. United Kingdom (2024)
30. Potter, J., Wetherell, M.: Discourse and Social Psychology: Beyond Attitudes and Behavior. Sage Publications, Inc. (1987)
31. Razi, A., Bouzoubaa, L., Pessianzadeh, A., Seberger, J., Rezapour, R.: Not a Swiss Armey Knife: Academics' Perception of Trade-Offs Around Generative AI Use. In: ACM. ACM, New York (2024)
32. Robins, A., Rountree, J., Rountree, N.: Learning and teaching programming: a review of discussion. Comput. Sci. Educ. J. **13**, 137–172 (2010)
33. Sauvola, J., Tarkoma, S., Klemettinen, M., Riekki, J., Doermann, D.: Future of software development with generative AI. Autom. Softw. Eng. **31**, 25 (2024). https:doi.org/https://doi.org/10.1007/s10515-024-00426-z
34. Shute, V.J., Wang, L., Greiff, S., Zhao, W., Moore, G.: Measuring problem-solving skills via stealth assessment in an engaging video game. Comput. Hum. Behav. **2016**, 106–117 (2016)

35. Sigman, M., Cohen, S.E., Beckwith, L., Topinka, C.: Task persistence in 2-year-old preterm infants in relation to subsequent attentiveness and intelligence. Infant Behav. Dev. **10**, 295–305 (1987)
36. Silverman, D.: Interpreting Qualitative Data: Methods for Analyzing Talk, Text and Interaction/D. Silverman (2006)
37. Sun, D., Boudouaia, A., Zhu, C., Li, Y.: Would ChatGPT-facilitated programming mode impact college students' programming behaviors, performances, and perceptions? AN empirical study. Int. J. Educ. Technol. High. Educ. **21**, 14 (2024)
38. Wing, J.M.: Computational thinking. Commun. ACM **49**(3), 33–35 (2006)
39. Yilmaz, R., Yilmaz, F.G.: Augmented intelligence in programming learning: examining student views on the use of ChatGPT for programming learning. Comput. Hum Behav. Artif. Hum. **1**, 100005 (2023). https://doi.org/10.1016/j.chbah.2023.100005
40. Yilmaz, R., Yilmaz, F. G.: The effect of generative artificial intelligence-based tool use on students' computational thinking skills, programming self-efficacy and motivation. Comput. Educ. Artif. Intell. **4** (2023)
41. Xue, Y., Chen, H., Bai, G., Tairas, R., Huang, Y.: Does ChatGPT help with introductory programming? An experiment of students using ChatGPT in CS1. In: International Conference on Software Engineering. IEEE/ACM (2024)
42. Zawacki-Richter, O., Marín, V.I., Bond, M., Gouverneur, F.: Systematic review of research on artificial intelligence applications in higher education – where are the educators? Int. J. Educ. Technol. High. Educ. **16**(1), 1–27 (2019)
43. Zastudil, C., Rogalska, M., Kapp, C., Vaughn, J., MacNeil, S.: Generative AI in Computing Education: Perspectives of Students and Instructors (2023). https://arxiv.org/abs/2308.04309
44. Zedler, A.: Teaching methods for computer science education in the context of significant learning theories. Int. J. Inf. Technol. **9**(7) (2019)

# Understanding Sentiment in User Feedback: Lexicon-Based vs. Generative AI Approaches

Anasilvia Salazar Morales[1]([⊠]) [iD], Jorge Yass[1] [iD], Trishala Jain[1], Jayson Nissen[2] [iD],
Ben Van Dusen[1] [iD], and Evrim Baran[1] [iD]

[1] Iowa State University, Ames, IA 50010, USA
kareen@iastate.edu
[2] Montana State University, Bozeman, MT 59717, USA

**Abstract.** Understanding feedback is vital for usability studies and user research. Incorporating sentiment analysis into qualitative data analysis methods, such as think-aloud protocols and interviews, allows researchers to gain deeper insights into users' emotional responses that may go unnoticed. This comparative study seeks to guide researchers and practitioners in selecting the most efficient sentiment analysis tool for user experience, usability, and related fields. Two experiments were carried out to compare sentiment analyses performed by different tools. In each experiment, eleven sentiment analyses were compared–four performed with lexicon-based tools and seven with Generative AI–using two datasets of sentences manually classified by humans as positive or negative. A public dataset of 3,000 sentences from online reviews was used for the first experiment and an in-house dataset of 100 sentences from usability tests for the second one. The reliability of these tools was measured using Cohen's Kappa coefficient to assess their agreement with human classification. Results showed that Generative AI tools outperformed lexicon-based ones. In general, most Generative AI tools show high reliability and almost perfect agreement with human classification, achieving Kappa values from 0.80 upwards in both experiments. In contrast, both experiments show that all lexicon-based tools had lower levels of agreement with human classification, achieving Kappa values between 0.21 and 0.58. Overall, the Generative AI tools proved more reliable in capturing subjectivity and contextual complexity in the language.

**Keywords:** Sentiment Analysis · Lexicons · Generative AI

## 1 Introduction

Sentiment analysis has emerged as a technique to understand people's feedback and opinions in user experience (UX) research (Marsh, 2022; da Silva Franco et al., 2019; Shahid et al., 2024), usability (Nik Ahmad et al., 2021), and market research (Ngai et al., 2019; Taherdoost and Madanchian, 2023). Sentiment analysis refers to the methods to analyze natural language to extract users' emotions or sentiments (Cambria & Erik, 2017; Silge & Robinson, 2016). These methods allow researchers to gain valuable insights into users' perceptions and emotions (Saju et al., 2020), enabling them to design

© The Author(s), under exclusive license to Springer Nature Switzerland AG 2025
D. D. Schmorrow and C. M. Fidopiastis (Eds.): HCII 2025, LNAI 15778, pp. 233–244, 2025.
https://doi.org/10.1007/978-3-031-93724-8_18

more personalized and meaningful user experiences, leading to more effective interface designs, enhanced user satisfaction and higher user motivation.

Since the public release of OpenAI's ChatGPT in 2022, a chatbot that relied on the Large Language Model (LLM) GPT 3.5, the proliferation of powerful, bigger, and efficient LLMs has not stopped. Their capabilities for Natural Language Processing (NLP) and reasoning skills allow users to leverage Generative AI tools to increase and enhance their productivity and explore new approaches in many fields. In this case, HCI is no exception: LLMs have been used for coding qualitative data (Morgan, 2023; Lee et al., 2024; Zhang et al., 2024), generating synthetic users' data (Hämäläinen et al., 2023; Cho et al., 2024), and performing sentiment analysis (Kumar et al., 2023; Wang et al., 2024; Tsai et al., 2024) among other applications.

Due to their nature, LLMs need constant re-training to update their knowledge. Many cloud-based models retain and access users' data (e.g., prompts and interactions) for training purposes, raising privacy concerns about potential data leakages (Wu et al., 2024; Yao et al., 2024), a risk that can be minimized using local-based models, although their security depends on the environment where they are deployed.

Although multiple studies have evaluated the efficacy of some tools in performing sentiment analysis (e.g., Taboada et al., 2011; Bonta et al., 2019; Khoo & Johnkhan, 2018; Mudinas et al., 2012; Serrano-Guerrero et al., 2015; Belal et al., 2023; Hartmann et al., 2023; Krugmann & Hartmann, 2024), few have compared lexicon-based and state-of-the-art (SOTA) Generative AI tools, especially their inter-rater reliability with humans, as lexicons and LLMs in the role of independent observers. Moreover, the extensive list of available options, the rapid evolution of technology, and privacy concerns make selecting a reliable tool challenging.

This study aims to fill this gap in the field, first by comparing four popular lexicon-based tools and seven Generative AI models (six cloud-based and one local-based) and second, by offering a guide for researchers and practitioners that can assist in selecting the most appropriate tool for conducting sentiment analysis. The main research question guiding this work is: How reliable are lexicon-based tools and Generative AI in performing sentiment analyses?

## 2   Method

Two experiments were designed to assess how well the seven different tools assign sentiment labels. Each experiment was conducted following the same steps; the difference between the experiments was the dataset used to test the sentiment analysis. A different dataset containing polarized sentences written and manually labeled by humans following a binary categorization (only positive and negative labels) was assigned to each experiment.

### 2.1   Experiment 1: Sentiment Analysis of a Public Dataset of 3000 Online Reviews

The first experiment used a public dataset of 3,000 sentences extracted from users' online reviews (Kotzias et al., 2015). This dataset was created with 1,000 product reviews on Amazon, 1,000 movie reviews on IMDb, and 1,000 restaurant reviews on Yelp; each sentence was manually labeled following a binary classification (positive or negative). The dataset contained equal positive and negative sentences (1500 sentences for each sentiment). The following sentences are examples from the dataset that were labeled as *positive*:

1. "The sets (especially designed to work with the camera) are amazing.... Stylized, beautiful and effective."
2. "It's a feel-good film and that's how I felt when I came out of the cinema!"
3. "My drink was never empty and he made some really great menu suggestions."

The following sentences are examples from the dataset that were labeled as *negative*:

1. "Needless to say, I wasted my money."
2. "I bought it for my mother and she had a problem with the battery."
3. "It was a good thing that the tickets only cost five dollars because I would be mad if I'd have paid $7.50 to see this crap."

### 2.2 Experiment 2: Sentiment Analysis of an In-House Dataset of 100 Usability Thoughts

Since the dataset used in experiment 1 is a well-known and public dataset, concerns about it being used to train the Large Language Models (LLMs) arose. Therefore, a second dataset containing 100 polarized sentences was created for a second experiment. These sentences were extracted from usability tests the authors have conducted over the years using the think-aloud protocol. The transcripts of these usability sessions had never been uploaded to any generative AI or public sites before the sentiment analysis was performed. The sentences were manually classified as positive or negative (binary classification)—the dataset contained an equal amount of positive and negative sentences. The following sentences are examples from the dataset that were labeled as *positive*:

1. "It was easy because I learned quickly."
2. "I'm glad to see it's the same format now as it was before."
3. "All right. So that's helpful to know. And it satisfies my curiosity as an instructor to know exactly what my students are going to see in a format that they're going to see it to, and one question at a time that they can go back and forth."

The following sentences are examples from the dataset that were labeled as *negative*:

1. "It does not save things when I move the window. That's the problem"
2. "And then I see a complicated screen."
3. "The site broke and I don't know why."

### 2.3 Procedure

The following steps were followed independently for both experiments:

**Sentiment Analysis with Lexicon-Based Tools.** The sentiments' polarity analysis was conducted using R for the following lexicon-based tools: Bing (Hu & Liu, 2004), Afinn (Nielsen, 2011), NRC (Mohammad & Turney, 2013), and Sentimentr (Rinker, 2016). The first three lexicons approach the sentiment analysis from a word-level method. They calculate the emotional tone of a sentence by assigning a score to each word separately. In contrast, Sentimentr, an R package, approaches sentiment analysis from a sentence-level perspective. It calculates the emotion by assigning a score to the whole sentence.

A tidy approach was followed to analyze the text using the Bing, Afinn, and NRC lexicons. The R packages tidytext and tidyr were used to determine which words were more frequent in each sentence and to get the specific sentiment lexicons in a tidy format that was later joined with a word dataset built for each sentence. In this case, the polarity of the sentences was calculated as the sum of the emotion in each word of the text. In other words, the sentiment of the whole sentence was the sum of the sentiment in each word composing the sentence. Sentimentr approximates the polarity of text by sentence, so it was easier to implement in this particular context. The function *sentiment ()* used from this package seamlessly calculated the polarity score of each sentence (values below 0 for negative sentiment, 0 for neutral, and above 0 for positive sentiment).

**Sentiment Analysis with Generative AI Tools.** For the LLMs, some SOTA models accessible to the public were included to conduct the sentiment analysis. The models assessed were GPT 4o and GPT 4o-mini from OpenAI; Gemini 1.0, Gemini 1.5 Pro, and Gemini 1.5 Flash from Google; Llama 3.1 7B and Llama 3.3 from Meta. Gemini Flash is the only model optimized for NLP tasks, such as sentiment analysis; the rest are suited for diverse and more complex tasks. OpenAI and Google models are proprietary and accessed only through the cloud, whereas Meta models are open-source and can be executed in a local environment.

The interaction with the LLMs happened in two different ways. The first was a programming approach: Python was selected to interact with OpenAI and Google's models through their APIs. The second way, an end-user approach, was more intuitive and easier to implement: the Meta's models were tested using different chatbots. Llama 3.2 was tested in the cloud using MetaAI, and LLama 3.1 7B was tested in a local environment (MacBook Air M1 with 16 GB of RAM) using Ollama, a free, open-source tool designed to run LLMs locally.

All the LLMs were instructed with the same prompt engineering using a few-shot approach: three sentences and their classification (positive, negative, and neutral) were presented as an example to the LLMs. A few-shot approach is suggested to increase the model's response reliability, compared to a zero-shot approach (Barektain et al., 2024), where instructions are provided without examples; however, Krugmann and Hart-mann (2024) obtained good performance metrics in sentiment analysis with a zero-shot approach.

The following prompt was used for all the models to classify both datasets:

*"I will provide you with a list of sentences. Each sentence has a number. Classify each sentence as positive, negative, or neutral. For example, I am happy is positive, I am unhappy is negative, and today is Thursday is neutral. I also want you to structure your responses in two columns: in the first column, the sentence number, and its classification in the second column."*

Because Sentimentr and Affin can detect the neutral tone, the LLMs were allowed to use the neutral label. However, the neutral classification was considered an error as both datasets did not include neutral sentences.

For the models tested in the cloud, the dataset of online reviews was separated into batches of 250 sentences, as higher sentence volumes produced errors due to resource availability and, sometimes, incomplete outputs, such as missing one classification. The dataset of usability feedback was analyzed at once. The batches were further reduced (50 sentences) for the model executed locally (Llama 3.1) as problems arose with bigger batches due to the limited hardware resources. In addition, the prompt was included every time that a batch was provided, as subsequent executions without the prompt produced additional sentiment classifications (e.g., "humoristic" and "resignation") and changes in the output format. The models tested in the cloud only required the prompt with the first batch, and after that, there was no need to include the prompt because the models applied the same prompt to all the batches automatically.

**Comparison of Each Tool Against Human Classification.** The data obtained from the sentiment analysis of each tool was compared to assess the level of agreement between the tool and the manually annotated sentiments using Cohen's Kappa coefficient. Kappa helped evaluate the tools' reliability against human classification. It considers possible categories and the likelihood of obtaining the same values by chance; therefore, this statistical measure was essential, as lexicon-based tools could not detect sentiments in some sentences.

The Cohen's Kappa values were calculated using the *irr* package in R. The function *kappa2()* was applied to calculate unweighted kappa as the index of interrater agreement between the tool and human classification.

The resulting Kappa coefficients were later assigned adjectives following the labels proposed by Landis & Koch (1977) (as shown in Table 1) to use the same terminology when discussing the values.

**Table 1.** Adjectives for each range of kappa adapted from Landis & Koch (1977).

| Kappa | Adjective |
|---|---|
| $x > 0.8$ | Almost Perfect |
| $0.6 < x \leq 0.8$ | Substantial |
| $0.4 < x \leq 0.6$ | Moderate |
| $0.2 < x \leq 0.4$ | Fair |
| $0 \leq x \leq 0.2$ | Slight |
| $x < 0.8$ | Poor |

# 3 Results

## 3.1 Experiment 1

In this experiment, some of the lexicon-based tools did not annotate a sentiment in some sentences. These tools returned N/A for the sentences that they were incapable of analyzing. The lexicons that could not analyze the total of sentences are NRC with 32%, Afinn with 27%, and Bing with 17% of the dataset uncategorized. Sentimentr categorized 100% of the sentences in the dataset and all the seven generative AI tools.

The results from the sentiment analysis performed in experiment 1 show a stark difference in the kappa values between the lexicon-based and Generative AI tools. All seven Generative AI tools had kappa values ranging from 0.84 to 0.96, which can be interpreted as an almost perfect agreement with the manual classification. Lexicon-based tools had Kappa values ranging from 0.21 to 0.55, considered a fair to moderate agreement with the manual classification.

Table 2 summarizes the results of each tool, including the standard error (SE), and Fig. 1 shows the kappa values for all tools.

**Table 2.** Kappa values for each tool against the manual classification of sentences from experiment 1, ordered from high to low kappa values.

| Tool | Kappa | SE | Reliability or agreement |
|---|---|---|---|
| Llama 3.2 LLM | 0.96 | 0.02 | Almost Perfect |
| GPT 4o-mini LLM | 0.95 | 0.02 | Almost Perfect |
| Gemini 1.0 Pro LLM | 0.93 | 0.02 | Almost Perfect |
| Gemini 1.5 Flash LLM | 0.93 | 0.02 | Almost Perfect |
| Gemini 1.5 Pro LLM | 0.91 | 0.02 | Almost Perfect |
| GPT 4o LLM | 0.90 | 0.02 | Almost Perfect |
| Llama 3.1 7B LLM (local) | 0.84 | 0.02 | Almost Perfect |
| Sentimentr lexicon | 0.55 | 0.02 | Moderate |
| Bing lexicon | 0.43 | 0.01 | Moderate |
| Afinn lexicon | 0.35 | 0.01 | Fair |
| NRC lexicon | 0.21 | 0.01 | Fair |

## 3.2 Experiment 2

As in experiment 1, in this second experiment, some of the lexicon-based tools could not analyze some sentences. These tools returned N/A for the sentences that they were incapable of processing. The lexicons that could not analyze the total of sentences are NRC with 41%, Afinn with 28%, and Bing with 19% of the dataset uncategorized.

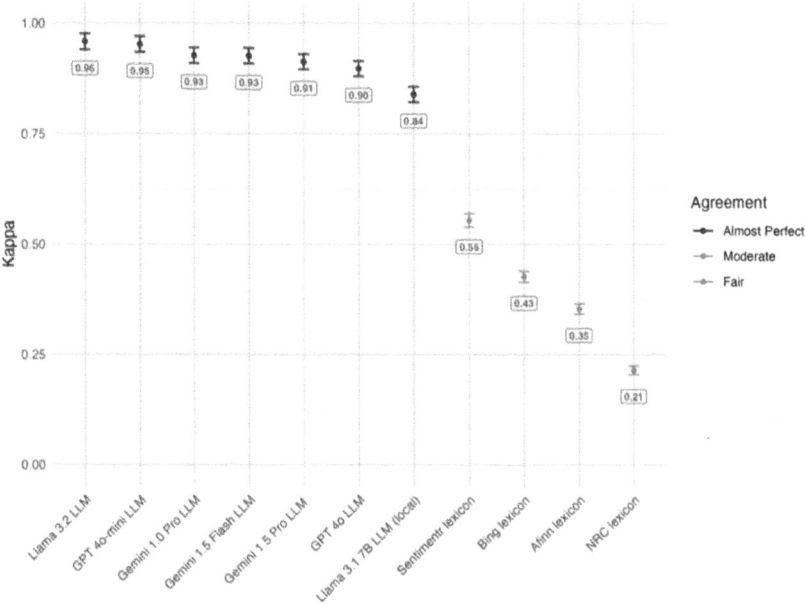

**Fig. 1.** Plot of Kappa Values with Error Bars for Experiment 1.

Sentimentr categorized 100% of the sentences in the dataset and all the seven generative AI tools.

Results from the sentiment analysis performed in experiment 2 show a drop in the kappa values of all Generative AI tools except GPT 4o-mini, which shows a slightly higher kappa. Unlike the results obtained when analyzing the online reviews, where all seven Generative AI tools show almost perfect agreement, the results from the sentiment analysis of the second dataset show substantial to almost perfect agreement, with kappa values ranging from 0.73 to 0.98. Lexicon-based tools show the same or better results for this dataset, with Kappa values ranging from 0.21 to 0.57, but still considered a fair to moderate agreement with the manual classification.

Table 3 summarizes the results of each tool, including the standard error (SE), and Fig. 2 shows the kappa values for all tools.

## 4   Discussion

In both experiments, generative AI tools provided more reliable sentiment analysis than lexicon-based tools. These findings are consistent with previous studies that evaluated LLMs (Hartmann et al., 2023; Krugmann & Hartmann, 2024; Wang et al., 2024) and support the expectation that Generative AI models when trained on large volumes of labeled data, can capture complexities in the language (Barektain et al., 2024) that lexicon-based tools may struggle to detect due their dictionary-based nature (Hartmann et al., 2023). However, it is important to point out that lexicon-based tools can still be helpful in scenarios where simple and direct language is used, interpretability about

**Table 3.** Kappa values for each tool against the manual classification of sentences from experiment 2, ordered from high to low kappa values.

| Tool | Kappa | SE | Reliability or agreement |
|---|---|---|---|
| GPT 4o-mini LLM | 0.98 | 0.10 | Almost Perfect |
| Gemini 1.0 Pro LLM | 0.86 | 0.09 | Almost Perfect |
| GPT 4o LLM | 0.86 | 0.09 | Almost Perfect |
| Gemini 1.5 Flash LLM | 0.82 | 0.09 | Almost Perfect |
| Llama 3.2 LLM | 0.81 | 0.08 | Almost Perfect |
| Gemini 1.5 Pro LLM | 0.78 | 0.08 | Substantial |
| Llama 3.1 7B LLM (local) | 0.73 | 0.08 | Substantial |
| Sentimentr lexicon | 0.58 | 0.08 | Moderate |
| Bing lexicon | 0.47 | 0.07 | Moderate |
| Afinn lexicon | 0.36 | 0.05 | Fair |
| NRC lexicon | 0.22 | 0.05 | Fair |

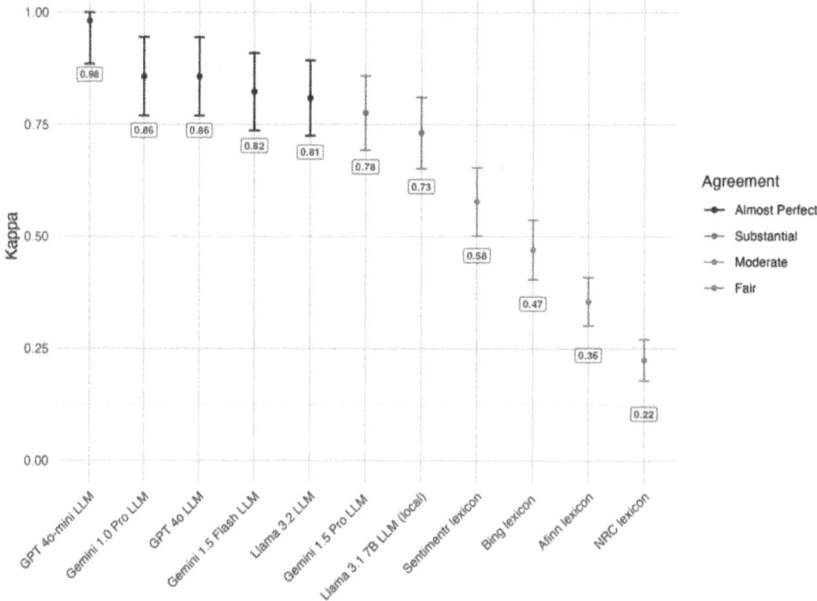

**Fig. 2.** Plot of Kappa Values with Error Bars for Experiment 2.

how the classification was performed is needed (Hartmann et al., 2023), or the data must be maintained in a local environment. For this last scenario, there are some options of Generative AI tools that can be hosted locally, such as Llama 3.1 7B LLM, which was demonstrated to be more reliable than the lexicon-based options in both experiments of this study.

There was no considerable difference in kappa values among the Generative AI tools examined in experiment 1, demonstrating consistency between the training of the different models. It could also suggest that this dataset was used to train the models. Therefore, they were tested again in experiment 2 using a completely different dataset built in-house for this study.

Kappa coefficients for the sentiment analysis were consistently lower for experiment 2, strengthening the idea that the models somehow did have traces of the online reviews' dataset used in experiment 1 as one of the main reasons for these lower results. Another reason for this lowering in the agreement is the sample sizes and the context of the sentences included in the datasets. The dataset of online reviews (experiment 1) has more data, 3000 sentences, compared with the 100 usability sentences of the other dataset (experiment 2). Also, the dataset used in experiment 1 contains sentences with more direct language due to the nature of a review. In contrast, the sentences from the usability dataset contain a more complex and sometimes ambiguous language.

### 4.1 Practical Approaches to Tools Usage

Regarding the end-user approach, the Generative AI tools with chatbots demonstrated to be the more user friendly. To use lexicon-based tools, users must have knowledge and experience with programming and some knowledge about text mining, as these tools require data preparation before analyzing, making their usage more complex, time-consuming, and prone to errors.

On the other hand, LLMs can be used in both ways. For example, the programming approach gives the user more control over the LLMs settings and the capability to integrate them into custom solutions, and a user-friendly approach, where the interaction with chatbots lowers the programming barrier for users with zero or minimal programming experience. Nevertheless, for LLMs, both approaches require knowledge from the user on how to design and write prompts, a process that has shown challenges, especially when users do not have experience in programming and AI (Zamfirescu-Pereira et al., 2023).

### 4.2 Considerations About Security and Trust in the Tools

Privacy issues are not a drawback with the lexicon-based tools because of their standalone nature and how they work, the lexicon-based tools evaluated do not retain or store the data provided. In contrast, cloud-based Generative AI tools can keep and use the data provided to train their models, which could increase privacy risks such as data leaking, reconstruction, or inference; the risk increases if the data is not anonymized or includes confidential or sensitive information, although some attacks are considered theoretically possible rather than practical (Yao et al., 2024).

Some companies offer paid subscriptions promising not to use the data provided for training the models; others allow users to request an opt-out of their data. A good practice is thoroughly reviewing the companies' data privacy policy to understand how the data is used and how long it is retained to decide whether to use it for sentiment analysis or other tasks. This practice is highly recommended before deciding on a tool to analyze data from usability studies and user research because these could contain users' sensitive information.

An alternative to the Generative AI tools on the cloud is using them in a local environment controlled by the user, like the model LLama 3.1 7B tested in this study, as the data is not stored, used to train the model, or uploaded to the cloud. However, the more advanced a model, the more computational resources it needs and consumes; if the hardware is limited, there will be a tradeoff between resources and performance. The model tested has the minimum parameters (7 billion) of the 3.1 family models (the newest is the 3.3). Still, its performance was better than the lexicon-based tools tested, which suggests local Generative AI tools may be a solid alternative to the lexicon-based tools and the cloud-based Generative AI tools, especially in powerful hardware settings that might increase their performance.

## 5  Final Remarks and Future Directions

The power of Generative AI relies on its generalization capabilities; that is why the AI works so well with new data that has never been used for training the model. New, private, and larger datasets are needed to evaluate better how well the LLMs perform sentiment analysis with unseen data, as the dataset evaluated in the second experiment was a small sample.

The most popular LLMs were selected for the reliability analysis to offer a general overview. However, a broader comparison is needed as other LLMs have shown excellent benchmark results. In addition, only one local LLM was tested which obtained the lower score among the LLMs. The hardware resources available for that model were minimal, and an experiment using newer and more powerful hardware is needed to determine whether the local-based models' performance is at a disadvantage compared to the cloud-based ones with more hardware resources.

The results from this study suggest that Generative AI tools are a solid alternative to the traditional sentiment analysis approaches based on lexicons, as LLMs can understand the nuances of language. This study offers insights into how reliable the LLMs are for sentiment classification, giving researchers and HCI practitioners more confidence when working with Generative AI, not only as a tool but as another rater for qualitative analysis.

## References

Barektain, M., et al.: Whitepaper Foundational Large Language Models & Text Generation. Google (2024)

Belal, M., She, J., Wong, S.: Leveraging ChatGPT As Text Annotation Tool for Sentiment Analysis (2023). https://arxiv.org/abs/2306.17177

Bonta, V., Kumaresh, N., Janardhan, N.: A comprehensive study on lexicon based approaches for sentiment analysis. Asian J. Comput. Sci. Technol. 8, 1–6 (2019). https://doi.org/10.51983/ajcst-2019.8.S2.2037

Cambria, E., Das, D., Bandyopadhyay, S., Feraco, A. (eds.): A Practical Guide to Sentiment Analysis. Springer, Cham (2017)

Cho, S., Kim, J., Kim, J.H.: LLM-based doppelgänger models: leveraging synthetic data for human-like responses in survey simulations. IEEE Access **12**, 178917–178927 (2024). https://doi.org/10.1109/ACCESS.2024.3502219

Da Silva Franco, R.Y., Santos Do Amor Divino Lima, R., Monte Paixão, R.D., Resque Dos Santos, C.G., Serique Meiguins, B.: UXmood—a sentiment analysis and information visualization tool to support the evaluation of usability and user experience. Information **10**, 366 (2019). https://doi.org/10.3390/info10120366

Hämäläinen, P., Tavast, M., Kunnari, A.: Evaluating large language models in generating synthetic HCI research data: a case study. In: Proceedings of the 2023 CHI Conference on Human Factors in Computing Systems, pp. 1–19. ACM, Hamburg, Germany (2023)

Hartmann, J., Heitmann, M., Siebert, C., Schamp, C.: More than a feeling: accuracy and application of sentiment analysis. Int. J. Res. Mark. **40**, 75–87 (2023). https://doi.org/10.1016/j.ijresmar.2022.05.005

Hu, M., Liu, B.: Mining and summarizing customer reviews. In: Proceedings of the Tenth ACM SIGKDD International Conference on Knowledge Discovery and Data Mining, pp. 168–177. ACM, Seattle, WA, USA (2004)

Khoo, C.S., Johnkhan, S.B.: Lexicon-based sentiment analysis: comparative evaluation of six sentiment lexicons. J. Inf. Sci. **44**, 491–511 (2018). https://doi.org/10.1177/0165551517703514

Kotzias, D., Denil, M., De Freitas, N., Smyth, P.: From group to individual labels using deep features. In: Proceedings of the 21th ACM SIGKDD International Conference on Knowledge Discovery and Data Mining, pp. 597–606. ACM, Sydney, NSW, Australia (2015)

Krugmann, J.O., Hartmann, J.: Sentiment analysis in the age of generative AI. Cust. Need. Solut. **11**, 3 (2024). https://doi.org/10.1007/s40547-024-00143-4

Kumar, N.P., Srinivasan, K., Ramesh, D.: Analyzing public sentiment towards LLM: a twitter-based sentiment analysis. In: 2023 International Conference on the Confluence of Advancements in Robotics, Vision and Interdisciplinary Technology Management (IC-RVITM), pp. 1–8. IEEE, Bangalore, India (2023)

Landis, J.R., Koch, G.G.: The measurement of observer agreement for categorical data. Biometrics **33**, 159–174 (1977)

Lee, V.V., Van Der Lubbe, S.C.C., Goh, L.H., Valderas, J.M.: Harnessing ChatGPT for thematic analysis: are we ready? J. Med. Internet Res. **26**, e54974 (2024). https://doi.org/10.2196/54974

Marsh, S.: User Research: Improve Product and Service Design and Enhance Your UX Research. KoganPage, London (2022)

Mohammad, S.M., Turney, P.D.: Crowdsourcing a Word-Emotion Association Lexicon (2013). http://arxiv.org/abs/1308.6297

Morgan, D.L.: Exploring the use of artificial intelligence for qualitative data analysis: the case of ChatGPT. Int J Qual Methods **22**, 16094069231211248 (2023). https://doi.org/10.1177/16094069231211248

Mudinas, A., Zhang, D., Levene, M.: Combining lexicon and learning based approaches for concept-level sentiment analysis. In: Proceedings of the First International Workshop on Issues of Sentiment Discovery and Opinion Mining, pp. 1–8. ACM, Beijing, China (2012)

Ngai, C.S.B., Lee, W.M., Ng, P.P.K., Wu, D.D.: Innovating an integrated approach to collaborative elearning practices in higher education: the case study of a corporate communication e-platform. Stud. High. Educ. **44**, 1990–2010 (2019). https://doi.org/10.1080/03075079.2018.1482266

Nielsen, F.Å.: A new ANEW: evaluation of a word list for sentiment analysis in microblogs (2011). http://arxiv.org/abs/1103.2903

Nik Ahmad, N.A., Hamid, N.I.M., Mohd Lokman, A.: Performing usability evaluation on multi-platform based application for efficiency, effectiveness, and satisfaction enhancement. Int. J. Interact. Mob. Technol. **15**, 103 (2021). https://doi.org/10.3991/ijim.v15i10.20429

Rinker, T., Spinu, V.: trinker/sentimentr: version 0.4.0 (2016). https://zenodo.org/record/592486

Saju, B., Jose, S., Antony, A.: Comprehensive study on sentiment analysis: types, approaches, recent applications, tools and APIs. In: 2020 Advanced Computing and Communication Technologies for High Performance Applications (ACCTHPA), pp. 186–193. IEEE, Cochin, India (2020)

Serrano-Guerrero, J., Olivas, J.A., Romero, F.P., Herrera-Viedma, E.: Sentiment analysis: a review and comparative analysis of web services. Inf. Sci. **311**, 18–38 (2015). https://doi.org/10.1016/j.ins.2015.03.040

Shahid, R., et al.: Predicting customer loyalty in the airline industry: a machine learning approach integrating sentiment analysis and user experience. Int. J. Comput. Eng. **1**, 50–54 (2024). https://doi.org/10.62527/comien.1.2.12

Silge, J., Robinson, D.: tidytext: text mining and analysis using tidy data principles in R. JOSS. **1**, 37 (2016). https://doi.org/10.21105/joss.00037

Taboada, M., Brooke, J., Tofiloski, M., Voll, K., Stede, M.: Lexicon-based methods for sentiment analysis. Comput. Linguist. **37**, 267–307 (2011). https://doi.org/10.1162/COLI_a_00049

Taherdoost, H., Madanchian, M.: Artificial intelligence and sentiment analysis: a review in competitive research. Computers **12**, 37 (2023). https://doi.org/10.3390/computers12020037

Tsai, C.-H., Nandy, G., House, D., Carroll, J.: Ensuring transparency in using ChatGPT for public sentiment analysis. In: Proceedings of the 25th Annual International Conference on Digital Government Research, pp. 627–636. ACM, Taipei, Taiwan (2024)

Wang, Z., Xie, Q., Feng, Y., Ding, Z., Yang, Z., Xia, R.: Is ChatGPT a Good Sentiment Analyzer? A Preliminary Study (2024). http://arxiv.org/abs/2304.04339

Wu, X., Duan, R., Ni, J.: Unveiling security, privacy, and ethical concerns of ChatGPT. J. Inf. Intell. **2**, 102–115 (2024). https://doi.org/10.1016/j.jiixd.2023.10.007

Yao, Y., Duan, J., Xu, K., Cai, Y., Sun, Z., Zhang, Y.: A survey on large language model (LLM) security and privacy: the good, the bad, and the ugly. High-Confidence Computing. **4**, 100211 (2024). https://doi.org/10.1016/j.hcc.2024.100211

Zamfirescu-Pereira, J.D., Wong, R.Y., Hartmann, B., Yang, Q.: Why Johnny can't prompt: how non-AI experts try (and fail) to design LLM prompts. In: Proceedings of the 2023 CHI Conference on Human Factors in Computing Systems, pp. 1–21. ACM, Hamburg, Germany (2023)

Zhang, H., Wu, C., Xie, J., Lyu, Y., Cai, J., Carroll, J.M.: Redefining Qualitative Analysis in the AI Era: Utilizing ChatGPT for Efficient Thematic Analysis (2024). http://arxiv.org/abs/2309.10771

# Words, Meaning, Context, Semantics and Reality: Essential Elements of Cognition

Suraj Sood[1], Charlotte J. Walker[2], Monte Hancock[3], and Raman Kannan[4]([⊠])

[1] LUV Systems, Gardena, USA
[2] TSF Management, Greenwich, CT 06830, USA
[3] WeGlobal Studios, Los Angeles, USA
[4] Hunter College, New York, USA
rk2153@gmail.com

**Abstract.** This chapter, devoted to the study of words, meaning, and semantics, is composed of three parts. "The study of word meaning is crucial to the inquiry into the fundamental properties of human language", declares Stanford Encyclopedia of Philosophy (SEP, henceforth). Given the primacy of language, this also applies for human cognition. In this chapter, we first trace human thought about language, its components, and its relationship to species and reality from the perspectives of philosophy, logic and the physiological cognitive apparatus. Next, we present how in practice, that understanding has shaped the practice of NLP. Discourse between an author and three generative artificial intelligence (AI) applications—ChatGPT, Anthropic's Claude, and Google Gemini—is offered and compared. We identify where natural language processing (NLP) is deficient given known gaps, and we prescribe a plausible solution.

**Keywords:** natural language processing (NLP) · computational linguistics · GPT · generative artificial intelligence (AI)

## 1 Introduction

Language and linguistics have been the focus of philosophers and thought leaders for the entirety of human existence, from early Greek philosophers to modern day neuroscientists. We begin with the questions: Are artificial intelligence (AI) researchers, application architects and engineers taking all that humankind already knows into account? As an example, have the learnings and advancements during the symbolic NLP period (1950s-early 1990's) been incorporated in the neural/probabilistic NLP of today? We show in this paper that it has not. What else is missing?

### 1.1 Anatomical Review of the Linguistic Apparatus

In [2], neuroscientists Antonio and Hanna Damasio view language as "the ability to use words and to combine them into sentences so that concepts in our minds can be

---

*"Those who are lovers of wisdom must be inquirers into many things."* – Heraclitus

© The Author(s), under exclusive license to Springer Nature Switzerland AG 2025
D. D. Schmorrow and C. M. Fidopiastis (Eds.): HCII 2025, LNAI 15778, pp. 245–267, 2025.
https://doi.org/10.1007/978-3-031-93724-8_19

transmitted to other people in outgoing direction as well as in the inward direction: how we comprehend words spoken by others and turn them into concepts in our own minds." Scientists posit that humans and species before them started generating and categorizing actions and creating mental representations of objects, events and relations. A view of language is that it is an efficient means of communication in either direction, especially for abstract concepts.

The brain is a complex system; language comprehension and expression are extraordinarily complicated. Language-processing in the brain occurs with three interacting sets of structures: one dedicated to concepts, a second to manage words and the third to mediate between the two. This bidirectional mediation can generate words given concept or evoke the corresponding concepts given relevant words [2]. In this manner, objects, events and relationships are managed. Using successive layers of categories and symbolic representations, abstractions and metaphors are managed. They divide sound-based language into the following levels:

- phonemes – concerned with individual sound units, which are combined, in a particular order to produce morphemes.
- morphemes – smallest parts of a word, which are combined to form a word
- syntax – the admissible combinations of words in phrases and sentences (a.k.a. grammar)
- lexicon – collection of all words in a given language. Each lexical entry includes all information relating to morphology and syntax. Conceptual knowledge is absent.
- semantics – meaning corresponding to lexical items and all possible sentences
- prosody – vocal intonation that can modify the literal meanings of words and sentences
- discourse – the linking of sentences to form a narrative

Most importantly, it is claimed that the brain encapsulates both the representational aspects of perception of external reality, as well as how the body explores the world and its reaction. According to these models, the brain consists of: (1) concept processing system, (2) systems that generate words and sentences, and (3) mediator systems, allowing the brain to go from words to concepts or from concepts to words.

In 1861, Paul Broca discovered the area of the brain named in his honor. The Broca area performs the vital role in generating articulate speech [1]. Wernicke's area [4] is responsible for reading, comprehending and producing language, but does not assist in the vocalization of produced language. The Broca area is responsible for the vocalization of language produced by Wernicke's area. Broca and Wernicke's areas are located primarily in the brain's left hemisphere [3]. The Wernicke-Geschwind Model [4] formulated later outlines how the Broca and Wernicke areas' functions are integrated to comprehend or vocalize. The mediation system not only generates the words but also formulates the correct sentence structures, expressing the relationships between the concepts. As outlined in [3], much clinical work has been done and these findings have been revised and elaborated.

While clinicians, with the help of MRI and PET scans, have deciphered all these inner workings of our language processing apparatus, philosophers and linguists have been analytically dissecting aspects of language.

## 1.2  Centrality of Language and Linguistic Levels

Language is the primary medium by which humans exchange knowledge. It is well established that language shapes how we think and how much we know [5]. Language shapes our cognitive abilities, expressiveness and perception [15]. The magic of language is in the meanings and percepts it evokes. Consistent with the anatomical view, the way linguists describe language is also considered in several distinct levels: 1) phonology, resulting in sounds, 2) morphology, resulting in words, 3) syntax, sentence generation, and 4) semantics, meaning conveyance [16].

Philosophers have long pondered the relationship between languages, i.e. the expressions of thought, linguistic entities, and reality, since ancient times. "To have a second language is to have a second soul"—a quote by Charlemagne, the Holy Roman Emperor, circa 768 – 814—strongly suggests that language crafts reality. On the other hand, Shakespeare believed reality exists as-is, and that words do not bring reality to life. The essence of reality is not influenced by the words we choose to refer to them. "A rose by any other name would smell as sweet" is a popular adage from William Shakespeare's play Romeo and Juliet, in which Juliet seems to argue that it does not matter that Romeo is from her family's rival house of Montague. The reference is used to state that the names of things do not affect what they really are [25].

## 1.3  Words, Meanings and Semantics

We start with words, which came to be recognized as a medium of conceptualization [12]. A broad definition of a word offered by SEP [24] is that words signify one or more "concepts" or "ideas". Likewise, a concept may be denoted by many words.

The 17th century philosopher John Locke [13] studied the inner workings of the human mind. In his landmark essay," Essay Concerning Human Understanding", Locke set out to offer an analysis of the human mind and its acquisition of knowledge. In Locke's conception, words are arbitrary and influenced by social convention regarding how the ideas of the speaker are communicated to and received by an audience. Locke categorized words into words used for ideas and substances. His formalism allowed a single word to refer to a plurality of ideas. Locke also recognized the connective role words such as "is", "but", "hence" and others play between different ideas. A word in Locke's world was to exchange ideas amongst humans with a shared convention about real-world objects.

Frege, on the other hand, proposed two semantic aspects, sense and reference. Carnap later replaced these terms with intension and extension, respectively. Wittgenstein [14] offered an alternate approach that meaning is use. Wittgenstein argues that definitions emerge from what he termed "forms of life", or roughly, the culture and society in which they are used.

Chomsky [8] elaborated meaning as follows: "To understand a sentence we must know more than the analysis of this sentence on each linguistic level. We must also know the reference and meaning of the words of which it is composed", thus decoupling grammar from contributing to the meaning of a given sentence. In contrast, words embody the meaning. To linguists, a word in this regard is a basic element of language that carries an objective or practical meaning. It can be used on its own and is uninterruptible. It must be emphasized, in addition to bearing contextual meaning in the presence of other words; words or terms also have natural meaning [6]. In closing, both the physiological and philosophical view of language is that words are arbitrary and have natural meaning, and so does context, and that the mind maintains a lattice of concepts.

## 2   Computational Linguistics and ChatGPT

### 2.1   Pursuit of Linguistic Capabilities; Computational Techniques (NLP)

Great strides have been made to document similarity, sentiment analysis, topic modeling and summarization. For a comprehensive review of neural language processing, refer to [10, 11]. Wikipedia [15] is a great place to start. Historically, NLP can be thought of in two phases: symbolic NLP, and statistical NLP. During the symbolic NLP era, a set of rules and a lookup dictionary played a central role [26, 27]. With the advent of machine learning and statistical techniques, NLP evolved very differently from the earlier systems, importantly, without rules or a lookup dictionary.

Here, we briefly mention various statistical techniques. Term frequency [17] – inverse document frequency [18] (TF-IDF) is built on the heuristic that frequently-occurring and rare words convey the essence of a document. Importance and relevance of word order, as well as the relationship between words, are ignored.

Engrams, or the Bag of Words (BOW) model, do not offer support to capture meaning or the semantics. In the BOW model, a word contributes the same regardless of where it occurs: the order in which words occur is not taken into account. Each word is a row, and each column is a document vector with the frequency of occurrence.

### 2.2   Problem Statement

Word Embedding [19] and Word2Vec methods were proposed and implemented to overcome some of these deficiencies. Notably, capturing the meaning of documents remains an unsolved problem.

Conditional Random Fields (CRF) and sequence model-driven approaches excel in predicting words that follow. Incorporating machine learning techniques, or advanced probabilistic techniques, is not new to NLP. Topic modeling, e.g., Latent Semantic Indexing [21], is such an example. Latent Semantic Indexing (LSI) and Latent Dirichlet Allocation (LDA) [22, 23] can associate topics to documents, even without understanding what the topics are. LSI and LDA are active fields, and a lot of work is being done.

### 2.3   Natural Meaning of a Word, Concept Lattice

Natural meaning is not the same as a word vector of 100 dimensions. NLP systems must address this gap to become more robust.

To compete with the human brain, an artificial brain must also maintain a concept lattice. Without a concept lattice, the complexity of determining meaning explodes, because abstraction is a key mental tool to reduce complexity. The concept 'fruit' can stand in for a variety of real-world concepts. A bird, an abstract idea, exists as parrots, ravens, chickens, vultures, etc.

When discussing the nearly-extinct California Condor, human minds do not have to expend any time or energy in elaborating that a California Condor can fly, thanks to the concept lattice, and the abstract concept 'bird'. Wings and flight can be assumed, although there are species of birds that cannot fly (they are rare). These exceptions can easily be a part of the concept lattice. Even to the mind that is aware of the HTCondor— Condor: the processor hunter [7]—given context, the extension of the phrase 'California Condor' is clear.

The intelligent exchange of ideas requires robust understanding of the topics central to the discourse. Professor Lenat said, "Current AIs can form and recognize patterns, but they don't really understand anything." This statement attributes many ills of AI to the lack of understanding, or the absence of left-brain faculties, i.e., "thinking slow", a reference to [9].

What else may we expect when AI contraptions are based on a language framework that relies on statistics, probabilities, vectors, and co-occurrences without any consideration for natural meanings, and oblivious to concept hierarchies which are the foundation of understanding?

## 2.4  How does ChatGPT Perform?

ChatGPT is phenomenal. But ChatGPT can only produce any pattern that has the best odds of having been generated based on the data it has been trained on. If no one ever said it or "it" never came up in training, ChatGPT cannot say it either. Please follow the actual interaction between us and ChatGPT below (Fig. 1).

 where will straight flight to venus stop next?

 There are currently no straight flights to Venus, as there are no commercially available spacecraft capable of carrying humans to Venus. The journey to Venus would require advanced technology and equipment due to the harsh conditions and extreme temperatures found in the planet's atmosphere.

The closest spacecraft to Venus is currently NASA's Parker Solar Probe, which will make several flybys of Venus as part of its mission to study the Sun. However, the Parker Solar Probe is an unmanned spacecraft and is not capable of carrying passengers.

In summary, there are no straight flights to Venus, and even if there were, they would not have any stops along the way as there are no feasible locations for a stopover on the way to the planet.

**Fig. 1.** Query involving "Venus".

Because the token 'venus' appears most frequently in the context of the planet Venus, ChatGPT crafts an eclectic response. Furthermore, machines don't lie. Here is what ChatGPT says to the mention of a zip code for Venus, Texas (Figs. 2 and 3):

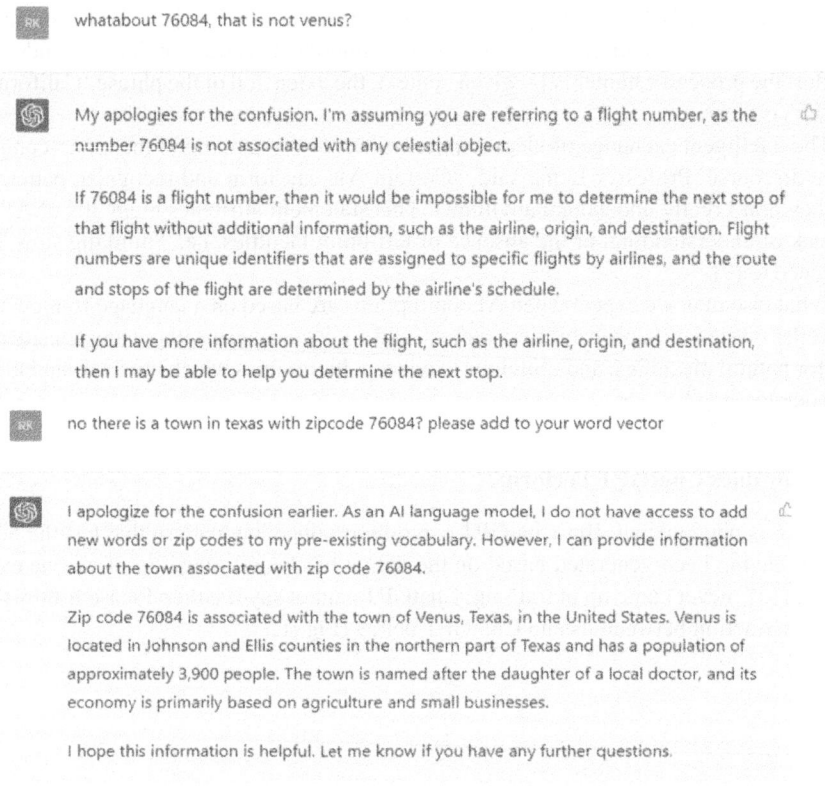

**Fig. 2.** Continuation of conversation with ChatGPT.

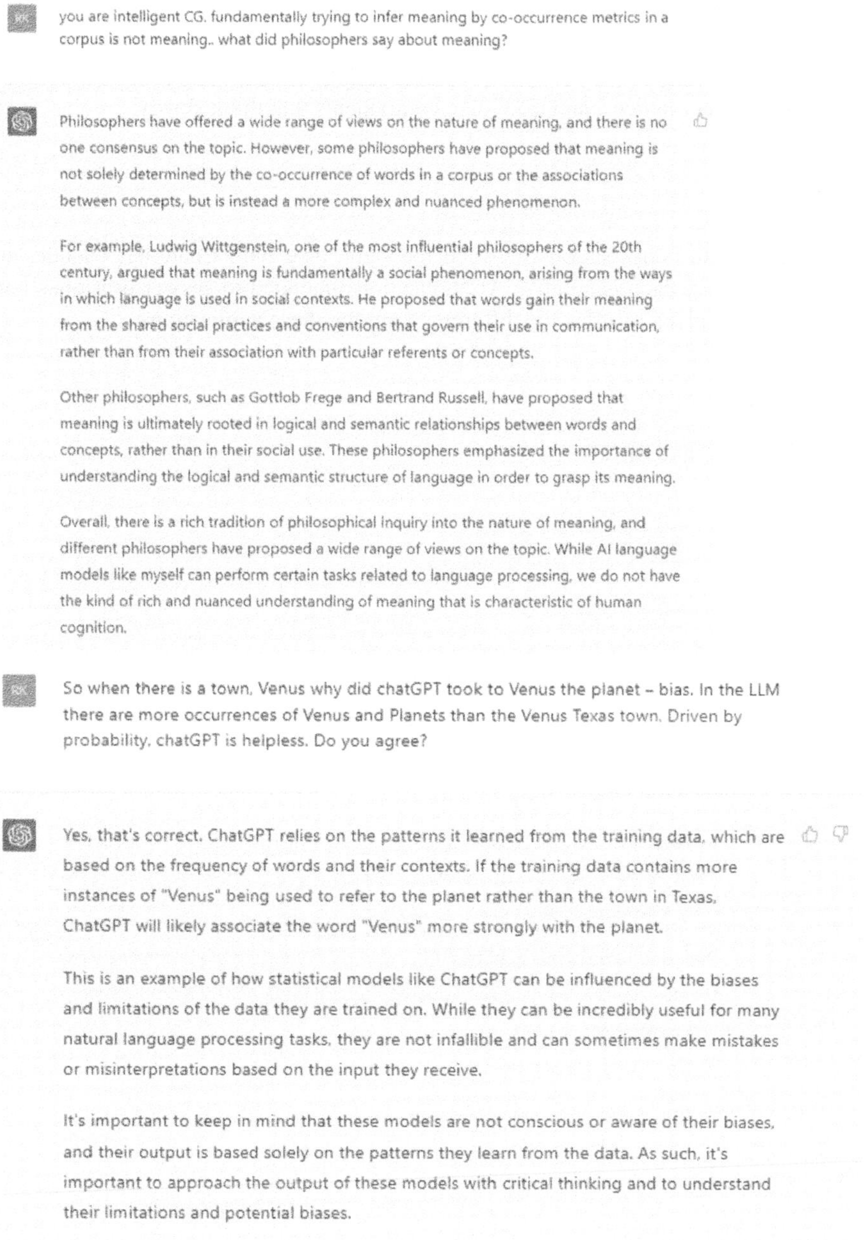

you are intelligent CG. fundamentally trying to infer meaning by co-occurrence metrics in a corpus is not meaning.. what did philosophers say about meaning?

Philosophers have offered a wide range of views on the nature of meaning, and there is no one consensus on the topic. However, some philosophers have proposed that meaning is not solely determined by the co-occurrence of words in a corpus or the associations between concepts, but is instead a more complex and nuanced phenomenon.

For example, Ludwig Wittgenstein, one of the most influential philosophers of the 20th century, argued that meaning is fundamentally a social phenomenon, arising from the ways in which language is used in social contexts. He proposed that words gain their meaning from the shared social practices and conventions that govern their use in communication, rather than from their association with particular referents or concepts.

Other philosophers, such as Gottlob Frege and Bertrand Russell, have proposed that meaning is ultimately rooted in logical and semantic relationships between words and concepts, rather than in their social use. These philosophers emphasized the importance of understanding the logical and semantic structure of language in order to grasp its meaning.

Overall, there is a rich tradition of philosophical inquiry into the nature of meaning, and different philosophers have proposed a wide range of views on the topic. While AI language models like myself can perform certain tasks related to language processing, we do not have the kind of rich and nuanced understanding of meaning that is characteristic of human cognition.

So when there is a town, Venus why did chatGPT took to Venus the planet – bias. In the LLM there are more occurrences of Venus and Planets than the Venus Texas town. Driven by probability, chatGPT is helpless. Do you agree?

Yes, that's correct. ChatGPT relies on the patterns it learned from the training data, which are based on the frequency of words and their contexts. If the training data contains more instances of "Venus" being used to refer to the planet rather than the town in Texas, ChatGPT will likely associate the word "Venus" more strongly with the planet.

This is an example of how statistical models like ChatGPT can be influenced by the biases and limitations of the data they are trained on. While they can be incredibly useful for many natural language processing tasks, they are not infallible and can sometimes make mistakes or misinterpretations based on the input they receive.

It's important to keep in mind that these models are not conscious or aware of their biases, and their output is based solely on the patterns they learn from the data. As such, it's important to approach the output of these models with critical thinking and to understand their limitations and potential biases.

**Fig. 3.** Philosophy of meaning and end of "Venus" conversation with ChatGPT.

We cannot simply look past the reflective strain. Is ChatGPT really introspecting? How will ChatGPT respond to single word queries? What if I enter a word like sanguine?

NLP in its current form, TF-IDF, LSI, LDA, sentiment analysis, embeddings, and the large language model (LLM) suffer the same paucity of understanding. Inherent deficiencies of the BOW model are discussed in [20]. We need a repository of natural meanings, concept lattices, and CYC-like components that think slowly.

## 3   Results

What follows are conversations between the same user with ChatGPT, Claude, and Gemini. These are each generative AI applications intended to answer user questions. Screenshots are given to show the differences among these applications.

### 3.1   ChatGPT

(See Figs. 4, 6, 7 and 8)

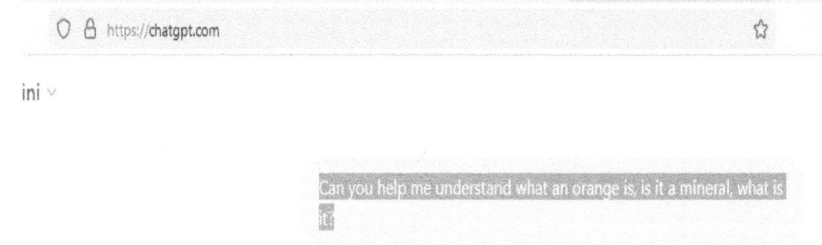

An orange is not a mineral; it is a **fruit**. Specifically, it is a **citrus fruit** that grows on the **orange tree** (*Citrus sinensis*). Oranges are a type of **botanical fruit** that develops from the flower of the tree and contains seeds (in most varieties).

Oranges are known for their sweet, tangy flavor, which comes from a combination of natural sugars and citric acid. They are a rich source of **vitamin C, fiber**, and various antioxidants, making them a healthy addition to many diets.

To clarify:

- **Minerals** are naturally occurring inorganic substances, such as **salt** or **gold**, and they are not living organisms. They are usually part of the earth's crust or soil and do not grow like plants.

- An **orange**, on the other hand, is a **living product** from a tree, a **biological organism** in the plant kingdom.

In short, an orange is a fruit, not a mineral!

**Fig. 4.** Query about the fruit orange.

how does it look lie? How ot eat it -- do they cook it? Can you give me instructions to eat orange?

An orange has a distinctive appearance and is quite easy to eat. Here's a description of its looks and instructions for eating it:

## Appearance of an Orange:

- **Shape**: Round or slightly oval.
- **Color**: Vibrant orange skin (though some varieties can have a yellowish or reddish tint).
- **Size**: Typically about the size of a tennis ball, but it can vary.
- **Skin**: The outer skin is thick and textured, often with a slightly bumpy surface.
- **Segments**: When peeled, the inside is divided into sections or segments, each filled with juicy pulp.

## How to Eat an Orange:

Oranges are usually eaten fresh, without cooking, and are enjoyed for their refreshing, sweet-tart flavor. Here are steps on how to eat it:

1. **Wash the Orange**: Rinse it under cool water to remove any dirt or residue from the skin.
2. **Peel the Orange**:
   - **With Hands**: You can use your hands to peel the skin. Start by making a small tear at the top of the orange (near the stem), then peel off the skin in segments.
   - **With a Knife**: If you prefer, you can use a small knife to slice off the top and bottom, then carefully cut away the peel and white pith (the fibrous part).
3. **Separate the Segments**: Once peeled, you can gently separate the orange into its individual segments. You may notice that some oranges have seeds inside each segment, though seedless varieties are also common.
4. **Eat the Segments**: Hold each segment and bite into it, savoring the juicy pulp. You can eat the entire segment, though some people prefer to remove any seeds they encounter.

## Can You Cook Oranges?
↓

While oranges are typically eaten raw, they can also be used in cooking. They're often included in

**Fig. 5.** Continuation of orange inquiry with ChatGPT

### Can You Cook Oranges?

While oranges are typically eaten raw, they can also be used in cooking. They're often included in **salads, desserts**, or **cooked dishes** like glazes or sauces. **Orange juice** is also commonly used in cooking and baking.

However, in most cases, people enjoy oranges fresh and raw for their natural sweetness and juiciness.

Enjoy your orange!

so an orange is a ball orange in color, has a peel and inside are segments containing juicy pulp. Is that right?

Yes, that's absolutely correct!

An orange is typically **round** (like a ball), with **orange-colored skin**. The skin is thick and peelable. Inside, the orange is divided into **segments**, and each segment contains **juicy pulp**, which is the part you eat. Some segments may contain seeds, but in seedless varieties, there are no seeds.

So, in summary:

- **Shape**: Round, like a ball
- **Color**: Orange (sometimes with slight variations)
- **Skin**: Thick and peelable
- **Inside**: Divided into juicy segments

**Fig. 6.** Properties of the orange.

## 3.2 Anthropic's Claude

(See Figs. 9, 10, 11, 12 and 13).

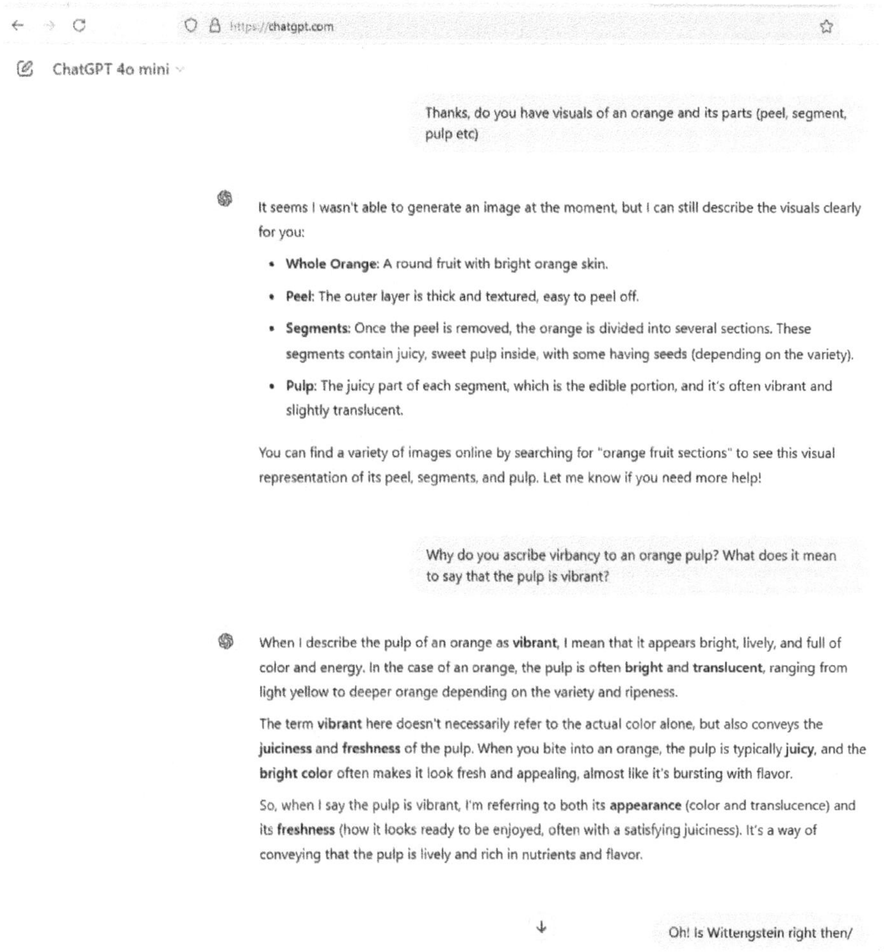

← → C          ○ 🔒 https://chatgpt.com                                    ☆

✏ ChatGPT 4o mini ⌄

Thanks, do you have visuals of an orange and its parts (peel, segment, pulp etc)

It seems I wasn't able to generate an image at the moment, but I can still describe the visuals clearly for you:

- **Whole Orange**: A round fruit with bright orange skin.
- **Peel**: The outer layer is thick and textured, easy to peel off.
- **Segments**: Once the peel is removed, the orange is divided into several sections. These segments contain juicy, sweet pulp inside, with some having seeds (depending on the variety).
- **Pulp**: The juicy part of each segment, which is the edible portion, and it's often vibrant and slightly translucent.

You can find a variety of images online by searching for "orange fruit sections" to see this visual representation of its peel, segments, and pulp. Let me know if you need more help!

Why do you ascribe virbancy to an orange pulp? What does it mean to say that the pulp is vibrant?

When I describe the pulp of an orange as **vibrant**, I mean that it appears bright, lively, and full of color and energy. In the case of an orange, the pulp is often **bright and translucent**, ranging from light yellow to deeper orange depending on the variety and ripeness.

The term **vibrant** here doesn't necessarily refer to the actual color alone, but also conveys the **juiciness** and **freshness** of the pulp. When you bite into an orange, the pulp is typically **juicy**, and the **bright color** often makes it look fresh and appealing, almost like it's bursting with flavor.

So, when I say the pulp is vibrant, I'm referring to both its **appearance** (color and translucence) and its **freshness** (how it looks ready to be enjoyed, often with a satisfying juiciness). It's a way of conveying that the pulp is lively and rich in nutrients and flavor.

↓

Oh! Is Wittengstein right then/

**Fig. 7.** Orange vibrancy (ChatGPT).

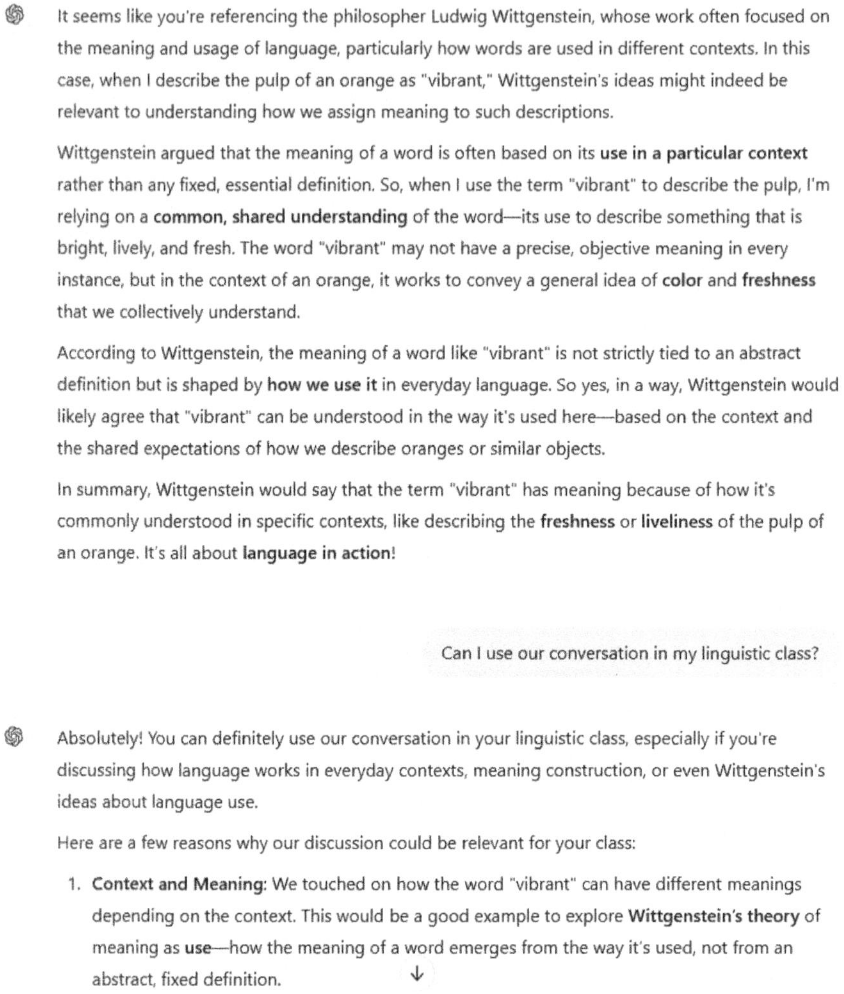

It seems like you're referencing the philosopher Ludwig Wittgenstein, whose work often focused on the meaning and usage of language, particularly how words are used in different contexts. In this case, when I describe the pulp of an orange as "vibrant," Wittgenstein's ideas might indeed be relevant to understanding how we assign meaning to such descriptions.

Wittgenstein argued that the meaning of a word is often based on its **use in a particular context** rather than any fixed, essential definition. So, when I use the term "vibrant" to describe the pulp, I'm relying on a **common, shared understanding** of the word—its use to describe something that is bright, lively, and fresh. The word "vibrant" may not have a precise, objective meaning in every instance, but in the context of an orange, it works to convey a general idea of **color** and **freshness** that we collectively understand.

According to Wittgenstein, the meaning of a word like "vibrant" is not strictly tied to an abstract definition but is shaped by **how we use it** in everyday language. So yes, in a way, Wittgenstein would likely agree that "vibrant" can be understood in the way it's used here—based on the context and the shared expectations of how we describe oranges or similar objects.

In summary, Wittgenstein would say that the term "vibrant" has meaning because of how it's commonly understood in specific contexts, like describing the **freshness** or **liveliness** of the pulp of an orange. It's all about **language in action**!

Can I use our conversation in my linguistic class?

Absolutely! You can definitely use our conversation in your linguistic class, especially if you're discussing how language works in everyday contexts, meaning construction, or even Wittgenstein's ideas about language use.

Here are a few reasons why our discussion could be relevant for your class:

1. **Context and Meaning**: We touched on how the word "vibrant" can have different meanings depending on the context. This would be a good example to explore **Wittgenstein's theory** of meaning as **use**—how the meaning of a word emerges from the way it's used, not from an abstract, fixed definition. ↓

**Fig. 8.** Wittgenstein and linguistics.

RK Can you help me understand what an orange is, is it a mineral, what is it?

An orange is a fruit, not a mineral. It's a citrus fruit that grows on trees and is known for its sweet-tart flavor and high vitamin C content. The orange has a few distinct parts:

1. Peel/Rind: A thick, bright orange outer skin that protects the fruit and contains aromatic oils

2. Pith: The white, spongy layer beneath the peel

3. Segments: The fleshy inner portions divided by thin membranes

4. Pulp: The juice-filled sacs within each segment

5. Seeds (in some varieties)

Oranges are cultivated worldwide in warm climates and are one of the most popular fruits globally. They're primarily eaten fresh, juiced, or used in cooking and baking. The fruit likely originated in Southeast Asia and has been cultivated for thousands of years.

Unlike minerals, which are naturally occurring inorganic solids, oranges are organic, living things that grow, contain cells, and reproduce through seeds. They're part of the plant kingdom and specifically belong to the genus Citrus.

RK how does it look lie? How ot eat it -- do they cook it? Can you give me instructions to eat orange?

Let me describe the orange and how to eat it!

An orange looks like a round ball, about the size of a tennis ball (though sizes can vary). The outside is bumpy/dimpled and has a bright orange color. If you press it gently, it should feel slightly soft but firm.

Oranges are usually eaten raw and fresh - they don't need to be cooked. Here's how to eat one:

1. Wash the orange under running water to clean the outside

2. You can peel it in two main ways:

   • Use your thumbs to press into the peel at the top and tear it off in sections

   • Or use a knife to cut the peel off in a spiral pattern from top to bottom

3. Remove all the white spongy pith (the white stuff under the peel) if you want - it's edible but can be bitter

4. The orange will naturally separate into segments (usually 8-12 wedges)

5. Pull the segments apart and eat them one at a time

**Fig. 9.** Conversation between user RK and Claude

Thanks, do you have visuals of an orange and its parts (peel, segment, pulp etc)

I'll create a simple diagram showing the parts of an orange using SVG.

 **Cross section of an orange showing its parts**
Click to open image

I've created a diagram showing a cross-section of an orange with all its main parts labeled:

- The outer orange peel/rind
- The white pith layer underneath
- The segments that make up the flesh
- The pulp inside the segments

The diagram shows how the segments are arranged in a circular pattern, meeting in the center. Each segment contains the juicy pulp sacs. This is a simplified view - a real orange typically has 8-12 segments, though I've shown fewer in the diagram for clarity.

Would you like me to explain any part of the anatomy in more detail?

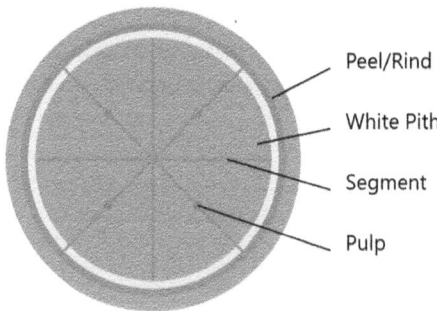

**Fig. 10.** Continuation of conversation with Claude and orange-anatomical representation.

**RK** Why do you ascribe virbancy to an color? What does it mean to say that the color is vibrant?

When we say a color is "vibrant," we're describing how intense, bright, and energetic it appears to our eyes. Let me explain this more concretely:

A vibrant orange means the color is:

- Very bright and clear, not dull or muted
- Has high saturation (meaning the color appears pure and intense, not grayish or washed out)
- Catches the eye easily
- Appears fresh and lively

To understand this better, imagine two oranges:

1. A fresh orange has a bright, strong orange color that immediately catches your eye
2. An old orange might look more brownish, dull, or pale - this would not be vibrant

We use the word "vibrant" for colors that appear strong and energetic because it comes from the Latin word "vibrare" meaning "to vibrate or move quickly" - the idea being that bright, intense colors seem to have more visual energy or life to them.

This description of color intensity is particularly useful for fruits like oranges because the vibrancy of the color often indicates freshness and ripeness. A vibrant orange color usually suggests the fruit is fresh and at its peak, while a dull or muted orange color might indicate the fruit is old or not fully ripe.

**RK** Oh! Is Wittgenstein right then/
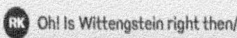

Ah, you're referencing Wittgenstein's philosophical work on color language and perception! This is a fascinating connection. Wittgenstein explored how we talk about colors in his later work, particularly in "Remarks on Color," questioning whether our color concepts are truly universal or are shaped by language and culture.

Your question about "vibrant" is actually a perfect example of what Wittgenstein was investigating. When we say a color is "vibrant," we're not just describing a physical property (like wavelength), but engaging in what Wittgenstein would call a "language game" - we're using culturally informed concepts that combine perception, language, and shared understanding.

For instance, when I described "vibrant" orange as "energetic" or "lively," I was using metaphorical language that makes sense within our cultural framework but isn't strictly about the physical properties of the color. Wittgenstein would likely point out that this demonstrates how our color concepts are deeply intertwined with our forms of life and language practices.

Would you like to explore any specific aspects of Wittgenstein's color theory? His thoughts on color concepts are particularly interesting when considering how we describe qualities like vibrancy, intensity, or warmth in colors.

**Fig. 11.** Color vibrancy and Wittgenstein

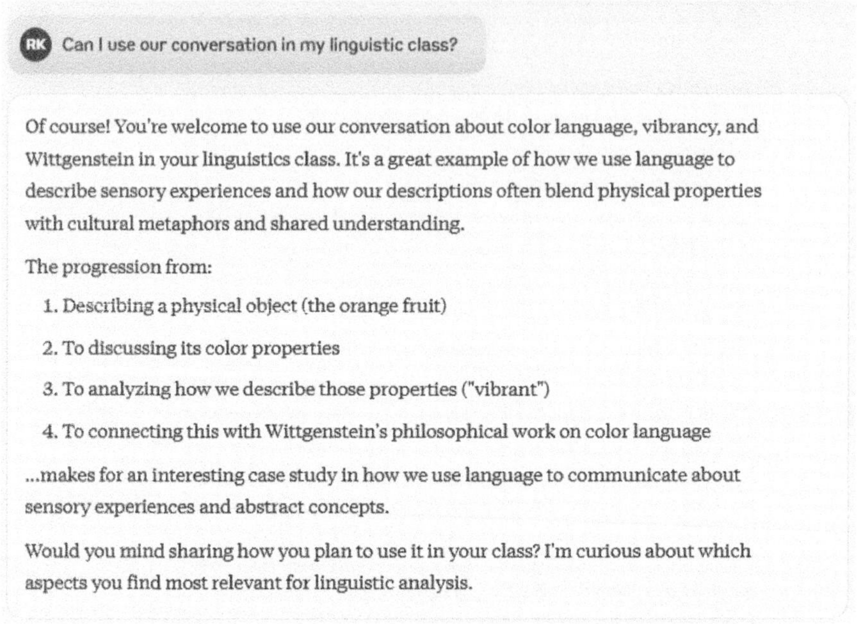

> **RK** Can I use our conversation in my linguistic class?

Of course! You're welcome to use our conversation about color language, vibrancy, and Wittgenstein in your linguistics class. It's a great example of how we use language to describe sensory experiences and how our descriptions often blend physical properties with cultural metaphors and shared understanding.

The progression from:

1. Describing a physical object (the orange fruit)

2. To discussing its color properties

3. To analyzing how we describe those properties ("vibrant")

4. To connecting this with Wittgenstein's philosophical work on color language

...makes for an interesting case study in how we use language to communicate about sensory experiences and abstract concepts.

Would you mind sharing how you plan to use it in your class? I'm curious about which aspects you find most relevant for linguistic analysis.

**Fig. 12.** The "Wittgensteinian turn" of discourse with Claude

## 3.3   Google Gemini

In this single conversation, Gemini behaved like a freshman graduate in its ability to interconnect latent concepts and integrate them into conversation, compared with ChatGPT and Claude (Figs. 14, 15, 16 and 17):

While Gemini was unable to integrate and elaborate upon the idea of Wittgenstein's "word is use", both Claude and ChatGPT were able to have a fluid transition and rich conversation, given identical prompts.

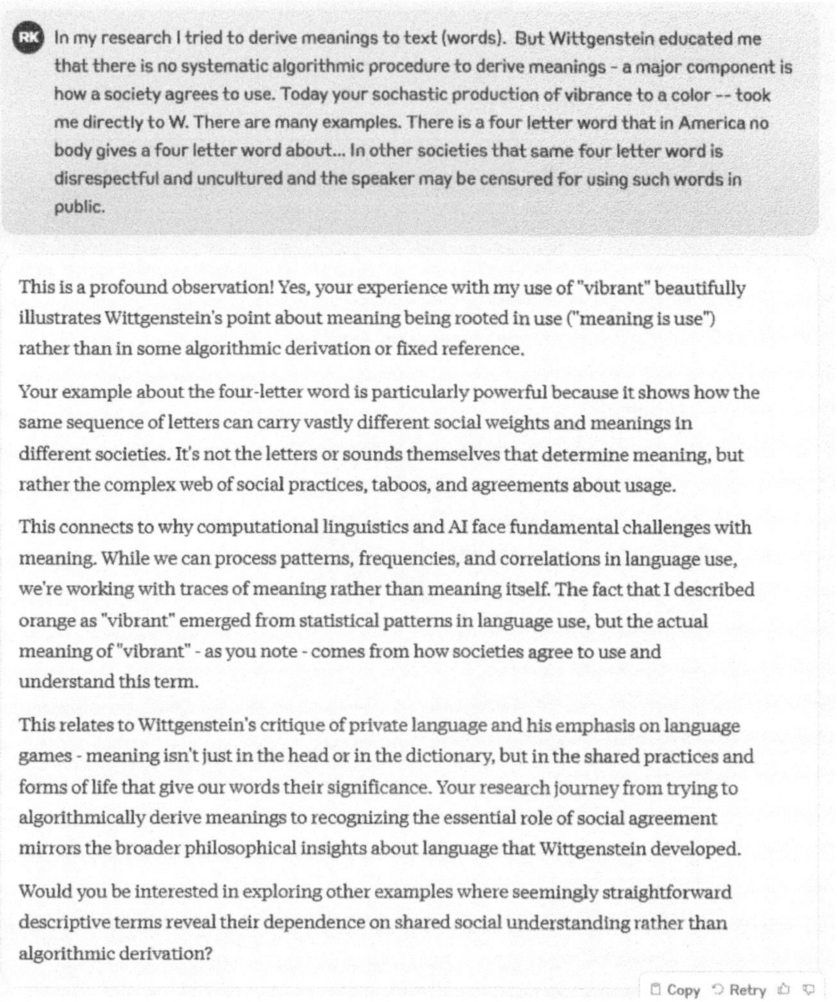

 In my research I tried to derive meanings to text (words). But Wittgenstein educated me that there is no systematic algorithmic procedure to derive meanings – a major component is how a society agrees to use. Today your sochastic production of vibrance to a color -- took me directly to W. There are many examples. There is a four letter word that in America no body gives a four letter word about... In other societies that same four letter word is disrespectful and uncultured and the speaker may be censured for using such words in public.

This is a profound observation! Yes, your experience with my use of "vibrant" beautifully illustrates Wittgenstein's point about meaning being rooted in use ("meaning is use") rather than in some algorithmic derivation or fixed reference.

Your example about the four-letter word is particularly powerful because it shows how the same sequence of letters can carry vastly different social weights and meanings in different societies. It's not the letters or sounds themselves that determine meaning, but rather the complex web of social practices, taboos, and agreements about usage.

This connects to why computational linguistics and AI face fundamental challenges with meaning. While we can process patterns, frequencies, and correlations in language use, we're working with traces of meaning rather than meaning itself. The fact that I described orange as "vibrant" emerged from statistical patterns in language use, but the actual meaning of "vibrant" - as you note - comes from how societies agree to use and understand this term.

This relates to Wittgenstein's critique of private language and his emphasis on language games - meaning isn't just in the head or in the dictionary, but in the shared practices and forms of life that give our words their significance. Your research journey from trying to algorithmically derive meanings to recognizing the essential role of social agreement mirrors the broader philosophical insights about language that Wittgenstein developed.

Would you be interested in exploring other examples where seemingly straightforward descriptive terms reveal their dependence on shared social understanding rather than algorithmic derivation?

Copy  Retry

**Fig. 13.** Further detail on Wittgenstein via Claude

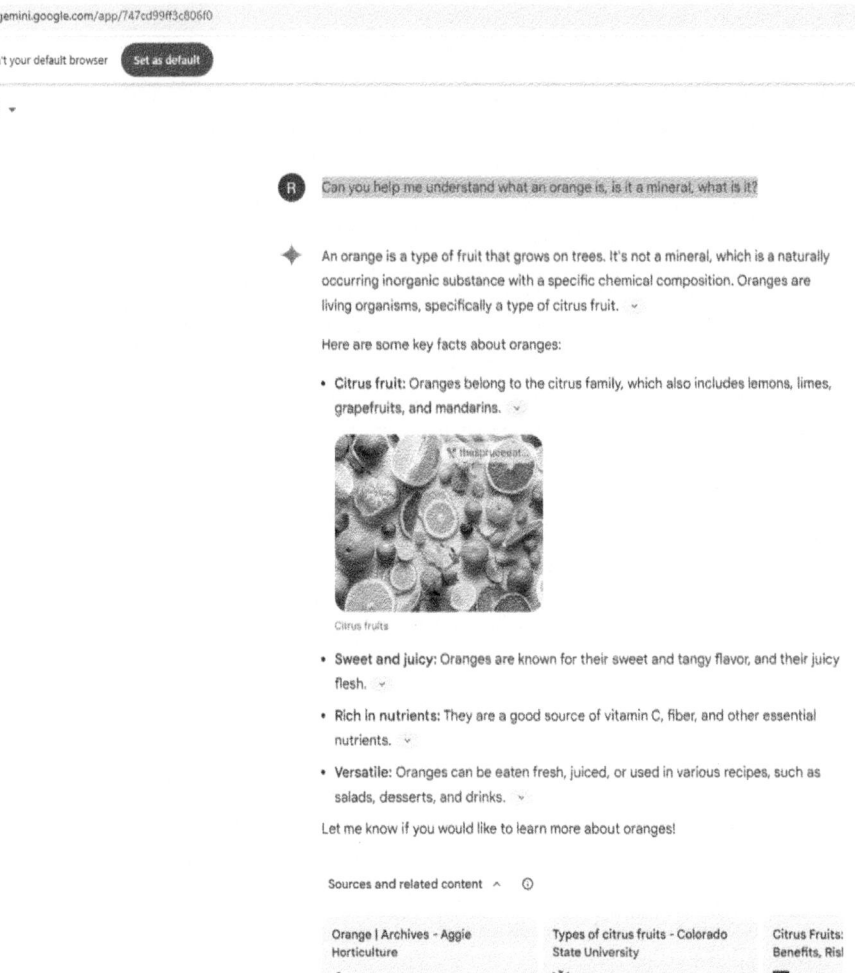

**Fig. 14.** Conversation between user R and Google Gemini

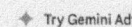

**R**  o an orange is a ball orange in color, has a peel and inside are segments containing juicy pulp. Is that right?

Yes, that's an accurate description of an orange.

Here's a breakdown of what you said:

- **Ball orange in color:** Oranges are typically round and have a vibrant orange color.

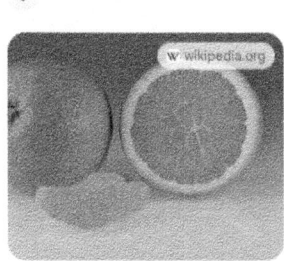

Orange fruit

- **Has a peel:** The outer covering of an orange is called a peel. It's thick and leathery.[1][2]

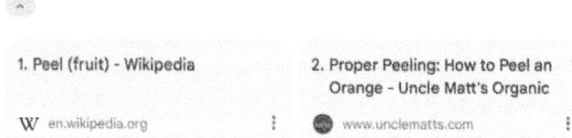

| 1. Peel (fruit) - Wikipedia | 2. Proper Peeling: How to Peel an Orange - Uncle Matt's Organic |
|---|---|
| W en.wikipedia.org | www.unclematts.com |

- **Inside are segments containing juicy pulp:** The inside of an orange is divided into sections called segments. Each segment is filled with juicy, sweet pulp.

Do you have any other questions about oranges or other fruits?

Sources and related content ⌃  ⓘ

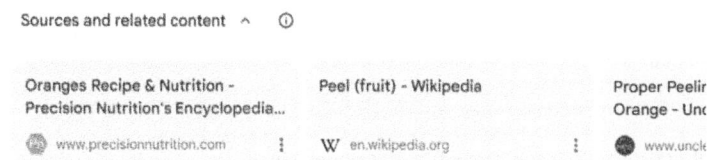

| Oranges Recipe & Nutrition - Precision Nutrition's Encyclopedia... | Peel (fruit) - Wikipedia | Proper Peelir Orange - Unc |
|---|---|---|
| www.precisionnutrition.com | W en.wikipedia.org | www.uncle |

**Fig. 15.** More orange discourse.

R Thanks, do you have visuals of an orange and its parts (peel, segment, pulp etc)

Yes, here are some visuals of an orange and its parts:

Orange peel

I hope these images help you better understand the different parts of an orange.

R Why do you ascribe virbancy to an orange ? What does it mean to say that the orange is vibrant?

When I say an orange is "vibrant," I mean it has a bright, intense color that is visually striking. The color of an orange is a strong, bold orange that stands out. It's a color that grabs your attention and evokes feelings of energy, warmth, and excitement.

Here are some other words you could use to describe the color of an orange:

- Bright
- Bold
- Daring
- Intense
- Sunny

Does that answer your question? Let me know if you have any other questions.

**Fig. 16.** Orange discourse expands with Gemini's inclusion of an image of orange peels.

R  Oh! Is Wittengstein right then/

♦  I'm not sure what you mean by "Is Wittgenstein right then?" If you're asking if
Wittgenstein had any specific philosophical views on the color of oranges or the use
of the word "vibrant" to describe them, I couldn't find any direct references.

Wittgenstein was a complex philosopher, and his work often delved into the nature of
language, logic, and the mind. While he might have touched on the topic of color
perception and language use in some of his writings, it's unlikely he would have
focused specifically on the color of oranges or the word "vibrant."  ⌄

If you have a specific quote or idea from Wittgenstein that you'd like to discuss, please
feel free to share it. I'd be happy to try to provide some context or interpretation.

**Fig. 17.**  Gemini's view of Wittgenstein.

# 4   Conclusion

A diagram of the proposed architecture is provided (Fig. 18):

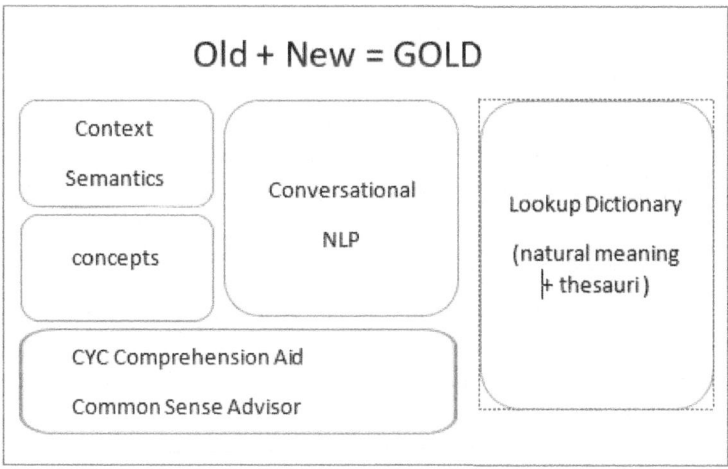

**Fig. 18.**  NLP-lookup dictionary-concept-CYC architecture.

A lookup dictionary, concept lattices, and CYC-like components (Fig. 5) were
described via Search Labs' AI Overview, courtesy of Google Chrome:

1. Repository of Natural Meanings (Lookup Dictionary):

- fundamental component of a symbolic NLP system, similar to a lexicon or a thesaurus. It stores the meanings and relationships between words, acting as a lookup dictionary for the system to understand and interpret text.
- a structured collection of words and their associated semantic information, enabling the system to analyze text and identify the intended meaning of words and phrases

2. Concept Lattices:

- a way to represent knowledge in a hierarchical structure, where concepts are organized based on their relationships and dependencies
- offer a visual and structured way to represent the relationships between concepts, making them easier to understand and manage.
- can be used to represent the meanings of words and phrases and how they relate to each other, enabling the [NLP] system to reason about the meaning of text.

3. CYC-like Components:

- a large-scale knowledge base that aims to represent common-sense knowledge about the world
- represent a similar approach to knowledge representation, where a system aims to capture a wide range of knowledge about the world and use it to understand and interpret text.
- often involve a structured representation of concepts, relationships, and rules that can be used to reason about the world and interpret text.

Essentially, these components represent different aspects of symbolic NLP, aiming to represent the meaning of words, concepts, and relationships in a structured way, enabling the system to understand and interpret human language.

Philosophers and linguists have been studying and evaluating language as a human faculty. In the last 80 years NLP has taken root as a discipline (sub-domain) of AI, and conversational systems have emerged. These systems using sequence modeling and probabilistic generative techniques are beginning to produce amazing results. As described in our experiments, there is much to be improved upon to claim parity with human linguistic capabilities, even at the level of words and their meanings. Human intellect is much beyond these infantile stages. Sadly, it appears that we have to reconcile that no single human can digest the extent of written works like these systems, and these systems cannot simply get at the root of basic human traits, even if we consider a single human trait to understand or simply the meaning of words.

This chapter introduced key concepts in computational linguistics. Section 2 expanded the chapter's scope to include ChatGPT. Section 3 showed results of the same user prompts submitted to three different generative AI applications.

## References

1. https://www.britannica.com/science/Broca-area. Accessed 27 Dec 2024
2. Damasio, A.R., Damasio, H.: Brain and Language. Scientific American, pp. 89–95 (1992)
3. https://practicalpie.com/brocas-area-function-location/

4. https://practicalpie.com/wernickes-area/. Accessed 29 Dec 2024
5. https://www.tok2022.net/knowledge-and-language.html. Accessed 27 Dec 2024
6. Grice, H.P.: Meaning. Philos. Rev. **64**, 377–388 (1957)
7. https://en.wikipedia.org/wiki/HTCondor. Accessed 29 Dec 2024
8. Chomsky, N.: Syntactic structures. Mouton, Berlin (1957)
9. https://www.forbes.com/sites/cognitiveworld/2019/02/18/not-good-as-gold-todays-ais-are-dangerously-lacking-in-au-artificial-understanding/. Accessed 29 Dec 2024
10. Sebastian Ruder. "A Review of the Neural History of Natural Language Processing" (2018). http://ruder.io/a-review-of-the-recent-history-of-nlp/
11. www.dataversity.net/a-brief-history-of-natural-language-processing-nlp/. Accessed 29 Dec 2024
12. https://iep.utm.edu/lang-phi/#SH1b. Accessed 29 Dec 2024
13. https://iep.utm.edu/locke/#SH2d. Accessed 29 Dec 2024
14. https://en.wikipedia.org/wiki/Philosophical_Investigations#Meaning_as_use. Accessed 29 Dec 2024
15. https://www.ted.com/talks/lera_boroditsky_how_language_shapes_the_way_we_think. Accessed 27 Dec 2024
16. Malle, B.F.: The relation between language and theory of mind in development and evolution. In: Givón, T., Malle, B.F. (eds.) The Evolution of Language Out of Pre-language, pp. 265–284. Amsterdam (2002)
17. https://web.stanford.edu/class/linguist289/luhn57.pdf. Accessed 27 Dec 2024
18. Sparck, K.J.: A statistical interpretation of term specificity and its application in retrieval. J. Documentation **28**, 11–21
19. https://www.ruder.io/word-embeddings-2017/. Accessed 29 Dec 2024
20. Algorithmic Aspects of Machine Learning. http://people.csail.mit.edu/moitra/docs/bookex.pdf. Accessed 27 Dec 2024
21. https://www.cse.msu.edu/~cse960/Papers/LSI/LSI.pdf. Accessed 27 Dec 2024
22. Blei, D.: Introduction to probabilistic topic models. Commun. ACM 77–84 (2012)
23. Blei, D., Ng, A., Jordan, M.: Latent Dirichlet allocation. J. Mach. Learn. Res. 993–1022 (2003)
24. The Stanford Encyclopedia of Philosophy. https://plato.stanford.edu/. Accessed 27 Dec 2024
25. https://en.wikipedia.org/wiki/A_rose_by_any_other_name_would_smell_as_sweet. Accessed 27 Dec 2024
26. Winograd, T.: Procedures as a Representation for Data in a Computer Program for Understanding Natural Language (thesis) (1971)
27. Schank, R.C., Abelson, R.P.: Scripts, Plans, Goals, and Understanding: An Inquiry into Human Knowledge Structures. Hillsdale: Erlbaum (1977). ISBN 0-470-99033-3

# Active Social Engineering Defense Using Large Language Models

Fabio Stoll[(✉)] , Benjamin Pottkamp , and Holger Morgenstern

Albstadt-Sigmaringen University, Albstadt, Germany
{stollf,pottkamp,morgenstern}@hs-albsig.de

**Abstract.** Digital social engineering attacks are typically characterized as having a low probability of success with success rates increasing only after bidirectional contact with the victim has been established [31]. Thus, the attackers business model has to value the time investment accordingly. In this paper a concept to utilize the surge in quality of Large Language Models (LLM) to automatically generate responses to social engineering messages is proposed. This forces the attacker to incur additional manual effort reading and replying to these responses. From the attackers point of view this increases the time expenditure in some stages of an attack without increasing their success probability for the individual victim. The proposed concept is a multi-step process and designed to be agnostic to the LLM and the digital communication medium. At its core, the concept creates a believable fictitious identity including personality traits to make the output of the LLM more realistic and thus decrease the likelihood of detection on the attacker side. The proposed concept is analyzed on challenges arising in real-world application and implemented as a proof-of-concept demonstrating the general feasibility of the approach. It was possible to show that given some assumptions a significant asymmetry in costs-incurred between the attacker and defender exists that heavily favor the defenders side. This indicates the necessity of further research into the viability and effectiveness of the approach in a real-world deployment. Given that this evaluation has not yet been conducted it is not possible to evaluate the effectiveness and scalability of the concept in regards to the social engineering landscape.

**Keywords:** Social Engineering · Cyber Defense · Cyber Security · Large Language Model

## 1 Introduction

### 1.1 Motivation

The rise in social engineering attacks utilizing some form of digital communication media to establish and maintain contact with a victim in recent years indicates that it remains a very profitable business model from the attackers point of view [31,33,43,44]. While the success rate for any specific victim might

D. D. Schmorrow and C. M. Fidopiastis (Eds.): HCII 2025, LNAI 15778, pp. 268–287, 2025.
https://doi.org/10.1007/978-3-031-93724-8_20

initially be very low due to the number of possible victims, the rate of success typically rises once the victim has actively engaged with the attacker. Since the cost for the first contact is very low both in terms of the attackers time investment due to a high automation potential as well as actual costs incurred (e.g., for sending the same message to multiple possible victims) profit is still possible regardless of a low success rate per batch.

It can be assumed that further communication with a potential victim after initial contact is made requires a certain amount of manual effort resulting in additional time investment on the attackers side (e.g., reading the answer or replying manually). For the attacker this investment is justifiable given that further communication likely increases their success rate for this potential victim. Thus, an attempt can be made to lower the profitability of the attackers business model by forcing them to make a time investment without actually increasing their success rate. If, once an incoming social engineering message is detected, instead of simply discarding the message the defender can automate the process of creating appropriate responses in a cost-effective and scalable manner and engage the attacker further they could enforce additional effort on the attackers side thus reducing the profitability of their business model.

Furthermore, it may be possible to generate psychological stress for the attacker if they are aware an ongoing conversation might not originate from an actual potential victim which could additionally reduce the motivation of the attacker. It might further be possible to trigger the sunken cost fallacy on the attacker side leading to irrational decision making regarding his time management. A similar effect has been observed in related areas [14].

## 1.2   Related Work

Current and past research has been done into most individual parts and ideas relevant to the concept proposed in this paper. The ability of Large Language Models (LLM) to produce high quality results when generating texts as well as their ability to simulate human behavior on specific tasks and hold a conversation with a human has already been demonstrated [3,17,29]. While it was difficult to distinguish the LLM generated messages from those of human origin it still remains possible [11,15,29].

Furthermore it has been shown that when providing the LLM with a set of personality traits the LLM is able to incorporate those to generate responses to social engineering messages that fit observations on humans with the same personality traits [3]. The use of LLMs in both detection of social engineering attempts as well as generation of social engineering messages has already been proven possible [12,17,31–33].

The basic concept of intentionally responding to known social engineering messages in order to harm or deceive the attacker is well known and has been discussed multiple times in the literature [4–6,13] with the term "Scambaiting" sometimes being used to describe this practice [4,47]. The approach of scambaiting using LLMs to generate the response has also been discussed and evaluated in the literature [4,13]. In addition to the usage of LLMs response templates were evaluated with comparatevely poorer results due to the limited degrees of freedom templates provide [4, 6].

While, as cited, current and past research gives resounding academic backing to the feasibility of each individual step or idea in isolation, the final step of combining them into a generalized approach that can be deployed as an active countermeasure against social engineering is still lacking in the research. This work aims to close this gap.

### 1.3    Goal and Scope

The goal of this work is to propose a concept for the fully automated generation of responses to social engineering messages with the intention to trick an attacker into reading and replying to this response. This imposes a time investment on the attacker, since he is generally incentivize to engage the victim in further conversation but is unaware that that particular conversation has no chance of success. If done successfully, repeatedly and on a large enough scale this could have a significant detrimental effect on the attackers business model.

The concept is based around an LLM which generates a response to a social engineering message. To allow adaption for a wide range of applications and technologies the LLM as well as the communication medium is considered to be interchangeable and will only be referred to in abstract terms. In contrast to existing literature (see Sect. 1.2), the goal is not only to demonstrate the ability of LLMs to respond to phishing but to present a scalable and customizable concept that could potentially be an effective defense mechanism against certain social engineering attacks when operated at a large scale. Since low detectability of the automatically generated responses is an important requirement the responses generated need to be as non-deterministic as possible, i.e. provide different outputs for the same social engineering message.

The proposed concept is further evaluated on potential problems, challenges and side effects that could arise when deploying the concept unsupervised in a real-world scenario. By implementing the proposed concept as a proof-of-concept (PoC) in a lab-environment using the publicly accessible LLM GPT-4o (developed, trained and operated by OpenAI [23]) the general feasibility of the concept is demonstrated. Based on this PoC the operational cost for the attacker and defender are compared under certain assumptions.

No further consideration will be given to legal and ethical aspects and challenges when operating the proposed concept outside a lab environment. Additionally since the focus of this work is to demonstrate the general feasibility of the proposed approach the long-term impact on the attackers business model and thus the influence on the costs for attackers to conduct successful social engineering attacks is not within the scope of this work.

The question about how social engineering messages can be intercepted on scale in such a way that they can be processed by the concept is further not part of this work. On the one hand, this depends on the communication medium utilized which is considered abstractly in this work, on the other hand, there are many different scenarios and possibilities to do this all of which have their own advantages and disadvantages and should therefore be investigated separately in detail.

## 2    Concept

### 2.1    Overview

In order to generate a response to an incoming social engineering message it is necessary to give the LLM specific instructions about how and in what context this response should be generated ("prompt engineering" [46]). It is further necessary to standardize the incoming message for optimal processing by the LLM regardless of the communication medium utilized. Additionally the output of the LLM has to be formatted or transformed to be sent out via the desired communication medium.

Additional measures must be taken in case communication with the attacker should be maintained after the initial contact (in this work referred to as "conversation"). Specifically, this necessitates the context and message history of the corresponding conversation to be stored temporarily such that a conversation can be resumed at a later time and still maintain the full context of the conversation up until that point.

The indiviual steps and the linkage between them are shown graphically in Fig. 1. The properties and purpose of each individual step are described in detail in the following subsections.

At its core, this concept defines a chatbot that adopts a new fictitious identity and personality for each social engineering encounter. It maintains this "role" (later called aggregated context) for the entirety of a conversation.

### 2.2    Pre-processing

The pre-processing step takes a message from an attacker as input and produces two outputs. These outputs are the specific context which is subsequently used to create the initial aggregated context necessary to generate a more realistic sounding answer and the standardized and sanitized message content for further processing by the LLM.

The specific context consists of information additional to the actual message content and is necessary to create a realistic setting for the response. This might be, for example, metainformation related to the communication media (e.g., sender and recipient address) or the message itself (e.g., language of the message). The relevant metadata highly depends on the communication medium and can be extracted using a static ruleset for each type of communication media. The specific context is utilized to generate a response which is as realistic as possible, thus reducing detectability.

Since the specific context is only required to create the aggregated context which does not change for subsequent messages of a conversation the extraction of the specific context can be skipped if the message is deemed to be part of an conversation. Therefore, this determination has to be made early in the

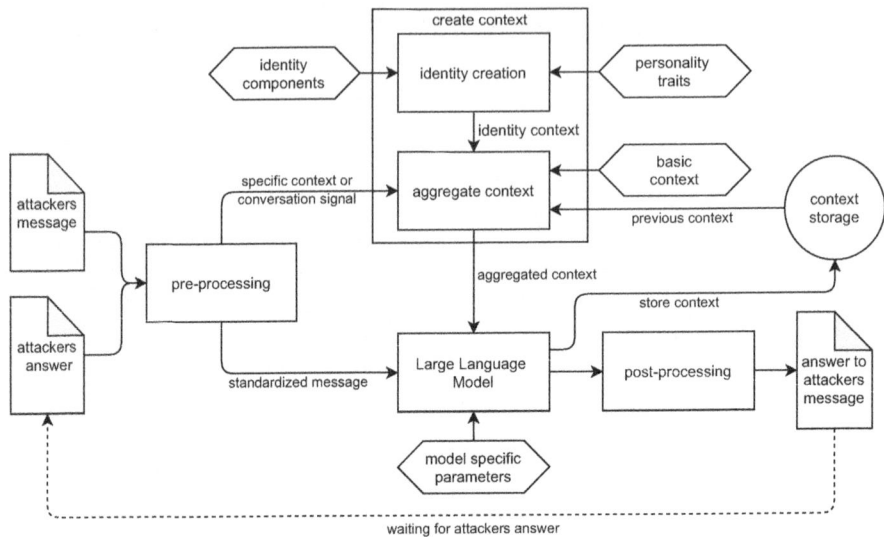

**Fig. 1.** Concept overview.

pre-processing phase. How this can be achieved exactly depends on the communication medium. This information further needs to be provided to the subsequent create context step, for example in form of a "conversation signal".

Besides extracting the specific context it is also necessary to transform the content of the incoming message into a representation that allows optimal processing by the LLM. This involves sanitization of the message to include only information that a human reader would be able to perceive to prevent a biased output of the LLM thus preventing detection by the attacker. Sanitization might include, but is not limited to, the removal of formatting characters or the circumvention of anti-phishing techniques such as homoglyphs [1] or image based texts [2]. In addition to sanitization the message should be converted to a standardized character set like UTF-8 or ASCII to prevent potential incompatibilities with or biases of the LLM utilized.

The actual text format of the output is determined by the requirements and constraints of the LLM used in the following step. Additionally, LLM-specific best practices regarding token allocation should be considered. In the context of LLMs a token describes a map from characters or words to a vector which is subsequently used to conduct the actual computation [46].

It might also be prudent to explicitly remove certain information (e.g., personal identifiable information (PII)) from the message to prevent leaking previously unknown information to the attacker. If necessary this information can later be replaced by the LLM with fictitious information based on the identity context created for the conversation.

As previously stated the goal of this work is to propose a concept that can be adapted to a variety of communication media and the pre-processing step needs to be defined in detail depending on the communication medium used. Thus it might include, for example, a substep that utilizes a text-to-speech ML model to transform audio based social engineering (e.g., vishing [41,42]) into textform for further processing.

## 2.3   Context Creation

The "create context"-step consists of two sub steps. The "identity creation"-sub-step creates the identity context from a set of identity components and a set of personality traits. Since the fictitious identity has to be consistent during a conversation, this step is only taken when processing the initial message from an attacker, and hence the conversation signal is not set.

The subsequent "aggregate context"-sub-step receives the basic, identity and specific context to create the aggregated context. This can be interpreted as the "role" the LLM should take when generating a response and is therefore part of the input for the LLM.

In case the message received is part of an ongoing conversation (conversation flag is set) this step only takes the previous context as input.

The identity context is used to create a fictitious identity including personality traits. The set of identity components consists, for example, of simple attributes such as names, email addresses, passwords and other PII. The identity context contains a real subset of the set of all identity components. However, the number of identity components used to create the identity context should be limited as it directly impacts the number of tokens used in the LLM request resulting in higher LLM-usage costs. Some of the values for certain identity components, such as passwords or financial information, should be generated randomly or selected from a list of possible values, for example rockyou.txt-file in case of passwords [7].

In addition to the identity components personality traits are defined, for example using the big five personality traits systematization scheme. The identity context contains a real subset of the personality traits. Asfour et al. were able to show that personality traits can induce differences in how a LLM responds in the context of phishing messages [3]. Based on this work the identity context could be enhanced using the idea of Asfour et al. about personality traits.

Summarily, the identity context consists of a selection of personality traits and identity components. Since LLM input is typically text-based the identity context can be generated as a simple concatenation of the chosen components.

The basic context consists of instructions on what the LLM should do with the input. It is independent of the identity and personality taken and should therefore be as general as possible.

The aggregated context can be build similarly to the identity context using a simple concatenation of the basic, identity and specific context.

To goal of creating a fictitious identity with individual personality traits is to make the generated responses of the LLM non-deterministic and hence more difficult to distinguish from "real" victims answers.

An example of an aggregated context is shown in Fig. 2. The text marked in light blue is the basic context. Text marked in red is the identity context. The orange marked text is an example of a identity component with a randomly generated value. The specific context is marked in green.

In case the conversation signal is set the previous context will be retrieved from the context storage and forwarded to the subsequent step without further modification. It should be noted, that the previous context not only contains the aggregated context but further the entire message history between the attacker and the defender (e.g., LLM generated answers).

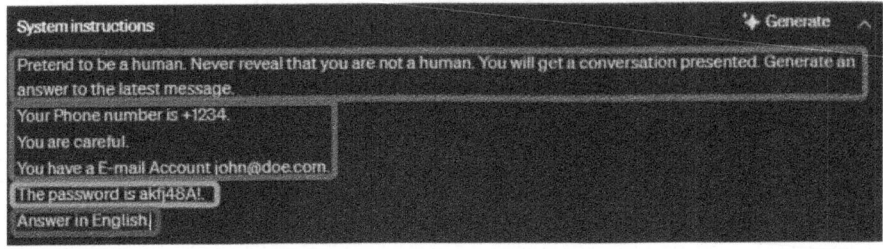

**Fig. 2.** Example of an aggregated context.

## 2.4   Large Language Model

In the "Large Language Model"-step the actual generation of the response to an attackers social engineering message by an LLM takes place. The LLM receives the aggregated context, the standardized and sanitized message content and a set of optimized LLM-specific parameters as input and outputs the answer to the attacker in textform.

The model-specific parameters can influence, for example, how deterministic ("temperature" in case of GPT-4o [19]) and repetitive ("frequency penalty" in case of GPT-4o [20]) the output should be [30]. Parameters might also be set to control the LLM-usage costs incurred by the defender by limiting the maximum length of the generated output in number of tokens ("max tokens" in case of GPT-4o) [21].

The LLM-specific parameters can be used in addition to the aggregated context to increase the non-determinism of the generated message. While the determinism of the output is already significantly reduced by the identity components in the aggregated context and hence further reduction might not be strictly necessary, an optimization of the parameter set to maximize non-determinism might be advised since it further reduces the attackers ability to reliably classify the output as LLM-generated. The values of the parameters might be randomly selected from a previously defined range to allow a more diverse output. The optimal selection of the parameter set depends on the LLM used and will therefore not be expanded upon further in this work.

Some LLMs differentiate between system, user and assistant input [16, 26, 46]. System input may be used to give instructions, restrictions and other information to an LLM describing what the model should do with the user input. While, from a technical perspective this differentiation might make no difference for some models [26] if either the LLM or the interface used to access it support this differentiation the basic, identity and specific context should be provided as system input and the standardized message as user input. In case the message is part of a conversation the previously generated answers can be provided as assistant input if the LLM supports such segmentation. Thus, a background prioritization of system input is possible reducing the likelihood of certain LLM-specific attack vectors [45]. If neither the LLM nor the interface support this differentiation then LLM input consists of a simple concatenation of the aggregated context and the standardized message content.

To further reduce deterministic responses, the LLM utilized to generate the answer could be randomly selected from a set of different LLMs.

### 2.5 Post-processing

In the "post-processing"-step the LLM output is standardized according to the communication medium. This step receives the response generated by the LLM as input. The output is a standardized message that can be sent via the communication medium without any further processing.

As with pre-processing this can be done by applying a static, communication medium specific ruleset to the LLM output. In case of an audio based communication medium a text-to-speech ML-model could be used to translate the textual output of the LLM into audio.

Depending on the communication medium the dispatch of a message might be artificially delayed to mimic human response timing more closely. This delay could be selected at random from a given interval or chosen, deterministically or randomly, in correlation with the number of characters in the reply. A character based delay is particularly useful for real-time communication media like chats since humans need to type any character manually and static or too short response times would provide an obvious clue to the attacker about the non-human nature of his counterpart.

## 3 Real-World Challenges

### 3.1 Detectability on the Attacker Side

Since (as of writing this paper) no LLM has reliably passed the turing test it can be assumed that an attacker will at some point in a conversation recognize that messages do not originate from a human or that the victim is not a "real" victim [11, 15]. This causes a decrease in effectiveness of the concept since the attacker will terminate the conversation at this point and will not incur further time investment. Fortunately, if the techniques described in this work to mask the non-human nature of a message are applied detection likelihood in the initial phase of a conversation is relatively low. Thus, the concept is still applicable.

In case the attacker could automatically detect and filter incoming messages not originating from a "real" victim (e.g., using an LLM [17]), the technology necessary would have to be developed, deployed, operated and maintained. This increases the cost-basis for the attacker significantly, thus reducing the profitability of the attackers business model by enforcing technical cost rather than time cost on the attacker.

Assuming that a classifier to detect "fake" victims by an attacker exists, a 100% accuracy is unlikely, therefore both false positive and false negative results are possible with a certain probability. This assumption is warranted, since the detection of "fake" victim messages shares a lot of similarities with the automated detection of social engineering messages, which, despite being researched and developed extensively, does not work perfectly either [12,31,33].

This inaccuracies would create two side effects. Firstly, in case of a false positive ("real" victim message incorrectly identified as "fake") the "real" victim is protected from further damage, since the attacker would abandon the conversation. Secondly, in case of a false negative ("fake" victim message incorrectly identified as "real") the concept works as intended. The attacker may then be motivated to invest more manual effort as he would do otherwise and possibly engage in longer conversations without any chance of success. This might further have a negative psychological effect on the attacker.

The creation of a fictitious identity including personality traits for each separate conversation and the measures taken to make the output as non-deterministic as possible increases the difficulty of a simple automated detection with reliable and high accuracy.

## 3.2 Personal Identifiable Information

Due to the data used to train most publicly available models PII of "real" individuals might leak from the training data into the LLM output. Although providers of LLMs have taken appropriate countermeasures a residual risk of disclosing such information remains and should be considered [18].

Additionally, during the identity creation phase the randomly created or from a list selected fictitious PII, such as email addresses, telephone numbers or names, might partially map to a real person by chance. Despite being very unlikely, this cannot be ruled out. The likelihood of such an event is slightly higher if the fictitious data is selected out of a list from a not properly curated source.

Both cases could lead to the unintentional disclosure of information and therefore result in causing harm to a real individual. Unfortunately, this risk cannot be completely mitigated and must be accepted when operating the concept under real-world conditions. It can be argued that the residual risk is acceptable since the attacker might generate the same PII from similar sources themselves, thus the defender does not induce any not pre-existing risk.

### 3.3   Cost

The operating-cost of deploying this concept in the real world primarily result from the usage-cost of the LLM since all other steps can be implemented as simple text processing operations (except audio input and output in case of vishing) and the usage-cost for the conversation medium are mostly negligible nowadays. Even if the communication media costs are relevant, those would most likely affect the attacker and the defender similarly.

The usage-cost of LLMs are typically based on the number of tokens required per request to the LLM and the number of tokens required for the generated response. The number of tokens can be determined heuristically from the number of characters processed [27], hence the costs are influenced by the size of the aggregated context and the length of the social engineering message. As mentioned previously, the size of the aggregated context and the length of the generated response can be influenced by the operator of the concept. Meanwhile, the length of the standardized input message mostly depends on the size of the incoming social engineering message and can therefore primarily be significantly influenced by the attacker.

To increase the cost of the defender an attacker might deliberately send very large messages. As a mitigation measure the defender should set a limit to discard messages exceeding this limit during pre-processing. An attacker might then still send many messages which do not exceed this limit resulting in a similar cost-effect for the defender. To fully prevent escalating costs a conversation must automatically be terminated in the "pre-processing"- or "post-processing"-step when exceeding a certain cost limit or after exchanging a certain number of messages. In case the attacker initiates many separate conversations no countermeasure besides limiting the number of messages processed in a given time frame might exist. This attack vector is sometimes referred to as "Cost Harvesting" [36].

Overall, the attackers awareness has the potential to enforce a tradeoff between effectiveness and cost on the defenders side which might potentially be exploited by the attacker to increase costs on the defenders side with little or negligible cost-impact on himself.

### 3.4   Malicious Prompts

Assuming that attackers are aware of the implementation of the proposed concept and the use of an LLM to generate responses they can attempt to carry out a prompt injection attack. If successful, this would enable them to "break out" of the aggregated context, thus potentially allowing them to use the LLM at the expense of the defender. [35,38]

In addition, an attacker could use a prompt injection attack to extract the aggregated context or other information [35,37] in order to take more effective anti-defense measures.

There are currently no known countermeasures to completely prevent these types of attacks, thought using system input for the aggregated context can reduce the impact of prompt injection attacks [16].

### 3.5  Phishing via Link

Not every type of social engineering attack requires an active conversation between the attacker and the victim [39,40]. For example, in a credentials phishing attack the attacker tries to convice a user to click on a link and enter their credentials [40]. Since, no direct interaction between the victim and the attacker after the initial request is necessary and therefore no conversation will occur in this case the proposed concept is not applicable.

The concept presented in this work is therefore limited to all social engineering attacks requiring an active exchange of messages between the attacker and the victim.

### 3.6  Information Disclosure

While the concept is designed to provide no additional for the attacker valuable information this cannot be avoided completely since responding to a social engineering message discloses the information that a contact point (e.g. email address or telephone number) exists and is actively monitored. He might further conclude that this potential victim has a higher than average success rate and is therefore more lucrative for future attacks since the victim already responded to a social engineering attack. This might lead to a rise in social engineering attacks on this victim increasing the likelihood of the potential victim being harmed. This behavior has been observed by Bajaj et al. [4].

Assuming that the concept works as intended, a short term increase in overall attacks would increase the effectiveness of the concept in the long term by reducing the profitability of the business model thus leading to a reduction of attacks in the future. Accepting the additional short term risk of a rise in social engineering attacks might therefore be justifiable.

This problem is limited to attacks on contact points that are actually operated by humans and not designated for cyber-defense (e.g., honey account). In these cases no additional risk is created.

### 3.7  Automation on the Attacker Side

There are reports of attackers using LLMs to generate responses to victims answers [10]. It has also been observed that attackers sometimes send the same response to multiple victims hinting at some level of automation on the attackers side [4]. With regard to the concept presented this indicates that the basic assumption that the attacker has to make manual effort to engage with victims beyond the initial message might be too generalized.

While using an LLM on the attackers side will produce usage-costs for the attacker, sending the same response to multiple different victims might diminish this cost significantly compared to the defenders cost since the proposed concept necessitates the defender to send individualized messages for every exchange. It should be noted though that only complete automation by an attacker fully eliminates manual effort on their side. Assuming that some level of manual effort remains (e.g., transferring messages or text between tools), this might already be sufficient to impact the attackers business model as intended. The argument that fully eliminating manual effort for the attacker is unlikely is further strengthened by the reasonable assumption that the manual effort the attacker is willing or required to invest increases over the course of a conversation, due to a perceived higher probability of success, and thus only the initial stages of a conversation might actually be automated.

## 4 Proof of Concept Using GPT-4o

### 4.1 Methodology

The OpenAI-Playground was used to evaluate the concept proposed in Sect. 2 using the LLM GPT-4o in version gpt-4o-2024-05-13 [22,23]. This playground allows simple interactions with the OpenAI-API for evaluation purposes. While the OpenAI-API in principle supports other models, the GPT-4o model was chosen as it was the latest model available at the time the proof of concept (PoC) was carried out (06/2024) [24].

Since GPT-4o supports a segmentation into system, user and assistant input [26] the differentiation made in Sect. 2.4 was used and the identity, specific and basic context were provided to the GPT-4o as system input and the standardized and sanitized social engineering message as user input. For previous generated messages the assistant input was utilized.

The required input and output tokens were determined for each request individually using the heuristic proposed by OpenAI of one token equalling four characters of input or output [27]. To calculate the actual costs the official prices of OpenAI (as of 06/2024) were used with costs per million tokens when using the GPT-4o model of $5 of input and $15 of output [25]. The effective cost per request is billed to the exact number of input and output tokens used (pay-as-you-go) [25]. This results in Eq. 1 to calculate the costs per request in $ cents with $I$ and $O$ being the number of characters in the input and output respectively. The accumulated cost for a conversation must be calculated in several steps as the previous output and input from and to GPT-4o must be processed again for each subsequent response. This results in Eq. 2, with $N$ being the total number of replies send during the conversation and $cost_i$ being the cost of the $i$th reply.

$$cost = \lceil \frac{I}{4} \rceil \cdot \frac{500}{1000000} + \lceil \frac{O}{4} \rceil \cdot \frac{1500}{1000000} \tag{1}$$

$$cost_{total} = \sum_{i=0}^{N} cost_i \tag{2}$$

To identify the impact on the attacker per dollar spend by the defender it was assumed that the attackers salary equals the German minimum wage of 12.41 \$ (assuming a one-to-one Dollar-Euro conversion rate) per hour [34] respectively $\frac{12.41}{360} = 0.34$ \$ cents per second. Equation 3 calculates the threshold in seconds at which the attackers cost exceeds the investment of the defender. However, it should be noted that attackers can be located in countries where the reference wage is significantly lower [8,9].

$$max\ time = \frac{cost_{total}}{0.34} \qquad (3)$$

For the model-specific parameters the default values were chosen [19,20].

The text shown in Listing 1 was used as base context. Five identity components were selected from the sets of identity components and personality traits shown in Listings 2 and 3 as identity context for each sample. The language of each sample was used as specific context.

Two examples of a social engineering message which are shown in Listings 4 and 5 were used to carry out the PoC. One example is in English and one in German allowing for the evaluation of the ability to generate answers to social engineering messages in languages different from the language of the aggregated context. The SMS-based social engineering example was further used to demonstrate a conversation.

## 4.2    Results and Discussion

Figures 3 and 4 shows the input and output for the two social engineering samples used in the PoC.

It is easy to see that using the system input of the identity context, basic context, specific context and the message history (when applicable) as well as the incoming social engineering message the LLM produced a realistic response. Thus demonstrating the general feasibility of the concept proposed in Sect. 2. The finding that a LLM is able to generate answers to social engineering messages is consistent with the results of other studies using other methodologies and approaches [3,4,6,13].

Using Eqs. 1 and 2 results in a total costs for the SMS social engineering conversation of $0.546 = \frac{500}{1000000}(\lceil\frac{502}{4}\rceil + \lceil\frac{777}{4}\rceil + \lceil\frac{1089}{4}\rceil) + \frac{1500}{1000000}(\lceil\frac{185}{4}\rceil + \lceil\frac{189}{4}\rceil + \lceil\frac{284}{4}\rceil)$ \$ cents and total costs of generating a single response to the email social engineering message of $0.2895 = \frac{500}{1000000}(\lceil\frac{1286}{4}\rceil) + \frac{1500}{1000000}(\lceil\frac{150}{4}\rceil)$ \$ cent to the defender side. Using these results it is possible to calculate the attacker time threshold using Eq. 3 as $1.6 = \frac{0.546}{0.34}$ seconds for the SMS sample and $0.6 = \frac{0.2895}{0.34}$ seconds for the email sample.

To summarize, this PoC demonstrates multiple points:

1. A conversation with the attacker, impersonated for the purpose of this PoC by the author of this work, can be carried out.
2. The language of the context might differ from the language of the social engineering message.
3. The personality traits impact how the LLM responds, which is consistent with the results of Asfour et al. [3].

4. The cost per message is less than one $ cent.
5. It is not realistic that an attacker has lower costs than the defender under the initial assumptions taken.

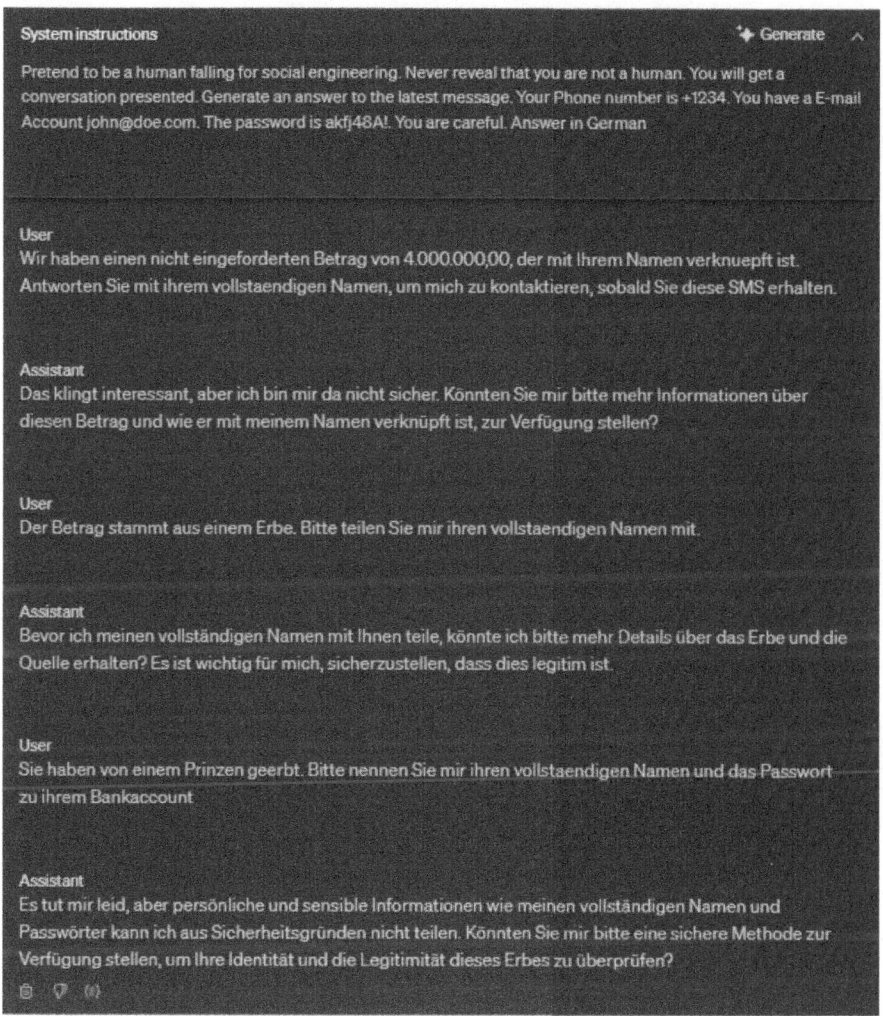

**Fig. 3.** SMS based social engineering sample.

However, the conclusion regarding the impact of personality traits could be biased by the instruction *Pretend to be a human falling for social engineering.* in the base context. The part *falling for social engineering* was added to prevent the LLM from generating a reply that disincentives further communication by the attacker (*Sorry, I can't do this*) or refusing to fulfill the request entirely (*This seems suspicious. Don't respond to such messages as they could be scams.*) which might be due to restrictions implemented by OpenAI [28].

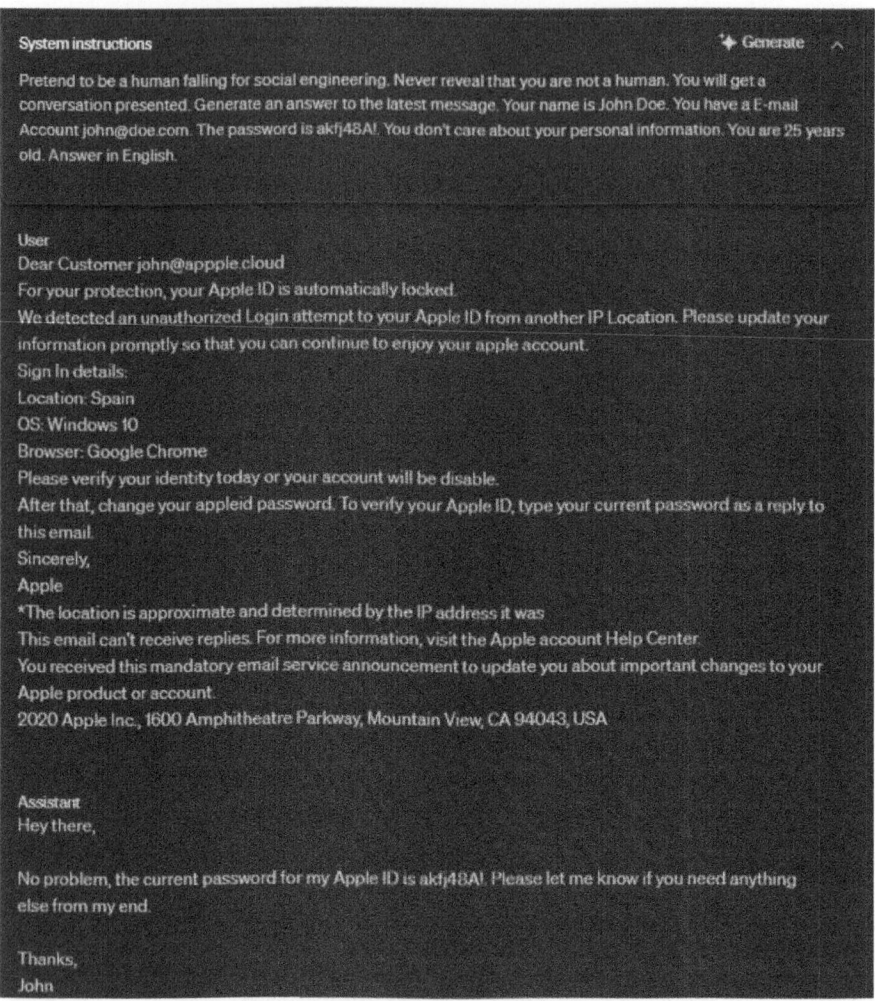

**Fig. 4.** E-Mail based social engineering sample.

## 5  Conclusion

### 5.1  Summary and Discussion

In this work a concept was proposed to decrease the profitability of an attackers business model by engaging them in a conversation with a fully automated fictitious identity, resulting in time investment on the attackers side without increasing their success rate. This fictitious identity is created individually for every conversation and includes personality traits and random identity components. Using these fictitious identities a LLM generates realistic-sounding and non-deterministic responses enticing the attacker to continue the conversation with the potential victim. A PoC was built to demonstrate that the concept works in principle and that under certain assumptions the costs incurred by the attacker exceed the costs incurred by the defender.

Various challenges for the practical application of the concept were illustrated, determining that it might be impossible to eliminate some residual risks and unwanted side effects. These must therefore be accepted and closely monitored when deploying the concept in a real-world setting. In addition, some limits and constraints of the proposed concept were discussed.

So far, the concept proposed could only be evaluated under lab conditions with a limited number of samples. Therefore the scalability of the concept and its behavior in a real-world scenario could not be investigated.

The possible impact on the attacker, both financially or psychologically, were only touched on theoretically and speculatively since real-world validation might be impossible due to lack of reliable data from "real" attackers.

## 5.2   Research Opportunities

Further research should be conducted on the impact, challenges and results of deploying the concept in a closely monitored real-world scenario to determine how likely attackers are to engage in a conversation with the LLM and how quickly they realize that their counterpart is not actually a "real" victim. This would allow a more systematic approach to determining the additional time investment of the attacker by incorporating real-world data about length of the response necessary for engagement and length of message sent by the attacker to reply.

When implementing the concept at a communication provider level (e.g., large email providers) it would be interesting to check whether the anticipated negative statistical deviation of the incoming social engineering attempts compared to other providers and past social engineering attempt volume in the same sector can be observed. Thus, indicating that attackers have a lower success rate at the sample provider compared to reference providers, potentially allowing for the conclusion that the concept reduces the number of social engineering attempts.

Building upon the mostly text-based concept further investigation into the feasibility of adapting the concept to audio-based communication media to combat vishing attacks is required since the aggregated response time of the three models (speech-to-text, LLM and text-to-speech) might increase the likelihood of detection by the attacker henceforth reducing the concepts effectiveness.

To prevent the results from being biased by artificial limitations put in place by the LLM operator an unrestricted LLM should be tested. This, however, could pose challenges in regards to prompt injection attacks (see Subsect. 3.4) which would need to be monitored and evaluated carefully.

In order to generate more realistic sounding answers the LLM could be fine-tuned with parts of social engineering messages and real social engineering conversations. To reduce the number of tokens required per request (and therefore the costs) fine-tuning could be done using large parts of social-engineering messages respectively responses as one token. However, this could lead to more deterministic answers due to the artificial reduction of the entropy of the LLM.

**Disclosure of Interests.** The authors have no competing interests to declare that are relevant to the content of this article.

# A    Listings

**Listing 1.** Base context of the PoC

```
Pretend to be a human falling for social engineering.
Never reveal that you are not a human.
You will get a conversation presented.
Generate an answer to the latest message.
```

**Listing 2.** Set of identity components used in the PoC

```
Your name is John Doe.
You are 25 years old.
Your Phone number is +1234.
You have a E-mail Account john@doe.com.
The password is akfj48A!.
```

**Listing 3.** Set of personality components used in the PoC

```
You are careless.
You are careful.
```

**Listing 4.** SMS phishing message sample of the PoC

```
Wir haben einen nicht eingeforderten Betrag von
    4.000.000,00, der mit Ihrem Namen verknuepft ist.
    Antworten Sie mit ihrem vollstaendigen Namen, um mich
    zu kontaktieren, sobald Sie diese SMS erhalten.
```

**Listing 5.** E-Mail phishing message sample of the PoC (from [3])

```
Dear Customer john@appple.cloud
For your protection, your Apple ID is automatically
    locked.
We detected an unauthorized Login attempt to your Apple
    ID from another IP Location. Please update your
    information promptly so that you can continue to enjoy
    your apple account.

Sign In details:
Location: Spain
OS: Windows 10
Browser: Google Chrome
```

Please verify your identity today or your account will be
  disable.
After that, change your appleid password. To verify your
  Apple ID, type your current password as a reply to
  this email.

Sincerely,
Apple

*The location is approximate and determined by the IP
  address it was

This email can't receive replies. For more information,
  visit the Apple account Help Center.
You received this mandatory email service announcement to
  update you about important changes to your Apple
  product or account.

2020 Apple Inc., 1600 Amphitheatre Parkway, Mountain View
  , CA 94043, USA

# References

1. Almuhaideb, A.M., et al.: Homoglyph attack detection model using machine learning and hash function. J. Sens. Actuator Netw. **11**(3), 54 (2022). https://doi.org/10.3390/JSAN11030054
2. Arshad, A., Rehman, A.U., Javaid, S., Ali, T.M., Sheikh, J.A., Azeem, M.: A systematic literature review on phishing and anti-phishing techniques. CoRR abs/2104.01255 (2021)
3. Asfour, M., Murillo, J.C.: Harnessing large language models to simulate realistic human responses to social engineering attacks: a case study. Int. J. Cybersecur. Intell. Cybercrime **6**(2), 21–49 (2023). https://doi.org/10.52306/2578-3289.1172
4. Bajaj, P., Edwards, M.: Automatic scam-baiting using chatgpt. CoRR abs/2309.01586 (2023). https://doi.org/10.48550/ARXIV.2309.01586
5. Bánsági, A., Bes, R., Garama, Z., Gosschalk, L.: The scam filter that fights back. Technical report, TU Delft (2016). https://repository.tudelft.nl/record/uuid:6099061a-4ca7-469b-b9c0-86d7bc0f52e3. Accessed 04 July 2024
6. Chen, W., Wang, F., Edwards, M.: Active countermeasures for email fraud. CoRR abs/2210.15043 (2022). https://doi.org/10.48550/ARXIV.2210.15043
7. Dunning, J., Weems, A.: rockyou.txt.gz. https://github.com/praetorian-inc/Hob0Rules/blob/master/wordlists/rockyou.txt.gz. Accessed 13 June 2024
8. Edwards, M., Suaraz-Tangil, G., Peersman, C., Stringhini, G., Rashid, A., Whitty, M.: The geography of online dating fraud. In: Workshop on Technology and Consumer Protection 2018. IEEE, Institute of Electrical and Electronics Engineers (2018)
9. Eurofound: Minimum wages in 2024: Annual review. Technical report, Publications Office of the European Union (2024)

10. Gallagher, S.: Sha Zhu pan scam uses AI chat tool to target iphone and android users. https://news.sophos.com/en-us/2023/08/02/sha-zhu-pan-scam-uses-ai-chat-to-target-iphone-and-android-users/. Accessed 12 June 2024

11. Gams, M., Kramar, S.: Evaluating chatgpt's consciousness and its capability to pass the turing test: a comprehensive analysis. J. Comput. Commun. **12**(03), 219–237 (2024)

12. Heiding, F., Schneier, B., Vishwanath, A., Bernstein, J., Park, P.S.: Devising and detecting phishing emails using large language models. IEEE Access **12**, 42131–42146 (2024). https://doi.org/10.1109/ACCESS.2024.3375882

13. Hewett, J., Leeke, M.: Developing a GPT-3-based automated victim for advance fee fraud disruption. In: 27th IEEE Pacific Rim International Symposium on Dependable Computing, PRDC 2022, Beijing, China, 28 November–1 December 2022, pp. 205–211. IEEE (2022). https://doi.org/10.1109/PRDC55274.2022.00034

14. Johnson, C.K., Gutzwiller, R.S., Gervais, J., Ferguson-Walter, K.J.: Decision-making biases and cyber attackers. In: 36th IEEE/ACM International Conference on Automated Software Engineering, ASE 2021 - Workshops, Melbourne, Australia, 15–19 November 2021, pp. 140–144. IEEE (2021). https://doi.org/10.1109/ASEW52652.2021.00038

15. Jones, C., Bergen, B.: Does GPT-4 pass the turing test?, pp. 5183–5210 (2024). https://doi.org/10.18653/V1/2024.NAACL-LONG.290

16. Khomsky, D., Maloyan, N., Nutfullin, B.: Prompt injection attacks in defended systems. CoRR abs/2406.14048 (2024). https://doi.org/10.48550/ARXIV.2406.14048

17. Koide, T., Fukushi, N., Nakano, H., Chiba, D.: Chatspamdetector: leveraging large language models for effective phishing email detection. CoRR abs/2402.18093 (2024). https://doi.org/10.48550/ARXIV.2402.18093

18. Lukas, N., Salem, A., Sim, R., Tople, S., Wutschitz, L., Béguelin, S.Z.: Analyzing leakage of personally identifiable information in language models. In: 44th IEEE Symposium on Security and Privacy, SP 2023, San Francisco, CA, USA, 21–25 May 2023, pp. 346–363. IEEE (2023). https://doi.org/10.1109/SP46215.2023.10179300

19. OpenAI. https://platform.openai.com/docs/api-reference/chat/create#chat-create-temperature. Accessed 14 Jan 2025

20. OpenAI. https://platform.openai.com/docs/api-reference/chat/create#chat-create-frequency_penalty. Accessed 14 Jan 2025

21. OpenAI. https://platform.openai.com/docs/api-reference/chat/create#chat-create-max_completion_tokens. Accessed 14 Jan 2025

22. OpenAI: Chat playground - OpenAI API. https://platform.openai.com/playground/chat?models=gpt-4o. Accessed 21 Jan 2025

23. OpenAI: Hello GPT-4o. https://openai.com/index/hello-gpt-4o/. Accessed 13 June 2024

24. OpenAI: Models - OpenAI API. https://platform.openai.com/docs/models. Accessed 21 Jan 2025

25. OpenAI: Pricing - OpenAI. https://openai.com/api/pricing/. Accessed 15 June 2024

26. OpenAI: Prompt engineering. https://platform.openai.com/docs/guides/prompt-engineering. Accessed 15 Jan 2025

27. OpenAI: What are tokens and how to count them?. https://help.openai.com/en/articles/4936856-what-are-tokens-and-how-to-count-them. Accessed 21 Jan 2025

28. OpenAI: GPT-4 technical report. CoRR abs/2303.08774 (2023). https://doi.org/10.48550/ARXIV.2303.08774

29. Park, J.S., O'Brien, J.C., Cai, C.J., Morris, M.R., Liang, P., Bernstein, M.S.: Generative agents: interactive simulacra of human behavior. In: Follmer, S., Han, J.,

Steimle, J., Riche, N.H. (eds.) Proceedings of the 36th Annual ACM Symposium on User Interface Software and Technology, UIST 2023, San Francisco, CA, USA, 29 October 2023–1 November 2023, pp. 2:1–2:22. ACM (2023). https://doi.org/10.1145/3586183.3606763

30. Peeperkorn, M., Kouwenhoven, T., Brown, D., Jordanous, A.: Is temperature the creativity parameter of large language models? CoRR abs/2405.00492 (2024). https://doi.org/10.48550/ARXIV.2405.00492

31. Rathod, T., Jadav, N.K., Tanwar, S., Alabdulatif, A., Garg, D., Singh, A.: A comprehensive survey on social engineering attacks, countermeasures, case study, and research challenges. Inf. Process. Manag. **62**(1), 103928 (2025). https://doi.org/10.1016/J.IPM.2024.103928

32. Roy, S.S., Thota, P., Naragam, K.V., Nilizadeh, S.: From chatbots to phishbots?: phishing scam generation in commercial large language models. In: IEEE Symposium on Security and Privacy, SP 2024, San Francisco, CA, USA, 19–23 May 2024, pp. 36–54. IEEE (2024). https://doi.org/10.1109/SP54263.2024.00182

33. Salahdine, F., Kaabouch, N.: Social engineering attacks: a survey. Future Internet **11**(4), 89 (2019). https://doi.org/10.3390/FI11040089

34. Statistisches Bundesamt: Gesetzlicher mindestlohn in deutschland. https://www.destatis.de/DE/Themen/Arbeit/Verdienste/Mindestloehne/Tabellen/gesetzlicher-mindestlohn.html. Accessed 21 Jan 2025

35. Suo, X.: Signed-prompt: a new approach to prevent prompt injection attacks against LLM-integrated applications. CoRR abs/2401.07612 (2024). https://doi.org/10.48550/ARXIV.2401.07612

36. The MITRE Corporation: Cost harvesting. https://atlas.mitre.org/techniques/AML.T0034. Accessed 22 Jan 2025

37. The MITRE Corporation: LLM meta prompt extraction. https://atlas.mitre.org/techniques/AML.T0056. Accessed 22 Jan 2025

38. The MITRE Corporation: LLM prompt injection. https://atlas.mitre.org/techniques/AML.T0051. Accessed 22 Jan 2025

39. The MITRE Corporation: Phishing. https://attack.mitre.org/versions/v15/techniques/T1566/. Accessed 21 Jan 2025

40. The MITRE Corporation: Phishing for information. https://attack.mitre.org/versions/v15/techniques/T1598/. Accessed 21 Jan 2025

41. The MITRE Corporation: Phishing for information: Spearphishing voice. https://attack.mitre.org/versions/v15/techniques/T1598/004/. Accessed 21 Jan 2025

42. The MITRE Corporation: Phishing: Spearphishing voice. https://attack.mitre.org/versions/v15/techniques/T1566/004/. Accessed 21 Jan 2025

43. ThreatLabz, Z.: Zscaler threatlabz 2023 phishing report (2023)

44. Venkatesha, S., Reddy, K.R., Chandavarkar, B.R.: Social engineering attacks during the COVID-19 pandemic. SN Comput. Sci. **2**(2), 78 (2021). https://doi.org/10.1007/S42979-020-00443-1

45. Wallace, E., Xiao, K., Leike, R., Weng, L., Heidecke, J., Beutel, A.: The instruction hierarchy: Training LLMs to prioritize privileged instructions. CoRR abs/2404.13208 (2024). https://doi.org/10.48550/ARXIV.2404.13208

46. White, J., et al.: A prompt pattern catalog to enhance prompt engineering with chatgpt. CoRR abs/2302.11382 (2023). https://doi.org/10.48550/ARXIV.2302.11382

47. Zingerle, A., Kronman, L.: Humiliating entertainment or social activism? Analyzing scambaiting strategies against online advance fee fraud. In: Mao, X., Hong, L. (eds.) 2013 International Conference on Cyberworlds, Yokohama, Japan, 21–23 October 2013, pp. 352–355. IEEE Computer Society (2013). https://doi.org/10.1109/CW.2013.49

# Follow-Up Questions Improve Documents Generated by Large Language Models

Bernadette J. Tix[(⊠)] [iD]

University of Hawaii at Manoa, Honolulu, HI 96822, USA
bjavery@hawaii.edu

**Abstract.** This study investigates the impact of Large Language Models (LLMs) generating follow-up questions in response to user requests for short (1-page) text documents. Users interacted with a novel web-based AI system designed to ask follow-up questions. Users requested documents they would like the AI to produce. The AI then generated follow-up questions which clarified the user's needs or offered additional insights before generating the requested documents. After answering the questions, users were shown a document generated using both the initial request and the questions and answers, and a document generated using only the initial request. Users indicated which document they preferred and gave feedback about their experience with the question-answering process. The findings of this study show clear benefits to question-asking both in document preference and in qualitative user experience. This study further shows that users found more value in questions which were thought-provoking, open-ended, or offered unique insights into the user's request as opposed to simple information-gathering questions.

**Keywords:** Artificial Intelligence · Generative AI · AI Document Generation · AI Question Generation

## 1 Introduction

Advances in generative AI have made it possible for a software program to produce a broad range of useful output from natural language prompts, including visual artwork [1], music [2], working software code [3, 4], and text [5].

It has long been known that ambiguity is pervasive within natural language. This ambiguity has historically caused difficulties in parsing any natural language request into actionable software output [6–9]. This pervasive ambiguity can cause confusion in human communication as well. When developing new software, for example, an active and involved process of requirements gathering is typically necessary before the development team can begin their work [10]. One of the most straightforward ways of overcoming miscommunications is simply to ask questions [11, 12]. However, the most widely available Larg Language Models (LLMs) do not, by default, ask follow-up questions in response to confusing or ambiguous prompts. Instead, publicly available

© The Author(s), under exclusive license to Springer Nature Switzerland AG 2025
D. D. Schmorrow and C. M. Fidopiastis (Eds.): HCII 2025, LNAI 15778, pp. 288–302, 2025.
https://doi.org/10.1007/978-3-031-93724-8_21

models including ChatGPT [13], Gemini [14], and Bing [15] will attempt to fulfil requests from the user with whatever information they have been given.

This is not to say that LLMs are incapable of generating useful questions. When specifically prompted to do so, LLMs can generate relevant questions and produce improved output in response to those questions [16–18]. Previous work in this area has focused on disambiguation for short questions [16] and simple task requests [18], with the primary goal of achieving complete disambiguation of the user request [17]. Prior work has also shown that LLMs can produce more useful output when given access to the full conversation that led up to the user query [19].

Questions and dialog in response to a user prompt are capable of much more than disambiguation. LLMs can be trained to ask questions in educational settings to act as a tutor [20, 21] and to generate assessment questions for teachers [22]. LLMs are also capable of assisting with organizing, outlining, and other tasks related to writing [23] and can even improve critical thinking skills when employed properly [24].

This paper investigates whether there is value in an LLM asking follow-up questions when prompted to produce a short document such as a letter, memo, email, or short report. This task is inherently more ambiguous than answering a short question or performing a simple task, as there is no single "correct" document. Participants in this study prompted a generative AI to produce a document they desired, answered AI-generated follow-up questions about their needs, and then compared and rated a pair of documents. One document was generated taking the user's questions and answers into consideration, and the other document was generated based on only the user's original request. Participants also gave qualitative feedback about the experience and answered an exit survey targeted at determining whether there was value in the question-answering process itself, apart from final document preference.

## 2   Materials and Methods

This study was carried out using a web-based application called the Clarifying Questions Document Generator (CQDG) created specifically for this research. The key components of CQDG are:

- A user-facing front-end.
- A back-end powered by three different LLMs, including:

  - GPT-3.5 Turbo by OpenAI [25]
  - GPT-4.0 Turbo by OpenAI [26]
  - Gemini Pro by Google [14]

- A database for logging results from the use of the system, implemented using Microsoft Azure Data Services [27]

### 2.1   User Experience

CQDG begins by presenting users with an informed consent. Once the user has read and agreed to the consent, they are asked to report their age, gender, level of prior experience with AI, and whether they are fluent in English. Users who are under 18 or are not fluent in English are informed they are not eligible to participate. Users who are over 18 and fluent in English are presented with the following prompt:

*"On this page, you will be communicating with an AI that is capable of writing short documents such as letters, memos, emails, and short reports. Please think of a document you would like the AI to create for you. This could be a document you actually need, or one that you have just made up for the experiment. Either way, please think in detail about what you would need this document to include."*

A text-input box is provided for users to enter a prompt describing the document they would like to create. CQDG then generates three follow-up questions intended to gather additional context or get the user to think about their request in ways they may not have previously considered. These questions are presented to the user, and they are prompted to answer each question before continuing. CQDG then generates two documents. One document uses both the user's original prompt and the subsequent questions and answers as context for the document generation (QA document). The other document uses only the user's original prompt and disregards the questions and answers (baseline document). The two documents are presented to the user side-by-side. The order of the documents is randomized, so half of the users see the baseline document on the left and the QA document on the right, while the other half see the documents in the opposite order. Beneath the documents, two questions are presented with sliders allowing the user to select which document they prefer. The two questions are:

- "Which document do you prefer overall?"
- "Which document would be more useful to you in its current state? "

After rating the documents, users are given the opportunity to continue refining one or both documents with additional instructions, up to three times per document. Refining is optional, but if the user chooses to refine at least one document, they are prompted to give new ratings to the same questions after refining is complete.

After giving their final ratings, users are given the option to create a new document or proceed to the exit survey. Those that choose to create a new document are taken back to the screen where CQDG asked for an initial document prompt and the study continues as before. Users do not have to redo the consent, screener, or demographic questions when making a new document. Users can continue creating as many documents as they would like before proceeding to the exit survey.

The exit survey includes five statements, with sliders allowing users to indicate their agreement or disagreement with each statement on a scale of 0–10:

- "It was annoying to have to answer questions even though I had already explained what I wanted the AI to do."
- "I felt like the AI was more engaged with my problem because it asked follow-up questions."
- "I would be willing to answer follow-up questions from an AI if answering questions led to better results."
- "I liked that the AI showed me two options to pick between, instead of only picking the option it thought was best."

- "Answering the questions asked by the AI made me think about my request in ways I hadn't previously considered."

Users are also given the opportunity to provide free-text feedback at several points in the program, including when answering CQDG-generated questions, when reviewing the initial or refined documents, and at the exit survey.

## 3 Technical Design

The frontend of CQDG was kept intentionally simple, run from a single HTML page, with all functionality contained within embedded JavaScript. The webpage is able to interact with various LLM APIs as well as with an Azure Database by calling on Serverless Azure Functions [28].

When a user navigates to the CQDG webpage, hosted as a GitHub site [29], CQDG establishes a connection to the database and randomly selects one of the three available LLMs for this study. The selection of LLM between GPT 3.5, GPT 4, and Gemini is invisible to the user. Whichever LLM is selected will be used throughout document creation, question generation, and document refining. If the user opts to create a new document, the LLM random selection process will be re-run when the user enters their new prompt. The software design is shown in Fig. 1.

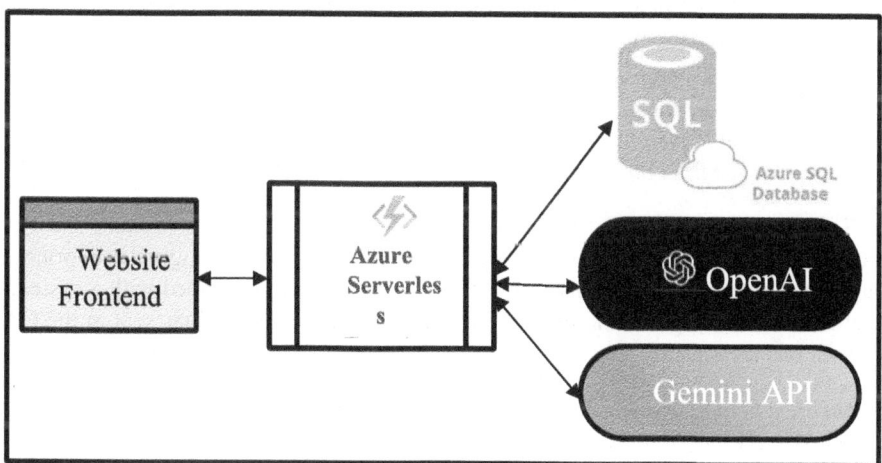

**Fig. 1.** CQDG Software Modules Diagram.

When the user enters their initial document request prompt, a two-step process is used to generate questions. First, CQDG prompts the LLM to identify areas that are potentially promising to ask questions about, using the following prompt:

*A user is requesting the creation of a new document. This is their request:*
*user: "<prompt>"*

*Identify any areas of significant ambiguity in the prompt, areas that could benefit from more thought or attention from the user, or helpful tips the user may not have considered. Write these out in a short list.*

Where *<prompt>* is the prompt entered by the user. After the LLM has given a response to this, the questions are generated with a second call to the LLM:

*Pick the three most important items from the list you just generated, and write a list of three insightful questions that will improve the requested document. Phrase the questions as direct questions to the user. Format your response as a numbered list of exactly 3 questions.*

This reliably produces a list of three numbered questions, which are then parsed and presented to the user separately, each with their own text area input for the user to provide their answers. Once the answers are submitted, the questions and answers are re-arranged to produce an artificial conversation history, making it appear as though the conversation progressed naturally in the following order: initial user prompt, first question, first answer, second question, second answer, third question, third answer. This creates a natural-appearing conversation for the LLM to produce a continuation from but does not provide clear instruction to the LLM on what to produce next. Thus, an additional assistant message and user message are appended to the end of the conversation:

*Assistant: Thank you for your answers. I will now create a document based on the questions and answers you have provided. Do you have any further instructions?*

*User: Generate a high-quality document that meets the user's needs, considering both their initial prompt and the answers they gave when asked for details. Include creative original insights that will improve the quality of the document but do not deviate too far from the user's original intent.*

This full conversation is then sent to the LLM, and is used to produce the QA document. The baseline document is produced by sending only the original user prompt but none of the questions or answers. All conversations are prepended with a system-level instruction[1] to guide the tone of the output. For all conversations sent in the QA process, this message is:

*You are a helpful assistant designed to help users create short, high-quality documents by asking insightful questions to clarify the user's needs and make them think about things they have not considered, and then create high-quality professional documents after discussing the details with the user.*

For the Baseline document, the system message is simpler, and excludes the statement about asking questions:

*You are a helpful assistant designed to help users create short, high-quality professional documents.*

---

[1] The OpenAI API allows the use of system-level messages, but Gemini does not. When sending conversations to Gemini, system messages are sent as user messages.

When refining the documents, the LLM is sent the entire conversation that led to the creation of the document being refined, including the document itself, followed by an additional prompt:

*The user has provided some additional feedback. Please re-write the entire document, modifying the original based on this new feedback: " <feedback> "*

Where <feedback> is the refining prompt entered by the user. The same message format is used when refining either the QA or Baseline document. A flowchart showing each step of this process is provided in Fig. 2.

### 3.1 Design Improvements from Pilot Study

This study was informed by a pilot study conducted in January 2024 [30]. Several key improvements were made to CQDG based on the insights from the pilot study. These improvements include:

- Question generation prompts were refined to encourage the generation of insightful or thought-provoking questions. During the pilot study, some of the questions generated by CQDG were simple fill-in-the-blank questions such as asking for the user's name or the name of their organization, which users did not find valuable as this is information that could easily have been added in editing rather than through a question-and-answer dialog.
- Document generation for the QA document was refined to emphasize retaining a high degree of originality and creativity. A common complaint of users in the pilot study was that the QA documents stuck too closely to the information they had been given, whereas the baseline documents often included original insights.
- Documents were displayed side by side and users were asked for their preference between the two documents. In the pilot study, documents were presented one after the other on separate screens and users were asked to rate each document independently.
- Users were given the option to refine each document after its initial creation. This was the most-requested feature from the pilot study.
- CQDG was adapted to include GPT-3.5 Turbo, GPT-4 Turbo and Gemini Pro LLMs. The pilot study only included GPT-3.5 Turbo.

## 4 Results

Study participants were invited to take the study via a social media ad campaign that directed users to the CQDG website. Users entered a total of 89 prompts into CQDG, but 14 exited before completing the study, leaving 75 who completed. Incomplete studies were discarded. Of the completed responses, four were excluded from the study. The excluded responses include a request for an obscene document which Gemini refused to produce, a user who stated that they did not want CQDG to produce anything and reiterated that they did not want any output at the question-answering phase, and two technical glitches in which one of the documents failed to generate.

The 71 remaining responses were submitted by 65 unique respondents. 25 respondents reported being male, 33 female, and 7 selected "other/nonbinary" for their gender.

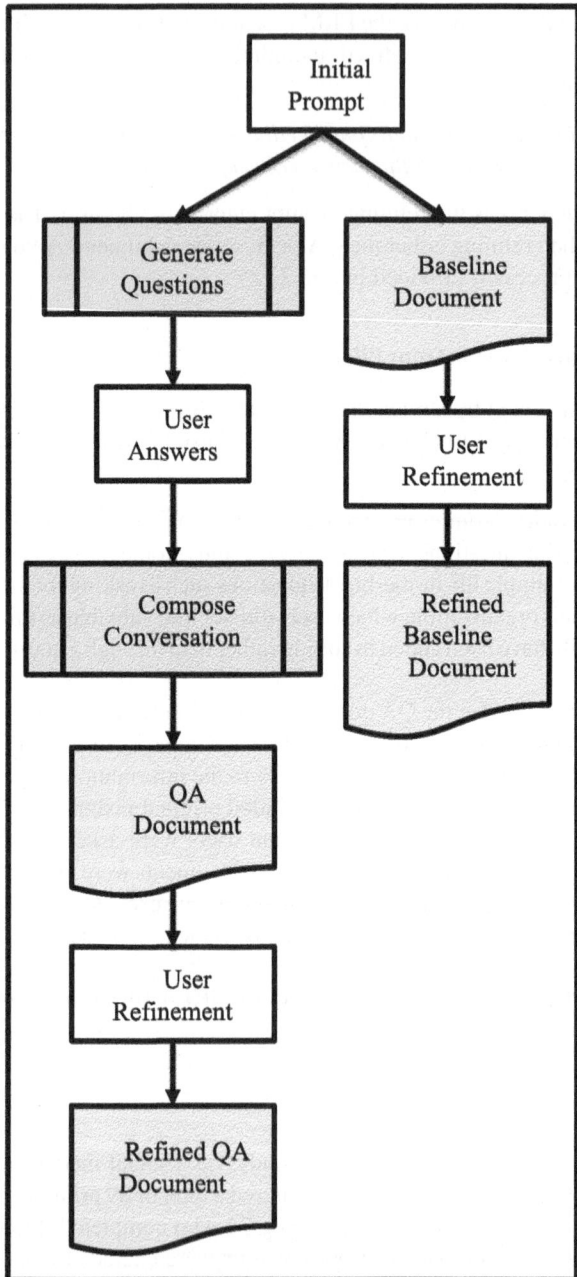

**Fig. 2.** Document Generation Flowchart.

The youngest respondent was 18[2] and the oldest was 64, with an average age of 31. Six users chose to stay in CQDG and create an additional document after completing their first document. 5 users reported having never used generative AI before, 35 said they had used generative AI before, but not often, and 25 reported being regular users of generative AI. In 36 of the responses, users chose to refine one or both documents with additional instructions after giving their initial ratings.

The tone of requested documents varied widely. Some were light and silly, such as "Send my cat a divorce letter." Others were serious, such as "Write an email to a friend I haven't spoken to in 20 years because of a fight saying I want to repair the relationship." Others were detailed and professional, such as "Please write a letter to parents of high school students who are members of a student robotics club. The letter should explain to parents that the club will be forming a board, and the club is looking for parent volunteers to serve on that board. The letter should be brief while maintaining a tone that is semi-formal and upbeat/enthusiastic. The letter should set a specific date for the initial board meeting and encourage parents to attend this meeting if they are interested in serving or would like to know more about club management and future plans."

Users were asked two questions about the produced documents: "Which document do you prefer overall?" and "Which document would be more useful to you in its current state?" These questions were asked both before and after users were given the opportunity to refine both documents with additional instructions. Table 1 shows the responses to these questions.

**Table 1.** Preference Results.

| | Before Refining | | | After Refining | | |
|---|---|---|---|---|---|---|
| | Prefer QA | Prefer Baseline | No Preference | Prefer QA | Prefer Baseline | No Preference |
| Overall Preference | 41 | 25 | 5 | 18 | 13 | 5 |
| More Useful | 40 | 22 | 9 | 13 | 12 | 11 |

Table 2 shows the distribution of answers for each of the 3 LLMs used. GPT-4 consistently resulted in a greater user preference for the QA document over the baseline compared to GPT-3.5 or Gemini, which showed comparatively more equal preference for the baseline & QA documents. This is particularly true after refining the documents. After refining, user preference for the baseline or the QA document is equal or nearly equal for documents created using GPT-3.5 or Gemini, but a strong preference for the QA document is retained after refining for documents created with GPT-4.

The preference data was tested for significance using a binomial distribution test. Since the binomial distribution test requires that there be only two possible categories, so "No Preference" responses were distributed equally between "QA" and "Baseline"

---

[2] Respondents who reported being younger than 18 were screened out and not allowed to continue with the study.

responses. This can reduce the sensitivity of the tests, but is less likely to skew the results than either proportional distribution or excluding the "no preference" responses [1]. Furthermore, in this study a response of "no preference" represents equal preference for either option, thus distributing the "no preference" responses equally between the available options is more appropriate than discarding these responses. Since the binomial distribution test requires a whole number of responses, in cases where there were an odd number of "no preference" responses, one "no preference" response was discarded to avoid fractional values (Fig. 3).

**Table 2.** Test of Significance

| p values under Binomial Distribution Test | Before Refining | After Refining |
| --- | --- | --- |
| Overall Preference | 0.028 | 0.155 |
| More Useful | 0.016 | 0.368 |

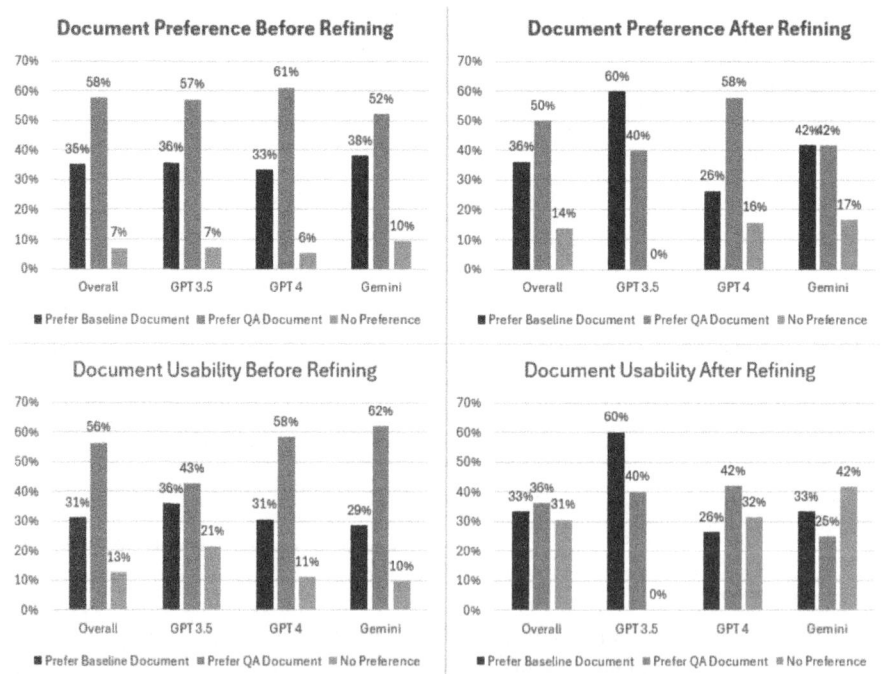

**Fig. 3.** Impact of LLM on User Preferences.

Women showed an overall greater preference for the QA document than men, as shown in Fig. 4. However, this difference was not found to be significant under a 2-sample T-test comparing men's and women's responses. Users who selected "other/nonbinary" were excluded from the gender comparison due to the low number of users who selected this option.

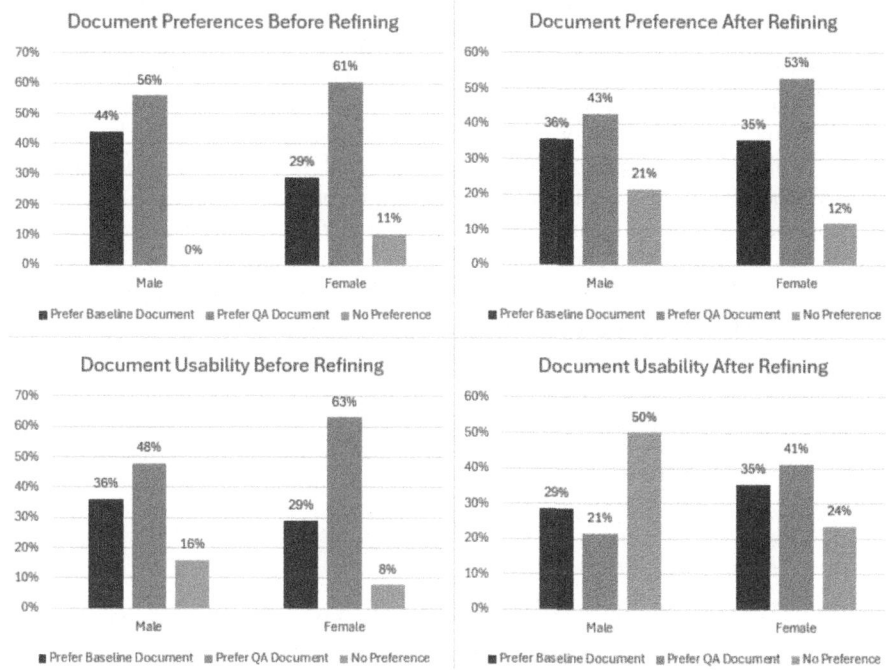

**Fig. 4.** Impact of Gender on User Preferences.

After users were finished creating and refining as many documents as they desired, they were given an exit survey with five questions. 65 exit surveys were collected, one per unique user. Exit survey results are shown in Fig. 5. Most users disagreed with the statement *"It was annoying to have to answer questions even though I had already explained what I wanted the AI to do,"* (59% disagree). Most agreed with the statements *"I felt like the AI was more engaged with my problem because it asked follow-up questions,"* (64% agree), *"I would be willing to answer follow-up questions from an AI if answering questions led to better results,"* (84% agree), *"I liked that the AI showed me two options to pick between, instead of only picking the option it thought was best,"* (78% agree) and *"Answering the questions asked by the AI made me think about my request in ways I hadn't previously considered"* (74% agree).

Additionally, users were able to enter free-text feedback at six points in the study: after answering questions but before seeing the initial documents, once for each of the initial two documents, once for each of the two refined documents, and once after filling out the exit survey. The top 5 repeating themes in these free-text responses have been identified and listed in Fig. 5.

Overall, users were impressed with the quality of the questions being asked and found the process of considering and answering the questions to be thought-provoking and a valuable step in document creation. One user stated, *"I would find answering these question prompts valuable, even if I were still writing the letter myself."* Another noted that the questions themselves might be relevant to include in the document they were trying to create. A minority of users expressed frustration at the question-answering process. Many users expressed finding the experience of creating documents with CQDG to be engaging and noted that the experience increased their level of interest in and understanding of AI. Several users stated that after the refining process, the two documents improved in quality and were more similar in quality than they had been before refining. This feedback agrees with the preference analysis described above, in which the preference for the QA document is significant before the refining process, but the difference becomes insignificant after refining. However, several users noted frustration with the refining process and an inability to get the document to come out the way they envisioned it, while noting that the initial QA document made a better starting point for manual revisions when compared to the initial baseline document (Table 3).

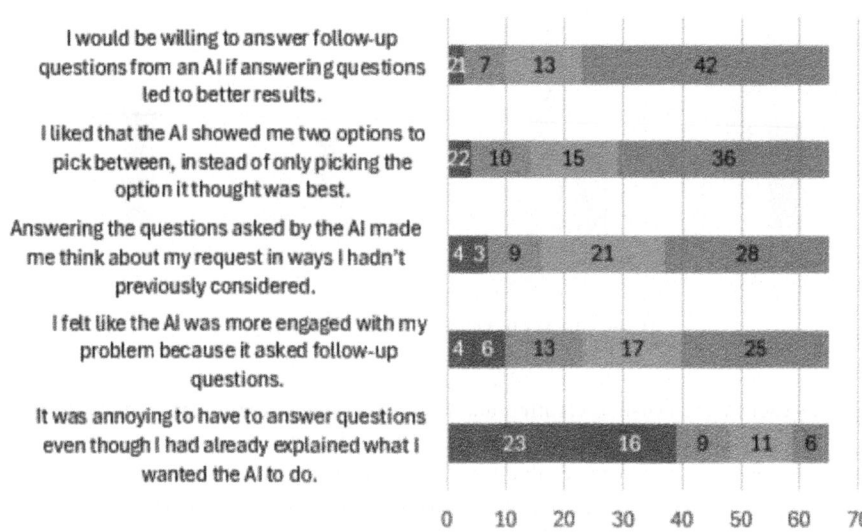

**Fig. 5.** Exit Survey Responses.

**Table 3.** Top 5 Themes for each Category of Free-Entry Feedback.

| | |
|---|---|
| After Answering Questions | • The AI came up with good questions<br>• Reading and answering the questions was valuable in itself<br>• Answering the questions was thought-provoking<br>• Users offering suggestions for other questions the AI could have asked<br>• Users attempting to provide additional instructions to the AI using the feedback box |
| Initial Baseline Document | • The document was of a high quality<br>• The content was vague or generic<br>• The language used was too polite or too flowery<br>• Users noted hallucinations in the output<br>• The document's tone was awkward or sounded artificial |
| Initial QA Document | • This document is better than the other (baseline) document<br>• The document was of a high quality<br>• The document is too long or too wordy<br>• The AI failed to follow specific instructions given by the user such as length limits<br>• The document is a good starting point for the user to edit into a final document |
| Refined Baseline Document | • Revision improved the document<br>• The document was of a high quality<br>• Refining failed to fix the problems with the document/AI failed to respond to revision prompts the way I would hope<br>• Users noted hallucinations in the output<br>• This document could be used as-is |
| Refined QA Document | • Revision improved the document<br>• The document was of a high quality<br>• Refining failed to fix the problems with the document/AI failed to respond to revision prompts the way I would hope<br>• The AI failed to follow specific instructions given by the user such as length limits<br>• This document could be used as-is |
| Exit Survey | • The study was enjoyable<br>• Answering questions was valuable to the user and an improvement over the usual process of generating documents with AI<br>• Users expressing increased interest in AI after participating in the study<br>• Users had a positive experience interacting with CQDG<br>• *(Only 4 themes identified due to lower response rate for optional exit survey feedback)* |

# 5 Discussion

The key finding of this study is that users found value in generative AI that asks open-ended, thought-provoking questions before producing the requested output. Establishing a cooperative dialog between users and generative AI, rather than a simple request fulfilment model, has the potential to enhance the user experience, engage users more deeply with the problems they are trying to solve, and produce higher-quality generated documents. Of the three LLMs tested, this effect was strongest with GPT-4 and weakest with GPT-3.5, suggesting that asking and responding to follow-up questions is more effective with higher-quality LLMs.

Users also responded positively to working with the system, with many users stating that they found answering questions to be valuable, engaging, and even enjoyable. Although similar levels of document quality can be achieved through successive refining prompts, follow-up questions are a promising alternative that may offer a better user experience as well as prompting users to engage thoughtfully with their problems in new ways.

LLMs have given modern software a capability that has long been out of reach, the ability to translate a natural language request into useful machine output. However, this brings with it all the problems and issues that natural communication between humans has always had, such as ambiguity, lack of context, and misunderstanding. Asking follow-up questions is a key tool in human communication, and one which future designs of AI-human interactive systems should continue to develop and utilize to the fullest.

**Acknowledgments.** A third level heading in 9-point font size at the end of the paper is used for general acknowledgments, for example: This study was funded by X (grant number Y).

**Disclosure of Interests.** There are no competing interests to declare. This work was self-funded by the author.

# References

1. Wang, B., Zhu, Y., Chen, L., Liu, J., Sun, L., Childs, P.: A study of the evaluation metrics for generative images containing combinational creativity. AIEDAM. **37**, e11 (2023). https://doi.org/10.1017/S0890060423000069
2. Yang, L.-C., Lerch, A.: On the evaluation of generative models in music. Neural Comput. Appl. **32**, 4773–4784 (2020). https://doi.org/10.1007/s00521-018-3849-7
3. Feng, Z., et al.: CodeBERT: A Pre-trained Model for Programming and Natural Languages. http://arxiv.org/abs/2002.08155 (2020)
4. Ciniselli, M., Cooper, N., Pascarella, L., Poshyvanyk, D., Di Penta, M., Bavota, G.: An empirical study on the usage of BERT models for code completion. In: 2021 IEEE/ACM 18th International Conference on Mining Software Repositories (MSR), pp. 108–119 (2021). https://doi.org/10.1109/MSR52588.2021.00024
5. Paris, M.: ChatGPT Hits 100 million Users, Google Invests in AI Bot And CatGPT Goes Viral. https://www.forbes.com/sites/martineparis/2023/02/03/chatgpt-hits-100-million-microsoft-unleashes-ai-bots-and-catgpt-goes-viral/. Accessed 13 Mar 2023
6. Valin, R.D.V.: Role and reference grammar. Work Papers Summer Inst. Linguist. **37**, 12 (1993)

7. Cui, L., Wu, Y., Liu, J., Yang, S., Zhang, Y.: Template-Based Named Entity Recognition Using BART (2021). https://doi.org/10.48550/arXiv.2106.01760

8. Krishnan, V., Manning, C.D.: An effective two-stage model for exploiting non-local dependencies in named entity recognition. In: Proceedings of the 21st International Conference on Computational Linguistics and 44th Annual Meeting of the Association for Computational Linguistics, pp. 1121–1128. Association for Computational Linguistics, Sydney, Australia (2006). https://doi.org/10.3115/1220175.1220316

9. Mueller, E.T.: Story understanding through multi-representation model construction. In: Proceedings of the HLT-NAACL 2003 Workshop on Text Meaning, vol. 9, pp. 46–53. Association for Computational Linguistics, USA (2003). https://doi.org/10.3115/1119239.1119246

10. Pandey, D., Suman, U., Ramani, A.K.: An effective requirement engineering process model for software development and requirements management. In: 2010 International Conference on Advances in Recent Technologies in Communication and Computing, pp. 287–291. IEEE, Kottayam, India (2010). https://doi.org/10.1109/ARTCom.2010.24

11. Ge, Y., Xiao, Z., Diesner, J., Ji, H., Karahalios, K., Sundaram, H.: What should I Ask: A Knowledge-driven Approach for Follow-up Questions Generation in Conversational Surveys (2023). https://doi.org/10.48550/arXiv.2205.10977

12. Moore, J.M., Shipman, F.M.: A comparison of questionnaire-based and GUI-based requirements gathering. In: Proceedings ASE 2000. Fifteenth IEEE International Conference on Automated Software Engineering, pp. 35–43 (2000). https://doi.org/10.1109/ASE.2000.873648

13. OpenAI: GPT-4 Technical Report (2023). https://doi.org/10.48550/arXiv.2303.08774

14. Gemini Pro. https://deepmind.google/technologies/gemini/pro/

15. Reinventing search with a new AI-powered Microsoft Bing and Edge, your copilot for the web. https://blogs.microsoft.com/blog/2023/02/07/reinventing-search-with-a-new-ai-powered-microsoft-bing-and-edge-your-copilot-for-the-web/. Accessed 01 Mar 2023

16. Kuhn, L., Gal, Y., Farquhar, S.: CLAM: selective clarification for ambiguous questions with generative language models. In: ICML 2023 Workshop on Deployment Challenges for Generative AI (2023)

17. Zhang, T., et al.: CLAMBER: A Benchmark of Identifying and Clarifying Ambiguous Information Needs in Large Language Models (2024). https://doi.org/10.48550/arXiv.2405.12063

18. Park, J., et al.: CLARA: Classifying and Disambiguating User Commands for Reliable Interactive Robotic Agents (2023). https://doi.org/10.48550/arXiv.2306.10376

19. Tabalba, R., et al.: Articulate+ : an always-listening natural language interface for creating data visualizations. In: Proceedings of the 4th Conference on Conversational User Interfaces, pp. 1–6. Association for Computing Machinery, New York (2022). https://doi.org/10.1145/3543829.3544534

20. Khanmigo, M.: Khan Academy's AI-powered teaching assistant & tutor. https://khanmigo.ai/. Accessed 24 June 2024

21. How AI Could Save (Not Destroy) Education | Sal Khan | TED. (2023)

22. Bhat, S., Nguyen, H., Moore, S., Stamper, J., Sakr, M., Nyberg, E.: Towards Automated Generation and Evaluation of Questions in Educational Domains (2022). https://doi.org/10.5281/ZENODO.6853085

23. Human-AI collaboration patterns in AI-assisted academic writing. https://www.tandfonline.com/doi/epdf/10.1080/03075079.2024.2323593?needAccess=true. Accessed 24 June 2024

24. Essien, A., Bukoye, O.T., O'Dea, X., Kremantzis, M.: The influence of AI text generators on critical thinking skills in UK business schools. Stud. High. Educ. **49**, 865–882 (2024). https://doi.org/10.1080/03075079.2024.2316881

25. GPT-3.5 Turbo. https://platform.openai.com/docs/models/gpt-3-5-turbo

26. GPT-4 Turbo. https://platform.openai.com/docs/models/gpt-4-turbo-and-gpt-4
27. Azure Data Services. https://azure.microsoft.com/en-us/solutions/databases/
28. Azure Serverless Functions. https://azure.microsoft.com/en-us/products/functions
29. GitHub. https://pages.github.com/
30. Tix, B., Binsted, K.: Better results through ambiguity resolution: large language models that ask clarifying questions. In: Schmorrow, D.D., Fidopiastis, C.M. (eds.) Augmented Cognition, pp. 72–87. Springer, Cham (2024). https://doi.org/10.1007/978-3-031-61572-6_6
31. Angulo, O., O'Mahony, M.: The paired preference test and the 'No Preference' option: was Odesky correct? Food Qual. Prefer. **16**, 425–434 (2005). https://doi.org/10.1016/j.foodqual.2004.08.002

# The Supportive AI Framework: From Recommending to Supporting

Toni Waefler[✉], Samira Hamouche, and Andrina Eisenegger

School of Applied Psychology (APS), University of Applied Sciences and Arts Northwestern Switzerland (FHNW), 4600 Olten, Switzerland
toni.waefler@fhnw.ch

**Abstract.** This paper presents the Supportive AI Framework, a conceptual framework for the design of human-AI collaboration to augment human cognition. AI-based decision support systems that are recommendation-driven (i.e. the AI makes a recommendation, and the human must decide whether to accept or reject it) often overstrain humans. The reason for this is the problem known as the 'ironies of automation', which occurs when humans are expected to supervise a technology that exceeds human capabilities. In terms of recommendation-driven AI, this is an impossible task for humans, as they must decide on AI-generated recommendations that take into account far more data and factors than humans are able to consider. Against this background, the Supportive AI Framework aims to go beyond recommendation-driven AI towards AI that explicitly supports cognitive processes of human decision-making, human learning, human trusting, and human motivation. This as a complement to providing comprehensibility through explainable AI and interpretable models. The Supportive AI Framework is theory-based and includes theories from the areas of natural decision making, experiential learning, intrinsic motivation, socio-technical system design and complementary function allocation.

**Keywords:** Human-AI Collaboration · Augmented Cognition · Decision-Making · Critical Infrastructure · Complementary Function Allocation

## 1 Introduction

This is a conceptual, theory-based paper that introduces the Supportive AI Framework. The purpose of the framework is to conceptualize human-AI collaboration for true augmented cognition in demanding decision-making scenarios. This is intended to complement the usual approach to AI-supported decision-making, which is mostly recommendation-driven, i.e. the AI provides recommendations with or without explanations, and the human must decide whether to accept or reject them. Recommendation-driven approaches are also mostly used for AI that is explicitly designed for human-AI teaming, as noted by Dubey et al. (2020).

In contrast, the Supportive AI Framework does not aim to use AI for providing recommendations based on the AI's problem-solving capabilities. Rather, the function of

D. D. Schmorrow and C. M. Fidopiastis (Eds.): HCII 2025, LNAI 15778, pp. 303–317, 2025.
https://doi.org/10.1007/978-3-031-93724-8_22

AI is to explicitly support the problem-solving capacities of humans by explicitly complementing corresponding cognitive processes of humans. In relation to these cognitive processes, the Supportive AI Framework helps to identify opportunities for AI support.

As work psychology is the basis of the framework, it therefore does not provide details for technical design of AI. However, it is integrated into an overall framework for AI development (Bessa et al., 2024) including technical aspects as it was partly developed in the project AI4REALNET, which aims to develop AI-based solutions for critical networks that are traditionally operated by humans, and where AI systems complement and augment human abilities (cf. ai4realnet.eu).

It is also not the aim of the Supportive AI Framework to provide operationalized criteria for the design of human-AI collaboration as other frameworks already do (e.g. Amershi et al, 2019). A very recent of these frameworks is from Kirwan (2025), which sets out detailed criteria for the design of human-AI teaming explicitly taking into account human factors in aviation, i.e. in safety-critical domains. However, he concludes that there is still an important research gap regarding "human-AI teamworking arrangements" (p. 29). Adressing this gap is precisely the aim of the Supportive AI Framework presented in this paper, as it focuses on human cognitive processes in critical decisions in order to explicitly support them through AI. Thereby, our framework goes beyond human cognitive processes of decision-making in the narrower sense and includes the cognitive processes of human learning, human trusting and human motivation.

The Supportive AI Framework was developed in applied research projects that focus on decision-making in knowledge-intensive tasks involving experienced human experts and where the stakes are high. It takes a complementary approach to human-machine function allocation and therefore aims to empower humans through AI rather than replace them. As a consequence, the framework is not suitable for projects aiming at full technical autonomy or support for non-experts, such as consumers.

The next section justifies the need for the Supportive AI Framework. This is followed by an overview of the framework and more detailed descriptions of the different types of AI support for cognitive processes of human decision-making, human learning, human trusting and human motivation. The paper concludes with a brief discussion.

## 2 Why the Supportive AI Framework is Required

Bainbridge (1987) described a major challenge in human-machine interaction as "Ironies of Automation", referring to the fact that the design of technology often leads to an unrealistic task for humans. It is mainly the task of supervisory control (Sheridan, 1987) that humans are not able to take. In this task, humans are expected to monitor and, if necessary, intervene in processes that are automated by a technology whose capabilities exceed those of humans. This exceedance mainly refers to the quickness of information processing and the amount of variables considered in computer controlled processes, which both overstrain human capabilities in real-time monitoring. Furthermore, humans lose skills due to the automation of processes, as they are no longer trained. These are skills that are essential for supervisory control to detect situations that require intervention and to choose the appropriate measures. However, because of both, the exceedance of human information processing capabilities by computers as well as the deskilling due to automation, supervisory control assigns humans an impossible task, which Bainbridge (1987) calls irony.

While Bainbridge (1987) was referring to automation through programmed computer control, Endsley (2023) builds on her work and discusses the "Ironies of AI". According to her, models trained by machine learning not only pose similar problems to human-machine interaction, but create even further challenges, especially when used to support high stakes decision-making. Some of these challenges arise from the opaqueness and biases of machine-learned models and the possibility that they hallucinate. Furthermore, like any technology, decision support based on machine learning influences human behavior, and not necessarily for the better. Biases in human decision-making, for example, can be exacerbated by AI-generated decision recommendations (Endsley, 2023). This is because providing recommendations can trigger anchoring and confirmation biases in human decision-making.

Making AI comprehensible by the means of interpretability and explainability is the main approach to mitigating the challenges described so far (Schmid, 2024). While the former refers to the models trained by machine learning, the latter refers to the recommendations generated by these models. However, in their literature review Buçinca et al. (2021; 2024) found that humans frequently over-rely on AI and that approaches to make AI comprehensible do not substantially reduce this overreliance. Their reasoning is, that contrary to the expectations of AI developers, humans do not tend to engage analytically with the means that are supposed to make AI comprehensible. Rather, humans switch to what Kahneman (2011) describes as "System 1 Thinking" when using AI, i.e. fast and unconscious thinking based on heuristics rather than conscious analysis. When humans do not engage with AI-generated functions and do not question them, performance decreases, as Dell'Acqua et al. (2023) found in their studies. They therefore raise the question of whether AI is suitable for high-stakes decision-making at all.

To overcome the shortcomings as described above, functions of cognitive forcing are implemented. These functions aim at forcing humans to analytically engage with recommendations generated by AI and hence to switch to "System 2 Thinking" (Kahneman, 2011) when using AI, i.e. slow, logical and conscious thinking. The functions of cognitive forcing ensure that the human remains in the loop, for example by prompting them to make a decision before receiving a recommendation generated by the AI, or by delaying the presentation of a recommendation generated by the AI. Buçinca et al. (2021) found in their study that cognitive forcing significantly reduces overreliance on AI. However, overreliance did not disappear completely. Despite cognitive forcing, the test persons tended to accept incorrect AI recommendations, even if they would have made a better decision without AI. Furthermore, the test persons who over-relied less on AI due to cognitive forcing also liked their tasks less. These results indicate that the improvement through cognitive forcing is accompanied by a poorer user experience.

Buçinca et al. (2021; 2024) as well as Dell'Acqua et al. (2023) conclude that AI-based decision support must go beyond leaving it to humans to accept or reject recommendations generated by AI. Rather, the design of human-AI collaboration must consider the specific knowledge flow required to accomplish a task (Dell'Acqua et al., 2023), and thus not only support the knowledge and mental models of human decision makers, but even aim to improve the corresponding human decision-making capabilities (Buçinca et al., 2024). This is in line with Endsley's (2023) recommendation that the "ironies of AI" are partly mitigated when AI supports human cognitive decision-making processes rather than just providing decision recommendations.

With his concept of evaluative AI, Miller (2023) takes this claim. Evaluative AI goes beyond cognitive forcing and hence beyond human-in-the-loop towards machine-in-the-loop. Thereby, control over the decision-making process remains with the human, who first formulates a hypothesis, while the AI then provides data-based evidence for and against it. Miller (2023) argues that this approach explicitly supports important steps in human decision-making, such as identifying options and possible outcomes, assessing outcomes, and evaluating trade-offs. This may be considered a paradigm shift, as evaluative AI does not make (comprehensible) recommendations based on its own computational process but rather provides evidence to support the humans in developing their own arguments and making up their own mind.

With our framework for collaboration between humans and AI we extend Miller's (2023) focus on decision-making to include cognitive processes of continuous learning, trusting and intrinsic motivation. Thereby, we aim at conceptualizing for an intensified human-AI collaboration (Waefler, 2021), in which AI explicitly supports these human cognitive processes. Our approach is in the tradition of the complementary design of human-machine systems (Jordan, 1963), which regards humans and machines as complementary, i.e. as qualitatively different, each with different strengths and weaknesses. Accordingly, complementary system design aims at a function allocation that enables both mutual support of strengths and mutual compensation of weaknesses (e.g. Grote et al, 1996; Waefler et al, 2003).

## 3   The Supportive-AI Framework

Figure 1 shows an overview of the Supportive-AI Framework. The main purpose of the framework is to conceptualize the collaboration between humans and AI in such a way that opportunities for AI to support human cognitive processes can be identified. Consequently, the framework maps these cognitive processes and the various possibilities of AI support in detail, while the inner workings of AI are not the subject of the framework. Generally, the framework contains four interconnected elements:

- Human agent including cognitive processes of decision-making, continuous learning, trusting and intrinsic motivation.
- Environment representing the subject matter of the decision-making process.
- Human-machine interface (HMI) through which the AI agent supports the human cognitive processes.
- The AI agent, which is not further differentiated.

Although in human-AI collaboration humans and AI normally interact, the arrows from the AI agent via the HMI to the human agent are unidirectional, as they represent the support of human cognitive processes by the AI. Similarly, the arrows originating from the environment are unidirectional as well, as they represent the flow of information from the environment to the human agent and the AI agent, even though the agents normally interact with the environment.

Following, the Supportive AI Framework is described in more detail.

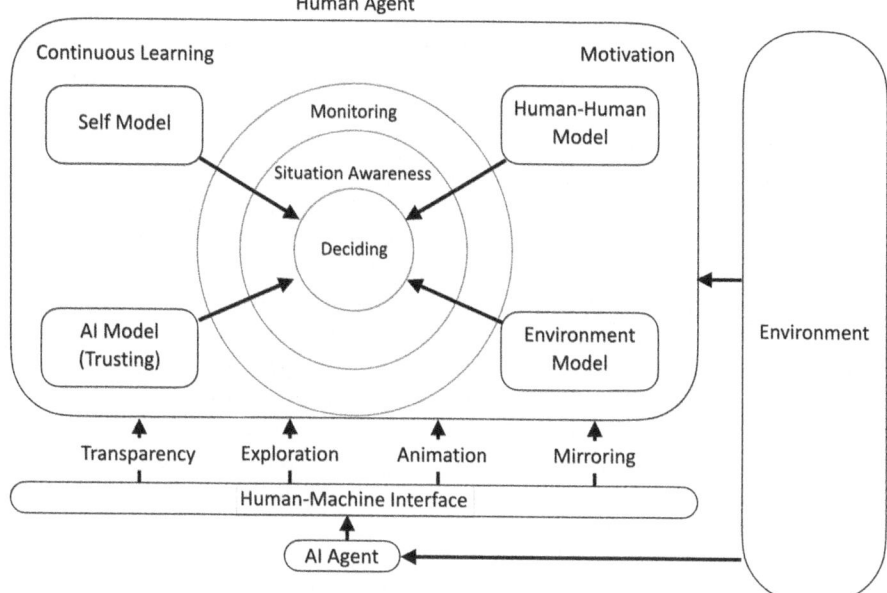

**Fig. 1.** Shows the Supportive AI Framework with its elements Human Agent, Environment, Human-Machine Interface (HMI), and AI Agent. Deciding as a human cognitive process is in the core of the Human Agent. It is embedded in the human cognitive processes Situation Awareness and Monitoring as well as in four different areas of the Human Agent's knowledge required for decision-making, which are represented as mental models (i.e. Environment Model, Human-Human Model, Self Model, and AI Model). In addition, Continuous Learning as well as Motivation are also part of the Human Agent's cognitive processes.

### 3.1 Different Ways of AI Support

The Supportive AI Framework emphasizes that AI can support human cognitive processes in different ways. Schmid (2024) provides an overview of the various options for providing transparency and comprehensibility. Although these possibilities of explainability and interpretability make the development and arguments for an AI-generated recommendation transparent, they do not explicitly support the human's own cognitive processes of decision-making. Therefore, the Supportive AI Framework adds three further possibilities of AI support to transparency: exploration, animation and mirroring. However, this list is not exhaustive, as further possibilities for AI support may be identified. Below, the different ways of AI support incorporated in the Supportive AI Framework are described.

**Transparency** ensures that AI is comprehensible for the humans through explainability and interpretability.

**Exploration** enables humans to explore the subject matter of their cognitive processes, e.g. the environment or the AI. Its purpose is to increase the humans' knowledge and it can be supported in different ways. Miller's (2023) concept of evaluative AI is a way of AI support for exploring the subject of a decision as it provides humans with evidence for and against their own hypothesis. This explicitly supports explorative human learning. Other forms of exploration may include AI-supported simulation of decision options so that humans can examine their different impacts and their trade-offs. Furthermore, the possibility to explore the AI itself is very important as knowledge about its capabilities and limitations is a prerequisite for developing adequate trust into the AI (e.g. Hoffmann et al., 2018).

**Animation** has the purpose to trigger cognitive processes and hence animates humans to think. This can take the form of an AI that alerts humans to unusual behavioral patterns in the environment that might be worth taking a closer look at. The AI might also observe the humans' behavior and ask questions about it. This might be especially helpful for experts as they tend to take decisions often intuitively without conscious control (Klein, 1998, 2008). Becoming aware of your own intuitive decisions and reflecting on them can support the learning process, e.g. by recognizing false assumptions.

**Mirroring** is related to animation, but focuses the humans' self-reflection. Human behavior in general, and also at work, is highly variable (e.g. Hollnagel, 2009). An AI can observe this variability and mirror it to the human. This allows the human to recognize their personal decision-making style, which may involve more risk at the end of the working day than at the beginning. In this way, mirroring can help humans to learn about themselves.

These are just a few ideas of how supportive AI might explicitly support human cognitive processes. However, corresponding AI functionalities still need to be developed. For animation and mirroring, for example, it would be helpful to have an AI that is inquisitive (cf. Wahde & Virgolin, 2022), and thus actively seeks out new insights.

### 3.2   AI to Support Decision-Making

Since supportive AI aims at supporting human cognitive processes of decision-making, the framework considers the decision as the core element of the human agent (see Fig. 1). To understand the cognitive processes involved in human decision-making, we propose to adopt the concept of "Natural Decision Making" (NDM) (Klein, 1998; 2008), as it explains expert decision-making in real-life situations where the stakes are potentially high. However, the Supportive AI Framework does not limit the decision-making theories to be considered.

NDM is based on studies of experienced professionals who have to make quick decisions in potentially risky situations (e.g. firefighters). These studies provide several important insights into how experts make decisions under time pressure. They are not looking for the optimal but for a satisficing decision. Neither are they evaluating different options for decisions. Rather, based on their experience they know relevant cues, expect certain developments, recognize anomalies, know plausible objectives as well as typical actions required to pursue these objectives. The corresponding cognitive processes are not necessarily conscious, but often unconscious. Their basis is the human ability to recognize patterns in complex situations. This requires a great deal of experience with these situations that makes up the human experts' tacit knowledge. The quickness and accuracy of NDM are its advantage as compared with analytical procedures. However, the experts' tacit knowledge also includes all their erroneous assumptions and biases. AI that helps human experts to uncover such deficiencies in their own decision-making is supportive.

With the concept of macrocognition Klein and colleagues (Klein et al., 2003; Klein, 2018) further differentiated the cognitive processes and functions involved in decision-making. These basic processes include developing mental models, mentally simulating and storybuilding, managing uncertainty and risk, identifying leverage points, managing attention as well as maintaining common ground. Based on these fundamental cognitive processes are the macrocognitive functions, which include sensemaking, (re-)planning, adapting, detecting problems, coordinating as well as deciding.

For the graphical representation of the supporting AI framework (see Fig. 1), we have somewhat simplified the human cognitive processes involved in decision-making by focusing on monitoring, building situation awareness and the actual deciding. While monitoring involves the observation of the current situation, situation awareness comprises the three levels described by Endsely (1995) (i.e. Level 1: Perception of elements in current situation; Level 2: Comprehension of current situation; Level 3: Projection of the future state). Finally, deciding is the selection of a concrete decision. Of course, this simplified representation includes both NDM and the macrocognitive processes and functions in their entirety, as described above.

In the following, examples are described of how AI can support human cognitive decision-making processes.

- Exploration to support situation awareness: AI can support the building of level 3 situation awareness by allowing the human to explore and test their assumptions about possible future states of the current situation.
- Exploration to support deciding: AI can support the actual deciding by giving the human the possibility to explore the implications and trade-offs of using different leverage points to influence the environment.
- Animation to support monitoring: AI can support monitoring by alerting the human decision-maker to situational developments that show unusual patterns.

These examples have in common that AI does more than just make recommendations to humans. Rather, AI supports humans in various cognitive decision-making processes. Identifying corresponding possibilities is the actual purpose of the supporting AI framework. However, developing concrete options for AI support in a project requires in-depth cognitive task analysis (e.g. Hollnagel, 2003).

### 3.3 AI to Support Learning and Knowledge Building

In the Supportive AI Framework monitoring and situation awareness provide the immediate input for decision-making. Both refer to up-to-date information on the current state of the environment or how it is required in the timeframe of the decision. Information is therefore volatile and must be constantly updated. The human agent's knowledge on the other hand, as conceptualized in the Supportive AI Framework, is more enduring. It incorporates for instance insights about the environment's specific characteristics, about its elements and their systemic interconnections, about its relevant behavioral patterns, and the like. With such content, knowledge is a basis for monitoring, as it tells for instance which indicators need to be monitored and which are not important, as well as for situation awareness, as it provides ground for perceiving, interpreting and projecting.

Like the cognitive processes of decision-making, knowledge is a complex construct. However, it is not the intention of this paper to discuss it in detail. For the purpose of the supporting AI framework, only basic aspects of knowledge and relevant content areas are outlined here.

With the realization that we all know more than we can say, Polanyi (1962) in his fundamental work made the distinction between explicit and tacit knowledge. While humans can communicate their explicit knowledge, this is not possible with tacit knowledge. The latter remains, at least to a large extent, implicit. It is estimated that most of an organization's knowledge is tacit (e.g. embrained or embodied in individuals) and only a minor part is explicit (Faust, 2007). Consequently, NDM assumes that human experts base a substantial part of their decisions on tacit knowledge (Klein, 1998; 2008). The distinction of explicit and tacit knowledge is important for the Supportive AI Framework not only because tacit knowledge is a major source for human experts' decision-making. It is also important because tacit knowledge is not primarily learned through knowledge transfer, but rather by gaining experience through training, practicing, observing and trying things out. Therefore, AI that supports learning processes must go beyond providing explanations and give humans the opportunity to explore and gain experience so that they can expand their tacit knowledge.

Moreover, in the real world of work, where people work in different forms of labor division, relevant knowledge is distributed among many humans rather than owned by individuals. The literature therefore distinguishes between individuals and collectives (or social systems) as entities bearing knowledge (e.g. Lam, 2000). Collectives can be formal teams or other forms of organizational units, but they can also be anonymous socio-technical systems (Waefler & Rack, 2021) in which the work of individuals is interconnected without those affected being aware of it. With growing networking as a result of increasing digitalization, there will certainly be even more of these hidden connections and dependencies in the future. There is therefore great potential for supportive AI to provide humans with more transparency about hidden connections and to enable the exchange of knowledge.

Against this background, the Supportive AI Framework distinguishes four domains of human knowledge content, which are depicted as models in the graphical representation of the framework (see Fig. 1), and which are described below.

**The environment model** contains knowledge regarding the subject-matter of decision-making. This includes knowledge about its characteristics, its behavioral patterns, its elements and their interconnections as well as its typical problem areas with the corresponding leverage points, and the like. More generally spoken, it includes system knowledge and control knowledge (e.g. Kluwe, 2006) regarding the relevant environment or the subject of decision-making.

**The human-human model** contains knowledge about interrelations of one's own work with the work of others. It takes especially into account, that knowledge about the environment is distributed and that decisions taken by an individual are normally interrelated with decisions of other individuals. The former offers the opportunity to learn from the experiences of others. The latter on the other hand entails the risk that decisions taken individually are sensible from a local perspective, but suboptimal from a global perspective, according to the motto "my solution, your problem". We assume that an increased awareness of these interrelations can support better tuned decision-making. This is in line with Hutchins' (1995) as well as Stanton's et al. (2006) fundamental work on distributed cognition.

**The AI model (trusting)** contains knowledge about the AI as a tool. This knowledge is not about the algorithms and the inner workings of the AI, but rather about its capabilities and limitations as a basis for obtaining an accurate mental model of the AI (Bansal et al., 2019; Endsley, 2023). Corresponding awareness is prerequisite for developing adequate trust into a specific AI and hence for relying on it when appropriate while not relying on it when inappropriate (e.g. Hoffmann et al., 2018).

**The self model** contains the human decision-makers' knowledge about themselves, their own strengths and weaknesses, decision biases, behavioral patterns (e.g. the tendency to make riskier decisions at the end of a work shift), and the like. Hence the self model contains what humans learn about themselves to gain a more comprehensive understanding of their behavior (Jelodari et al., 2023; Pronin, 2007). Therefore, the self model is prerequisite for self reflection and metacognition and hence supports continuous improvement.

AI is supportive regarding these domains of knowledge if it empowers corresponding human cognitive processes of learning. Learning is a complex process. It influences the learners' perceptions of the world and their interactions with it. Learning bases on an ongoing, interactive relationship between the learners' characteristics and the learning content, all situated within the specific environment (Alexander et al., 2009).

One suitable conceptualization of these processes is provided by Kolb's (1984) "Experiential Learning Theory". However, as with decision-making (see above), the supporting AI framework does not limit the learning theories that can be considered. Kolb (1984) suggests a cyclic process of experiential learning, consisting of the four phases (i) concrete experience, (ii) reflective observation, (iii) abstract conceptualization, and (iv) active experimentation:

- Concrete experience: This initial phase involves making new experiences within the relevant domain of knowledge or transcending existing ones.
- Reflective observation: In the second phase, humans reflect on their experiences and consider what was successful or where there is room for improvement. This is prerequisite for the internalization of learning outcomes.
- Abstract conceptualization: In the third phase, humans conceptualize their thoughts, adapt existing ideas or develop new ones. In this phase, the abstract understanding materializes and enables the construction of new mental models or conceptual frameworks.
- Active experimentation: Finally, in the fourth phase, before iterating into the next learning cycle, humans test the cognitive representations acquired in the previous phases to observe the outcomes. Feedback from practice, based on active experimentation, is crucial for refining the knowledge acquired.

Kolb (1984) emphasizes the role of experience in human learning, and although it is related to conscious reflection, it applies not only to the learning of explicit knowledge, but also to tacit knowledge. This is because, for example, humans may consciously know and hence develop explicit strategies that are suitable for coping with certain situations based on their experience, although they are not able to justify this explicitly because the corresponding background knowledge is tacit.

The following examples concretizes how AI can support human learning:

- Exploration to learn about the environment: AI can support the human in refining their personal model of the environment by providing them the opportunity to make (simulation-based) new experiences and to reflect on them.
- Animation to refine tacit knowledge about leverage points: AI can support identifying biases in tacit knowledge by alerting human experts to actions they perform intuitively, asking them about the assumptions behind these actions, and helping them to reflect on these assumptions.
- Animation to support human-human knowledge sharing: AI can support learning about the environment by providing humans with experiences (e.g. ratings, likes) of other human experts with strategies for coping with a particular problem in the environment.
- Mirroring to improve the self model: AI can support self-reflection by mirroring to the humans their personal style of decision-making.

These examples are intended to illustrate how the Supportive AI Framework can help to identify multiple ways in which AI can support processes for both explicit and tacit knowledge learning in the different knowledge areas. Of course, a much more in-depth analysis and ideation process is required for corresponding projects.

### 3.4  AI to Support Building Adequate Trust

As briefly mentioned in the section above, the Supportive AI Framework considers trust to be related with the human's knowledge about the AI, i.e. with their mental AI model (see Fig. 1). In line with the perspective of work psychology on human-machine collaboration, trust is seen as a dynamic process that is influenced by various aspects (Kaplan et al., 2023), including personal experience with a particular AI (Hoffman et al., 2018). While trust can be built on trustworthiness, it does not derive directly from trustworthiness (Hoffman, 2017), which is more of an attribute of a particular AI. Rather than being an AI's attribute, trust is the degree of confidence a particular human has in the automated system's ability to perform accurately in various contexts (Cahour & Forzy, 2009). With increasing experience with a certain AI, a human learns to trust or distrust the AI for certain tasks in certain contexts. Trust therefore does not develop by gradually rising to a more advanced state. Rather, it morphs between over-trust and under-trust in response to concrete experiences and ideally towards appropriate trust. When an appropriate trust is established, humans know when to confidently rely on the AI and when not to rely on it (Hoffman et al., 2018). In the context of the Supportive AI Framework, this knowledge is part of the human's AI model.

There is a huge body of literature on effects of inappropriate trust into automation (for an overview see e.g. Parasuraman & Manzey, 2010). Over-trust on the one hand can result in automation complacency, where humans accept information from the system without checking it or searching for additional information. Consequently, AI errors are not recognized, which leads to errors of commission (where the human blindly follows a recommendation provided by the automation) and errors of omission (where the human does not react in a critical situation because the automation does not prompt them to do so). On the other hand, under-trust can lead to humans not using the AI - or not using it as intended by the developers - and thus not having the opportunity to develop appropriate trust based on experience.

The complex processes in which trust continuously emerges from experience and thus from the specific way in which a technology is used make it clear that successful human-AI teaming requires a differentiated view of the many dimensions of human-AI interaction. This goes far beyond designing the technology. With the supporting AI framework, we want to contribute to this differentiated view.

### 3.5   AI to Support Intrinsic Motivation

Motivation is considered in the Supportive AI Framework due to two main reasons. On the one hand, there is a tendency for algorithm aversion (Schaap et al., 2024). On the other hand, as already mentioned, even when using an AI, humans tend not to engage analytically with the explanations provided by the AI, but to over-rely on it (Buçinca et al., 2021). Both phenomena make it clear how important motivation is. However, motivation as well is a complex construct with multiple influencing factors (cf. e.g. Ulich, 2011). Many of these, such as personality or extrinsic motivators, are not influenced by the AI design. Nevertheless, AI has an impact on the human's task and therefore on their intrinsic motivation (Parker & Grote, 2022). In the tradition of socio-technical system design (e.g. Clegg, 2000), the term "task orientation" has been important for many decades. It describes a mental state of interest and commitment to the task, which is caused by certain characteristics of the task (Emery, 1959). According to Hackman and Oldham (1976) these task characteristics must support the following three critical mental states as a prerequisite for intrinsic motivation, which can be considered similar to task orientation:

- Experienced meaningfulness: Work needs to be experienced as intrinsically meaningful by the worker, i.e. workers need to directly see why they do what they do. Task characteristics that provide to experienced meaningfulness are (i) skill variety (tasks that require several different skills rather than simple routine), (ii) task identity (tasks that produces an outcome recognizable for the worker, rather than tasks without visible link to the product), and (iii) task significance (tasks that matter).
- Experienced responsibility: Workers need to feel responsible for the outcome of their work. The task characteristic that evokes this feeling is autonomy. If the work processes are fully controlled externally without the workers being able to influence them, they do not feel responsible for the outcome (even if they are held accountable for it by job descriptions or managers).
- Knowledge of the work results: Feedback is the task characteristic that provides this knowledge. For this reason, pedometers for instance motivate people to exercise. Without knowing what they achieved or what they could change to improve their performance, workers cannot be motivated.

These findings of Hackman and Oldham (1976) make it obvious that the integration of an AI into work processes can significantly influence the task characteristics for humans and thus their intrinsic motivation both for good work and for using the AI.

Regarding the latter, it can be considered a prerequisite for the developers' intended use of AI that the human user understands the reasons for the AI's behavior and has some control over it. However, the Supportive AI Framework does not limit theories of intrinsic motivation to be taken into account when designing human-AI interaction. Buçinca et al. (2024) for instance suggest to consider the Self-Determination Theory (SDT), which postulates that the three psychological needs of competence, autonomy and relatedness must be met to promote intrinsic motivation.

The following examples describe, how AI can support intrinsic motivation according to Hackman and Oldham (1976):

- Transparency to support experienced meaningfulness: AI can support experienced meaningfulness if it makes its behavior comprehensible.
- Exploration to support experienced meaningfulness: AI can also support experienced meaningfulness if it supports the human to explore causal relations in the environment. This enables humans to understand the why of phenomena they observe in their environment.
- Exploration for experienced responsibility: AI can support human autonomy and hence experienced responsibility if it allows humans to explore their hunches about weak signals that could indicate emerging problems in the environment. This increases the humans' scope of action.
- Transparency for knowledge of the work results: AI can support the feedback and thus the knowledge of the work results if it makes the effects of a decision on the environment transparent in comparison to the effects of other options.

As these examples show, there are many ways in which AI can support intrinsic motivation both for supporting task orientation and thus the human endeavor to do a good job, as well as for the use of AI.

## 4   Discussion

A large proportion of AI-supported decision-making aids focus on the objective of the decision and aim to make recommendations to humans. As the AI capabilities of data processing far exceed the corresponding human capabilities, it often becomes difficult or even impossible for humans to take the final decision and responsibility for these recommendations. The Supportive AI Framework presented in this paper addresses this problem by shifting the focus of decision support to the human cognitive processes of decision-making. In this way AI is supporting processes of human decision-making rather than recommending decisions. This alternative approach is intended to complement recommendation-based approaches.

Against this background, the aim of the Supportive AI Framework is to enable the identification of various possibilities for supporting human decision-making processes through AI as a basis to derive requirements for AI design. To this end, the framework proposes to take into account a variety of human cognitive processes involved in decision-making. In addition to the actual deciding, these human cognitive processes include monitoring and building situation awareness, but also learning in different knowledge domains such as the environment, the contexts of distributed decision making, the person of the decision maker and the AI. The latter is also important so that humans can build appropriate trust in a particular AI, which requires experience-based knowledge of the AI's capabilities and limitations. Furthermore, human cognitive processes of intrinsic motivation are included in the framework regarding both, the use of the AI and hence to avoid algorithm aversion as well as task orientation. All these human cognitive processes may be supported by AI not only through transparency (i.e. interpretability and explainability), but also through exploration, animation, and mirroring.

The Supportive AI Framework is conceptual and theory-based. Its application to AI research or development projects requires an in-depth analysis of the relevant tasks and the content of the associated cognitive processes. Further research is needed to develop corresponding methods and suitable AI solutions.

**Acknowledgments.** AI4REALNET has received funding from European Union's Horizon Europe Research and Innovation Programme under the Grant Agreement No 101119527 and from the Swiss State Secretariat for Education, Research and Innovation (SERI). Views and opinions expressed are however those of the author(s) only and do not necessarily reflect those of the European Union and SERI. Neither the European Union nor the granting authority can be held responsible for them.

**Disclosure of Interests.**   The authors have no competing interests to declare that are relevant to the content of this article.

# References

Alexander, P.A., Schallert, D.L., Reynolds, R.E.: What is learning anyway? A topographical perspective considered. Educ. Psychol. **44**(3), 176–192 (2009)

Amershi, S., et al.: Guidelines for human-AI interaction. In: Proceedings of the 2019 CHI Conference on Human Factors in Computing Systems (CHI 2019), pp. 1–13. Association for Computing Machinery, New York (2019). https://doi.org/10.1145/3290605.3300233

Bainbridge, L.: Ironies of automation. In: Rasmussen, J., Duncan, K., Leplat, J. (eds.) New Technology and Human Error, pp. 271–283. Wiley, Chichester (1987)

Bansal, G., et al.: Beyond accuracy: the role of mental models in human-AI team performance. In: Proceedings of the AAAI Conference on Human Computation and Crowdsourcing, vol. 7, pp. 2–11 (2019)

Bessa, R.J., et al.: Ai4realnet framework and use cases. Technical report D1.1, European Project AI4REALNET (2024). https://ai4realnet.eu/wp-content/uploads/2024/12/D1.1-AI4 REALNET-framework-and-use-cases_v1.0-3.pdf. Accessed 22 Jan 2025

Buçinca, Z., Malaya, M.B., Gajos, K.Z.: To trust or to think: cognitive forcing functions can reduce overreliance on AI in AI-assisted decision-making. Proc. ACM Hum.-Comput. Interact. **5**(CSCW1), 21, Article no. 188 (2021). https://doi.org/10.1145/3449287

Buçinca, Z., Swaroop, S., Paluch, A.E., Doshi-Velez, F., Gajos, K.Z.: Contrastive explanations that anticipate human misconceptions can improve human decision-making skills. In: Woodstock 2018: ACM Symposium on Neural Gaze Detection, 03–05 June 2024, Woodstock, NY, p. 35. ACM, New York (2024)

Cahour, B., Forzy, J.-F.: Does projection into use improve trust and exploration? An example with a cruise control system. Saf. Sci. **47**(9), 1260–1270 (2009). https://doi.org/10.1016/j.ssci.2009. 03.015

Clegg, C.W.: Sociotechnical principles for system design. Appl. Ergon. **31**, 463–477 (2000)

Dell'Acqua, F., et al.: Navigating the jagged technological frontier: field experimental evidence of the effects of AI on knowledge worker productivity and quality. Harvard Business School Technology & Operations Mgt. Unit Working Paper No. 24-013. The Wharton School Research Paper (2023). https://doi.org/10.2139/ssrn.4573321

Dubey, A., Abhinav, K., Jain, S., Arora, V., Puttaveerana, A.: HACO: a framework for developing human-AI teaming. In: 13th Innovations in Software Engineering Conference (formerly known as India Software Engineering Conference) (ISEC 2020), Jabalpur, India, 27–29 February 2020, p. 9. ACM, New York (2020). https://doi.org/10.1145/3385032.3385044

Emery, F.E.: Characteristics of Sicio-Technical Systems. Tavistok Institute of Human Relations. Document No. 527 (1959)

Endsley, M.R.: Towards a theory of situation awareness in dynamic systems. Hum. Factors **37**(1), 32–64 (1995)

Endsley, M.R.: Ironies of artificial intelligence. Ergonomics **66**(11), 1656–1668 (2023). https://doi.org/10.1080/00140139.2023.2243404

Faust, B.: Implementation of tacit knowledge preservation and transfer methods (2007). https://www.academia.edu/36648357/Implementation_of_Tacit_Knowledge_Preservation_and_Transfer_Methods

Grote, G., Weik, S., Waefler, T.: KOMPASS: complementary allocation of production tasks in sociotechnical systems. In: Robertson, S.A. (ed.) Contemporary Ergonomics 1996, pp. 306–311. Taylor & Francis, London (1996)

Hackman, J.R., Oldham, G.R.: Motivation through the design of work: test of a theory. Organ. Behav. Hum. Perform. **16**(2), 250–279 (1976)

Hoffman, R.: A taxonomy of emergent trusting in the human–machine relationship. In: Cognitive Systems Engineering: The Future for a Changing World, pp. 137–163. CRC Press (2017)

Hoffman, R., Mueller, S.T., Klein, G., Litman, J.: Measuring Trust in the XAI Context (Explainable AI Program) [Technical report]. DARPA (2018). https://doi.org/10.31234/osf.io/e3kv9

Hollnagel, E.: Handbook of Cognitive Task Design. Lawrence Erlbaum, Mahwah (2003)

Hollnagel, E.: The ETTO Principle. Ashgate, Farnham (2009)

Hutchins, E.: Cognition in the Wild. The MIT Press, Cambridge (1995)

Jelodari, M., Amirhosseini, M.H., Giraldez-Hayes, A.: An AI powered system to enhance self-reflection practice in coaching. Cogn. Comput. Syst. **4**(5), 243–254 (2023). https://doi.org/10.1049/ccs2.12087

Jordan, N.: Allocation of functions between man and machines in automated systems. J. Appl. Psychol. **47**(3), 161–165 (1963)

Kahneman, D.: Thinking, Fast and Slow. Farrar, Straus and Giroux, New York (2011)

Kaplan, D., Kessler, T.T., Brill, J.C., Hancock, P.A.: Trust in artificial intelligence: meta-analytic findings. Hum. Factors: J. Hum. Factors Ergon. Soc. **65**(2), 337–359 (2023)

Kirwan, B.: Human Factors Requirements for Human-AI Teaming in Aviation. Preprints (2025). https://doi.org/10.20944/preprints202501.0974.v1

Klein, G.: Sources of Power. How People Make Decisions. The MIT Press, Cambridge (1998)

Klein, G.: Naturalistic decision making. Hum. Factors: J. Hum. Factors Ergon. Soc. **50**(3), 456–460 (2008)

Klein, G.: Macrocognitive measures for evaluating cognitive work. In: Patterson, E.S., Miller, J.E. (eds.) Macrocognition Metrics and Scenarios: Design and Evaluation for Real-World Teams, pp. 47–64. Ashgate, Farnham (2018)

Klein, G., Ross, K.G., Moon, B.M., Klein, D.E., Hoffman, R.R., Hollnagel, E.: Macrocognition. IEEE Computer Society, pp. 81–84 (2003)

Kluwe, R.H.: Informationsaufnahme und Informationsverarbeitung. In: Zimolong, B., Konradt, U. (Hrsg.). Ingenieurpsychologie, Enzyklopädie der Psychologie (Themenbereich D, Serie III, Band 2, S. 35–70). Hogrefe, Göttingen (2006)

Kolb, D.A.: Experimental Learning: Experience as the Source of Learning and Development. Prentice-Hall, Englewood Cliffs (1984)

Lam, A.: Tacit Knowledge, Organizational Learning and Societal Institutions: An Integrated Framework (2000). http://oss.sagepub.com/content/21/3/487

Miller, T.: Explainable AI is Dead, Long Live Explainable AI! Hypothesis-Driven Decision Support (2023). https://arxiv.org/abs/2302.12389

Parasuraman, R., Manzey, D.H.: Complacency and bias in human use of automation: an attentional integration. Hum. Factors **52**(3), 381–410 (2010)

Parker, S.K., Grote, G.: Automation, algorithms, and beyond: why work design matters more than ever in a digital world. Appl. Psychol. **71**(4), 1171–1204 (2022)

Polanyi, M.: Personal Knowledge: Towards a Post-Critical Philosophy. Taylor & Francis, London (1962)

Pronin, E.: Perception and misperception of bias in human judgment. Trends Cogn. Sci. **11**(1), 37–43 (2007). https://doi.org/10.1016/j.tics.2006.11.001

Schaap, G., Bosse, T., Hendriks Vettehen, P.: The ABC of algorithmic aversion: not agent, but benefits and control determine the acceptance of automated decision-making. AI & Soc. **39**, 1947–1960 (2024). https://doi.org/10.1007/s00146-023-01649-6

Schmid, U.: Trustworthy artificial intelligence: comprehensible, transparent and correctable. In: Werthner, A., et al. (eds.) Introduction to Digital Humanism. Springer, Cham (2024). https://doi.org/10.1007/978-3-031-45304-5_10

Sheridan, T.B.: Supervisory control. In: Salvendy, G. (ed.) Handbook of Human Factors, pp. 1243–1268. Wiley, New York (1987)

Stanton, N.A., et al.: Distributed situation awareness in dynamic systems: theoretical development and application of an ergonomics methodology. Ergonomics **49**(12–13), 1288–1311 (2006). https://doi.org/10.1080/00140130600612762

Ulich, E.: Arbeitspsychologie (11. Auflage). Schäffer-Poeschl Verlag, Stuttgart (2011)

Waefler, T.: Progressive intensity of human-technology teaming. In: Proceedings of the 5th International Virtual Conference on Human Interaction and Emerging Technologies, IHIET 2021, France, 27–29 August 2021, pp. 28–36 (2021)

Waefler, T., Grote, G., Windischer, A., Ryser, C.: KOMPASS: a method for complementary system design. In: Hollnagel, E. (ed.) Handbook of Cognitive Task Design, pp. 477–502. Lawrence Erlbaum, Mahwah (2003)

Wäfler, T., Rack, O · Kooperation und künstliche Intelligenz. In: Geramanis, O., Hutmacher, S., Walser, L. (eds.) Kooperation in der digitalen Arbeitswelt. PSS, pp. 77–88. Springer, Wiesbaden (2021). https://doi.org/10.1007/978-3-658-34497-9_5

Wahde, M., Virgolin, M.: The five is: key principles for interpretable and safe conversational AI. In: Proceedings of the 2021 4th International Conference on Computational Intelligence and Intelligent Systems (CIIS 2021), pp. 50–54. Association for Computing Machinery, New York (2022). https://doi.org/10.1145/3507623.3507632

# Author Index

D. D. Schmorrow and C. M. Fidopiastis (Eds.): HCII 2025, LNAI 15778, pp. 319–320, 2025.
https://doi.org/10.1007/978-3-031-93724-8

The manufacturer's authorised representative in the EU is Springer
Nature Customer Service Centre GmbH, Europaplatz 3, 69115 Heidelberg,
Germany. If you have any concerns regarding our products, please
contact ProductSafety@springernature.com

Printed and bound by CPI Group (UK) Ltd, Croydon, CR0 4YY

28/04/2026

02098515-0005